LAW AND LEADERSHIP

T0300449

Emerging Legal Education

Series Editors:
Paul Maharg, *University of Northumbria, Newcastle upon Tyne, UK*,
Caroline Maughan, *University of the West of England, Bristol, UK* and
Elizabeth Mertz, *University of Wisconsin-Madison/American Bar Foundation, USA*

Emerging Legal Education is a forum for analysing the discourse of legal education and creating innovative ways of learning the law. The series focuses on research, theory and practice within legal education, drawing attention to historical, interdisciplinary and international characteristics, and is based upon imaginative and sophisticated educational thinking. The series takes a broad view of theory and practice. Series books are written for an international audience and are sensitive to the diversity of contexts in which law is taught, learned and practised.

Other titles in this series:

The Moral Imagination and the Legal Life
Beyond Text in Legal Education
Edited by Zenon Bańkowski and Maksymilian Del Mar

The Arts and the Legal Academy
Beyond Text in Legal Education
Edited by Zenon Bańkowski, Maksymilian Del Mar and Paul Maharg

Affect and Legal Education
Emotion in Learning and Teaching the Law
Edited by Paul Maharg and Caroline Maughan

Law and Leadership
Integrating Leadership Studies into the
Law School Curriculum

Edited by

PAULA MONOPOLI
University of Maryland Francis King Carey School of Law, USA

SUSAN McCARTY
University of Maryland Francis King Carey School of Law, USA

Routledge
Taylor & Francis Group

LONDON AND NEW YORK

First published 2013 by Ashgate Publishing

Published 2016 by Routledge
2 Park Square, Milton Park, Abingdon, Oxfordshire OX14 4RN
711 Third Avenue, New York, NY 10017, USA

First issued in paperback 2016

Routledge is an imprint of the Taylor & Francis Group, an informa business

British Library Cataloguing in Publication Data
Law and leadership : integrating leadership studies into
  the law school curriculum. -- (Emerging legal education)
  1. Leadership--Study and teaching (Higher) 2. Lawyers--
  Training of. 3. Law schools--Curricula. 4. Practice of
  law.
  I. Series II. Monopoli, Paula A., 1958- III. McCarty,
  Susan.
  340'.0711-dc23

Library of Congress Cataloging-in-Publication Data
Law and leadership : integrating leadership studies into the law school curriculum / [edited by] Paula Monopoli and Susan Mccarty.
     p. cm. -- (Emerging legal education)
  Includes bibliographical references and index.
   ISBN 978-1-4094-5021-4 (hardback) 1. Law--Study and teaching--United States.
2. Leadership--Study and teaching--United States. I. McCarty, Susan. II. Monopoli,
Paula A., 1958-
  KF273.L39 2012
  340.041'173--dc23

                                                                  2012026366

ISBN 13: 978-1-138-25286-8 (pbk)
ISBN 13: 978-1-4094-5021-4 (hbk)

*To Martha Barnett, who taught me to lead, and
To Deborah Rhode, who continues to lead the way.
P.A.M.*

*To my mother, who showed me that a woman's place was wherever she
wanted it to be, and to Greg, who helped me find it. And to my boys,
Danny and Tommy, who help me enjoy being there.
S.G.M.*

Contents

List of Figures   *xi*
List of Tables   *xiii*
Notes on Contributors   *xv*
Foreword by James MacGregor Burns   *xxi*
Preface by Donald J. Polden   *xxiii*
Acknowledgments   *xxvii*
Copyright Acknowledgments   *xxix*

Introduction   1
Paula A. Monopoli and Susan G. McCarty

PART I: LAWYERS AS LEADERS

1   Leadership Studies for Lawyers of the Future   5
     Phoebe A. Haddon

2   The Nexus between Leadership Theory and Law   19
     Georgia Sorenson

3   Leadership Competencies in Law   35
     Larry Richard

4   Leaders in the Changing Legal Economy   55
     Alexina Jackson

5   Private Practice and Leadership   69
     Maura DeMouy

6   Policy and Government Leadership   81
     Mickey Edwards

PART II: WHY LEADERSHIP STUDIES IN LAW SCHOOL?

7   Why Law Schools Should Emphasize
      Leadership Theory and Practice   91
      Leary Davis

8   An Argument for Leadership Education in Law Schools   125
      Diane Hoffmann

9   Thinking Like a Lawyer versus Thinking Like a Leader   141
      Michael Kelly

PART III: DEVELOPING A CURRICULUM: AN INTERDISCIPLINARY APPROACH

10   Charting a New Professional Responsibility Course in a
      Post-Carnegie World   167
      Brenda Bratton Blom, Lydia Nussbaum and Bonnie Allen

11   Developing Leadership through Discussion and Passion:
      A Law Student's Perspective   197
      Avery M. Blank

12   Recovering Relational Lawyering:
      Building Ethical Leaders through Mentorship   203
      Brenda Bratton Blom and Dorcas R. Gilmore

13   Reflections on Team Production in
      Professional Schools and the Workplace   213
      Robert J. Rhee

14   Law, Leadership, and the Literary Canon   223
      Alan D. Hornstein

15   Acknowledging Uncommon Relationships:
      Changing How We Teach Students to be Leaders   233
      Susan Leviton, Kerry Cooperman and Jeremy Grant-Skinner

16   Teaching Gender and Leadership   253
      Paula A. Monopoli

Appendix: Leadership Education in the Legal Academy:
    Principles, Practices and Possibilities.
    A Report from the James MacGregor Burns Academy of
    Leadership—University of Maryland   263
    Judy Sorum Brown and Bonnie Allen

Index   *283*

List of Figures

2.1	Periodic table of leadership studies	26
3.1	The basic principle of person-job fit	38
7.1	Relative importance of technical and leadership competence over time	94
7.2	Three special kinds of knowledge	99
7.3	Knowledge and the insensitive line	100
7.4	Knowledge and the sensitive line	102
7.5	Motivators	104
7.6	Three professional apprenticeships	113
7.A1	A model of the legal professionalization process	122

List of Tables

2.1   Ten-year review of articles published in *Leadership Quarterly*   31

3.1   Hogan Personal Inventory traits and scores   45
3.2   Hogan Personal Inventory traits and scores for sample of
      successful lawyers   45

7.A1 Skills emphasized in Hughes et al.,
      Leadership: Enhancing the Lessons of Experience,
      and their relevance to law practice, law firm management and
      leadership, and civic engagement   124

Notes on Contributors[1]

Bonnie Allen serves as Director of Access to Justice Partnerships at the Mississippi Center for Justice. She also has an independent consulting practice focused on resource development and leadership development in the field of public interest law. Allen holds a J.D. from the University of Florida College of Law, a master's degree in Theological Studies from Garrett-Evangelical Theological Seminary, and a B.A. from Rhodes College. She has served as executive director of several national and local nonprofit organizations, including the Center for Law and Renewal based at the Fetzer Institute. Allen previously taught as an adjunct clinical law instructor at the School of Law.

Avery M. Blank graduated *magna cum laude* from Colgate University and received her J.D. from the School of Law. At the School of Law, she was a 2010–2011 Rose Zetzer Fellow in the Women, Leadership and Equality Program and an Articles Editor of the *University of Maryland Law Journal of Race, Religion, Gender and Class*. Blank interned with the Office of General Counsel in President Obama's White House Office of Administration. She currently works as a Law and Policy Analyst for the University of Maryland Center for Health and Homeland Security.

Brenda Bratton Blom is a Law School Professor and former Director and Co-Director of the Clinical Program at the School of Law. Professor Blom worked in public interest law firms after graduating from law school, joining the Maryland faculty in 1998. She teaches the Community Development Clinic, the Community Justice Clinic, and in 2008, she developed a course in Professional Responsibility for clinical students. Her interests include nonprofit and community organizations, the impact of our policies on incarceration and criminal law on low income communities, restorative and community justice, professionalism and moral formation, the teaching of professionalism, and the role that solo and small firm lawyers have on the delivery of legal services. Professor Blom has a Ph.D. from the University of Maryland Baltimore County.

---

1 In this volume, all references to the "School of Law" shall mean the University of Maryland Francis King Carey School of Law.

Judy Sorum Brown, Ph.D. is a Senior Scholar at the Center for Public Policy and Private Enterprise at the University of Maryland. Her work revolves around themes of leadership, change, learning, dialogue, diversity, and renewal. Dr. Brown is particularly interested in the practice of leadership across boundaries, including the boundaries among the public sector, the non-governmental sector, and private enterprise.

James MacGregor Burns is the Emeritus Woodrow Wilson Professor of Government at Williams College. He is a Pulitzer Prize-winning presidential biographer, the author of more than two dozen books, and a pioneer in the field of leadership studies.

Kerry Cooperman is a 2009 graduate of the School of Law, where he was a member of the Juvenile Law Clinic. As part of the Clinic, he taught a tenth-grade law course at the Baltimore Freedom Academy in the spring of 2008. He was a fellow in the Center for Research in Crime and Justice at NYU School of Law in 2009–2010 and is currently a litigation associate at Stroock & Stroock & Lavan LLP in Manhattan.

Leary Davis is Founding Dean and Emeritus Professor of Law at Elon University School of Law and a member of the Center for Creative Leadership's Legal Sector Practice Group. He practiced law for nine years before entering legal education as founding dean of Campbell University School of Law. An elected member of the American Law Institute and a fellow of both the College of Law Practice Management and the American Bar Foundation, Dean Davis received B.A. and J.D. degrees from Wake Forest University and an LL.M. from Columbia University.

Maura DeMouy is an adjunct professor and teaches the Women, Leadership and Equality Workshop at the School of Law. She also serves as Coordinator for its LEAD Initiative, which seeks to prepare students for the challenges of modern practice through enhanced teaching of leadership, ethics, and democracy-building. She received her B.A. in French and economics from Washington University and her J.D., with honors, from the School of Law. Following graduation, DeMouy clerked for the Honorable Catherine C. Blake of the United States District Court for the District of Maryland. She then spent four years in private practice.

Mickey Edwards is a Vice President of the Aspen Institute and the Director of the Aspen Institute-Rodel Fellowships in Public Leadership. Congressman Edwards was a member of Congress from Oklahoma for 16 years. Since leaving Congress, he has taught at Harvard, Georgetown, and Princeton universities and he is a Senior Leadership Fellow at the School of Law.

Dorcas R. Gilmore is an Assistant General Counsel in the NAACP Legal Department. She is an advocate for racial and economic justice. Gilmore began her legal career as a Skadden Fellow and Staff Attorney at the Community Law Center, Inc. She serves on the Governing Committee of the ABA Forum on Affordable Housing and Community Development Law and on the Board of Directors of the Women's Law Center of Maryland, Inc. Gilmore graduated from the School of Law, where she was an inaugural Leadership Scholar as the 2004 Gilbert and Jaylee Mead Public Interest Scholar. She is also a graduate of the Honors Degree Program at Rollins College.

Jeremy Grant-Skinner is an education consultant with TNTP, a national nonprofit that works to end educational inequality by ensuring that more kids learn from excellent teachers. He graduated in 2008 from the School of Law, where he was a member of the Juvenile Law, Children's Issues, and Legislative Advocacy Clinic for two years, teaching at and supporting the law school's partnership with the Baltimore Freedom Academy. He is also an alumnus of New York University, Johns Hopkins University, and Teach For America, and taught for several years in Baltimore's public schools.

Phoebe A. Haddon is the Dean of the School of Law, a position she assumed in 2009 after a distinguished 25-year career at Temple University Beasley School of Law. The author of two casebooks and numerous articles on constitutional and tort law, she received the 2011 Great Teacher Award from the Society of American Law Teachers. She served as a law clerk for the U.S. Court of Appeals for the Third Circuit; practiced at Wilmer, Cutler & Pickering in Washington, D.C.; and holds an LL.M. from Yale University, a J.D. from Duquesne University, and a bachelor's degree from Smith College.

Diane Hoffmann is a Professor of Law and Director of the Law and Health Care Program at the School of Law. She is also a former Associate Dean of Academic Programs, responsible for the school's academic curriculum and dual degree programs. Her research interests include issues at the intersection of law, health care, ethics, and public policy such as advance directives, pain treatment, termination of life support, genetics, regulation of research, and of managed care. She has published several major articles in this area. Professor Hoffmann received her B.A., *magna cum laude,* from Duke University, her M.S. in Health Policy and Management from Harvard School of Public Health, and her J.D. from Harvard Law School. Professor Hoffmann is an elected member of the American Law Institute.

Alan D. Hornstein is Emeritus Professor at the School of Law, where he also served as Associate Dean and Acting Dean. He has taught at Fordham, New York, and Brooklyn Law Schools and was Distinguished Visiting Professor at Touro Law Center. Professor Hornstein has been a visiting faculty member at St. John's

College Graduate Institute in Liberal Education and held the Paschal P. Vacca Chair in Liberal Arts at the University of Montevallo. He was a Special Reporter and Consultant for the Maryland Rules of Evidence Project and produced annual editions of the Maryland Evidence Courtroom Manual (2000–2007). He is the author of *Appellate Advocacy in a Nutshell* and numerous articles on law and law-related subjects. Professor Hornstein is a Fellow of the American Bar Foundation and an elected member of the American Law Institute.

Alexina Jackson is an associate in the Washington, D.C. law office of Crowell & Moring LLP. She is a member of the Government Contracts practice group, focusing on claims and fraud litigation and counseling matters related to investigations, suspension and debarment, and compliance. Prior to law, Ms. Jackson worked in New York, Brazil, Spain, and France as a strategy consultant, primarily in technology and strategic industry and country development. Ms. Jackson graduated from the University of Pennsylvania with B.A.s in International Relations and Economics, *magna cum laude*, Phi Beta Kappa, and the School of Law, *magna cum laude*, order of the coif. She was a Rose Zetzer Fellow in the Women, Leadership and Equality Program.

Michael Kelly was Dean of the School of Law from 1975 to 1991. He later served as the University Vice President of Georgetown University, has been Senior Fellow at the Zicklin Center for Business Ethics Research at the Wharton School at the University of Pennsylvania, a Visiting Scholar at the Organization Studies Department of the Sloan School of Management at MIT, and a senior manager at the Center for Applied Research, a management consulting firm working with nonprofit and for-profit corporations. He currently serves on the board of the National Senior Citizens Law Center, an organization that specializes in issues affecting older Americans of modest or negligible means as a back-up center working in support of legal aid and other lawyers serving elderly clients. Dean Kelly is a member of the board and the executive committee of both CareFirst Inc., a nonprofit health insurer, and Union Theological Seminary in New York City.

Susan Leviton is a Professor at the School of Law. She is Founder and Honorary Chair of Advocates for Children and Youth, a statewide child advocacy organization. In the past, Professor Leviton was the chairperson of the Maryland Human Relations Commission. Presently, she is on the Board of the Open Society Institute and on the Board of the Baltimore Freedom Academy, a charter school. She presently runs a clinic where students represent children in the Juvenile Court and in Special Education proceedings and teach law-related advocacy courses to high school students at the Baltimore Freedom Academy.

Susan G. McCarty is the Managing Research Fellow at the School of Law. She is a graduate of Wellesley College and the School of Law, order of the coif. As Managing Research Fellow, McCarty directs the work of fellows who research and edit for faculty and prepare their books and articles for publication.

Paula A. Monopoli is Professor of Law at the School of Law. She is a graduate of Yale College and the University of Virginia School of Law, and she is an elected member of the American Law Institute. Professor Monopoli also founded the School of Law's Women, Leadership and Equality Program in 2003. Her previous books include *American Probate: Protecting the Public, Improving the Process* (Northeastern University Press, 2003) and *Contemporary Approaches to Trusts and Estates* (with Gary, Borison, and Cahn) (Aspen Publishing, 2011). Professor Monopoli is an Academic Fellow of the American College of Trust and Estates Counsel.

Lydia Nussbaum is on the faculty at the University of Baltimore School of Law, teaching in the Mediation Clinic for Families. Prior to joining the University of Baltimore, she worked at the School of Law as a Fellow for the Leadership, Ethics, and Democracy Building Initiative (LEAD), co-teaching a Professional Responsibility seminar for clinical students, and working on a variety of projects to help prepare law students for the challenges of legal practice. Ms. Nussbaum earned her J.D. from the School of Law and her B.A. from Cornell University. Before entering the legal profession, Nussbaum taught high school history.

Donald J. Polden is Dean and Professor of Law at Santa Clara University School of Law. Dean Polden is a well-known scholar in the areas of employment law and legal education. He has been at the forefront of the movement to introduce leadership studies as part of the curriculum in American law schools.

Robert J. Rhee is Marbury Research Professor of Law and Co-Director of the Business Law Program at the School of Law. He clerked on the federal circuit, served as a trial attorney in the U.S. Department of Justice, and as an M&A investment banker in London and New York. He is an active scholar and writes in the areas of business and risk analysis. He has taught law in the Netherlands, the United Kingdom, and Korea, and business ethics at the University of Maryland Robert H. Smith School of Business.

Larry Richard is the Principal Consultant at LawyerBrain LLC. Prior to founding LawyerBrain, Dr. Richard was a Managing Director and the Chair of the Leadership and Organization Development practice at Hildebrandt Baker Robbins, the world leader in management consulting to the legal profession. Based in the Philadelphia area, Dr. Richard earned his law degree from the University of Pennsylvania Law School and his Ph.D. in psychology from Temple University. An expert on lawyers' personalities and law firm leadership, he has published numerous articles and book chapters on law practice and behavioral science, and speaks and writes frequently on the subject.

Georgia Sorenson is a Visiting Research Professor of Leadership Studies at the School of Law. She founded the James MacGregor Burns Academy of Leadership at the University of Maryland at College Park, and also held the position of Distinguished Leadership Scholar and Research Professor. She has also served as the Inaugural Chair and Professor of Transformational Leadership for the U.S. Army, as a Visiting Senior Scholar at the University of Richmond's Jepson School of Leadership Studies and has held a faculty appointment at Williams College. Her policy experience includes being appointed Senior Analyst for Employment in the White House and roles in the Commission on Civil Rights and the National Institute of Education. An architect of the leadership studies field, Dr. Sorenson is co-editor (with George Goethals and James MacGregor Burns) of the four-volume multi-award-winning *Encyclopedia of Leadership*, published by SAGE Books (2004). Her most recent theoretical work (with Goethals) is *The Quest for a General Theory of Leadership* (Elgar, 2006). Dr. Sorenson serves on the editorial board of numerous refereed journals including *Leadership* (U.S. Editor), *Leadership Quarterly* (Associate Editor) and *Leadership Review*. Her most recent book, *Strategic Leadership, A General's Art* (with Mark Grandstaff) on military leadership, came out in early 2009 and she has a forthcoming book, *The Power of Invisible Leadership: How a Compelling Common Purpose Inspires Exceptional Leadership* (with Gill Hickman) to be released by SAGE in 2013.

Foreword

From Classrooms to the Professions

The last century will be known as a quest for leadership. It was a time of great leaders—from Roosevelt to Aung San Suu Kyi—as well as profound failures—from Kim Jong Il to Muammar Al-Qaddafi. It was a time when many gave considerable thought to understanding the art and science of leadership as well the practical need to create a culture of developing leaders. Some of our great thinkers—Bernie Bass, Jerry Hunt, Ed Hollander, Ron Walters, Joe Rost, and others—moved our thinking forward. We now focus on leadership and leaderships, much more than leaders, and understand the essential role of followers, situation, and context in the leadership process.

We are in desperate need of good leadership, as any daily newspaper attests. Answering this call, the twentieth century produced a renaissance of leadership development. Over the last 40 years, some 700 programs have emerged in higher education in the US and countless others across the globe. Leadership studies is one of the fastest growing interdisciplinary areas in higher education.

The twenty-first century marks the cusp of our work as we bring leadership and leadership scholarship to the professions, in the many schools and venues in which we train and educate those who serve the common good. Schools of medicine, law, nursing, architecture, social work, pharmacy, and business are incorporating leadership education and there is new work between the interstices of the professions, such as law and medicine, or business and pharmacy, where much of the cutting-edge new work resides.

Research has shown that leadership learning is developmental and sequential. Across the world we have programs in elementary schools, high schools, colleges, and graduate studies. We have school and university programs founded by parents, students, faculty, business leaders, presidents, kings, and queens.

A few pioneering efforts are now emerging in professional schools and in professional associations and societies. This is our frontier and our vision—to launch books, journals, and curricula focused tightly on those who will be leaders in their professional domains.

We do not ordinarily associate leadership with the law, but some of the great legal theorists and jurists in America—Oliver Wendell Holmes comes to mind—have been leadership thinkers as well.

This volume represents a significant rallying call to those in legal education who understand that attorneys are at the vanguard of leadership responsibilities, particularly in the public sphere. From the founding fathers onwards, lawyers have dominated public leadership roles at the local, congressional, and presidential level. It's not surprising. Where rule of law predominates, there will always be those who are trained to read, write, and practice law. And lead.

As Sarat and Scheingold have noted on the first page of their book, *Cause Lawyers and Social Movements* (Palo Alto: Stanford University Press 2006: 1), the last half of the twentieth century in the United States and elsewhere was also dominated by the law's role in social change, from the civil rights struggle, to equal rights for women, the environmental rights efforts, and gay rights. "They pressed the claims of oppressed people and disadvantaged groups and reminded Americans of our shared aspirations and ideals." In short, they used their legal education to reform and extend equal rights in dramatic ways.

The legal academy has come late to these efforts, compared with schools of business, nursing, and medicine, to name a few. This volume, produced by a pioneering group of leadership educators working to transform the legal curriculum, aims to rectify this.

James MacGregor Burns
Williamstown, Massachusetts

Preface

Leadership matters in nearly all aspects of public life and in many areas of private life. This adage has been true for many years in the areas of governmental affairs and political life as well as in business and commerce. Simply stated, there is a perceived need for leaders and for leadership in most areas of our society—including many professional and occupational disciplines—because societal and economic problems and their solutions are increasingly complicated, transnational, and require coordination and agreement. There are significant challenges to the order and functioning of world economies, to political alliances that foster cooperative resolutions to international disputes, and to the formation of coherent strategies for solving problems. Addressing these challenges requires leaders of the first order.

Recently, there has been greater recognition of the importance of leadership in disciplines such as medicine and law. There are thousands of programs and courses of study in many academic and professional disciplines that prepare individuals for leadership roles and responsibilities. Airport bookstores are jammed with dozens of contemporary treatments on the theory and practice of leadership, on effective leaders, and the growing need for better leadership. There is even consideration of the Zen of leadership. Nearly every business school undergraduate and graduate program has required courses in leadership and the development of leaders' skills. However, noticeably missing from this list of devotees and practitioners of leadership education, at least until now, have been lawyers, judges and law teachers. There are various reasons for this gap between the state of leadership education in law and in many other disciplines. No strong and clear case has been made for the notion that lawyers are not able to lead or that leadership and lawyers' work are incompatible. Many aspects of the work that lawyers do require leadership skills and attributes (Heineman 2006). In fact, as has become abundantly clear, there are important reasons why lawyers need formal education in leadership roles and responsibilities as well as practical training in leadership skills (Rhode 2010).

We are now witnessing an important movement toward leadership education for lawyers and in law schools. A great deal of the emphasis for this movement toward leadership skills and education for lawyers, judges and law students has come from the few law schools that have created leadership education programs and courses. Also, importantly, there has been an increase in scholarship—academic and practical—advocating the case for leadership education and for the development and demonstration of leadership attributes and abilities of lawyers and judges. Some of the scholarship applies leadership theories and approaches gathered from the business or corporate leadership literature to lawyers who are leaders and leadership education for lawyers and law students.[1] Some of the emerging literature provides a comprehensive treatment of topics on leadership by lawyers (Rhode and Packel 2011), while other literature emphasizes the topology of leadership skills and how they can be acquired, mastered, and demonstrated (Cullen 2009). Roughly a dozen American law schools now offer courses in leadership skills and theory, with the goals of informing law students of lawyers' leadership responsibilities and preparing them for leadership roles after law school.[2] A few law schools have "executive education" programs in leadership for lawyers, aimed at law firm leaders who wish to advance their leadership and management skills within the firm.

Some of the recent motivation for greater leadership education for lawyers is the result of the significant challenges to law practice, the legal profession, and legal education. There are profound changes occurring in the ways that law is practiced, how legal education is expected to prepare tomorrow's lawyers, and the organizations that lawyers form and lead to serve their clients.[3] Without question, there is a great need for strong, clear and effective leadership in the legal profession and in legal education to meet these challenges and articulate the case for a responsive, competent, and ethical legal profession.

This book, *Law and Leadership: Integrating Leadership Studies into the Law School Curriculum*, is a collection of readings and resource materials that will provide enormous assistance to the movement toward leadership education for lawyers and in law schools. The articles are a product of the University of Maryland Francis King Carey School of Law's commitment to leadership education and, more particularly, a national conference planned and sponsored by the School of Law in 2008 and a working group that grew out of that conference. Maryland's initiative in leadership education was supported by a significant grant from the Fetzer Institute to initiate and implement a national program in leadership by lawyers. This initiative—denominated as Leadership Ethics and Democracy (LEAD)—brought together resources and talent within the School of Law and the University, including the nationally recognized leadership program, the James MacGregor Burns Academy of Leadership, to address the key topics advanced in

---

1   For example, Cullen (2009) draws heavily on the work of James Kouzes and Barry Posner in their Leadership Challenge series of leadership education texts.

2   Some of those schools are at: Elon University, University of Maryland, Santa Clara University, St. Thomas University (Minnesota), Georgetown University, and University of Denver.

3   These challenges are many and include concerns about the teaching mission of law schools and their ability to prepare new lawyers for the challenges of tomorrow's law practice workplace, the effects of the recent economic recession on lawyers' work and economic viability, significantly reduced employment opportunities for new lawyers, and others. Important treatments of those trends are: Morgan (2010), Susskind (2008), and Sullivan et al. (2007).

this book, including lawyers as leaders in the profession and in communities, cross disciplinary approaches to leadership education, and leadership in the context of lawyers' service to the profession.

The book is organized around three fundamental themes: the roles that lawyers play as leaders; why leadership should be taught in law schools; and what a sound leadership education curriculum should look like in law schools. These are *the* critical topics being discussed in the movement toward leadership education in law schools and in law firms and towards an articulated description of lawyers' leadership skills and aptitudes. The authors, many of whom were key presenters at the 2008 conference at the School of Law and members of the ongoing working group, demonstrate a depth of knowledge and creative thinking about why we should think of lawyers as leaders, how best to educate lawyers for leadership positions, and the educational responsibilities of law schools and legal educators. However, the authors also illuminate and take on some of the "hard spots" in a comprehensive concept of educating lawyers for leadership roles. For example, it is relatively easy to view lawyers in leadership roles when they use their skills and prestige to serve on boards or as officers of professional organizations. However, in considering the customary contexts in which lawyers work (e.g., representing clients in business transactions, appearing as advocates in proceedings, etc.), the leadership roles are more complicated because lawyers have specific professional responsibilities to their clients that in many respects are different from the relationship between business leaders and their constituents. Moreover, lawyers' professional relationships with clients in a corporate transaction are fundamentally different than the relationship in criminal litigation, so the context of lawyer as leader of the client or the client's case is more nuanced and it is more difficult to fit within traditional leadership theories (for example, transformational leadership).

The authors also point out that law schools have developed pedagogical approaches to educate law students "to think like lawyers," but thinking like a lawyer is not the same thing as thinking like a leader. These distinctions and contradictions do not eviscerate the core theme of the book (and the movement toward useful theories of leadership by lawyers) that lawyers do lead and, like many other professionals, need leadership education to be more effective leaders and lawyers. Indeed, several articles in the book serve to make the inquiry into understanding how lawyers lead and the debate about whether lawyers serving as lawyers can be leaders more rigorous and more important.

The book also shares some successful examples of curricular ideas and pedagogy in law school leadership education courses. These descriptions illustrate the creative methods that leadership educators can bring to courses that introduce leadership education to law schools. The book will serve to induce other legal educators to design and teach leadership courses and build the lawyering skills curriculum nationally.

I hope that the readers of *Law and Leadership: Integrating Leadership Studies into the Law School Curriculum* share my enthusiasm, not only for the timeliness and comprehensive nature of the book, but also for its promise to materially advance the discussion of leadership education in law schools and in the legal profession.

Donald J. Polden
Dean and Professor of Law, Santa Clara University

References

Cullen, R. 2009. *The Leading Lawyer: A Guide to Practicing Law and Leadership.* St. Paul, MN: Thomson Reuters/West.

Heineman, B., Jr. 2006. Law and Leadership. *Journal of Legal Education*, 56(4): 596–614.

Morgan, T.D. 2010. *The Vanishing American Lawyer*. New York: Oxford University Press.

Rhode, D. 2010. Law and Leadership. *The Professional Lawyer*, 20(3): 1, 12–17.

Rhode, D. and Packel, A.K. 2011. *Leadership: Law, Policy and Management.* New York: Wolters Kluwer.

Sullivan, W.M., Colby, A., Wegner, J.W., Bond, L. and Shulman, L.S. 2007. *Educating Lawyers: Preparation for the Profession of Law*. San Francisco: Jossey-Bass.

Susskind, R.E. 2008. *The End of Lawyers?: Rethinking the Nature of Legal Services*. New York: Oxford University Press.

Acknowledgments

This book was inspired by a partnership between the University of Maryland Francis King Carey School of Law and the Fetzer Institute. In 2008, the Fetzer Institute entered into a collaborative project with the School of Law that became known as the Leadership, Ethics and Democracy (LEAD) Initiative. One of the projects included in the Initiative was the Lawyers as Leaders component. This project focused on developing a course of leadership studies for the School of Law. This work was informed by a group of legal academics, judges, and lawyers in private practice, corporations, nonprofits, and government in an ongoing leadership forum. This working group met over the course of three years to discuss what leadership meant in the legal profession, why (or why not) law schools should integrate leadership into the curriculum, and how it should do so. We heard from experts in the field, and we heard from faculty and students who were pioneers in designing new courses to explore how leadership was connected to law. We are grateful to all of the members of the working group listed below, to the people who spoke with us, to the students who were brave enough to enroll in these new courses, and to the Fetzer Institute for supporting our work. We want to thank Maura DeMouy in particular for her tireless work on behalf of the Initiative and Megan McDonald and Alice Johnson, who supported our work administratively.

Paula A. Monopoli
Susan G. McCarty

Leadership Forum Working Group

This book would not be possible without the members of the Leadership Forum Working Group. Their dedication and hard work are very much appreciated.

Bonnie Allen	Christopher Awad
José Bahamonde-González	Clinton Bamberger
Barbara Bezdek	Brenda Bratton Blom
Christopher Brown	Andrew Canter
Cait Clarke	Dawna Cobb
Adam Connolly	Diane D'Aiutolo
Leary Davis	Suzzanne Decker
Maura DeMouy	Leah Durant
John Frisch	Robert Gonzales
David Gray	Justin Hansford
Terry Hickey	Matthew Hjortsberg
Diane Hoffmann	Alan Hornstein
Alexina Jackson	Deborah Jennings
Sherri Keene	Michael Kelly
Teresa LaMaster	Susan McCarty
Michael Millemann	Paula Monopoli
Dana Morris	Larry Nathans
Lewis Noonberg	Laurie Norris
Lydia Nussbaum	Irma Raker
Robert Rhee	Larry Richard
Reena Shah	Georgia Sorenson
Heather Spurrier	Donna Hill Staton
Mark Treanor	Frank Wu

Copyright Acknowledgments

The authors thankfully acknowledge permission to reprint materials from the following works:

Ayers, W. 2004. *Teaching Toward Freedom: Moral Commitment and Ethical Action in the Classroom*. Boston: Beacon Press. Republished with permission of William Ayers, from *Teaching Toward Freedom: Moral Commitment and Ethical Action in the Classroom* (2007); permission conveyed through the Copyright Clearance Center, Inc.

Browne-Ferrigno, T. and Muth, R. 2004. Leadership Mentoring in Clinical Practice: Role Socialization, Professional Development, and Capacity Building, *Educational Administration Quarterly*, 40(4): 468–94. Copyright © 2004 by the University Council for Educational Administration, reprinted by permission of SAGE Publications.

Churchill, W.S. 1940. Speech before the House of Commons. Reproduced with permission of Curtis Brown, London, on behalf of the Estate of Sir Winston Churchill. Copyright © Winston S. Churchill.

Day, D.V. 2000. Leadership Development: A Review in Context, *Leadership Quarterly*, 11(4): 581–613. Reprinted from *The Leadership Quarterly*, 11(4), Day, D.V., Leadership Development: A Review in Context, 582, 605, Copyright 2000, with permission from Elsevier.

Gardner, H. 1983. *Frames of Mind: The Theory of Multiple Intelligences*. New York: Basic Books. Reprinted by permission of Basic Books, a member of the Perseus Book Group.

Jacobi, M. 1991. Mentoring and Undergraduate Academic Success: A Literature Review, *Review of Education Research*, 61(4): 505–32. Copyright © 1991 by American Educational Research Association. Reprinted by permission of SAGE Publications.

Kohl, H. 1994. *"I Won't Learn from You": And Other Thoughts on Creative Maladjustment*. New York: New Press. Herbert Kohl, from *I Won't Learn From You* (Minneapolis: Milkweed Editions, 1994). Copyright © 1994 by Herbert Kohl. Reprinted with permission from Milkweed Editions. www.milkweed.org.

Kouzes, J.M. and Posner, B.Z. 2002. *The Leadership Challenge*. 3rd edition. New York: Jossey Bass. This material is reproduced with permission of John Wiley & Sons, Inc.

Khurana, R. 2007. *From Higher Aims to Hired Hands, The Social Transformation of American Business Schools and the Unfulfilled Promise of Management as a Profession.* Princeton: Princeton University Press. Copyright © 2007, Princeton University Press.

Kronman, A. 1993. *The Lost Lawyer: Failing Ideals of the Legal Profession.* Cambridge, MA: Belknap. Reprinted by permission from the publisher from *The Lost Lawyer: Failing Ideals of the Legal Profession* by Anthony T. Kronman, p. 150, Cambridge, MA: The Belknap Press of the Harvard University Press. Copyright © 1993 by the President and Fellows of Harvard College.

Lerman, L.G. 2002. The Slippery Slope from Ambition to Greed to Dishonesty: Lawyers, Money, and Professional Integrity, *Hofstra Law Review*, 30(3): 879–922. With permission of the Hofstra Law Review Association.

Luban, D. 2007. *Legal Ethics and Human Dignity.* New York: Cambridge University Press. Reprinted with the permission of Cambridge University Press.

Mathews, R.E. 1953. The Lawyer, Law Schools and Responsible Leadership, *Rocky Mountain Law Review*, 25(4): 482–9. Reprinted with permission of the University of Colorado Law Review.

Newman, J. 2007. Appreciate Your Associates: Make Your Firm a Workplace of Choice, *Legal Management*, March/April, 47–54. Joan M. Newman, Joan Newman & Associates LLC. 2007. Appreciate Your Associates. Make Your Firm a Workplace of Choice, *Legal Management*, March/April, 47–54. Reprinted with permission from *Legal Management*, 6(2), published by the Association of Legal Administrators, www.alanet.org.

Rhode, D.L. 2000. *In the Interests of Justice: Reforming the Legal Profession.* New York: Oxford University Press. By permission of Oxford University Press, Inc.

Tatum, B.D. 2003. *Why Are All the Black Kids Sitting Together in the Cafeteria?* 5th anniversary edition. New York: Basic. Copyright © 1997 Tatum, Beverly Daniel. Reprinted by permission of Basic Books, a member of the Perseus Book Group.

Tyler, T.R. and Lind, E.A. 1992. A Relational Model of Authority in Groups, *Advances in Experimental Social Psychology*, 25(1): 115–91. Reprinted from *Advances in Experimental Social Psychology*, 25(1), Tyler, T.R. and Lind, E.A. *A Relational Model of Authority in Groups*, 115–91, Copyright © 1992, with permission from Elsevier.

Introduction

Paula A. Monopoli and Susan G. McCarty

Lawyers have always been leaders. If leadership is defined as the ability to persuade others to embrace your ideas and to act upon them, then lawyers are remarkably well suited to be leaders. We learn the art of persuasion the very first year of law school. So why is it that legal academics find it so odd that a new generation of students is clamoring for leadership studies in law schools?

Perhaps it is that we have never articulated the nexus between what we do—teach our students how to "think like lawyers"—and the skills that effective leaders deploy. This book is an effort to reflect upon that nexus. It is a collection of essays by law professors, professors of leadership studies, deans, a former congressman, law students, and lawyers in private practice, nonprofits, and government.

The book proceeds in three parts. Part I explores the *what*: What is leadership in the context of the legal profession? What are its particular challenges in legal academia, in private practice, in the nonprofit sector and government? Part II explores the *why*: Why do our students need to study leadership in law school and why are they demanding that we offer it as part of the curriculum? And, finally, Part III explores the *how*. Faculty who have designed new courses grounded in leadership, and who are integrating leadership into their existing courses, reflect on how to effectively blend law and leadership in doctrinal, clinical, and experiential classrooms.

Each part begins with a foundational essay that lays the groundwork for the essays that follow. In Part I, Phoebe A. Haddon, dean of the University of Maryland Francis King Carey School of Law, describes the significance of leadership studies for both future lawyers and legal education and Maryland's leadership in this area. Georgia Sorenson explores the nexus between leadership theory and law. Her chapter is followed by Larry Richard's analysis of the nature of lawyers and the competencies they require to be effective leaders. Alexina Jackson lays out a new model of practice and the leadership skills required of lawyers to succeed in this new environment. Specific leadership challenges in various sectors of the profession are then explored in the context of private practice and government by Maura DeMouy and Mickey Edwards.

Part II is anchored by Leary Davis, founding dean of Elon Law School, another institution on the cutting edge of integrating leadership into the law school curriculum. He analyzes why law schools are resistant to embracing the discipline of leadership studies and lays the foundation for the chapters that follow. These chapters further evaluate the need for leadership education in law school and whether or not it is a compatible discipline. They include Diane Hoffmann's argument for leadership education in law schools and Michael Kelly's analysis of how teaching students to think like lawyers—what we say we do in law schools—differs from teaching them how to think like leaders, and whether we can or should do the latter in law school.

Finally, in Part III we turn to how we actually integrate leadership into our law school classes. This process calls for an interdisciplinary approach where we borrow from our colleagues in other disciplines like philosophy, political science, business, economics, social psychology, and literature. Brenda Bratton Blom, Lydia Nussbaum, and Bonnie Allen anchor this section with their description of an innovative new approach to teaching professional responsibility and ethical leadership. Avery M. Blank describes the new Maryland course in leadership theory from a student's perspective. Blom and Dorcas R. Gilmore then explore the development of leadership concepts in the context of mentoring and professional identity formation. Robert J. Rhee explores how concepts so important to the modern lawyer, like working in teams and taking risks, can be integrated into the law school classroom. Alan D. Hornstein discusses how literature can be used to illuminate leadership issues within the context of law. Susan Leviton, Kerry Cooperman, and Jeremy Grant-Skinner explore learning leadership skills by teaching them to others. And, finally, Paula A. Monopoli reflects on teaching gender and leadership in the context of legal education.

Taken together, these chapters create a blueprint for others in legal education to evaluate whether leadership studies can and should be integrated into the modern law school curriculum and, if so, how it may be done.

PART I
Lawyers as Leaders

Chapter 1

Leadership Studies for Lawyers of the Future

Phoebe A. Haddon[1]

There is a nascent movement among American law schools to introduce leadership studies into the curriculum (Polden 2008, Rhode and Packel 2011). This is not surprising; more than a decade ago, business schools had undertaken a similar movement, making it a hallmark of their teaching and curriculum (Doh 2003: 57). Undergraduate schools have also focused attention on leadership studies, advertising curricular offerings that are designed to set their students apart from others.[2]

At the outset of each of these movements, faculty have often expressed skepticism about the ability to actually teach or even define what leadership means. They have questioned whether there is intellectual rigor in what is studied and argued that much of what a leader does—or why a leader emerges—is defined by character and context rather than knowledge (Posner 1993: 1924). Because our understanding of successful leadership emerges in diverse situations, the capacity of an individual to lead successfully may actually be unpredictable; certainly there is little consensus on the skills and attributes of leadership without a discussion of the context for its exercise (Rhode 2010).

Lawyers become leaders in a variety of settings, and it is time for law schools to address leadership in an academic way. But can we do a better job of answering the questions posed by the skeptics? What is our conception of leadership for lawyers? What can law schools offer in theory and practice that equips lawyers to become effective leaders? What purpose is served by offering leadership education in law school as contrasted with the undergraduate experiences to which many students by now have been exposed? Should we postpone such study until students are in practice or in other post-law school professional work?

Leadership studies are relatively new to legal education. As a result, they may be treated as though at the margins of curricula, and thus expendable or at risk of

---

1   I would like to thank Rachel Granfield and Jane Wilson for their work in researching and editing this chapter.
2   More than a decade ago, Gregory H. Williams, then president of the Association of American Law Schools, decried the lack of leadership training in law schools and pointed out the large number of leadership development programs in other areas of academia: nearly 700 such programs, mostly at undergraduate institutions (Williams 1999).

faculty decisions, leaving them with insufficient resources to create a sustained impact on student and professional development.[3] *In these times of scarce resources and burgeoning debt, how do we justify new and untested programs about leadership? Why would we expect foundations or other donors to support this work?*

As others have done, the University of Maryland Francis King Carey School of Law's Leadership, Ethics and Democracy (LEAD) Initiative has struggled to answer the skeptics. Lawyer and leader are not synonyms, and legal education as it presently stands may actually impede the development of some kinds of leadership, especially the relational conceptions that we know to be important in most contexts where lawyers lead. In this chapter, I consciously use the term *leadership* rather than *leader*, which has tended to connote the individualism and hierarchy that can disable lawyers and other leaders from successfully engaging others in their enterprise.

Delineating a concept of leadership appropriate for legal education and its pedagogy is a challenge. Any law school, public or private, must grapple with the question of what leadership means in the context of legal education and how it may be (and whether it must be) integrated into the law curriculum.

I have struggled with this challenge personally in self-reflection as I serve as dean and strive to lead effectively, as well as when I respond to skeptics on my faculty and among legal educators when I talk about the value of leadership studies for law students.

In thinking about this chapter, I have considered what special insights lawyers bring to leadership positions: are they successful because of their legal education or because of the experiences to which they have been exposed as lawyers along their professional paths? Are lawyers more predisposed to leadership because of personalities, acculturation, or professional development?

What is it that we seek in leadership studies for law students whom we expect to be leaders of the future? What are our objectives in such a program of study? What kind of leaders are we trying to shape?

Though I do not have the full answer to this set of questions, I am convinced that teaching leadership in law school is valuable "because our core skills, properly conceived, of understanding how values, rules and institutions interrelate with social, economic and political conditions is as central to the demands of leadership as any other professional or disciplinary background" (Heineman 2006: 19).

---

3   Insight from a conversation with Dr. Georgia Sorenson, founder of the James MacGregor Burns Academy of Leadership, formerly housed at the University of Maryland, College Park.

The Maryland Experiment

LEAD faculty began with a broad definition of leadership in the formative stages of the project. They did not narrowly define leadership as leading from *only* a position of authority, because leadership skills can be used in virtually any position. Leadership can include individual skills as well as group skills. For lawyers, leadership can start while in law school and develop further in practicing lawyers and as lawyers become leaders in society. Lawyers exhibit leadership within big firms, small firms, the private sector, the public sector, and the nonprofit sector.

In leadership studies, one must also consider the set of skills, personal qualities, ethics, and organizational dynamics that define effectiveness in a given context (Rhode 2010). It is questionable how helpful this abstract, big-tent description can be.

Maryland used the LEAD Initiative to develop a leadership curriculum that included three core courses,[4] a large group of elective courses, and opportunities for experiential learning, such as client advocacy at the Mississippi Center for Justice and teaching at the Baltimore Freedom Academy—experiences that are documented in this book.

Our hope was that by learning about the experiences of public leaders in seminars like Law and Public Leadership for Social Change, law students would be better able to model "the ability and the responsibility to lead, ethically and morally, in their law firms, communities, and the profession" (Polden 2008: 359). In contrast with the media image of lawyers, as well as with public figures who have lost their ethical moorings, students would have the opportunity to interact with political and community leaders who remain energized and passionate as they are caught up in the demands of their work. Such classroom experiences would help model what I have defined as a public calling to which all lawyers should aspire (Haddon 1994).

Given my commitment to the legal profession's public calling, I believe that law schools have a particular responsibility to prepare students for the leadership positions they are likely to hold throughout their lives and careers. This is especially true in a rapidly changing profession, when a leader must secure stable points for guidance. To me, the development of professional integrity is inseparable from the development of leadership skills because, in this time of dramatic change,

---

4 The core courses, taken in sequence, were Foundations of Leadership: Theory and Praxis, an introduction to leadership theory taught by Dr. Georgia Sorenson; Law and Public Leadership for Social Change, offered by former U.S. Congressman Mickey Edwards, now a vice president of the Aspen Institute and the director of its fellowship program for elected officials; and Professional Responsibility and Practice: The Rules and Reality, a new ethics course taught by Professor Brenda Bratton Blom, which was integrated with the clinical program. Each of these faculty members have written in depth about their courses in this book.

it is impossible to prepare students for the specific challenges they will face as leaders decades from now. Well-developed moral values provide the compass that allows effective leadership even in times of uncertainty. Law school leadership programs strive to provide students with the skills and values that will help them navigate the unknown challenges they will face.

To date, the evidence suggests that the Maryland leadership initiative was a success, particularly with students.[5] Going forward, we must engage the entire law school community in a discussion of leadership and professional identity. This may be somewhat easier at Maryland, given its longstanding commitment to clinical legal education and its requirement that all full-time students engage in "sustained reflective practice," which combines the actual practice of law with the mastery of legal theory.

The Future of Leadership Initiatives in Legal Education

There are several reasons why I am confident that the integration of leadership studies into legal education will grow—at Maryland and elsewhere—despite the challenges I have identified.

Both the Profession and the Public See Lawyers as Problem-solvers

Both the profession and the public perceive lawyers to be problem-solvers (Brest and Krieger 1999, Menkel-Meadow 1999, Reno 1999). Lawyers historically have been linked to leadership in the area of law reform as well as in articulating and addressing client problems before courts and other decision-makers. Because legal reasoning is a skill associated with lawyers and understood as foundational to problem-solving, "thinking like a lawyer" has sometimes been conflated with "thinking like a leader" in these contexts and beyond (Fuller 1948: 189, 201, 203).

In Chapter 9 of this volume, Michael Kelly challenges the assumption that lawyers are better leaders than members of other professions, although he also identifies productive intersections of lawyering and leadership that may be helpful in the education of young lawyers, which I will discuss later.

At bottom, Kelly and others who are skeptical of leadership studies are concerned that much of the literature removes leadership from the contexts in which it occurs. Others point to an academic preoccupation with legal reasoning at the expense of other important lawyering skills that could be used to measure leadership potential and thus indicate the need for leadership studies.

In some law schools, classes focus on creative thinking and problem-solving, team-building, persuasion (beyond advocacy), how to motivate others, and tactics

---

5   Students used terms such as "transformative," "magical," "out of this world," "phenomenal," and "amazing" to describe their experiences with the courses and other opportunities that are part of the LEAD Initiative.

for achieving cooperation—skills that have not traditionally been identified as necessary for professional legal training (Polden 2008: 358).

The academy's acceptance of a broader conception of skills training has its roots in the seminal work of the MacCrate Report (ABA Section of Legal Education and Admission to the Bar 1992) and more recently the Carnegie Report (Sullivan et al. 2007). Robert MacCrate's committee recognized that legal education's preoccupation with legal reasoning (principally through the case method of study) had marginalized important skills training necessary to prepare students for the practice of law. This approach can also be traced to the Lon Fuller/Karl Llewellyn debate about whether reading and studying appellate case law sufficiently prepares students for the difficult problem-solving challenges that lie ahead in practice (Fuller 1948, Llewellyn 1948).

A 2011 article in the *Chronicle of Higher Education* suggests that students come to undergraduate school and later graduate school without the lived experiences that lead them to understand the need for and value of compromise (Bacow et al. 2011). The MacCrate Report famously championed the idea that skills training, along with legal analysis, should be required in legal education and in the selection and graduation of competent students who are prepared to become lawyers (ABA Section of Legal Education and Admission to the Bar 1992).

The MacCrate Report recognized the problem of "the missing client" in legal education and spurred the rise of clinical education, as well as simulations and stories about clients in the traditional classroom. Schools use all of these methods in an attempt to prevent law from being taught as an abstract mental exercise without relevant details of situations and the people in them, as well as the social or ethical consequences of legal conclusions. Clinical education recovers relational lawyering, often through leadership mentoring (Blom and Gilmore: Chapter 12, this volume). For law students, both the exposure to the client in the clinic, as well as the connection to the clinical teacher, foster an understanding of leadership that is relational and built on teamwork rather than hierarchical and authoritative.

More recently, the Carnegie Foundation for the Advancement of Teaching's *Educating Lawyers: Preparation for the Profession of Law* has also recognized the shortcomings of a legal education that predominantly values analytical reasoning without adequate attention to skills training or opportunities for ethical reflection. The Carnegie Report praised the way that American law schools afford their students powerful intellectual and analytical tools. But it recognized "the increasingly urgent need to bridge the gap between analytical and practical knowledge, and a demand for a more robust professional integrity," as well as the shaping of professional identity important for all professions (Sullivan et al. 2007: 12).

Building on the recognition of lawyering skills as a foundation for leadership studies, Santa Clara Law has developed a broad array of what it characterizes as fundamental lawyering skills and values, including listening, teamwork, and reflection, as a way to complement pedagogy that is solely focused on legal reasoning (Polden 2008: 358).

This development also is supported by the trend within the legal profession itself to place greater value on individuals with a demonstrated ability to listen, to successfully recruit others in working toward a common cause, and to inspire others to achieve what appear to be unattainable goals.

Law schools at Elon, Santa Clara, and Maryland universities have pioneered leadership studies. The Santa Clara program grew from a course, some scholarship about the concept of leadership by lawyers, discussions of the importance of educating law students for leadership roles, and leadership skills training for student leaders. It relied upon the interest of a single faculty "champion" and the resources of its business school to develop the program (Polden 2008).

The Santa Clara leadership initiative was justified by this private law school's mission—"educating lawyers of competence, conscience and compassion" who are prepared to "meet the challenges of a legal profession that is increasingly global, technologically sophisticated, and culturally diverse" (Polden 2008: 354). The institutional focus on leadership reflects the belief that it is a fundamental lawyering skill that students will need as they assume leadership roles in their communities and in their profession throughout their careers (Polden 2008: 354). Not only is there controversy about whether leadership curriculum is necessary or valuable in our law schools, there is even more skepticism about the assumption that "leadership skills and attributes are fundamental lawyering skills ... and values" (Polden 2008: 353).

Changes in the Profession

The reality of the legal profession's restructuring has also given rise to interest in leadership studies in law schools among practitioners and others who remain critical of legal education's persistent failure to train students about the realities of practice.

Moreover, the current economic climate has led legal employers to reevaluate the skills they seek in their newest hires. Clients are unwilling to absorb the costs of training new associates. As a result, firms are looking for practice-ready graduates who have had not only significant legal skills training and experiential learning opportunities, but who are individuals with vision and who have developed their competency as leaders able to work well with clients and colleagues in finding solutions to problems (Borden and Rhee 2011, Segal 2011).

Many firms have relied on the work of consultants to gain insights into the personality traits that will predict whether a given lawyer is compatible with a firm's culture (Richard: Chapter 3, this volume). This trend is often ignored or disparaged by legal educators who believe that law schools should not react to changes in the profession. They challenge the proposition that changes in the business model underlying the practice of law are structural rather than cyclical, or even that they are relevant to teaching and scholarship in the academy (Stevenson 2012).

But not all skeptics about the value of leadership studies dismiss news about the restructuring of law firms. Michael Kelly, for example, argues that to prepare students for future practice, law schools should recognize that the changes in the profession share one crucial component: they are "driven by fierce competition, massive consolidation, and obsession with compensation by owners of private firms" (Chapter 9, this volume). Kelly observes that most organizational decisions in firms and other sites of law-related work are driven by perceptions of what is needed to serve present and future clients, with special attention paid to competition, compensation, and consolidation. Such decisions are designed to strengthen and preserve the organization by insulating it from market vicissitudes and uncertainties, stabilizing its client base and retaining the attorneys who will best recruit and retain clients.

Firms of all sizes and in-house corporate offices are implicated in Kelly's description of the organizational terrain that new lawyers will face. These organizations are increasingly sophisticated about their needs and responsive to client cost-reduction goals.

Kelly further observes that legal ethics, and especially the growth of issue conflicts, have deeply fragmented the profession, widening social, ideological, and economic divisions. "Law is now a profession divided, balkanized by the causes and interests of practice organizations beholden to their clients" (Kelly 2011: 446).

Kelly is reluctant to adopt the business school model of leadership studies or a leadership skills-based approach. However, the restructuring of the profession is a consequence of the growth of law-related organizations and the stratification of the profession. Such organizations depend on their ability to protect their client base from outside competition for survival; they are not primarily concerned about their clients' interests. Kelly argues that the fluidity of these legal organization arrangements is important for students to understand and to be able to navigate once they have graduated (Chapter 9, this volume).

Kelly believes law schools should provide opportunities for students to learn about organizational dynamics. This would enable them to grasp the dominant role of organizations and recognize that negotiating organizational life in the law is now an important element of a successful career.

Greater understanding of organizations also would enable students to become active, analytical observers and participants in their own organizations, regardless of whether students seek out a large or small practice or plan to work in public or private entities. This kind of training would also enhance students' understanding of clients' and adversaries' organizations and enable them to assess professional opportunities in fields outside the law.

Focusing analytically on the organizations of practice will enrich and enlarge for students the ethical dimensions of professional responsibility, according to Kelly. Studying organizations, particularly law practice organizations, can reveal the present limitations of our conception of legal ethics. Given the fragmentation and divergence of the profession, a consideration of "vertical professionalism" is important to address the impact of organizations across the profession (Kelly 2011: 449). With Kelly's insights, leadership curricula could be developed to emphasize:

- organization dynamics critical for professional development,
- an understanding of organizations' importance in ethical training,
- the reality of different types of organizations, such as small and large practices, private for-profit and nonprofit organizations, and law reform and defense associations.

If legal education presently does not acknowledge changes in the profession, and if focusing on legal reasoning equips graduates poorly for the reality of organizations, practice environments, and other contexts in which lawyers work, why should leadership studies or other leadership-related exposure be the solution or one of the solutions? Kelly adds an ethical dimension to the introduction of legal education to organizational studies—it provides opportunities to reconsider the value of ethics and reflect on what one should do in ethically ambiguous or controversial situations. There is also a professional identity dimension—having studied organizations in this way, students can determine for themselves whether the profession offers for them a life well led.

Legal Education as Part of the University—A Call to Repair the Social Fabric

In a 2011 article in the *Chronicle of Higher Education*, leaders of three of the more than a dozen universities who have come together to pool resources and expand their problem-solving capacity issued a call for all universities to join with neighbors in the cities and regions in which they are located to address problems. The invitation starts with the premise that a university or institution of higher learning is a place where complex problems ought to be explored and new ideas offered (Bacow et al. 2011).[6] This invitation touched me deeply, for it speaks to the public calling about which I have written here and elsewhere. It justifies a kind of leadership cultivation that is likely to be sustainable, and also resonates with Guido Calabresi's admonition to scholars in the law school and elsewhere not to be afraid to look into dark places to uncover truth (Calabresi 1979: 429).

As the *Chronicle*'s essayists assert, there is pressure on higher education to improve its response to the needs of society. Though some would say publicly supported higher education has a special responsibility, all academic institutions of higher education benefit from some public support—especially in legal education, where tremendous amounts of tuition revenue are financed through government

---

6   This *Chronicle* commentary was by college presidents Lawrence S. Bacow (Tufts University), Shamsh Kassim-Lakha (founding president of Aga Khan University and former minister of Pakistan), and Saran Kaur Gill (deputy vice chancellor for industry and community partnerships at the National University of Malaysia—part of a consortium of 12 universities).

loans.[7] Universities are, moreover, increasingly asked or see themselves as obligated to help the neighborhoods in which they reside. Every university, public or private, urban or rural, is a member of its larger community.

Universities like those of the essayists also see themselves as committed to strengthening the civic role of higher education, abandoning the ivory tower to become socially important enterprises linked both in reality and symbolically to their neighborhoods (with connections that may be local, regional, statewide, national, and even international in different contexts). In this vision of the university, there is an obligation to the society that supports them and gives them justification for existence.

These presidents call on other institutions like theirs to move away from insularity, producing scholarship in "splendid isolation." Rather, they believe universities should engage in theoretical and practical problem-solving of crucial and current social issues with local neighbors as collaborative agents of social change.

Universities themselves will benefit if they work on such crucial social issues as health, education, challenges of urban and rural living, climate change, and development of civil society. Their students, faculty, and partners are likely to find audacious alternatives by working together, whether as mentor and mentee or as client and lawyer, in relationships of trust.

Projects should be local, national, and global in focus—built on collaboration and sharing of ideas and resources (including but not limited to material assets). Under this consortium framework, students and faculty commit themselves to identifying a pressing, socially important issue. The university then allocates resources to develop the interdisciplinary and multidisciplinary tools needed to create effective strategies and solutions.

The School of Law is located in downtown Baltimore and sees its relationship with the larger community—on a scale as macrocosmic as the international level and as microcosmic as the blocks around 500 West Baltimore Street—as strong and ongoing. The LEAD Initiative, including its newly established international law clinic, which provides students with local projects in Namibia, China, and Mexico, has the capacity to fit this model. Our ongoing faculty and student commitment to work in Mississippi and New Orleans in the aftermath of Hurricane Katrina also can be a useful platform for reconceiving leadership studies. Our clinics in Baltimore and across the state also often involve collaborative work with local neighbors.

Aside from the socially important work they invite, there is tremendous potential for reimagining universities and reframing their scholarship in this light.

---

7 In 2010, law students borrowed at least $3.7 billion to pay for their educations (Henderson and Zahorsky 2012). Some amount of this sum went toward their living expenses, but even if only half was used for tuition, law schools still received at least $1.85 billion in loan-funded tuition payments. Though some of these funds are private loans, the majority come from the U.S. Department of Education.

There are powerful opportunities in this kind of work for learning lessons from others which can truly transform lives—those of both the local recipients, as well as the teachers and students who come together. The consortium representatives argue that significant improvement in learning flows from these projects and they palpably improve the level of assistance available to those who have been victimized by the problem at hand. Moreover, such partnerships continue to produce ideas and sustainable community engagement long after faculty and students have moved on.

The academy also benefits. The essayists report that teaching is transformed by new ideas from students and community members, challenging the traditional hierarchy of leadership and learning. The writers' institutions, while acting locally, have tremendous influence nationally and internationally, enhanced through collaborative outreach.

This influence is built on the notion that civically engaged universities— including law schools—must be an important voice in shaping the public policy of the nation. This is understandable in terms of the resources utilized by such institutions and the potential benefits that flow from their work, especially if they engage partners, such as businesses and nonprofit groups, and seek the support of foundations and industry willing to endow chairs and fund research in socially important issues.

Alliances among higher education institutions and their neighbors are ideal platforms for generating knowledge and program development that connect scholarship and research with practical problem-solving. These alliances benefit from a two-way flow of knowledge and resources that increases the efficacy of individual projects and the level of innovation. Such collaborations also offer students rich educational opportunities and exposure to mentors.

Students engaged in such projects will have not only immeasurable opportunities for job preparation, professional development, and personal growth, but also a chance to become "citizen leaders who can apply knowledge directly to pressing problems and recognize areas of need" as universities "put learning into context and increase the relevance of education" (Bacow et al. 2011).

Such projects foster a new and attractive conception of higher learning institutions generally and law schools in particular. Institutions are under increased pressure by states to demonstrate a return on investment and to diversify, to counter the perception of serving only the elite or those fortunate enough to be enrolled. The presidents observe: "looking ahead, discussions about investments in higher education must include not only access and internationalization, but also aligning university resources with local, regional, and national needs" (Bacow et al. 2011). At the same time, universities and other institutions can continue to be deeply committed to educating students and the serious scholarly pursuit of knowledge.

This model—and the supporting arguments for change—resonate for me because they fit my understanding of lawyers as leaders imbued with a public calling. They also offer a richer understanding than the other models I have discussed here as a justification for leadership studies and the provision of learning contexts that support the development of leadership in law students by:

- promoting a sense of civic responsibility,
- offering field work that provides the lived experiences important to shaping leaders,
- providing multiple perspectives that can foster creative problem-solving,
- encouraging interdisciplinary thinking and offering multidisciplinary tools for problem-solving.

Leadership initiatives such as those discussed in this volume can answer this need. They can offer experiences from the global to the local level through clinics that provide fertile environments for engaging law students and faculty teaching leadership in this light.

The Entrepreneurial University: *Grutter*'s Implications

The U.S. Supreme Court in *Grutter v. Bollinger* recognized the use of race in law school admissions decisions as a legitimate compelling state interest in diversity, because lawyers often become leaders in the community and in their professional lives. The Court, in justifying its decision, noted the importance of students' being exposed to other cultures and the importance in the law school context of the appearance of an open and fair admissions process. The leadership links to lawyering that I have discussed support a continued commitment to diversifying the profession and the student population.

The problem of the stunted student remains with us. Many such law students come from racially isolated places and live lives that are not as shaped by struggle as those of their clients or other members of the community they may serve as leaders. Such students are in need of leadership-shaping experiences to broaden their understanding of life and provide opportunities for learning about compromise and failure that might lead them to be more creative and risk-taking as leaders. The proposed reconception of the university or other places of higher learning, as demonstrated by LEAD and other law schools' leadership initiatives, helps to address such shortcomings. The initiatives offer opportunities for collaboration and teamwork and provide alternative perspectives on how the law shapes and can address social issues, all of which will promote the development of ethical lawyer leadership.

In an ideal world, leadership skills would be taught at all levels of education: the ability and willingness to listen, to compromise, and to work inclusively are valuable at all stages of life, and research shows that leadership capacity is largely learned, whether formally or informally, rather than instinctual (Rhode 2010). In law, where leadership is not merely expected but often inevitable, it is even more important for future partners, policymakers, and professors to learn how to lead. Far too often, individuals with great legal acumen find themselves promoted into leadership positions without any management training or development (Rhode 2010). The past decade's series of major law firm failures are perhaps less surprising in this light: Good leadership cannot guarantee success, but it can decrease the risk of failure.[8]

Good and ethical leadership should be taught and learned—and it can be. Indeed, it is and has been for quite some time, though the legal profession has dragged behind its colleagues in this regard. But lawyers can no longer neglect the teaching of this essential skill set, which is just as important to practice as a knowledge of legal ethics and substantive law. We have only to open our eyes to the possibilities.

References

ABA Section of Legal Education and Admissions to the Bar. 1992. *Legal Education and Professional Development—An Educational Curriculum: Report of the Task Force on Law Schools and the Profession: Narrowing the Gap.* Chicago: American Bar Association.

Bacow, L.S., Kassim-Lakha, S. and Gill, S.K. 2011. A University's Calling: To Repair the Social Fabric, *Chronicle of Higher Education* [Online], 13 January. Available at: http://chronicle.com/article/A-Universitys-Calling-to/125946 [accessed 7 September 2012].

Borden, B.T. and Rhee, R.J. 2011. The Law School Firm, *South Carolina Law Review*, 63(1): 1–12.

Brest, P. and Krieger, L.H. 1999. Lawyers as Problem Solvers, *Temple Law Review*, 72(4): 811–32.

Calabresi, G. 1979. Bakke as Pseudo-Tragedy, *Catholic University Law Review*, 28(3): 427–44.

Doh, J. 2003. Can Leadership be Taught? Perspectives from Management Educators, *Academy of Management Learning and Education*, 2(1): 54–67.

Fuller, L.L. 1948. What the Law Schools Can Contribute to the Making of Lawyers, *Journal of Legal Education*, 1(2): 189–204.

Grutter v. Bollinger, 539 US 306 (2003).

Haddon, P.A. 1994. Education for a Public Calling in the 21st Century, *Washington Law Review*, 69(3): 573–86.

---

8   At the time of this writing, the most recent and prominent example was Dewey & LeBoeuf LLP, which, deeply in debt and reeling from the departure of two-thirds of its partners, had just laid off its associates and secretarial staff and filed for bankruptcy (Lattman 2012). Though the economic downturn was a factor in the firm's failure, many believed that poor leadership, lack of transparency, and concomitant poor morale were what pushed Dewey & LeBoeuf to its fall (Longstreth and Raymond 2012).

Heineman, B.W. Jr. 2006. *Lecture at Yale Law School: Law and Leadership* [Online], 27 November. Available at: http://www.law.yale.edu/documents/pdf/ News_&_Events/HeinemanLecture.pdf [accessed 7 September 2012].

Henderson, W.D. and Zahorsky, R.M. 2012. The Law School Bubble: How Long Will It Last if Law Grads Can't Pay Bills?, *American Bar Association Journal*, January. Available at: http://www.abajournal.com/magazine/article/the_ law_school_bubble_how_long_will_it_last_if_law_grads_cant_pay_bills/ [accessed 7 September 2012].

Kelly, M. 2011. A Gaping Hole in American Legal Education, *Maryland Law Review*, 70(2): 440–50.

Lattman, P. 2012. Dewey & LeBoeuf Files for Bankruptcy, *New York Times Dealbook* [Online], 28 May. Available at: http://dealbook.nytimes. com/2012/05/28/dewey-leboeuf-files-for-bankruptcy/ [accessed 7 September 2012].

Llewellyn, K.N. 1948. The Crisis in Legal Education, *Journal of Legal Education*, 1(2): 211–20.

Longstreth, A. and Raymond, N. 2012. The Dewey Chronicles: The Rise and Fall of a Legal Titan, *Thomson Reuters News & Insight* [Online], 11 May. Available at: http://newsandinsight.thomsonreuters.com/Legal/News/2012/05_-_May/ The_Dewey_chronicles__The_rise_and_fall_of_a_legal_titan/ [accessed 7 September 2012].

Menkel-Meadow, C. 1999. The Lawyer as Problem Solver and Third Party Neutral: Creativity and Non-Partisanship in Lawyering, *Temple Law Review*, 72(4): 785–810.

Polden, D.J. 2008. Educating Law Students for Leadership Roles and Responsibilities, *University of Toledo Law Review*, 39(2): 353–60.

Posner, R.A. 1993. The Deprofessionalization of Legal Teaching and Scholarship, *Michigan Law Review*, 91(8): 1921–28.

Reno, J. 1999. Lawyers as Problem-Solvers: Keynote Address to the AALS, *Journal of Legal Education*, 49(1): 5–13.

Rhode, D.L. 2010. Lawyers and Leadership, *The Professional Lawyer*, 20(3): 1–15.

Rhode, D.L. and Packel, A.K. 2011. *Leadership: Law, Policy and Management*. New York: Wolters Kluwer.

Segal, D. 2011. What They Don't Teach Law Students: Lawyering, *New York Times* [Online], 19 November. Available at: http://www.nytimes. com/2011/11/20/business/after-law-school-associates-learn-to-be-lawyers. html?_r=1&pagewanted=all [accessed 7 September 2012].

Stevenson, D. 2012. Should Law Schools Focus on Lawyering Skills? *Circuit Splits* [Online], 16 May. Available at: http://www.circuitsplits.com/2012/05/ should-law-schools-focus-on-lawyering-skills.html [accessed 7 September 2012].

Sullivan, W.M., Colby, A., Wegner, J.W., Bond, L. and Shulman, L.S. 2007. *Educating Lawyers: Preparation for the Profession of Law*. San Francisco: John Wiley & Sons.

Williams, G.H. 1999. AALS President's Message: Teaching Leaders and Leadership, *AALS Newsletter* [Online], April. Available at: http://www.aals.org/presidentsmessages/leaders.html [accessed 7 September 2012].

Chapter 2
The Nexus between Leadership Theory and Law

Georgia Sorenson

> ... Graduates of law schools should aspire not just to be wise counselors but wise leaders; not just to dispense "practical wisdom" but to be "practical visionaries"; not just to have positions where they advise, but where they decide.
>
> Ben W. Heineman, Jr.

Leadership and the Human Condition

"Leadership is part and parcel of the human condition," as ubiquitous as life itself (Harvey 2006: 39). It is a scientific metaphenomenon: central to all cultures and all times.[1] Its form may vary, but its centrality as a social science construct and a fact of daily life is indisputable.

As social animals, we form groups for survival, childrearing, and to achieve common purposes and social order. As collectivities, we go to war and wage peace, build institutions and develop legal systems—and always leadership and leaders are vital to our efforts. As leadership scholar Michael Harvey has written, the power of leadership is "a mystery as modern as the nation-state and as ancient as the tribe" (Harvey 2006: 39). Thus the need for leaders—and its corollary, followers—is both historical and immutable.

Leadership is timeless but its practice remains time and contextually bound. Leadership scholars and researchers agree that context, history, follower characteristics, economics, and other situational factors impact the necessity and possibility of leadership. As legal scholar Michael Kelly remarks, "[l]ike politics, all leadership is local. It involves an almost unimaginable array of different groups or organizations, ... fields or markets, histories and challenges and understandings of the meaning of success." Thus, understanding leadership is highly contextual—it looks different depending upon the circumstances.

Human beings have always been interested in leadership. Confucius sought laws of order between leaders and subordinates,[2] and between states and within

---

1   See Bass and Bass (2008), which details anthropological reports of indigenous groups in Australia, Fiji, New Guinea, the Congo and elsewhere. There are no known societies where leadership is absent (Bass and Bass 2008: 3).

2   Leadership is a culturally nuanced construct. In China, for example, the word "leader" is a relatively recent concept, and quite different from Western ideas. The Chinese

government. Plato described an ideal republic with philosopher-kings dispensing wise counsel and judicious leadership, asserting that the ideal leader would be "noble, truthful, just, and courageous" (Burton forthcoming: 6). The first histories of civilizations—Herodotus, Thucydides, Xenophon, Sima Qian, the Griots of ancient Africa, and others—are the stories of leaders. In the sixteenth century, the Italian Niccolo Machiavelli, departing from a normative tradition to a descriptive one, wrote about the more practical side of leadership. In contrast with Plato, Machiavelli's ultimate aim was to reform structures (in his case, government or principalities) rather than focus on the individual leader. Hobbes in the seventeenth century, Carlyle, and later Laswell, Russell, Follett, Rawls, Burns, and others examined power, influence, and leadership in modern life.

Normative and Descriptive Work on Leadership

For the most part, these early works on "leaderships" (used to denote the study of leaders rather than the leadership process) use a normative approach, seeking to provide an ethical and constructive view of how leaders and followers "ought" to behave. Plato, Confucius, and even popular writers today like Stephen Covey exemplify the normative tradition.

In contrast to the normative approach, the descriptive approach looks at leadership[3] behavior in a relatively value-neutral way. It examines not what we would like leaders to do or what they should do, but what they actually do.

The descriptive approach utilizes primarily the methods of social sciences, notably observational and empirical approaches, deriving findings from fields such as political science, psychology, and sociology. Since 1945, empirical research on leadership has dominated the leadership discourse, especially since the 1990s, when computerized statistical analysis made possible multivariate analysis to examine relationships between leader/follower/situation variables. Leadership researcher Bernard Bass estimates that there are at least 10,000 studies using the empirical method, ranging from experimental small group laboratories to longitudinal cross-cultural methods like Bob House's Globe Project.

In many ways, the legal profession relies on the descriptive approach and traditional law schools are more inclined to use descriptive approaches to case law and precedent. But some legal scholars suggest legal education needs to develop both parts of the legal mind and to produce lawyers who can function both as

---

concept Lingdau is someone who is in charge, and by definition connotes positional authority, acquired through "political power, money, connections, corruption or force," according to Zhang and Baker (2008: 51). Thus in China, "leaders" have subordinates rather than "followers."

3   There are some scholars who eschew the descriptive approach, seeking to reserve the term "leadership" for more noble and ethical endeavors, and suggest that in some descriptive studies terms such as "tyrant," "despot," or "autocrat" be used instead.

"of counsel" and "of leadership." Ben W. Heineman suggests the normative inquiry would broaden their range: "We need lawyers who can create and build, not just criticize and deconstruct. Lawyers must be able to ask and answer 'what ought to be' questions, not only 'what is' questions—and in their answers they must respect the tensions between competing values that are inherent in most important decisions" (Heineman 2007).

Jurisprudence, if not legal education, does have a long history of normative scholarship, with legal philosophers asking such questions as "what is the purpose of law," "what is the moral foundation of law," and "what is justice and its relationship to law." Philosophical approaches such as Kant's deontological theory of law and, more recently, legal scholar Ronald Dworkin's law of integrity add to the mix (Dworkin 1986). Too, theories of distributive equality as well as critical legal studies approach the training of lawyers with such a view.

In short, both the descriptive and normative traditions of leadership studies and jurisprudence have relevance to a transformed law school curriculum. The descriptive approach can take the form of courses such as my own on Leadership Theory and Praxis, and the normative approach is a natural for a professional ethics curriculum, recommended by the recent Carnegie Commission report and others.

It is wise to remember the wisdom of the past and that these are not especially new ideas. As early as 1953, Robert E. Mathews, former President of the Association of American Law Schools, asserted "leadership is an integral function of membership in the legal profession. It is as much of a part of being a lawyer as is appearance in court, office consultation and representation in negotiation" (Mathews 1953: 482).[4]

A Natural Alliance: Leadership Education and the Law

The 2006 report of the Carnegie Foundation, *Educating Lawyers: Preparation for the Profession of Law*, calls for comprehensive reform of legal education, with ethics, leadership studies, clinical and experiential education, and other approaches better integrated into the law school experience (Sullivan et al. 2007: 53).

In an interesting parallel, a group of leadership scholars and researchers were working around the same time as the Carnegie authors, attempting to synthesize the leadership research to make it more useful to leaders in the professions and in everyday life.

From 2001–2005, these scholars from multiple disciplinary backgrounds[5] were invited by eminent leadership scholar James MacGregor Burns to explore the interstices between leadership theories. Our quest was to see if a general theory of leadership, much like general theories in physics or economics, might be achievable,

---

4   Reprinted with permission of the *University of Colorado Law Review*.
5   Psychology, history, anthropology, philosophy, education, political science, the law, English literature, and business management were represented.

and beyond that, to make leadership knowledge useful to others. Working over several years, the narrative of that group's work was published in 2006 in *The Quest for a General Theory of Leadership* (Goethals and Sorenson 2006).

At the heart of the group's inquiry was a seminal question, which asks, "given that leadership is integral to the human condition, what makes leadership necessary? And what makes leadership possible?"

The scholars' conclusion was that the quintessential aim—what made leadership necessary—was to enlarge the space for human freedom and imagination. With freedom allowing unbounded moral and creative imagination, all things were possible.

Interestingly, the American Bar Association's motto is "Defending Liberty, Pursuing Justice." It is both congruent with and slightly different from the aims of leadership, as described by the scholars in the general theory group. On the one hand, the implication is that the law defends the liberty that good leadership is pushing to continually enlarge, and defends what has been advanced by good leadership, collective and otherwise.

But the general theory leadership scholars included a second aim of leadership—"to expand the space for human imagination." Are individual and collective rights in place to secure the freedom to imagine new possibilities, speak truth to power, and to create societies based on fairness, beauty, and reciprocal care? Human imagination has wrought extermination camps, child abuse, and lethal wars, too. David Gurnham, in his book *Memory, Imagination, and Justice*, makes a compelling though controversial claim that imagination is the creative force behind legal reform (Gurnham 2009). Indeed, he suggests that imagination is the means by which we pursue justice.

I confess that after reading Gurnham's work, my imagination led me to envision our group of leadership scholars and a like-minded group of creative law professors, exploring liberty, justice, and imagination in a productive new partnership. These and other imaginations bring us to the nexus of this book.

Lawyer–Leaders?

Are lawyers leaders? Does our curriculum foster leadership development and knowledge? Should it? While these questions are the subject of this book and will be addressed in detail in the following chapters, as a leadership scholar and researcher the answer to this question seems obvious to me: lawyers are already leaders, both in the public and private sphere. Legal education lags significantly behind other professions in fostering leadership knowledge and development, and we do an injustice to our students by not addressing this critical need.

Leadership as a role in a group is both given (by the group or by formal authority) and taken (by individuals). While lawyers may eschew leadership roles, most people see lawyers as public leaders, whether they choose to be leaders or not. As attorney and chemist Beau Burton asserts,

Tocqueville proposed that the [American] public believes that political leaders should be drawn from high status occupations, and law is perceived as a high status occupation. In addition, the perceived reputations of lawyers and legislators overlap since their role is to pursue the interests of their client or constituency regardless of their personal beliefs. Thus, the view of a lawyer as an advocate and representative of or for a client is a positive trait in a political leader." (Burton forthcoming: 6)

Still, there is plenty of data to suggest that lawyers have and do play significant leadership roles—both given and taken.

Public Sector Lawyer–Leaders

From our earliest history, lawyers have been public leaders. On July 4, 1776, 56 individuals signed the Declaration of Independence; 25 of them were lawyers. In addition, there were 55 framers of the United States Constitution; 39 of them were lawyers.

Since 1789, lawyers have accounted for 40–65% of Congress, 25 of 43 (58%) presidents, and 100% of the judiciary. Today, law degrees account for nearly 40% of all the degrees in the House of Representatives. The law degree is the primary degree in the Senate at 57%, although in recent years those numbers have fallen slightly.[6]

In light of the fact that lawyers account for less than 1% of the U.S. population (as of 2009, there were 1,180,386 lawyers in the U.S. according to the American Bar Association), lawyers not only lead, one could argue that they are overrepresented in the public leadership.

In part this is due to sound legal training in the understanding of the law, which is the primary business of Congress and the Supreme Court, and certainly is central to the Executive Branch agencies as well. Lawyers also lead at the state and local levels of government.

But, as former Congressman Mickey Edwards suggests, most law schools give little or no attention to the task of either encouraging or training their students to take on such a role. "They provide superb instruction in the art of private legal services: estate planning, criminal defense, tort claims, corporate structure—but do little to prepare their charges to step onto the larger stage of devotion to public service or the eradication of injustice."

---

6   See Blom and Gilmore (Chapter 12 this volume). While the exact numbers have varied slightly from election cycle to election cycle, and the percentage has declined since 1930, still, nearly half are lawyers.

Private Sector Lawyer–Leaders

We might expect lawmakers to be trained as lawyers, but we are beginning to see the same phenomenon in the private sector.

In a much-quoted recent article in the *ABA Journal*, Mark Curriden found that nine of the Fortune 50 companies have a lawyer as chief executive, up three-fold from just a decade ago (Curriden 2010). Further, 10.8% of the CEOs of companies in the Standard & Poor's 500 stock index have law degrees.

Not surprisingly, with Sarbanes-Oxley and in the current turbulent economic environment, companies in highly litigious fields or with significant governmental regulatory oversight are seeking lawyer–leaders as CEOs. Attorneys, who are famously risk-averse, are finding that skill in risk management in today's business environment makes an attractive CEO candidate.

Nonprofit Lawyer–Leaders

We suspect the same trend in nonprofits and there is anecdotal evidence to support a trend of more attorneys leading nonprofits,[7] but systematic data is not available, either from the nonprofit sector or from the Bureau of Labor Statistics (Johnston and Rudney 1987: 28). We do know that every year, 11% of law school graduates decide to use their law degree in a nontraditional area, often in the nonprofit sector.

The question that remains with me, if lawyers are public and private sector leaders, and, as Alan Hornstein says, "legal education *is* leadership education," because "successful applicants to law are among the intellectual elite of their college generation" and in time they will become or be seen as leaders—is this really the education of future leaders without any leadership education? Or is this credentialing the elite and leaving the rest to fate? Why are we, as legal educators, leaving leadership education to chance? If we have many of the best and the brightest, who are destined to be or to be seen as leaders, why do we avoid giving them the preparation and tools they deserve?

To paraphrase scholar Deborah Rhode, are we as faculty not the leaders of these future leaders?

If so, how do we begin?

---

7   In fact, the nonprofit trade association, the National Council of Nonprofits, has as its CEO an attorney, Tim Delaney—as well as its two vice presidents.

Research on Leadership:
People, Places, Events, Context, History, and Conditions

The word "leader" first appeared in the English language in the 1300s; it stems from the root "leden" meaning "to travel" or "show the way" (Sorenson 2000). In fact, the term "leadership" (as opposed to "leader") did not find its way into common parlance until the late nineteenth century. Indeed, the scientific study of leadership (as opposed to the study of leaders) arose initially in the United States and almost exclusively since the turn of the twentieth century. Despite its relatively recent pedigree, leadership research has produced a half century of robust scholarly and empirical research and emergent paradigms are spurring new research.

This chapter briefly describes the transition in the research from a focus on leaders and their traits and behaviors to the leader-follower dynamic and finally the effect that context has on leadership outcomes. These are the key shifts in the research and most theories find themselves embedded within this thinking. Following is a short discussion of transformational leadership, which incorporates all the elements and is one of the most robust lines of research inquiry today.

What is important to note at the outset, is that as each new theory emerges in the scholarly community, it generally extends the previous work rather than supplants it. Thus theories of traits and behaviors expanded to include leaders' relationship to followers, which in turn yielded to new thoughts about context, power, and so forth. At the same time, as the research agenda moves beyond its original conceptions, in the last 10 years it has looped back to bring some of the earlier work into focus once again (traits, inherited, etc.). On a recent invitation to China, accompanied by Fred Fiedler, Chinese officials asked about leadership as it relates to efficiency and productivity—their interests—foci relegated until of late to economists in the United States. Earlier theories may be culturally compatible with developing countries and transformational leadership of interest to knowledge workers and networked organizations. This is to say that usefulness of leadership research also is embedded in the developmental needs of the country/organization/individual.

Figure 2.1 was constructed by Tom Wren, a historian, attorney, and leadership scholar as well as a member of the general theory group, and illustrates in a basic way the theories, methodologies, and contextual issues arrayed in a periodic table of leadership research. While it is beyond the scope of this chapter to discuss each "element," a review of some of the basic research trends may lay out possible avenues for leadership and law scholars to explore.

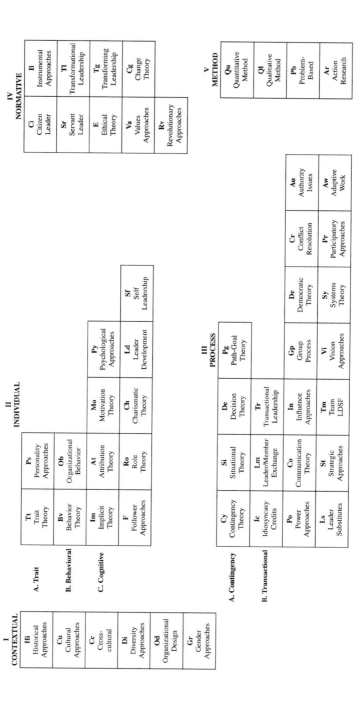

Figure 2.1   Periodic table of leadership studies

Source: J. Thomas Wren (2006), "Periodic Table of Leadership Studies" taken from "A Quest for a Grand Theory of Leadership" in George R. Goethals and Georgia L.J. Sorenson (eds), *The Quest for a General Theory of Leadership*, Cheltenham, UK and Northampton, MA: Edward Elgar Publishing Ltd, p. 13.

Trait Theories

For the most part, leadership research of the first five decades of the last century focused on leaders themselves, and has come to be called the era of the "Great Man Theories" (Bass 1974: 37–8). Early observational studies of the industrial giants in America (presumably these were all men) were premised on the concept that these unique traits and abilities, fueled by social status or inherited money, set these leaders apart. These were essentially the study of individual leaders—solo "leaderships" rather than "leadership."

Hereditary properties such as intelligence, height, and self-confidence were identified as distinguishing characteristics. Whether idealistic or normative, leadership research sought to identify traits or abilities that set leaders apart from non-leaders.

In a retrospective analysis of the leadership trait models, Peter Northouse found certain traits and personality constructs, notably intelligence, self-confidence, determination, integrity, and sociability, were common to all trait models (Northouse 2007: 18).

But at the same time, "Great Man" theories research failed to produce a set of traits that leaders must possess to be effective across all situations. One need only to look to some modern day examples such as Donald Regan, who was remarkably successful on Wall Street and as CEO of Merrill Lynch, but was unable to effectively parse the political environment as Secretary of the Treasury under Ronald Reagan (and was subsequently fired). Ulysses Grant as General was a very different leader than Ulysses Grant as President. As Ralph Stogdill presciently pointed out as early as 1948, one cannot identify traits of leaders separate from their environment. Leaders who are successful in one environment may be unsuccessful or even disastrous in another.

Despite this failing and later critiques of its ethnocentric and sexist premises, trait theory represents the first systematic and empirical study of leadership. In time, the trait approach gave way to a more complex view of leadership.

Behavioral Approach

As the notion of leadership traits and "Great Men" was dispelled, behavioral scientists looked to measurable and observable behaviors of leaders in an attempt to deconstruct leadership. In effect, their operating hypothesis was that the behaviors of effective leaders differed from those of ineffective leaders.

Psychologists at Ohio State and the University of Michigan contributed pioneering research in the behavioral understanding of leadership (Stogdill and Coons 1957). The Ohio State profiles comprised years of study of two-dimensional variables, most notably "consideration" and "initiating structure" (simply said, people skills and task orientation), but these studies failed to either explain or predict leader behavior (Korman 1966).

The Southern Illinois University Leadership Symposia, originating in 1971, produced four important volumes: *Current Developments in the Study of Leadership* (1973); *Contingency Approaches to Leadership* (1974); *Leadership Frontiers* (1975); and *Leadership: The Cutting Edge* (1977). During this period, particular attention was paid to the relationship between leaders and the group, with implications for the organizational workplace. Like the Ohio State studies, two variables were correlated—"consideration" and "task performance" for example—but the behavior was much more interpenetrating and complex than it appeared.

Follower Research

The U.S. military has been a significant funder and user of leadership research (Sorenson 2010). The early work of Ed Hollander, funded by the Navy, examined characteristics of followers and extended the field of leadership to leader-follower relations. His psychological construct of "idiosyncratic credit" (the leader's earned trust from the follower by demonstrating competence and respect for group members and norms over time) helps to demonstrate why some leaders achieved strong results with their team or platoon. The interaction between technical and interpersonal competence is a key theme of leadership theory, as Leary Davis points out.

Robert Kelley's earlier work, and later his book, *The Power of Followership* in 1992, extended the thinking of many scholars and practitioners about the importance of strong followers in any leadership context (Kelley 1992). His model followed two behavioral dimensions, independent critical thinking on the part of followers and an active-passive dimension. His discussion of alienated, passive, conformist, pragmatic, and exemplary followers has been useful to leaders and to leadership scholars in understanding the complexity of the leader-follower relationship.

A fascinating study in 2002 by James Kouzes and Barry Posner examined successful leadership by asking followers rather than leaders to rank the "qualities you most look for and admire in a leader" (Kouzes and Posner 2002). Subjects—over 1 million people in over 20 years in a variety of settings—were given 20 behavioral and personality traits to rank order. What they found with remarkable consistency across countries (Japan, U.S., Australia, Canada, Korea, and Mexico) and within industries was a high agreement on the following leader competencies: honest, forward-thinking, competent, and inspiring.

Situational and Contingency Approaches

In the late 1960s researchers began to incorporate situational factors into the study of leadership. The premise was that the demands of the environment, or situation, determined the emergence of leaders—the result of time, place, and circumstances.

Fred Fiedler developed a contingency theory (the leader's effectiveness was contingent on situational features and follower characteristics) by studying good and bad leadership under a variety of conditions. Leadership style was measured using the two-factor task-oriented and relationship-motivated styles, coupled with the leader's power position in the organization (the degree to which the leader is authorized to hire, fire, and reward subordinates) and an assessment of leader-subordinate relationships (loyalty, confidence, trust in the leader, etc.).

Fiedler's work was grounded in significant empirical work, both his own and replication studies (Northouse 2007, Peters et al. 1985, Strube and Garcia 1981). As Northouse discusses, Fiedler's work had strong predictive power, that is, the ability to determine the right match between a leader's style and the particular work context (Northouse 2007: 117). In effect, Fiedler moved leadership thinking beyond the traits and behaviors of individual leaders to a force field of co-determinant factors. Importantly, contingency theory revealed that a leader who is effective in one situation might not be effective in another, and "organizational fit" was an important dimension.

Transforming Leadership

James MacGregor Burns and Bernard Bass's work on transformational leadership has led a significant research stream in thinking about leadership. Burns challenged researchers to abandon the leader-focused model and to take up the study of leadership aimed at realizing goals mutually held by leaders and followers. To do so, he suggested, involves greater attention to the role of followers as well as the motivations of potential opponents and competition from other actors. Burns speaks of "the reciprocal process of mobilizing, by persons with certain motives and values, various economic, political, and other resources, in a context of competition and conflict, in order to realize goals independently or mutually held by both leaders and followers" (Burns 1978: 425). In short, Burns characterized leadership as a process and not a person.

The key, Burns felt, was in the hypersensitive force field of motivation rather than simply in "economic" or "ideological" or "institutional" analysis. His leadership model is not a linear sequence of stimulus-response "sets" or "stages" or even a network of sequential and cross-cutting forces as can be found in situational theories, but a rich and pulsating stream of leadership-followership forces flowing through the whole social process.

Until Burns's seminal 1978 book, *Leadership*, the goal of good leadership was seen as "effectiveness." Burns transformed our view of leadership by insisting that great leadership had moral dimensions. "Moral" to Burns did not mean the everyday virtues or daily ethical choices, but adherence to the great public values such as liberty, justice, and equality. Adherence to these public values was the purview of great leadership, he felt, and his historical work on Franklin and Eleanor Roosevelt helped to inform his thinking. This moral judgment, addressed by David Luban and Michael Millemann, can be learned and taught successfully in law schools, as they have shown (Luban and Millemann 1995).

Burns made a distinction between two different but compatible leadership behaviors—transforming and transactional. He defined transactional leadership as "everyday brokerage" and the process whereby "one person takes the initiative in making contact with others for the purpose of an exchange of valued things" (e.g., jobs for votes) (Burns 1978: 19). Transforming leadership, on the other hand, he asserts, is based on efforts that are "planned, articulated, systemic, enduring, measurable, and based on core public values."

Research psychologist Bernard Bass's work on transformational leadership, while somewhat different from Burns's, contributes a significant research legacy to transformational leadership. His transformational leadership instrument, the LMX, has been used since the early 1980s in measuring four factors of transformational leadership (idealized influence, inspirational motivation, intellectual stimulation, and individualized consideration) and two transactional factors (contingent reward and management by exception). While there has always been some dispute among researchers about some overlap of the items, a meta-analysis of 39 research studies by Lowe, Kroeck and Sivasubramaniam in 1996 found that transformational leaders were perceived to be more effective and have better work outcomes than those who exhibited primarily transactional leadership behaviors (Lowe et al. 1996). His instrument has been used in thousands of settings both in the U.S. and abroad, and a content analysis of refereed journals found that transformational and charismatic leadership research represents one-third of the articles published in *Leadership Quarterly* over the last 10 years (Lowe and Gardner 2001).

Articles accepted and published by *Leadership Quarterly*, by research area, can extrapolate a snapshot of where leadership research is today.

Table 2.1   Ten-year review of articles published in *Leadership Quarterly*

Type of Research	% of Publication
Trait	8.5
Leader Motive Profile	4.0
Behavioral	2.5
Contingency	12.0
Substitutes	4.5
Cognitive	3.5
Path-Goal	2.5
Multi-level	9.0
LMX	6.5
Leadership Information Processing	8.0
Neo-Charismatic	26.0
Transformational	18.0

Source: Reprinted from *Leadership Quarterly*, 11(4), Lowe, Kevin B. and Gardner, William L., Ten Years of the Leadership Quarterly: Contributions and Challenges for the Future, 480, table 5, Copyright © 2000, with permission from Elsevier.

The Future of Leadership Studies in the Professions: Leadership and Law

Larry Richard today has undertaken the most exciting empirical work on leadership and lawyers. Richard and his colleagues, using a competency-based model utilizing the framework of McClelland (Leader Motive Profile), found successful attorneys as a group were less sociable, more skeptical, more urgent, more analytical, more autonomous, and more defensive than the general public by a wide margin (Richard: Chapter 3, this volume). Richard's work promises to make the fit between the individual lawyer and law practice more successful by integrating what we know about leaders, followers, context, and situations.

Given that lawyers in our society are leaders, how can we support our students to also demonstrate and learn collaboration, social competence, ethical considerations, self-knowledge, openness, and the wisdom of those who work with leaders—that is that they want leaders who are honest, forward-thinking, competent, and inspiring?[8]

If, as Burton attests, lawyers tend to be highly competitive, risk-averse, and skeptical (Burton forthcoming), these are exactly the qualities that companies and firms are seeking in the economic downturn. Are there ways in which lawyer–

---

8   Law faculty and scholars such as Deborah Rhode, Ben Heinemann, Paula Monopoli, Don Polden, Leary Davis, Phoebe Haddon, Mike Millemann, and Larry Richard and others are integrating leadership research and practice into their schools by speaking out, offering courses taught by leadership scholars, developing school-wide leadership curriculum, practice, and development.

leaders can experience and adopt the full range of leadership competencies, to ride out the recession but also to transform the conditions that caused it in the first place?

Bringing leadership theory to the professions and to schools of law is an exciting enterprise. As academics, educators, and scholars, we have much to learn from the on-the-ground practice of leadership—in social movements, in Congress, in landmark court decisions, in nonprofits, and in law schools.

This chapter leaves you with a challenge and a question, offered by my friend and colleague, James MacGregor Burns, as he encourages us to learn from the practices of leaders in their own environment and to deploy our own moral imagination and leadership for common purpose:

> The amazing events that unfolded in Montgomery[9] and the state and nation are that the people in action embraced every major aspect of leadership and integrated it: individual leadership, collective leadership, intra-group and inter-group conflict, conflict of strongly held values, power aspects, etc.—and ultimately produced a real change leading to more change. They made our country a better country …

> If those activists could integrate the complex processes and elements of leadership in practice, in reality, should we not be able to do so in theory? (Burns 2006: 239)

Leadership scholarship in the professions offers us the chance to educate, support and encourage, and learn from leadership in the field. Law schools now have some critical elements to lead this transformation—pioneering schools that put leadership studies at the core of their teaching and learning, a core group of faculty around the country pushing for change in the curriculum, empirical work about lawyers and leadership by Richard and others, the Carnegie Report, a professional association supporting these efforts, a new law and leadership journal, the Fetzer Institute, an early ally in legal transformation, and now, a book by law faculty to provide support and encouragement to the emergent vision.

References

Bass, B. and Bass, R. 2008. *The Bass Handbook of Leadership*. 4th edition. New York: Free Press.

Bass, B.M. 1974. *Bass and Stogdill's Handbook of Leadership*. 3rd edition. New York: Free Press.

---

9   Burns is referring to a pivotal event in the American Civil Rights movement when African American seamstress Rosa Parks refused to sit in the back of a public bus, and her personal protest launched the citywide Montgomery, Alabama bus boycott.

Burns, J.M. 1978. *Leadership*. New York: Harper and Row.

Burns, J.M. 2006. Afterword, in *The Quest for a General Theory of Leadership*, 234–9.

Burton, B. (forthcoming). The Chemistry of Leadership in Law, *Journal of Leadership and Law*.

Curriden, M. 2010. CEO, Esq. *American Bar Association Journal* [Online], May. Available at: http://www.abajournal.com/magazine/article/ceo_esq/ [accessed 30 January 2012].

Dworkin, R. 1986. *Law's Empire*. Cambridge, MA: Belknap.

Goethals, G. and Sorenson, G.L.J. (eds). 2006. *The Quest for a General Theory of Leadership*. Northampton, MA: Edward Elgar.

Gurnham, D. 2009. *Memory, Imagination, Justice: Intersections of Law and Literature*. Aldershot: Ashgate.

Harvey, M. 2006. Leadership and the Human Condition, in *The Quest for a General Theory of Leadership*, 34–45.

Heineman, B.W. Jr. 2007. Lawyers as Leaders, *Yale Law Journal Pocket Part* [Online], 116: 266–71. Available at: http://yalelawjournal.org/the-yale-law-journal-pocket-part/professional-responsibility/lawyers-as-leaders/ [accessed 1 September 2012].

Johnston, D. and Rudney, G. 1987. Characteristics of Workers in Nonprofit Institutions, *Monthly Labor Review*, July, 28–33.

Kelley, R. 1992. *The Power of Followership*. New York: Doubleday.

Korman, A.K. 1966. "Consideration," "Initiating Structure," and Organizational Criteria: A Review, *Personnel Psychology*, 19(4): 349–61.

Kouzes, J.M. and Posner, B.Z. 2002. *The Leadership Challenge*. 3rd edition. New York: Jossey Bass.

Lowe, K.B., Kroeck, K.G. and Sivasubramaniam, N. 1996. Effectiveness Correlates of Transformational and Transactional Leadership: A Meta-Analytic Review of the MLQ Literature, *Leadership Quarterly*, 7(3): 385–425.

Lowe, K.B. and Gardner, W.L. 2000. Ten Years of the Leadership Quarterly: Contributions and Challenges for the Future, *Leadership Quarterly*, 11(4): 459–514.

Luban, D. and Millemann, M. 1995. Good Judgment: Ethics Teaching in Dark Times, *Georgetown Journal of Legal Ethics*, 9(1): 31–88.

Mathews, R.E. 1953. The Lawyer, Law Schools and Responsible Leadership, *Rocky Mountain Law Review*, 25(4): 482–9.

Northouse, P. 2007. *Leadership Theory and Practice*. Thousand Oaks, CA: Sage.

Peters, L.H., Hartke, D.D. and Pohlmann, J.T. 1985. Fiedler's Contingency Theory of Leadership: An Application of the Meta-Analysis Procedures of Schmidt and Hunter, *Psychological Bulletin*, 97(2): 274–85.

Sorenson, G. 2010. Leadership Beyond the Battlefield, *The Public Manager*, 39(4): 5–7.

Sorenson, G. 2000. An Intellectual History of Leadership Studies. Paper delivered at the 2000 Annual Meeting of the American Political Science Association, Washington, D.C. Copyright by the American Political Science Association and reprinted in *Reflections on Leadership*, edited by R. Coutu. University Press, Lanham, MD, 2007.

Stogdill, R.M. and Coons, A.E. 1957. *Leader Behavior: Its Description and Measurement*. Columbus: Ohio State University.

Strube, M.J. and Garcia, J.E. 1981. A Meta-Analytic Investigation of Fiedler's Contingency Model of Leadership Effectiveness, *Psychological Bulletin*, 90(2): 307–21.

Sullivan, W.M., Colby, A., Wegner, J.W., Bond, L. and Shulman, L.S. 2007. *Educating Lawyers: Preparation for the Profession of Law*. San Francisco: Jossey-Bass.

Zhang, H. and Baker, G. 2008. *Think Like Chinese*. Annandale, N.S.W.: Federation Press.

Chapter 3

Leadership Competencies in Law

Larry Richard

Social scientists have always been interested in exploring ways to predict human behavior. This fascination has led to considerable research in many areas. One such area that is of growing interest to the legal profession is the ongoing effort to study what predicts effective leaders. Law firms are years behind their corporate counterparts in applying predictive methods to determine who among the firm's lawyers will be the most effective leaders. However, the changing external environment has increased the importance of leadership in law firms, and has led many firms to develop a greater interest in using such methods to find and develop their future leaders. But the very traits that make lawyers good lawyers can actually make it more challenging for them to be good leaders. This chapter explores the evolution of such predictive methods and how law firms can use them to identify and develop institutional leaders.

I. The Evolution of Predictive Methods for Effective Leaders

In the 1960s and 1970s, investigators looked at a number of personality traits as possible predictors of effective leaders, as well as at IQ and other cognitive measures, such as measures of general knowledge. By the early 1970s, most of these hoped-for predictors had fallen out of favor, either because their predictive value was too weak, or because they introduced potential racial or socioeconomic bias, or both.

In the late 1960s and early 1970s, psychologist David McClelland at Harvard developed some groundbreaking theories about what motivates people. In 1973, Professor McClelland was consulted by the U.S. Information Service for assistance in doing a better job selecting candidates to become Foreign Service Information Officers. The USIS had apparently been using an IQ measure to screen candidates with little success.

McClelland's simple innovation was to use a technique known today as "criterion-based sampling"—that is, to interview a sample of clearly successful FSIOs as well as a sample of clearly less successful ones, and then to analyze their similarities and differences in order to form a testable hypothesis about the possible differentiators (McClelland 1973).

Because McClelland was doing pioneering exploratory research, and little guidance was available from the past, he was open to looking at every potential variable as a possible predictor—thoughts, attitudes, beliefs, behaviors, knowledge, traits, learned skills, innate talents, self-image or social role, motives, values, demographic characteristics, etc. The two key questions that he must have asked were: (1) Which bundle of these best predicts excellent behavior? and, (2) How can we accurately measure each such predictor?

The essence of this approach is to search for the differentiating characteristics and behaviors of people whose behavior is excellent. The term "differentiating," of course, implies that the characteristic or behavior is not found among what McClelland called "typical performers."

Since differences alone do not necessarily imply causation, it was necessary to test the hypothesis that grew out of the interviews. For those behaviors or qualities that are teachable, the USIS could take a select group of underperformers and train them in the identified skills, thoughts, behaviors, etc., and then track their performance over time to see if the training led to an improvement.

For those behaviors or qualities that are more likely innate, the required hypothesis-testing step was to hire some people who seemed to have the desired qualities and a control group of people who didn't, and then to track their performance to see if the candidates *with* the desired qualities outperformed those without.

As McClelland developed his methodology, he created what has come to be called the behavioral event interview (BEI). This involved an extensive, exquisitely detailed interview lasting four or five hours with each candidate in the "excellent" or "average" interview pool. The purpose was to go back in time and identify the actual behaviors, thoughts, feelings, motives, etc., of the individual at the time that they did something "excellent"—or, by contrast, did something that was clearly not excellent. McClelland believed that he would obtain higher-quality data by focusing on behaviors and attitudes that the individual had already, in the past, activated, rather than by asking an individual in the present to describe what makes them excellent. Likewise, careful study of past successful behaviors was deemed more fruitful than having the individual respond to a structured questionnaire or personality test in the present.

The BEI methodology resulted in a number of successful projects, and caught on as a methodology. Successful BEIs are highly dependent on the interviewer following a careful set of principles in the interview, not unlike the rules of evidence in a courtroom. As a consequence, today, BEIs are usually conducted by individuals who have been thoroughly trained by experts, many of whom trace their academic lineage back to McClelland and his group.

It should also be noted that since BEIs produce lots of information about what got a leader "from there to here," that is, it is based on a look back at historical information, there is always the possibility that the effective leader of the future will need to rely on a different set of competencies. Modern approaches to competency modeling address this concern by surveying "expert panels" (usually individuals inside your organization, sometimes external client groups) to identify any competencies that might need to be added to the model in order to adapt to a changing role or a changing environment. Naturally, any competencies added to the model in this way are likely to be less statistically predictive of excellence than those derived through BEIs.[1]

It's quite cumbersome to keep repeating the collection of various predictors— attitudes, learned skills, innate talents, motives, behaviors, etc.—and thus the shorthand "competency" has emerged as a catch-all label for the set of qualities and behaviors that describe a person who is excellent at something.

In the leadership field, many corporations over the years have conducted internal research to identify the competencies that predict excellence in leaders in their particular culture. Because this is a time-consuming and expensive process, a number of commercial vendors have emerged over the last 40 years (Lominger, PDI, etc.) who have studied these competencies and distilled them into "competency dictionaries" that offer a less expensive, quicker shortcut for those organizations wishing to utilize a set of leadership competencies without going through the burden of conducting their own research.

For those readers unfamiliar with competency modeling, there are a few other features that are worth noting, at the expense of declaring the obvious.

A competency framework, if scientifically developed, can then be used for selecting candidates, initial orientation, internal promotions (e.g., from a lower-level leadership role to a senior leadership role), training and development, performance management, evaluation and feedback, and succession planning. In many organizations, instead of developing a separate competency model just for leaders, a general competency model is developed for individual contributors, and certain individual competencies, at higher levels, are identified as criteria which particular leaders need to meet.

McClelland's idea is actually rooted in a broader principle that has been validated over and over again in the field of vocational psychology—the better the congruency of fit between an individual and the role that individual plays, the more effective and satisfied the individual will be in that role (Edwards 1991, Holland 1973, Kristof-Brown et al. 2002).

A competency is by definition measurable. The most common way to measure it is to identify the specific behavior that an outside observer would see a leader doing. Since the underlying elements that make up a competency can be composed of many possible human qualities,[2] it is vital to describe a competency in terms of the behaviors one would see. When the component is a behavior, a skill or a talent, this is easy.

---

1   A number of authors have proposed that certain competencies will be needed going forward due to increasing complexity, uncertainty and globalization. See, for example, Joiner and Josephs 2007, Institute for Corporate Productivity 2009, a study by The Conference Board, "Bridging the Leadership Gap," described in Bill Dee, "The New Leadership Competencies," http://www.hartsfieldadvisors.com/leader.pdf, Hernez-Broome and Hughes 2004.

2   Thoughts, attitudes, beliefs, behaviors, knowledge, traits, learned skills, innate talents, self-image or social role, motives, values, demographic characteristics, etc.

Most competency applications work from the basic principle of Person-Job fit

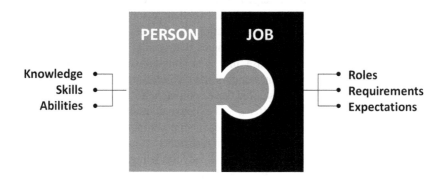

Figure 3.1   The basic principle of person-job fit
Source: Graphic by Mark Kizilos of Experience-Based Development Associates, LLC.
Courtesy of Mark Kizilos, Thomson-Reuters.

But when it's an attitude, a belief, a personality trait, etc., it's necessary to identify the *behavior* that the leader typically exhibits as a consequence of the internal state they are experiencing. Thus, for example, if an excellent leader always asks themselves, "What's the risk if I take no action at all?", and an average leader doesn't seem to ask this question, the competency model needs to offer actual behaviors, based on careful observations of actual excellent leaders in action, to describe what someone who asks that question of themselves actually behaves like.

Most good competency models today use behaviorally anchored rating scales (BARS) rather than the more common Likert-scaled items.[3]

Competencies are often divided into "technical" and "behavioral" competencies, or sometimes "cognitive" and "emotional" competencies. (These two continua are actually very similar in practice.) Technical or cognitive competencies usually refer to a leader's mastery of certain technical knowledge or one's use of some form of analytical skill. Behavioral or emotional competencies, by contrast, refer

---

3   BARS describe each increment in terms of measurable behaviors, for example, "1. Is able to understand what someone means when they reference 'project management.' 2. Is able to recognize when a situation calls for project management. 3. Is able to use project management techniques when appropriate."

A Likert-type scale uses an undifferentiated continuum, for example, "Is skilled at project management: 1 2 3 4 5."

to a leader's mastery of various people skills. Most competency models emphasize behavioral competencies by a 3:1 ratio. In most cases, this is because (a) behavioral skills are usually more operative in getting other people to move in the direction of the leader's vision, and (b) because knowledge-based industries recruit talent for their analytical skills to begin with, and this creates a talent pool of people who all, or nearly all, have high amounts of these cognitive skills. Statisticians call this a "restricted range" problem—that is, if everyone has a good analytical mind, then "good analytical mind" as a criterion will not be very powerful in sorting the excellent leaders from the average ones. Some amount of variance is necessary in order for a criterion to work well as a predictor.

I have already described the BEI approach to identifying competencies. This approach can be time-consuming and expensive. In addition, lawyers, who have a well-developed sense of "mastery," often believe that logic alone can lead them to solve any problem. This sometimes means that they dismiss the value of the scientific method. As a result, when law firms have in the past developed competency models,[4] they have often opted to poll their partners for a list of the qualities of an excellent lawyer instead of conducting formal BEIs. In the corporate world, studies have shown that these informal or "focus group" approaches to the development of competency models often err on the side of leaving out about half of the competencies identified in a BEI approach.[5] Moreover, the competencies that they do identify using the focus group approach often over-represent the technical/cognitive competencies and under-represent the behavioral/emotional competencies. This is ironic since it is the latter which, for leadership in particular, are the more powerful and effective predictors.

In most competency modeling projects, when BEIs are conducted, they end up discovering that excellent performers do excellent behaviors more often, for a longer time, and/or in more contexts, than average performers.

While competency models in different organizations often share many of the same or similar elements, it is the 5% or 10% that are different that may be critical for the particular organization. In other words, a competency model needs to fit the culture of the organization that it serves, and it needs to be congruent with the "dialect" spoken inside that organization, metaphorically speaking. The part of the model that takes into account this tailored aspect may end up being just a small part of the overall model, but it's a critical part.

Each competency in a well-developed competency model needs to be limited to a single behavior. Combining skills or behaviors, even ones that logically go together, makes it hard to measure and hard to discern which of the skills/behaviors was in fact mastered.

The development of a competency model is not done in a vacuum. In any organization, the development of a competency model ultimately means that

---

4   This has mainly been done in connection with the development of competency models for associate performance and promotion, not for leadership.

5   David McClelland himself conducted such a study.

many people down the road will be asked to change their behavior. Putting competency models into practice is easy to recommend but hard to do in practice because people will naturally resist the changes they portend, even if in the long run those changes are beneficial. Consequently, any organization that is planning to introduce a competency model is well advised to pay attention not only to the technical aspects of what the model should contain, but to the "process" aspects of how to introduce the entire process of competency development and implementation into the organization. Experts with training in industrial/ organizational (I/O) psychology or organization development (OD) are most likely to be able to help here.

Finally, thoughtful leaders often make the mistake of trying to ensure that their competency model includes every possible component. By striving for thoroughness, they often sacrifice practicality and usability. No matter how thorough a competency model, it is useless if no one can easily remember the core components. I would rather see a model with four critical components that actually make a real-world difference when mastered than a comprehensive 30-component model that covers every possible skill or quality that a leader might need to have. Strive for balance here.

II. The Legal Profession and Leadership Competencies

The legal profession has lagged behind corporate America by decades in several respects:

- Law firms generally did not pay much attention to leadership until the late 1990s or later. (Some still ignore the subject.)
- Lawyers are smart and are trained to believe that they can master any new field through force of logic. As a result, many law firms that began exploring leadership showed little interest in formally identifying leadership competencies. They simply selected leaders based on convenience criteria like "Which partner has the biggest book of business?" or "Which partner has the most seniority?"
- In the past 10 years, an increasing number of law firms have paid more attention to leadership selection and development and have approached it in a more serious way. Some have built competency models from scratch; others have worked with outside vendors to adapt existing models to their law firms.

Research published by John Kotter, at Harvard Business School, shows that the internal felt need for leadership increases as the degree of external uncertainty increases. We live in a time of increasingly rapid and nonstop change, so if Professor Kotter is right, the need for leadership should be on the rise. Law firms, which for many years were relatively unaffected by market ups and downs, are now being directly buffeted by external changes, and I believe that today's law firm leaders are taking much more seriously the notion that law firms need well-trained leaders.

A good leadership competency model, tailored to the unique role that lawyer–leaders play, will be helpful both in selecting lawyers to serve in leadership roles, and in developing lawyers who serve in those roles.

Most leaders in law firms are practicing lawyers, and most spend the majority of their time practicing law and perform their leadership roles part-time. Any model will need to take this fact into account.

There is also evidence from the research on leadership in the corporate world that the relevant competencies will vary depending on the level in the organization at which the leader serves. In particular, the span of control has an effect on the kinds of tasks that a leader will engage in. Leaders that are in charge of a small, face-to-face group of, say, five to ten people will employ a different skill set than leaders in charge of a thousand people.

What kinds of competencies drive leadership in the corporate world? And how similar or different are the essential leadership competencies needed by lawyers in leadership roles?

John Zenger and Joe Folkman have done careful and extensive original research on the competencies that drive leadership success in the corporate world. They've identified 16 competencies in five clusters[6] that predict leadership success (Zenger and Folkman 2009: 12–14):

Character
  1. Displaying high integrity and honesty
Personal capability
  2. Technical and professional expertise
  3. Solving problems and analyzing issues
  4. Innovation
  5. Practicing self-development
Focus on results
  6. Focus on results
  7. Establish stretch goals
  8. Take responsibility for outcomes/initiative
Interpersonal skills
  9. Communicating powerfully and prolifically
  10. Inspiring and motivating others to high performance

---

6   Research on competencies shows that many competencies correlate with one another. See the work of Richard Boyatzis at Weatherhead School of Management, Case Western Reserve University. For this reason, most competency models aggregate the competencies into a smaller number of clusters. Clustering is also beneficial from the standpoint of adult learning theory—cognitive psychologists tell us that we can only retain four to seven bits of information in our mind at one time (Miller 1956).

11. Building relationships
12. Developing others
13. Collaboration and teamwork
<u>Leading organizational change</u>
14. Developing strategic perspectives
15. Championing change
16. Connect internal groups with the outside world

In a more recent study, they concluded that competency 10, "Inspiring and motivating others to high performance," is the "most powerful predictor of someone's being seen as an extraordinary leader" (Zenger et al. 2009: 5). This is consistent with Jim Kouzes and Barry Posner's research on what makes leaders effective. In their most recent book, they concluded that "[t]he capacity to imagine and articulate exciting future possibilities is the defining competence of leaders" (Kouzes and Posner 2010). John Kotter's research leads to a similar conclusion— the number one competency is the ability of a leader to emotionally evoke a "sense of urgency" in their constituents (Kotter 2008).

When I led the Leadership and OD practice at Hildebrandt International, we conducted our own research with law firm leaders. Our studies showed that the competencies that predict effective leadership in law firms bear some distinct similarities to those that drive leaders in the corporate world. In addition, there are two atypical competencies that are essential to leaders in law firms but which are not typically found in leadership competency models in the corporate world.

Zenger and Folkman's five clusters are:

- character
- personal capability
- focus on results
- interpersonal skills
- leading organizational change.

Our research shows that leaders in law firms need to have:

- integrity
- self and other development
- focus on results
- leading change.

If you think of our second bullet as really embracing two elements—self-regulation plus a set of other-oriented skills—then at the cluster level, there is a great deal of similarity between our model and Zenger and Folkman's corporate model. This is not surprising in light of Kouzes and Posner's research, which suggests that many of the qualities that make leaders effective are universal, cutting across cultural and geographic boundaries. In fact, they have found that the cluster that includes integrity, character, honesty, and trustworthiness is not only nearly universal, but it is the number one competency in every country in which they have gathered data. It's hardly surprising to find it at the top of our model for law firm leaders as well.

In what ways do the needed competencies for law firm leaders differ from those found in corporate America? The differences lie in the individual competencies within the clusters.

One of the competencies that distinguishes law firm leaders is "Demonstrates confidence and resilience." This is no doubt related to the fact that lawyers, as a general rule, are extremely low in "resilience," as we will see in the next section of this chapter. Leaders who are lawyers themselves, and who are leading other lawyers, need to either have higher-than-average resilience, or else learn to manage their low resilience while in their leadership role.

The second atypical competency in the law firm leader competency model is "Influences in a sophisticated way." Leaders in law firms generally do not have the advantage of the hierarchical chain of command commonly found in corporations. Moreover, the constituents of law firm leaders are generally their peers, that is, other partners, and associates in training to become partners. Without positional authority, leaders in law firms must by necessity develop a sophisticated ability to influence those they lead, using informal but complex influencing strategies. This competency reflects that reality.

III. The Lawyer Personality and Leadership Competencies

Some competencies are learnable. Others are more innate. Most are a combination. The more innate the competency is, the less productive it becomes to "develop" existing leaders, and the more fruitful it is to hire people with those competencies to begin with.

Very few law firms consider leadership competencies at the point of hire, but they should. You can hire people who have both learned and innate competencies; you can only train people in learned competencies, and even then, you can only train those with both the motivation and the aptitude.

Personality traits can constitute a component of a competency, but more powerfully, personality influences just about every competency. Since personality is more genetic than learned (and far more genetic than psychologists believed even as recently as 15 years ago (Hur and Bouchard 1995)),[7] it may make sense to

---

7   Note that while the pendulum is moving back towards more biological explanations for psychological phenomena, at the same time, recent discoveries in cognitive neuroscience suggest that just because a feature is genetically based does not necessarily mean it is immutable. For example, see Dr. Richard Davidson's new book, *The Emotional Life of the Brain* (2011), in which he presents evidence that conscious thought can influence whether genes are activated ("expressed") or not.

favor selection over training as the preferred method for finding leaders with the right competencies.

At the opening of this chapter, I noted that reliance on personality fell out of favor as a predictor of human behavior. Because of that shift, there was a distinct falloff in the research literature on studies attempting to link personality to leadership. For a while, the conventional wisdom held that personality didn't predict any leader behaviors at all. More recently, studies have shown that while individual traits may not predict leader behavior all that well, traits in combination can do an excellent job.

Moreover, during the past 20 years, there have been remarkable advances in psychometrics due to faster computers and more sophisticated statistical packages. The net result of these advances has been the emergence of several personality measurement tools that have proven themselves in both identifying leaders and in developing leaders (Kaiser and Overfield 2010a, 2010b).

Over the past decade, I've gathered personality data on thousands of lawyers, including leaders as well as rank-and-file lawyers. Taking these data as a whole, there are several trends that stand out:

- People who enter the legal profession and stay (that is, they become partners) have a number of personality traits that are atypical compared with the general population. Stated another way, certain traits that are infrequently found in the general population are over-represented among lawyers.
- These over-represented traits seem to help lawyers to be more effective in their roles as lawyers.
- These same traits may make it more challenging for lawyers to be effective in leadership roles.

Let's look at the traits that distinguish lawyers from the general public.

We've used a number of assessment tools to measure the mental landscape of lawyers, including measures of personality, values, emotional intelligence, career interests, optimism, and attitude towards change. Two of the personality measures, in particular, are quite germane to selecting and developing leaders—the Hogan Assessment suite and the Caliper Profile.

The Hogan Assessment suite has become one of the leading tools in the corporate world in leadership selection and development.

In 2009, we conducted a large-scale study of lawyers' personality traits using the Hogan tool with a cross-section of lawyers in successful large law firms. We actually gathered our data shortly after the economy had plunged into a recession and the legal profession had laid off over 20,000 lawyers. Because we only tested lawyers who survived this shakeout, arguably they represent the more successful lawyers.

The Hogan test consists of three components—the HPI (Hogan Personality Inventory); the MVPI (Motives, Values and Preferences Inventory); and the HDS (Hogan Development Survey).

The HPI is the centerpiece of the test, and measures seven key personality traits. Each trait is measured on a percentile scale, from 0% to 100%.

Table 3.1 shows the traits, along with the average score for each trait based on a sample of 156,614 individuals they've tested (in effect, a cross-section of the general population).

Table 3.1   Hogan Personal Inventory traits and scores

Scale	HPI norm group (n = 156,614)
Adjustment	54.0
Ambition	57.0
Sociability	52.9
Interpersonal sensitivity	61.7
Prudence	53.7
Inquisitive	53.1
Learning approach	55.1

Table 3.2 shows the average scores for our sample of successful lawyers (includes both partners and associates).

Table 3.2   Hogan Personal Inventory traits and scores for sample of successful lawyers[8]

Scale	Successful lawyers (n = 1,510)
Adjustment	42.7
Ambition	51.6
Sociability	54.3
Interpersonal sensitivity	39.3
Prudence	47.8
Inquisitive	51.9
Learning approach	69.1

---

8   Tables 3.1 and 3.2 are both Copyright 2007, Hogan Assessment Systems, Inc. Used with permission. The Hogan Personality Inventory is a registered trademark of Hogan Assessment Systems.

Note that lawyers score significantly lower than the general public on Interpersonal Sensitivity and significantly higher on Learning Approach.

People with low scores on Interpersonal Sensitivity can be described as tough-minded, skeptical, direct, argumentative, blunt, not nurturing, plain-speaking (that is, not prone to sugarcoating bad news).

People with high scores on Learning Approach can be described as enjoying learning for its own sake, appreciating education, tend to stay up to date, like to "know stuff." Every study of lawyers that's been published finds lawyers high in this or a related trait. People drawn to the legal profession enjoy analyzing, problem-solving, using their cognitive gifts. This is equally true of leaders and rank-and-file lawyers.

These two traits serve lawyers well in what they do. A high Learning Approach provides them with an interest in immersing themselves in learning and analyzing, which is at the heart of what lawyers do. The low Interpersonal Sensitivity trait is compatible with the objective, blunt, logical approach that lawyers need to take in order to advise their clients on the law. Law is rule-based, not sentiment-based, and a personal style that emphasizes the logical side of things makes more sense. This is as true for litigators as it is for transactional lawyers. Litigators are expected to be able to argue any side of a proposition, depending on whom they represent. The lower range of the Interpersonal Sensitivity scale seems compatible with these demands.

But how do these traits work when lawyers undertake a leadership role?

Leadership is a fundamentally interpersonal role. Leaders are effective to the extent that they gain the trust of their followers and build rapport with their followers. Low scores on Interpersonal Sensitivity are not fatal for leaders, but they can certainly make it harder or less comfortable for such a leader to consistently act in ways that build trust and rapport. John Kotter has emphasized the importance of leaders developing the skill of evoking an *emotional* response in order to get constituents on board with the leader's vision (Kotter and Cohen 2002). Lower scores on Interpersonal Sensitivity are likely to be associated with a more cognitive approach and a less emotional one.

Likewise, leaders need to act with imperfect information. While a high Learning Approach score might aid a lawyer–leader in gathering lots of information and comfortably sifting through it, it also raises the danger of "analysis paralysis" and information overload.

The implications for the selection and development of leaders in law firms is that the pool of potential leaders is more likely to be over-represented by individuals with scores on these two traits that are better for lawyering than for leadership. Law firms will either need to select atypical candidates, or else devote resources to training and coaching their leaders in how to manage these personality traits and how to lead effectively despite them.

One subset of our Hogan data was a group of nearly 100 leaders of large firms. Most were managing partners or the equivalent in AmLaw 100 firms. The data from this sample were interesting.

One trait stood out among our leaders—88% of our sample of leaders had an Ambition score of 47 or higher on a scale of 0 to 100. The average Ambition score for our sample was 67; the average for the public is 57. The average for rank-and-file lawyers is 51.6. High scores on "Ambition" are associated with an outwardly confident style, leader-like behavior, and a competitive, driven quality. High scorers more often will vie for leadership positions. One possible inference to be drawn from these data is that lawyers whose personalities are more naturally leader-like more often step into leadership roles. This is consistent with most job-person fit theories in vocational psychology.

Further confirmation of this inference can be seen if we look at the 12% of leaders with lower Ambition scores. The theory predicts that they would be less inclined to seek out leadership roles. Yet all of these individuals in our sample are in leadership roles. Informal interviews with a sampling of these leaders revealed that most of them reported being drafted into their role as managing partner. Thus, their entry into the role was prompted by an outside request *despite* their low Ambition score.

This doesn't necessarily mean that a high Ambition score is a prerequisite to becoming a leader. A low-scoring individual could also become one, and do well in the role. The difference is that for the high-scoring individual, the qualities represented by the high Ambition trait are a comfort zone; for the low-Ambition leader, he or she may have to struggle to direct others, to maintain a confident front, etc.

Likewise, just because a person has a high Ambition score doesn't necessarily mean that he or she will invariably apply for a leadership role. Many other factors besides personality may dictate that choice. But it does tell us that once in that role, there is likely to be a level of comfort with being a leader.

Additional insight can be gained by looking at the data we have gathered using the Caliper Profile. Like the Hogan, the Caliper Profile is a personality assessment tool that was developed for use in the business world. In 1997, I began testing lawyers with this tool, and to date, have tested over 5,000 lawyers with it, including 140 law firm leaders.

The Caliper Profile measures 18 independent traits:

Assertiveness
Aggressiveness
Ego drive
Empathy
Urgency
Self-structure
External structure
Risk-taking
Cautiousness
Conscientiousness
Skepticism

Resilience
Gregariousness
Sociability
Idea orientation
Abstract reasoning
Accommodation
Flexibility

Since 1964, the publisher of the Caliper Profile has tested over 4 million individuals, mostly people in knowledge worker roles in the business world. Like the Hogan, each trait is measured on a percentile scale. The lowest score one can get is 1%; the highest is 99%. All traits have an average score of 50% for the general population.

Our research showed that lawyers in medium to large business law firms have traits that look very similar to those of the general public—for 12 of the 18 traits. (People often express surprise that lawyers are no different from the general public on Empathy or on Conscientiousness.)

However, lawyers scored significantly higher than the public on three traits:

- skepticism
- abstract reasoning
- urgency

And they scored significantly lower than the public on three other traits:

- sociability
- external structure
- resilience

Each of these traits contributes to the ability of lawyers to be effective at their craft, but can actually make it more challenging to be effective as a leader.

Skepticism

Lawyers are skeptical. They are trained to think this way in law school, and in addition, the profession attracts a group of people with higher than average scores on the Caliper "Skepticism" scale. Research shows that low-scoring law students drop out, thus concentrating the high-Skeptical group. This dropout pattern continues during the associate years. By the point at which associates become partners, high-Skepticism lawyers are well over-represented.

Martin Seligman, the well-known professor of psychology at the University of Pennsylvania, has tested a number of lawyers to measure their level of optimism or pessimism, a quality that is undoubtedly related to what the Caliper "Skepticism" scale is measuring. He notes that they have the highest level of pessimism of any occupational group he has tested (Seligman 1991).

People with a high score on Skepticism can be described as doubting, argumentative, mistrustful, and not willing to give the benefit of the doubt. These qualities actually serve most lawyers pretty well in their practice. Lawyers are frequently expected to challenge otherwise accepted ideas, documents, statements, or orthodoxies on behalf of their clients. It's a lawyer's job to ask "What bad things could happen if … ?" so that they can then protect their client from possible harm. Some of my clients have actually argued that a lawyer is not doing a proper job if they are not sufficiently Skeptical.

By contrast, Skepticism is less of an asset in a leadership role. Leaders need to build trust and be seen as people that others want to voluntarily follow. Skepticism has a reciprocal quality—when someone is Skeptical with you, you are less likely to trust him or her. Leaders need to behave in a trusting and trustworthy way. The Skepticism trait may make that more challenging, especially for a lawyer–leader who needs to move between the two roles fluidly.

Law firm leaders that we have studied are less Skeptical than rank-and-file lawyers are.

Abstract Reasoning

This trait, while not identical, is in the same family as the Hogan trait Learning Approach. Lawyers as a group score fairly high on Abstract Reasoning. They like analyzing issues, solving problems, using their intellect.

As noted above, this may be useful in a leadership role as well as in a lawyering role, but it also has a potential downside in a leadership role, that is, used to excess, the trait can lead to over-analysis and inaction. It can also lead lawyer–leaders to favor the cerebral over the emotional in instances where evoking an emotional response would be more effective.

Law firm leaders that we have studied are no different in Abstract Reasoning than rank-and-file lawyers are.

Urgency

Lawyers score high on Urgency. People with high Urgency scores are impatient. They finish others' sentences. They cut in line. They tap their fingers. They have a strong need for closure and need to spring into action to complete a transaction, a conversation, an errand, etc.

This trait is vital for lawyers. Numerous studies have shown that the business clients of large law firms value "responsiveness" above all other qualities in the lawyers they hire. When a client asks for help from their law firm, they want immediate help with their problem. A lawyer with a high Urgency score is naturally suited to respond quickly and to make "Urgency" a part of their client service repertoire.

In a leadership role, Urgency can certainly be an asset in the sense that Urgent leaders are more likely to move initiatives forward faster than leaders with low scores. However, as noted above, leadership is an inherently interpersonal activity. Leaders are most effective when they can build rapport with their constituents, listen to their constituents, build trust, and get those constituents on board with the leader's vision. An Urgent leader may make their constituent feel "not listened to" or taken for granted. Even though it may be unrealistic, people want their leaders to be interested in them. Good leadership is not just about "telling"—it's also about listening. And a high Urgency score can make listening well a bit of a challenge.

Law firm leaders that we have studied are no different in Urgency than rank-and-file lawyers are.

Sociability

People who score high on this trait are interested in connecting with people. They are willing to disclose information about themselves in order to increase intimacy over time in a relationship. They are true "people" people. (Low-scoring individuals are more private, slower to warm up, and less interested in intimate connections, especially with people they don't know well.) Lawyers score low on this trait.

Because of the impersonal, objective, transactional nature of much law practice, low scores on this trait serve lawyers in many instances. (Although in today's business climate, a good argument can be made that this is no longer the case.)

In a leadership role, being willing to connect with constituents is a desirable skill to have.[9] Once again, lawyers with low Sociability scores may find it more challenging to build the level of connected relationships that will most effectively build trust and buy-in.

Law firm leaders that we have studied are slightly more Sociable than rank-and-file lawyers are.

External Structure

A person who is low in External Structure really can be thought of as being high in Autonomy. Low scorers tend to pay little attention to rules, procedures, and hierarchies. They don't like being told what to do by others. Lawyers as a group have one of the lowest External Structure scores of any occupational subgroup.[10]

---

9   Look at the "Interpersonal Skills" cluster of competencies in Zenger and Folkman's model, or at the examples given in Kotter's *Heart of Change* or *A Sense of Urgency.*

10   Professor Tom Davenport at Babson College (he was at Harvard Business School when he published this research) has described the tendency for knowledge workers in general, and professionals in particular, to value Autonomy more than other people in society (Davenport 2005). But among professionals, lawyers are near the top of the Autonomy-loving group.

One of the responsibilities of a lawyer is to maintain independence. This is even built into the code of ethics in most jurisdictions—a lawyer, in their representation of a client, should not be influenced by or be beholden to any other person or entity. Law firms are famously described as places where managers grow gray trying to "herd cats."

Because lawyers are educated in how laws and societal rules are made, and because they are the ones who, on behalf of clients, challenge those rules, they may develop an insouciant attitude towards rules themselves—"Rules are for other people; I don't want anyone telling me what to do however."

This may work in the day-to-day role of a lawyer, but a leader is a role model. People normally place a lot of weight on the actions of their leaders. If a leader behaves in too autonomous a fashion, it may send the wrong signal to that leader's constituents.

Law firm leaders that we have studied are less Autonomous (that is, higher on External Structure) than rank-and-file lawyers are.

Resilience

A person who scores high on this trait is relatively thick-skinned in the face of criticism, rejection, or setbacks. They recover quickly from such incidents, and they manage their emotional responses well.

Low scorers are more reactive. They are prone to over-explaining why they did things the way they did them. They may feel easily hurt by criticism or rejection. They frequently get defensive and take things personally. It's harder for them to recover from setbacks readily, and their skills in managing their emotional responses are not as good as those of high scorers. Lawyers score low on this trait—as a group, they consistently average at around the 30th percentile (compared with the 50th percentile for the general public.) But the distribution of scores is not a classic bell curve; rather, scores are dramatically skewed to the lower end—year in and year out, approximately 90% of the lawyers that we measure on this trait have a Resilience score at or below the 50th percentile! This is a very low-Resilience group.

I have strained to see how this serves lawyers in their role as lawyers. While I can think of several possibilities,[11] none are very convincing.

There are two important implications of this low Resilience score for lawyers in leadership roles:

1. When leaders themselves behave in a low Resilience way—acting defensive, hurt, or thin-skinned—others who interact with them may be put off and may elect not to deliver bad news to them out of concern that "they won't take it well." Moreover, leaders get criticized more than others

---

11 For example, maybe it serves lawyers to be defensive because it puts them on alert to possible injustices? Plausible, but improbable.

do. A leader who reacts defensively to criticism is essentially denying the critic's validity, which may further distance the critic.

2. When lawyer–leaders are leading other lawyers, they have to assume that they are leading a profoundly low Resilience constituency. The tactical approach one should take in leading low Resilience people is quite different from how one might lead people with average Resilience scores.[12]

Law firm leaders that we have studied are significantly more Resilient than rank-and-file lawyers are.

In contrast to these six traits on which lawyers differ from the public, there are three other traits on which leaders score higher than average, even though rank-and-file lawyers score "average" on these traits: Empathy, Risk-taking, and Flexibility.

Empathy, in Caliper parlance, has more to do with cognitive "perspective taking"—the act of wondering how things look from another's shoes—rather than the more emotional version of empathy (as in "I feel your pain").

It makes sense that leaders would naturally consider the views of others, even though lawyers in general are not particularly drawn to this trait.

Risk-taking, in Caliper parlance, is actually related to one's desire to lead an adventurous life (or, by contrast, low scorers like to play it safe). Lawyers are relatively notorious for being risk-averse. I've actually been surprised to see this trait average out in the middle for lawyers—my personal experience, and feedback from many clients over the years, suggests that lawyers should score low on this trait. Be that as it may, it's clear that lawyers in leadership roles are a little more willing to take risks, which is what leaders need to do.

Flexibility is just what it sounds like—high scorers are open to changing their minds as new information comes in. This may be the "type O blood" of personality—for no matter how strong one of your other traits may be, if you are Flexible, you can successfully adapt in a given situation despite strong proclivities to behave in an unhelpful manner.

Leaders take risks. Sometimes those risks don't work out. When that happens, they need to do something different. A low-Flexibility leader might be more inclined to simply re-do the first effort only with more vigor. More effective leaders will try a different approach.

---

12 For example, in giving feedback to an individual, if the feedback recipient is low in Resilience, it is vital that the feedback-giver emphasize the recipient's strengths, and focus on how the individual can be even more effective going forward. While attention to the recipient's shortcomings may be honest and valid, if the feedback is not heard, it won't be very helpful.

IV. Law Firm Leadership is Evolving

In summary, human behavior, with all its subjectivity, can nevertheless be studied and to some extent predicted using qualitative methods such as competency modeling and behavioral event interviews. When applied to the field of leadership, these methods can help identify, recruit, and develop individuals who are more likely to perform towards the "excellent" end of the spectrum of leadership.

Law firms that move in the direction of using such methods need to take into account the personality traits of lawyers because personality has a significant effect on all aspects of competency development, leadership training, and leadership performance. Moreover, most lawyers in leadership roles continue to practice law as their main job, and perform leadership functions as a "second job." More important, the very traits that make them good lawyers can make it more challenging for them to be good leaders.

There is some evidence that some firms are beginning to establish full-time leadership roles filled by former practicing lawyers who give up their practice and serve as leaders full-time. We have very sketchy data so far suggesting that firms that have done so seem to be selecting lawyers who are better suited to these leadership roles than the average lawyer might be. This is a healthy trend, but there is a lot more that firms can do to increase the quality and effectiveness of their leaders.

Militating against this progress is the fact that the legal profession has historically been very slow to change. Leadership is all about managing change, so the die has been cast.

As law firms become more comfortable with the idea of empowering their lawyers to enter into and perform well in leadership roles, and as they take more seriously the science behind the selection and development of leaders, there will be significant opportunities for firms to improve their competitive capacity by building a highly competent leadership pipeline.

References

Davenport, T.H. 2005. *Thinking for a Living: How to Get Better Performance and Results from Knowledge Workers.* Boston: Harvard Business School Press.

Edwards, J.R. 1991. Person-Job Fit: A Conceptual Integration, Literature Review, and Methodological Critique, in *International Review of Industrial and Organizational Psychology*, edited by C.L. Cooper and I.T. Robertson, Vol. 6. New York: Wiley and Sons.

Hernez-Broome, G. and Hughes, R.L. 2004. Leadership Development: Past, Present and Future, *Human Resource Planning*, March, 24–32.

Holland, J.L. 1973. *Making Vocational Choices: A Theory of Careers.* Englewood Cliffs, NJ: Prentice-Hall.

Law and Leadership

Hur, Yoon-Mi and Bouchard, T.J., Jr. 1995. Genetic Influences on Perceptions of Childhood Family Environment: A Reared Apart Twin Study, *Child Development*, 66(2): 330–45.

Institute for Corporate Productivity (i4cp) 2009. *The Top Five Leadership Competencies of Tomorrow* [Online], 8 October. Available at: http://www.pr.com/press-release/184309 [accessed 9 September 2012].

Joiner, W.B. and Josephs, S.A. 2007. *Leadership Agility: Five Levels of Mastery for Anticipating and Initiating Change.* San Francisco: Jossey-Bass.

Kaiser, R.B. and Overfield, D.V. 2010a. The Leadership Value Chain, *Psychologist-Manager Journal*, 13(3): 164–83.

Kaiser, R.B. and Overfield, D.V. 2010b. Assessing Flexible Leadership as a Mastery of Opposites, *Consulting Psychology Journal*, 62(2): 105–18.

Kotter, J.P. 2008. *A Sense of Urgency.* Boston: Harvard Business Press.

Kotter, J.P. and Cohen, D.S. 2002. *Heart of Change: Real-Life Stories of How People Change Their Organizations.* Boston: Harvard Business School Press.

Kouzes, J.M. and Posner, B.Z. 2010. *The Truth About Leadership: The No-Fads, Heart-of-the-Matter Facts You Need to Know.* San Francisco: Jossey-Bass.

Kristof-Brown, A.L., Jansen, K.J. and Colbert, A.E. 2002. A Policy-Capturing Study of the Simultaneous Effects of Fit with Jobs, Groups, and Organizations, *Journal of Applied Psychology*, 87(5): 985–93.

McClelland, D.C. 1973. Testing for Competence Rather than for "Intelligence," *American Psychologist*, 28(1): 1–14.

Miller, G. 1956. The Magical Number Seven, Plus or Minus Two: Some Limits on Our Capacity for Processing Information, *Psychological Review*, 63(2): 81–97.

Seligman, M.E.P. 1991. *Learned Optimism.* New York: A.A. Knopf.

Zenger, J. and Folkman, J. 2009. *The Extraordinary Leader: Turning Good Managers into Great Leaders.* New York: McGraw-Hill.

Zenger, J.H., Folkman, J.R. and Edinger, S.K. 2009. *The Inspiring Leader: Unlocking the Secrets of How Extraordinary Leaders Motivate.* New York: McGraw-Hill.

Chapter 4

Leaders in the Changing Legal Economy

Alexina Jackson

Law firms are not known for dynamic business strategies or cutting-edge entrepreneurial models. Instead of anticipating changes in the legal economy and leading the charge with creative solutions, most law firms are cornered into new business models as pressure builds from clients, employees, and finances. But as new legal business models emerge, lawyers will be called on to adapt and think of their employers and clients through a wider lens. The individuals who become leaders in the changing legal economy will likely be those lawyers who are able to identify and communicate a vision of their own careers that demonstrates partnership with their employers and clients. The firms that become leaders will likely be those firms that realize the qualities of partnership and vision embodied by the talented lawyers that they employ.

While the ability to find and communicate vision has been a skill of leadership from time immemorial, the emerging legal economy will require successful lawyers (and firms) to more frequently bring leadership skills to the table. And although not every successful lawyer will be a star in the field, attention to leadership skills should increase job performance as well as job satisfaction for any attorney. This calculation alone should provide clients, employers, and educators with the incentive to teach and encourage the development of leadership skills by lawyers. This chapter briefly explores the changing legal economy, the qualities of successful firms, and the skills of leaders. The leadership skills that lawyers should be taught are mentioned in conclusion and left for further contemplation.

I. The Changing Legal Economy: New Demands on Firms

Law firms encounter pressure to evolve their way of doing business from various sources. Clients are looking for law firms with which to partner and establish lasting relationships (Comodeca and Everett 2010). Attorneys are asking their employers to invest in them and provide flexibility in work environment and career trajectory (Shannon 2010a). The financial limits of an economy (perhaps) emerging from recession amplify client and employee demands and clarify the incentives for firms to respond to these demands in competition for client business and employee talent (Zahorsky 2012).

Large and small clients alike are asking their law firms to team with them and share in the risk and reward of business endeavors (Comodeca and Everett

2010). When a firm is willing to partner with a client over time, the client receives relevant, targeted work product that recognizes the unique dynamics of the client's business. However, lasting relationships require both investment by the client to teach the firm about its business and investment by firms in employee skills and non-billable client development (Shannon 2010a). Because of these relationship costs, clients might ask their partner firms to undergo pre-qualification, create firm-wide relationships across practice areas and geographies, and tie the firm's financial reward to the client's own success in a matter (*DuPont Legal Model* n.d.).

Clients who pre-qualify firms to receive legal business sometimes look not only to past performance metrics or ranking in an area of law, but also compliance with ethical and social standards that the client holds important (*DuPont Legal Model* n.d.). For law firms traditionally concerned with substantive skills above others, a client's attention to ethical and social standards can require a significant shift in the firm's focus. A client might look to the firm's contribution to its community through *pro bono* involvement or internships. A client can also take interest in the diversity of a firm's workforce and its promotion of diverse attorneys into leadership positions. Also of interest to some clients is the availability of flexible work arrangements that allow employees to more closely achieve the ever-evasive work–life balance. As some clients begin to condition access to legal work on these "softer" standards, in addition to substantive skills, firms will need to develop business models that integrate these standards and to teach the "soft" skills required to actualize the changes at all levels of the firm hierarchy.

Another change to the law firm business model can come from clients' requirements for firm-wide, lasting relationships. As client business widens its aperture to capture multiple practice areas and geographies, relationships shift from models of single-partner ownership to firm-wide investment (Zahorsky 2012). Firm-wide client relationships require commitment to understanding the client's business more completely, not just at the level of a single matter (Zahorsky 2012). This understanding will enable a firm to identify opportunities and spot risks for the client, and link them to competitive legal strategies. Investment in the client relationship could require the firm to make an ethical and social commitment to community, diversity, and flexible work arrangements. Investment will certainly entail development and retention of talented, well-rounded attorneys, including early involvement in client relationships and, possibly, appointment of mid-level attorneys to client secondments, rotating them among the firm's clients so they develop broader client relationships. (Shannon 2010a, Smith 2011).

Perhaps the most discussed change to the law firm business model is the alternative fee arrangement (Loomis 2009). Indeed, this change is already so commonplace that the word "alternative" may soon disappear, in acknowledgement that many clients hesitate to accept pure hourly fees. Instead, clients now often tie the compensation of a firm to the success of a suit, negotiation, or other engagement (Comodeca and Everett 2010). This means that early projects can serve as investments in sustaining the longer-term client relationship (Comodeca and Everett 2010). If ramp-up costs are shared between the client and law firm, the client might not subsidize the learning curve of lawyers who are getting to know the client or the law.

The alternative fee arrangement also requires a law firm to align its objectives more closely with its client's (Zahorsky 2012). A billing arrangement can motivate a firm to seek settlement of a suit because it is not only the best outcome for the client, but it is also a good result for the firm. A billing arrangement can shift a firm's focus from profitability through ever-increasing billable hours to providing the right person for the job for the right amount of time—in short, prioritizing creativity and productivity over simple accumulation of hours. Risks are shared between client and firm, as are costs. Finally, alternative fee arrangements have ethical value because they align client and firm outcomes (Zahorsky 2012).

But it is not only clients that require changes to law firm business models. Whether attributed to generational differences, technological advances, or shifting dynamics in personal relationships, employees also pressure firms to increase their employee investment, including greater flexibility in work environment and career trajectory (Shannon 2010b). Increased investment in employees is warranted, as they are the firms' biggest asset. Clients benefit from, and desire, well-rounded attorneys who receive training in substantive law *and* "soft" skills (Shannon 2010b). Attorneys seek access to a variety of work, including access to a variety of partners, so a career is not made or broken on the portfolio, skills, or kindness of a single partner. For similar reasons, attorneys desire formal and informal mentoring (Vorro 2012). Such investment should include diverse mentors and role models so junior attorneys can envision a path to their own success (Vorro 2012).

Attorneys seek increased flexibility in work environment, which can include hours and location of work. Certainly attorneys believe that there is a base salary that is the deserved minimum for the sacrifices made in a law firm environment, such as longer hours, unpredictable schedules, and availability to client and partner demands. However, there is a diminishing return to increased pay. Stated differently: incremental increases in hours require much more pay to be desireable to an employee. Sensitivity to long hours can be offset somewhat by a firm's flexibility in the location of an attorney's work. Technology allows for such flexibility, enabling employees to more effectively balance work with other things of importance in the attorney's life. An attorney's need for flexibility in hours and location of work may also fluctuate during their career (Fortney 2010, New York State Bar Association 2011, Project for Attorney Retention).

Although one might argue that employee demands of firms carry little water during an economic downturn, this is not purely so. Difficult economies present their own set of pressures for law firms, but also magnify those of clients and employees (Pearlstein 2011). Perhaps obvious is that, as firms compete for more limited client funds, competition drives firms to conform to client objectives and demands (Wald 2012). Potentially less obvious is that, although employment becomes a scarce resource in a downturned economy, firms need to maintain employee morale in difficult times, and to do so with more limited resources (Alexander 2012, Volkert 2012). A downturned economy creates incentives to:

1. Use creative alternative fee arrangements that create predictable costs for clients and predictable revenue for firms (Comodeca and Everett 2010). Although non-hourly fee arrangements can place more risk on a firm than an hourly fee, the firm might secure more clients if it does not require the client to accept the entirety of the risk. These arrangements also encourage productivity from employees.
2. Develop and retain talent because turnover is expensive (Tucker 2009). The economic pressure to avoid costs of finding and training new talent underlines employee demands for investment and flexibility. Also, a downturned economy creates incentives for firms to provide reduced-hour arrangements coupled with reduced pay.
3. Take advantage of economies of scale and outsourcing (Rampell 2011). This, however, must be in delicate balance with client and employee interests as economies of scale and outsourcing can risk firm culture and reduce the payoff from investment in client and employee relationships (Rampell 2011). However, used in a targeted and thoughtful manner, a large firm that outsources may be positioned to not only better weather economic downturn, but also provide a variety of services at a reasonable cost.

The pressures of the changing legal economy result in opportunities for competitive differentiation among firms that helps secure clients or retain employee talent. Market pressures, however, require all parties—clients, employees, and firms—to share in the risk of business success or failure. There will be those who chase market success and those who do not. The desire to succeed in the new market drives change in firm business models.

II. New Demands Require New Firm Business Models

As the desire to secure limited client and employee resources drives change, firms should develop business models that emphasize market competitive qualities. To meet the pressures for improved client-firm and employee-employer relationships, a firm could develop a teaming business model that shares the risks and rewards of success. To better ensure profitability, a firm might look to economic models that thoughtfully diversify pricing structures, portfolios of work, and employee compensation. To extend the concept of partnership to clients and employees, a firm could adopt a broad partnership model that allows for firm-wide service to clients, as well as diversified ways of compensating and evaluating employee talent.

A. Reasons to Develop a Teaming Business Model

To share in the risks and rewards of business, firms would benefit from business models that identify mechanisms in both the firm's business and the client's business that maximize market opportunities and mitigate against risks (Bayley 2010). A team-based business model focuses on relationship-building and shared outcomes. It emphasizes a firm's understanding of its client's business as a whole, and not just the context of a single matter or engagement. Teaming relationships—strategic in approach and requiring considerable investment—tend to be long term in nature (Zahorsky 2012).

When a firm thinks of its client relationships in a long-term, relationship-building manner, it aligns its interests with those of its clients (Zahorsky 2012). This means that a firm must carefully select its clients. Many firms already do this when they consider conflicts of interest and the future revenue potential of a client. But a teaming relationship requires even broader thinking. A firm should consider the client as a partner that provides opportunities that strategically benefit (not only financially benefit) the firm in its own business. The firm needs to learn to say "no," even when considerable money is on the table. A firm that strategically invests in its clients also generates unique value to the client through in-depth knowledge and understanding of the client's business dynamics and needs. Understanding that goes beyond a single matter generates superior outcomes for the client, and with greater efficiency (Zahorsky 2012)—these are the benefits that retain clients.

Similarly, if a firm wants to share the risk and reward of investment with its employees, it cannot see the relationship as a one-way street. If an employee is to invest in a firm career, the firm must return investment in the employee (Harvard Business School 2010). Firms that insist on a single model for employment will likely have higher turnover rates. When the firm begins to think of its employees as long-term investments, it is better situated to retain people with a variety of talents through a variety of life and career cycles. The value of the firm's investment in human assets can be realized by shifting assets in line with the cycles. Asset-shifting avoids requiring employees to leave their career to secure change in the nature of their employment.

For example, most employees that stay with a single employer for an extended period of time will encounter the need for career change. The need for change may come about because of family pressures, career satisfaction, or the desire to engage in multiple life pursuits (Mullins 2009). If a firm considers an employee to be a long-term investment, and finds utility in retaining an employee with diverse interests, skills, and backgrounds, the firm might adopt creative models of employment such as: reduced or alternative hour schedules; working from remote locations; externships or leaves of absence to develop desired skill sets (including client secondments, *pro bono* litigation, government employment, and continuing education), and; transition to management-type positions within the firm. A firm that allows its employees to find opportunities for change within its relationship with the firm is likely to secure loyalty and a natural desire from employees to invest in their place of employment (Harvard Business School 2010).

B. Reasons to Develop a Diversified Economic Model

Client and employee demands can also require firms to take on some economic risk. The risk can be hedged against by using economic models that thoughtfully diversify pricing structures, work portfolios, and employee compensation (Bayley 2010). To respond to client demands for new billing arrangements, a firm might secure profitability by responding to diversified pricing methods with diversified portfolios of work. Alternative fee arrangements, whether project-based, fixed-fee, performance-based, piece-work, or some other arrangement, shift risk to firms (Comodeca and Everett 2010). The task of pricing a project becomes difficult and unpredictable. A firm may be required to generate an "up-front" estimate of the cost to conduct discovery, file summary judgment papers, mediate a joint venture, or complete due diligence (Zahorsky 2012). Although a firm can develop "typical" pricing models through estimates based on past experience, significant risk remains in the uncertainty of whether a particular matter's discovery is more or less expensive than average, or whether a certain attorney or judge is assigned to the matter.

The unpredictable nature of alternative fee arrangements, therefore, requires firms to think creatively and remain flexible (Loomis 2009). A firm's ability to combine creativity and flexibility should allow it to take the risks needed to meet client demands, yet hedge those risks enough to ensure business sustainability. In hedging risks, a firm should consider them as part of a firm-wide equation. A firm might achieve sustainable pricing by diversifying its matter portfolio across the firm to include a variety of pricing structures (Bayley 2011). A firm can consider undertaking projects or organizing its business to enable economies of scale in services to a single client or among various clients (Zahorsky 2012). For a single client, this can mean sharing the client relationship across firm practice groups or cross-selling work. For multiple clients, this might mean generating a single product or skill set that proves valuable to various clients without implicating conflicts of interest.

Responding to employee demands, a firm could hedge against losing investments made in employee talent by diversifying forms of compensation. Creative models of employee compensation can enable a firm to strategically invest in its employee talent and retain effective employees (Harvard Business School 2010). Compensation structures can balance employment awards such as money, time, flexibility of working conditions, and other nonmonetary benefits such as healthcare, leave, and training. For employees at different points in their careers and lives, and according to financial, developmental, or family demands, the benefits offered by an employer will have varying value (Harvard Business School 2010). A compensation structure that recognizes variations between employees and variations within an employee's career can provide more or less of each type of employment benefit according to the value perceived by the employee. A firm might also benefit from creative compensation systems because it can hedge against the risks of client demands for new pricing structures by selecting from its portfolio of employees to best match the pricing bargain struck with the client.

Certainly, a firm is wise to balance the extent to which it diversifies its employee compensation structure with the cost of managing the diversity. The principal point, therefore, is that a successful, profitable firm should choose to retain employee talent of various types, and at various points in life, through a diversified approach to compensation—in short, by recognizing that "one size" really does not "fit all." A firm that can thoughtfully compensate its employees will encourage an environment of shared investment, in the firm and the employee, where risk and reward are carried by employee and firm alike.

C. Reasons to Develop a Broad Partnership Model

As firms react to market demands for long-term partnership with clients and employees, they will likely need to evolve the traditional firm partnership model into one built on a broader base. This is not to say that firms will necessarily move away from a partnership business form, but rather, that partnership as an organization of independent actors may be a less effective model. Firm efforts must be well coordinated to cross-sell work, diversify pricing portfolios, and treat client and employee relationships as investments over time (*The Economist* 2011). A firm should, therefore, act more like a single business than a collection of actors. Some firms "up-source" significant business decisions to their management boards to achieve this structure, relinquishing a certain amount of independent action (Zahorsky 2012). Geographic and subject-specific committees can also allow attorneys to collaborate and share relationships within the firm (Comodeca and Everett 2010).

Over time, a broad model of partnership—where client and employee relationships accrue to the firm and not to a single partner or group—will likely become an effective model. As clients encourage cross-selling across practice and geographical areas, or they pre-qualify firms in a way that evaluates diversity initiatives and considerations of firm culture, the firm becomes the point of interface for a client, not a single partner or group (*The Economist* 2011). Also, if firms respond to employee demands for greater flexibility in compensation and career path, employee evaluations and opportunities will need to appear consistent and credible—balancing individuality and consistency is more effective within a firm-wide model (New York State Bar Association 2011). In short, a single partner or group might no longer be the *de facto* interface with a client or employee; rather, a broad model of partnership in which the firm mediates the client or employee relationship is more likely to take the lead.

Not all firms will construct the same business model; indeed, it would be surprising for firms to create identical business models. Business model variations result from a variety of choices, including decisions to target different markets, lead in different practice areas, and prioritize unique cultural features (Bayley 2011, Poor 2012). However, if a firm is to become, or remain, a leader in an evolving legal marketplace, it will have to adapt to the demands of the marketplace with changes in focus and business model.

III. Successful Lawyers Align Skills with New Business Models

It is perhaps not surprising that when firms adapt to remain market competitive—or, in aspiration, to lead the market—their employees must develop skills that are increasingly relevant to the new firm business models. Successful attorneys should keep an eye on relationship-building with clients and the firm. A creative and pragmatic attorney will be able to identify opportunities to increase firm profitability and client business success. The attorney who realizes the breadth of opportunity across a client engagement, a firm, and a career is likely to find a satisfying career that also creates value for those around her.

The leader in the new legal economy will be able to build relationships, recognize opportunities, and understand the big picture. The successful attorney will realize that each of these skills requires reflection on one's desires and abilities, as well as how personal goals interface with firm and client needs. To leverage these skills, the attorney should bring entrepreneurial thinking to her career, identifying how to create opportunities where personal, firm, and client needs overlap. To actualize these skills, the leader-attorney will need to communicate and demonstrate how personal, firm, and client needs fit into a bigger picture.

First, leadership will require the ability to build relationships, both within a firm and with clients (Rubenstein 2008). This is not a new skill of leadership by any means, but in an environment that emphasizes deeper investment in client relationships, an attorney's ability to build and manage relationships should become even more important. To be successful at relationship-building, an attorney must first know something about herself. She should have an idea of what her career goals are, or at least the general direction in which she wants to head. She benefits by identifying the boundaries of her path—what is on it and what is off it—and understanding the limits of her strengths and weaknesses. The successful attorney should realize that a career is a long-term project, as are relationships, and that the effort made today will pay dividends in the future. This attorney, therefore, will likely be community-minded and understand that contributing to those around her, at the firm and within a client base, will be a source of growth and propel her career forward. Indeed, she will recognize that the core of relationship-building is shared investment (Hamilton and Monson 2011).

The successful attorney will also invest wisely in relationships at her firm (Hamilton and Monson 2011). She should diligently study the organizational dynamics of her firm and identify the partners, counsel, associates, and staff that will help energize her career (Vorro 2012). Recognizing that her career will rise as her firm rises, she will likely contribute to firm-building and invest in those around her. By building strong relationships within her firm, an attorney can realize that, during changes in her career, she should be able to grow and make changes to her career path within the firm, or even leave the firm with goodwill in place to return. Certainly, the successful attorney should understand that her reputation travels with her, and that guarding the integrity of her reputation, as much by saying "yes" to the right projects as by saying "no," can be appropriate.

Long-term thinking on the part of an effective lawyer should assist overall career success. This is not to imply that an attorney will know the path of her career from beginning to end. But she should recognize that early investment in her client relationships is necessary to her success (Hamilton and Monson 2011). As a junior attorney, she can invest in those relationships through substantive work product, participating in client pitches and presentations, or attending client dinners when possible. When she receives opportunities for direct client contact, the attorney should listen to the client and understand the client's business concerns—both in the instant matter and in the greater context of the client's business. The attorney will not only do this because there is a billable hour connected to the effort, but also because it is a direct investment in the client relationship.

Second, leadership will require the ability to recognize opportunities—within the attorney's career, for his firm, and for the firm's (his) clients. The attorney who only focuses on the instant matter will fail to see the proverbial forest for the trees. As it relates to his own career, the successful attorney should create opportunities for himself, not wait for things to happen for him. He should be able to envision a role for himself within his legal community. Identifying the contributions he can bring to a matter, his firm, or his client, the attorney will identify mentoring opportunities that advance his development in line with his goals and strengths. He should insure that the opportunities he takes also ameliorate his weaknesses. These opportunities should enable the attorney to develop experience and confidence in substantive and "soft" interpersonal skills.

The ability to recognize good opportunity should not be limited to his own career—rather, a leader identifies how he can create value for his firm and his clients (Association of Corporate Counsel 2010). He can recognize market change and learn the nature of his firm's and client's business, goals, issues, and culture. A successful attorney can identify case-related or business needs of the firm and client, and share those ideas with a proposal of how he fits into a plan to meet those needs. The attorney should be practical and pragmatic in his plans, aware of situations that warrant investment of resources. However, he should also understand the need for creativity and flexibility as plans, strategies, and opportunities are most effective when they allow one to be responsive to change (Smith 2009).

Third, leading attorneys will be able to take an identified opportunity and translate it into something understood by others. In the context of her own career, the attorney should take the image she has of her career path (often non-linear, but thematically connected) and identify interim goals to achieve along the path. As she aligns those goals with the needs of her firm and her clients, she creates her niche, presenting her unique value proposition and demonstrating her unique competitive advantage. This requires the attorney to listen to her firm members and clients, and to understand their needs—or identify needs not yet identified—so she can communicate her value and goals within that framework.

Translating one's career goals into valuable, attainable opportunities for a firm and client requires entrepreneurial spirit and sufficient courage to take risks (Riskin 2005). As an entrepreneur, the successful attorney should grow the relationships she needs and gather the information that allows her to identify opportunities that she can render valuable to her career, her firm's growth, and her client's success. The entrepreneur is excited to find a nexus of interest between herself, the firm, and the client because it is at this nexus that positive outcomes for all parties are found.

Courage will set apart the successful attorney because she will need to be able to face the risks associated with communicating her vision (Riskin 2005). Certainly not all ideas grow as we envision them, and this is particularly intimidating for a junior attorney or an attorney setting out on a new challenge in her career. Courage (and strong communication skills) enable the attorney to communicate her goals and take on the challenge of reaching the goal. This can include the courage to express her value and how she thinks her skills and interests will be most effectively leveraged. She might also require courage to identify issues and opportunities for her firm and her clients, discussing them in a productive, pragmatic, and value-driven framework. In this way, the successful attorney evolves into a true "counselor."

IV. Conclusion: Encouraging Skills Development in Leaders

As clients, employees, and firms share in the risk and reward of success, there is incentive to teach and encourage the development of leadership skills among lawyers. Certainly a strong foundation in the law, its subject matter and practice, remains a basic measure of competency (Garth and Martin 1993). However, "soft" skills and the ability to understand business dynamics will likely prove to be leadership skills held by successful attorneys. An attorney who understands the pressures of the new legal economy—to share in the risks and rewards of business, to creatively approach pricing models and thoughtfully diversify sources of profit, and to operate as part of a larger team—will acquire a frame onto which he can apply his unique leadership skills, creating value for himself, his firm, and his clients.

This chapter does not identify how leadership skills should be taught, nor does it translate the skills into the language of academia. However, when integrating leadership studies into the law school curriculum, the leadership skills of the successful attorney, described above, likely include the following:

1. Skills of self-reflection:
   a. assess strengths and weaknesses
   b. identify goals and desires, both long term and interim

    c. prioritize goals and desires
    d. create a vision of one's career and role in the organization
    e. take responsibility for success or failure
    f. express sincerity and integrity
    g. remain a well-rounded individual with interests outside of work.

2. Entrepreneurial skills:
    a. consider situations with a "big picture" lens and a "detail" lens
    b. identify and create opportunity instead of waiting for opportunity
    c. build partnerships and relationships, including mentoring and sponsorship relationships
    d. think as a member of a team or community
    e. bring perspective to a situation with pragmatic, practical, and creative thinking
    f. adapt to new situations—be flexible and strategic
    g. act with courage, taking considered risk.

3. Communication skills:
    a. listen actively to colleagues and clients
    b. understand a diversity of perspectives
    c. connect various points of information and package it in a manner relevant to the target audience
    d. demonstrate the value of an idea or opportunity
    e. promote oneself, colleagues, and clients
    f. network in a manner consistent with one's goals and vision
    g. connect with others, considering their strengths, weaknesses, and aspirations.

References

Alexander, J. 2012. *Maximizing Morale: How to Have More Great Days at Work* [Online]. Available at: http://www.alanet.org/conf/2012/handouts/CM40_Maximizing_Morale.pdf#search=%22volkert%20morale%22 [accessed 21 May 2012].
Association of Corporate Counsel. 2010. *51 Practical Ways for Law Firms to Add Value* [Online]. Available at: http://www.acc.com/legalresources/resource.cfm?show=939328 [accessed 21 May 2012].
Bayley, R.E. 2010. Balancing the Risks and Rewards of Alternative Fees. *Law Practice* [Online], 36(6): 32–4. Available at: http://www.americanbar.org/publications/law_practice_home/law_practice_archive/lpm_magazine_articles_v36_is6_pg32.html [accessed 21 May 2012].

Bayley, J.R. 2011. *The Law Firm Crisis: Changing Business Models* [Online]. Available at: business.gwu.edu/files/james-bailey-law-firm-crisis-3-11.pdf [accessed 24 July 2012].

Comodeca, J.A. and Everett, S.R. 2010. Alternative Fee Arrangements: Risk Sharing Requires A Strong Partnership. *The National Law Review* [Online]. Available at: http://www.natlawreview.com/article/alternative-fee-arrangements-risk-sharing-requires-strong-partnership [accessed 21 May 2012].

The DuPont Legal Model [Online]. Available at: http://www.dupontlegalmodel.com/the-dupont-legal-model/ [accessed 9 September 2012].

The Economist. 2011. Bargain Briefs: Technology Offers 50 Ways to Leave your Lawyer. *The Economist* [Online], 13 August. Available at: http://www.economist.com/node/21525907 [accessed 21 May 2012].

Fortney, S.S. 2010. Leaks, Lies, and the Moonlight: Fiduciary Duties of Associates to their Law Firms, *St. Mary's Law Journal*, 41(4): 595–616.

Garth, B.G. and Martin, J. 1992. Law Schools and the Construction of Competence, *Journal of Legal Education*, 43(4): 469–509.

Hamilton, N. and Monson, V. 2011. The Positive Empirical Relationship of Professionalism to Effectiveness in the Practice of Law, *Georgetown Journal of Legal Ethics*, 23(1): 139–83.

Harvard Business School. 2010. *Retaining Employees*. Cambridge: Harvard Business School Publishing.

Loomis, T. 2009. Talkin' Revolution; GCs Say the Pressure is on to Kill the Billable Hour. But has it Reached the Tipping Point? *Corporate Counsel* [Online], 1 September. Available at: http://www.law.com/jsp/cc/PubArticleCC.jsp?id=1202432923584 [accessed 21 May 2012].

Mullins, J. 2009. Career Planning the Second Time Around, *Occupational Outlook Quarterly*, 53(2): 12–15.

New York State Bar Association. 2011. *Report of the Task Force on the Future of the Legal Profession* [Online]. Available at: http://www.nysba.org/AM/Template.cfm?Section=Task_Force_on_the_Future_of_the_Legal_Profession_Home&Template=/CM/ContentDisplay.cfm&ContentID=48108 [accessed 21 May 2012].

Pearlstein, S. 2011. Why Howrey Law Firm Could Not Hold it Together, *The Washington Post* [Online], 19 March. Available at: http://www.washingtonpost.com/business/economy/why-howrey-law-firm-could-not-hold-it-together/2011/03/16/ABNTqkx_story.html [accessed 21 May 2012].

Poor, J.S. 2012. Re-Engineering the Business of Law. *New York Times Dealbook* [Online], 7 May. Available at: http://dealbook.nytimes.com/2012/05/07/re-engineering-the-business-of-law/ [accessed 24 July 2012].

Project for Attorney Retention [Online]. http://www.attorneyretention.org/ [accessed 9 September 2012].

Rampell, C. 2011. At Well-Paying Law Firms, a Low-Paid Corner, *The New York Times* [Online], 23 May. Available at: http://www.nytimes.com/2011/05/24/business/24lawyers.html?pagewanted=all [accessed 21 May 2012].

Riskin, G.A. 2005. *The Successful Lawyer: Powerful Strategies for Transforming Your Practice*. Chicago: ABA Publishing.

Rubenstein, H. 2008. *Leadership for Lawyers*. Chicago: ABA Publishing.

Shannon, M.P. 2010a. Between Law School and Real World Practice: Filling the Gap for Associates, *Law Practice*, 36(1): 60–61.

Shannon, M.P. 2010b. Building a Better Game Plan: Best Practices for Training and Developing Lawyers, *Law Practice*, 36(5): 28–30.

Smith, M. 2011. The Joy of Secs (Secondments), *LexisNexis Communities: Legal Business* [Online], 22 September. Available at: http://release.allnet.com/community/legalbusiness/blogs/people/archive/2011/09/22/the-joy-of-secs-secondments.aspx [accessed 21 May 2012].

Smith, R.B. 2009. The Struggles of Lawyer-Leaders and What They Need to Know, *NYSBA Bar Journal* [Online], March/April, 38–40. Available at: http://www.ccl.org/leadership/pdf/landing/NYSBAJournalMarApr09.pdf [accessed 21 May 2012].

Tucker, K. 2009. Keeping Employees Motivated in a Troubled Economy is Critical, *AZ Business Magazine* [Online], 1 August. Available at: http://aznow.biz/workforce/employees-motivated-troubled-economy [accessed 21 May 2012].

Volkert, C.A. 2012. Morale Busters to Avoid in Troubled Times. Association of Legal Administrators. *Alanet.org* [Online], 23 March. Available at: http://www.alanet.org/careers/articles/Morale_Busters_to_Avoid_in_Troubled_Times.pdf#search=%22morale%20busters%20to%20avoid%20in%20troubled%20times%22 [accessed 21 May 2012].

Vorro, A. 2012. Mentoring Helps Attorneys at all Levels Advance their Careers: Programs Allow Seasoned Attorneys to Impart their Wisdom to the Next Generation, *Inside Counsel* [Online], 27 March. Available at: http://www.insidecounsel.com/2012/03/27/mentoring-helps-attorneys-at-all-levels-advance-th?page=3 [accessed 21 May 2012].

Wald, E. 2012. Smart Growth: The Large Law Firm in the Twenty-First Century, *Fordham Law Review*, 80(6): 2867–915.

Zahorsky, R.M. 2012. Facing the Alternative: How Does a Flat Fee System Really Work? *ABA Journal* [Online], 1 March. Available at: http://www.abajournal.com/magazine/article/facing_the_alternative_how_does_a_flat_fee_system_really_work/ [accessed 21 May 2012].

Chapter 5

Private Practice and Leadership

Maura DeMouy

Even in today's increasingly diversified legal work landscape, most lawyers still work in private practice (U.S. Department of Labor 2010–2011).[1] But, should they? Despite being one of the most likely places a lawyer will work after law school, modern private law firm practice, with its crushing hours commitment, undiversified workplace, poor training, and lack of collegiality is not the most likely place a lawyer will find a satisfying and rewarding work environment or build the leadership skills needed to succeed over the long haul.

Moreover, the current economic downturn appears only to have increased the likelihood that many private firms will continue to push these issues under the rug. The bleak economic climate has increased client demands on firms to keep their eyes on the bottom line—pressuring them to cut costs while increasing efficiency. This need to be more efficient at a lower cost is difficult to meet for private law firms that have operated for decades under the billable hours system, which actually discourages strategic planning and efficiency and instead rewards working as many hours as possible so as to generate as many billable hours as possible.

Although these private practice challenges and client pressures currently appear to be working against each other, the converse could be true instead. Solving much of what currently makes law firm life unsatisfying likely would help law firms meet the efficiency and value demands that clients are placing on them and create the work–life balance that lawyers seek. Without the pressure to bill an unreasonable number of hours, constant fear of upheaval from lawyer departures, poor training and lack of collegiality, law firms and their lawyers would be better able to focus more on efficiency, creativity and strengthening their relationships with clients, their families and their communities. Moreover, when law firms are better able to retain and develop the diverse, talented pool of attorneys they initially hire, they will do better for their clients and the profession as a whole.

---

1 Galanter and Henderson (2007: 1869) analyze the most recently available data from the American Bar Foundation's *The Lawyer Statistical Report* and show that as of 2000, 74% of lawyers in the U.S. were in private practice. The National Association for Law Placement (2011), in its most recent survey of law school graduates' employment categories (class of 2010), indicates that 50.9% of those graduates went to work in private practice. The second greatest number of graduates, only 15.1%, worked in business.

In light of clients' increasing pressure to change the way law firms do business, the time has never been better for addressing these challenges throughout the profession. Instead of viewing these persisting and ever increasing challenges as problems, the time has come for law firms to view them as opportunities to do business more strategically, more profitably and in ways that improve the lives of the lawyers they employ, reach better resolutions for the clients they serve and better support the communities of which they are a part.

Unfortunately, recognizing the wisdom of making fundamental changes in the way law firms operate will not make such change happen. Successfully making the changes necessary for law firms to address these challenges that have become such a routine part of law firm life will be difficult. Firms will need to employ the basic skills of leadership, envisioning the changes they want to see and implementing the changes in ways that engage as many members of the firm as possible in a heartfelt way, to achieve these goals.

I. Private Practice Challenges: Persistent and Worsening

The challenges of private law practice have persisted for some time now and have been well explored in professional reports and academic literature. As has been identified (oftentimes, over and over again), some of the primary factors that contribute to making private law firm practice a less than ideal work environment (particularly for the younger lawyer) are: the "instability" of the modern private law firm as an institution because of increased lateral lawyer mobility; competition and pressure to lower costs;[2] the unrelenting demands of billable hours requirements (still the most common way of billing private clients);[3] the lack of meaningful flexible or part-time work options;[4] the lack of diversity among lawyers in private

---

2   Galanter and Henderson (2007: 1890) explore the current state of the modern large private law firm and the factors such as increased lateral movement, increased competition and expanding markets that are contributing to increased instability and fragility for firms as institutions.

3   Liss and Kelly (2002) identify 15 costs of billable hours, including lack of time for pro bono work, decreased firm collegiality, placement of the lawyer in conflict with client's best interests and discouragement of investment in technology that makes the lawyer more efficient. Fortney (2005: 173) reports on a 2005 national survey focused on work–life issues and billable hours pressure and notes the pervasive comments from the survey respondents "on the tyranny of the billable hour" that often leads to padding of hours, inefficiency, compromised performance and ultimately associate attrition.

4   Williams and Calvert (2002: 375–8) point out that most law firms' current part-time or flexible work policies are ineffective because those who use them suffer negative consequences in terms of career advancement, choice of work assignments, and treatment from colleagues.

law firm practice;[5] the disappearance of firm collegiality and culture that served to create helpful practice and ethical norms in the profession;[6] the rapidly vanishing commitment to training and mentoring young lawyers;[7] and the high rates of associate turnover.[8]

Moreover, today's economic slowdown appears only to have made matters worse. Layoffs, hiring uncertainties, compensation uncertainties, and more lawyers vying for less work increase anxiety and pressure for the firm and its lawyers. Attorneys are less likely to ask for flexible work options when work is harder to come by. Partners are less likely to spend time developing and training younger lawyers when the client is refusing to pay for time spent this way.

The first factor in the list above, institutional instability, might be the most damaging to any hope of change. The instability has resulted from increased competition created by a decreased demand for more routine services, increased lateral movement (lawyers no longer spend their entire careers with one firm) and expanding markets. Gone are the days when clients committed to the private law firm as an institution in what was usually a lifelong relationship. Today, seeking less expensive ways to meet their legal needs, clients use in-house counsel, ready-made "shelf" documents or paralegals to perform many routine legal matters. When they do hire private law firm attorneys, the clients typically are looking for an attorney with expertise in a complex subject. As a result, as compared with the past, clients are bonding more with the individual "expert" lawyer than the firm for which that individual attorney works. This phenomenon has led to a shift in the balance of power away from the private law firm to these individual lawyers,

---

5   Djordjevich (2010) notes that when conducting a national diversity assessment for the ABA's 2009 Report, *Diversity in the Legal Profession: The Next Steps*, it was found that although women are half of the U.S. population and law school classes, they are only 18% of law firm equity partners; minorities, which are one-third of the U.S. population, only represent 10% of the lawyer population and 6% of law firm equity partners.

6   Schiltz (1999: 931–2) describes the collegiality at big law firms as an illusion because of the increased "competition, stress, … loss of institutional loyalty and sense of belonging."

7   "[O]ne-on-one mentoring is disappearing in big firms for a number of reasons, including the pressure to bill hours, the pressure to attract and retain clients, the pressure to minimize legal costs, the increasing size of law firms, and the increasing mobility of lawyers." (Schiltz 1999: 927–8).

8   For example, Johnson (2008: 51) cites the NALP Foundation's conclusion "that 53.4% of entry-level associates leave their law firms within fifty-five months of their start dates." Heineman and Wilkins (2008) report: "The larger law firms are reported to be losing 30, 40, 50 percent of associates after three to four years—with half to two-thirds of the defections due to associate, not firm, choice … . The After the JD study of 4,000 graduates in the class of 2000—conducted jointly by the American Bar Foundation, Harvard Law School's Program on the Legal Profession, and others—indicates such churn."

commonly known as "free agents" or "stars."[9] The newly competitive market that these free agents have created includes firms of all sizes and pedigrees. For example, large private law firms face competition not just from other large firms, but also from spin-off entities and smaller firms, where clients often find the same high-quality lawyers, but at a cheaper cost. These smaller firms correspondingly face competition from firms of all sizes as well.

In addition to increased lawyer mobility, in part because of the recent economic downturn (although many of these pressures already were at work even before the economy deteriorated), clients increasingly are asking their law firms to share more of the costs of legal work, for example by offering work under a fixed-fee arrangement that encourages the law firm to keep costs down and bear the costs of any overages or by refusing to bear the costs of training for younger lawyers (Thies 2010).[10]

If law firms are to survive in a market where upheaval and change are the norm and clients are pushing more and more of the costs of doing business back on the firm, they need to meet these challenges as strategically and successfully as they can. To date, it appears that many law firms are struggling to keep up.[11]

The remaining factors—onerous billable hours requirements, lack of flexible schedules and diversity, decreasing collegiality and training and the corresponding increased attrition—and many firms' failure to address them—arguably flow from the firm's instability. These factors have serious implications both for the firm's employees and its clients, in light of the profound effects that dissatisfaction and poor productivity in the workplace have on the delivery of quality legal services.

Indeed, the effects of the typical law firm's draconian work environment cannot be overstated. The personal toll on individual lawyers is tremendous. When compared with other professions, lawyers' rates of substance abuse and anxiety-related mental illness are higher, and their rates of job satisfaction are

---

9   Galanter and Henderson (2007: 1906–1907) describe the difficulties of achieving a better work environment for the collective whole "when rainmaking partners located in multiple offices throughout the world are free to exit at any time with clients in tow."

10   Jones and Palazzolo (2011) report that in a September 2011 *Wall Street Journal* survey, "[m]ore than 20% of the 366 in-house legal departments that responded are refusing to pay for the work of first- or second-year attorneys, in at least some matters. Almost half of the companies, which have annual revenues ranging from $25 million or less to more than $4 billion, said they put those policies in place during the past two years, and the trend appears to be growing."

11   For example, Ribstein (2010: 770–74) explores the difficult market pressures on firms today and describes the recent demise of many large firms. The *Economist* (2011) explained that the failure of Howrey & Simon, one of the world's 100 largest law firms, was due in part to trends that are putting pressure on the legal industry such as clients' refusal to pay for "work of green trainees," clients' emphasis on alternative billing arrangements, the global emerging markets and technology growth and concluded that "[n]ot all firms will survive, and those that do will not prosper equally."

lower.[12] Given the crushing workloads, the lack of alternative schedules, the lack of diversity, decreased training for young associates, and increased firm instability, it is not surprising that so many lawyers are so miserable. Nor is it hard to imagine that these conditions affect the quality of their work and ultimately the justice the profession delivers.

These conditions also cause law firms to suffer in some very concrete monetary ways. First, as already described above, firms that are unable to deal with the current pressures from the marketplace—to offer alternative fee arrangements and train young associates in a cost-effective way, for example—are not succeeding (Ribstein 2010, *The Economist* 2011).

Second, even those firms that are not failing are worse off because the costs of losing dissatisfied attorneys are high. Firms invest significant amounts of money in hiring and training their lawyers and in assisting the lawyers in developing client relationships. Firms do this because they expect to reap the benefits of having a team of well-trained experts and solid client connections. When a lawyer decides to leave a firm, they take all of the expertise and sometimes established client relationships along. Estimates of a large law firm's cost for the loss of one associate range from $200,000 to $400,000.[13]

Third, because of their failure to address attrition and diversity, firms are actually losing clients. Attrition and diversity are factors that large corporations are taking into account when deciding whether to hire or continue working with law firms. Those firms with high rates of attrition and without diversity are not getting the business.[14] Wal-Mart has fired law firms or pulled work from those that

----

12 Pearce (2005: 214) states: "It is no surprise that the rates of substance abuse and anxiety-related mental illness are far higher for lawyers than for other occupations, or that according to most surveys job satisfaction is far lower" (citations omitted). Rhode (2005: 66 note 90) reports: "An estimated one-third of American attorneys suffer from depression or from alcohol or drug addiction, a rate two-to-three times higher than the population generally." Hall (1992) notes that 52% of responding lawyers were unhappy. But Heinz et al. (1999) argue that lawyers, like members of all professions, are generally satisfied.

13 Newman (2007): "The cost of attrition is also extremely high. According to *The American Lawyer*, some firms estimate the cost of attrition per associate at between $200,000 and $400,000. Further, not only does associate attrition adversely affect associate morale, but mid-level associate departures also leave gaps in the experience level of the law firm associate pool. These gaps cannot be filled by younger associates, and they impact the cost effectiveness of staffing client projects." (Joan M. Newman, Joan Newman & Associates LLC. 2007. Appreciate Your Associates. Make Your Firm a Workplace of Choice, *Legal Management*, March/April, 47–54. Reprinted with permission from *Legal Management*, 26(2), published by the Association of Legal Administrators, www.alanet. org.) See also Williams and Calvert (2002: 366), providing estimates for the costs of losing an associate ranging from $200,000 to $500,000 and explaining what those costs cover.

14 Hiott-Levine and Branigan (2006: 24) note that clients see "that high lawyer turnover affects the overall quality of legal services" and that "clients increasingly

have not demonstrated sufficient diversity (Donovan 2006). In 2004, Sara Lee's chief legal officer, Roderick Palmore, led a hundred corporations to sign a "Call to Action" in which the companies committed to make law firm hiring decisions based on the diversity performance of those firms.[15]

As one journalist explained in an article about companies' demands for greater diversity, "The fact is that diversity is no longer just the right thing to do. It's an essential factor to compete in today's business climate. So it should be no surprise that corporate clients will expect their outside counsel to share diversity as a core value" (McDonogh 2005). These companies' call for diversity is grounded in good data. In a recent study of teams conducted by MIT, Carnegie Mellon, and others, those teams with men and women outperformed all-male teams on a variety of problem-solving exercises (Weisul 2011).

Nonetheless, on the whole, most firms large and small have not taken much initiative in addressing these issues. Given the potential benefits of addressing them in a meaningful way, it is unclear why the majority of private law firms appear only to have made sporadic, unsustained attempts at solving them.

As an example, the American Bar Association's Commission on Billable Hours released its report detailing the devastating effects of billable hours on the profession and its clients in 2001–2002—10 years ago (Liss and Kelly 2002). The *American Lawyer*'s 2010 survey of leaders of its top 200 firms indicated, however, that although managing partners are using alternative billing arrangements more frequently, the "vast majority of legal work continues to be done on a billable-hour basis" (Zillman 2010).

And, although large billable hour requirements seem directly linked to associate departures from firms, the firms continue to be caught in what one commentator, Joshua Johnson, called "a sick cycle" (Johnson 2008: 54).

> [A]s billable hours expectations increase, associates are more likely to leave their law firms, and firms are forced to recruit even more aggressively [with higher salaries] because of their failure to retain the associates they hire. Attrition thus begets pay raises, which in turn yield more attrition as billable hours requirements rise. (Johnson 2008: 55)

Johnson concludes that firms keep the cycle going because the associate problem is analogous to an economic phenomenon referred to as the "tragedy of the commons" (Johnson 2008: 55–6). The tragedy of the commons results when a group has access to a shared resource or good, such as a piece of land, without any community or universal limitations or rules in place to govern use of the resource

---

scrutinize law firms' attrition rates and quality of life issues and seek outside counsel that demonstrably value greater diversity (including women)."

15   Palmore's Call to Action followed up on an earlier effort in 1999 by then Bell-South General Counsel, Charles Morgan, entitled "Diversity in the Workplace: A Statement of Principle," which over 500 corporations signed (Donovan 2006).

(Johnson 2008: 76–7). Each individual with access to the shared resource likely will use it as best suits his or her own economic needs without regard to the effect on others trying to use the resource, until the resource is depleted for all.

In the modern law firm, associates are a shared resource. Partners have every incentive to work them hard and realize payment for as many billable hours as they can get out of as many associates as they can. Conversely, without loyalty to, or investment in, the firm as an institution, the firm's whole client base, or the community, partners have little or no incentive to invest in activities benefiting the firm that might appear to cost them personally, such as spending time mentoring, developing flexible work schedules, or ensuring diversity goals are being met.

The solution to a tragedy of the commons is developing a plan that neutralizes the individual impulses, which impose significant costs on the firms, their employees, the profession, and the expression of their values as a whole. With a vision of the changes that need to be made, backed by the collective will to see the change through to fruition, these issues can be addressed. To put it another way, leadership is needed to address these issues in a meaningful way.

II. Throwing Money at the Problems Has Not Solved Them

The typical law firm response to unhappiness in the workplace has not demonstrated much long-term foresight. Firms appear to have tried to solve the problem by simply raising salaries or partner compensation. As described above, this approach kicks off a "sick cycle" that does not provide any long-term solutions. Thus, although this approach is straightforward and easily administered, thus far, based on current attrition levels, it does not appear to be working.

Addressing the complicated interplay of creating a balanced, satisfying life for the firm's lawyers while ensuring that client, community, and professional needs are met requires more sophisticated solutions that will require vision, planning, and firm participation to implement. Interestingly, corporations have been much more successful in navigating the balance between clients', employees', and the business's needs and expectations than law firms. Companies that have chosen to offer employees "a life" (instead of more money) through flexible work schedules and other nonmonetary measures have had much more success in keeping their employees and saving money (Rhode 2005: 367).

Addressing these challenges more directly (not with increased pay) could be a powerful antidote to the market forces that are making the modern firm such an unreliable, uncollegial and unpleasant place. Using alternative billing arrangements that de-emphasize number of hours worked in favor of the quality of the result delivered to the client would reward creativity, a problem-solving approach, and expertise, not a rote number of (likely inefficient) hours worked. Flexible schedules and commitments to diversity would increase creative problem-solving for clients, attorney loyalty and retention, and decrease the costs of hiring and training replacement lawyers. Increased collegiality and training would improve attorney satisfaction with their work, loyalty to the firm, client outcomes, and the profession overall. Moreover, satisfied lawyers and their firms would be more likely to build strong, strategic client relationships.

III. Leadership Can Make a Difference

The reality is that change is hard. Current private law firm structures are often too entrenched and too familiar to succumb to calls for change from outside the law firm (Liss and Kelly 2002: 11). Without strong leadership, these changes simply won't occur.

Leadership can bring change where it otherwise looks impossible. It mobilizes groups to improve situations where individual efforts might fail. Most successful leaders employ variations of the "five practices" first identified by United States leadership experts James Kouzes and Barry Posner: modeling the way, inspiring a shared vision, challenging the prior way of doing things, enabling a group to act, and encouraging the heart or encouraging people to "align with their values" (Kouzes and Posner 2007: 14–23).[16] These practices build a sense of common identity and purpose that help individuals accomplish common goals with benefits that lead to satisfaction at work and in life (Kouzes and Posner 2007: 23).

Frustrated with private law firms' slow pace at addressing these challenges successfully, diverse groups have sprung up to call for change. A few examples: The Project for Attorney Retention, an initiative of the Center for WorkLife Law at University of California Hastings College of Law, is working to minimize "unwanted attrition among lawyers" through research and publications that promote ways of increasing flexibility and diversity in the legal workplace and has many legal employers supporting its efforts (http://www.attorneyretention.org/). CBS[17] Senior Vice President and Assistant General Counsel Laurie Robinson founded Corporate Counsel Women of Color to foster diversity in law practice (http://www.ccwomenofcolor.org/). In January 2007, Stanford Law students started a grassroots movement, "Building a Better Legal Profession," which publishes data on large private law firms' billable hours, pro bono work, diversity, and more in an effort to educate young lawyers about their options and help them make better choices (http://www.betterlegalprofession.org/). In 2008, prominent women alumni of the University of Texas School of Law established the Center for Women in Law to work with academia, businesses, and law firms to help women advance in law practice (http://www.utexas.edu/law/centers/cwil/). And, at the University of Miami, Michele DeStefano and Michael Bossone created a virtual collaborative academic initiative they call Law Without Walls that selects students from top law schools and partners them with academic and practitioner mentors,

---

16   This material is reproduced with permission of John Wiley & Sons, Inc.

17   A United States-based network television broadcaster and media company with operations world-wide.

subject experts, and entrepreneurs to solve legal practice related problems such as exploring alternatives to the billable hour, embracing technology and globalization to improve law practice and more (http://www.lawwithoutwalls.org/).

Moreover, those private law firms that have decided to focus on leadership to reinvigorate the institution of the law firm, and thereby benefit all of their employees, their clients, and the communities they serve, are finding that the rewards are many. For example, Miles & Stockbridge P.C., a mid-size regional firm with its head office in Baltimore, Maryland, has a chairman, John Frisch, who devotes a significant amount of his time to developing a vision of the firm as a team, committed to knowing its clients' businesses and valuing its employees. He also is responsible for making sure this vision is executed. According to Frisch, the success for the firm and all of its employees has been "exciting" (University of Maryland School of Law's Leadership, Ethics and Democracy Initiative Newsletter 2011). Moreover, the firm is getting clients' "most challenging and difficult work," which is "most satisfying and interesting for [the] lawyers and most lucrative for the firm."

The current overemphasis on number of billable hours to determine a lawyer's value to a firm, the lack of commitment to retaining and developing a diverse, talented pool of lawyers, poor training, and increased competition and specialization are slowly splintering the collegial, unified institution the private law firm once was. This splintering of the private law firm members' loyalties has prevented law firms from effecting change that aligns with the values of the firms, their employees, and the profession as a whole. As a result, firms continue to struggle with achieving work–life balance, including time for pro bono and community service, achieving diversity, ensuring proper mentoring and training, and ultimately in performing quality work for the clients they serve. This affects not just the delivery of legal services on individual matters, but the quality of justice in our society as a whole. Firms willing to employ leadership principles to establish common goals and achieve them will be able to reverse these trends. Lawyers' lives, the profession, and the quality of justice will all benefit as a result.

References

American Bar Association. 2010. *Diversity in the Profession: The Next Steps* [Online]. Available at: http://www.americanbar.org/content/dam/aba/ migrated/2011_build/diversity/next_steps_final_virtua_accessible_042010. pdf [accessed 30 January 2012].

Djordjevich, V. 2010. Outgoing ABA President Carolyn Lamm Discusses Next Steps to Achieving a More Diverse Legal Profession, *National Law Review* [Online], 12 August. Available at: http://www.natlawreview.com/article/ outgoing-aba-president-carolyn-lamm-discusses-next-steps-to-achieving- more-diverse-legal-pro [accessed 30 January 2012].

Donovan, K. 2006. Pushed by Clients, Law Firms Step Up Diversity Efforts, *New York Times*, 21 July, C6.

Fortney, S.S. 2005. The Billable Hours Derby: Empirical Data on the Problems and Pressure Points, *Fordham Urban Law Journal*, 33(1): 171–92.

Galanter, M. and Henderson, W. 2007. The Elastic Tournament: A Second Transformation of the Big Law Firm, *Stanford Law Review*, 60(6): 1867–930.

Hall, M.J. 1992. Fax Poll Finds Attorneys Aren't Happy with Work, *Los Angeles Daily Journal*, 4 March, 3.

Heineman, B.W. Jr. and Wilkins, D.B. 2008. The Lost Generation?, *The American Lawyer*, 30(30): 85.

Heinz, J.P., Hull, K.E. and Harter, A.A. 1999. Lawyers and Their Discontents: Findings from a Survey of the Chicago Bar, *Indiana Law Journal*, 74(3): 735–58.

Hiott-Levine, N.M. and Branigan, K.S. 2006. Women in the Legal Profession: The Quest to Overcome Barriers to Advancement Continues—Working Toward Meaningful Solutions, *Commerce Magazine*, Summer, 22–4.

Johnson, J. 2008. Associate Attrition and the Tragedy of the Commons, *The Crit*, 1(1): 48–95.

Jones, A. and Palazzolo, J. 2011. What's a First-Year Lawyer Worth?, *Wall Street Journal*, 17 October, B1.

Kouzes, J. and Posner, B. 2007. *The Leadership Challenge*. 4th edition. San Francisco: John Wiley & Sons.

Law Firms: A Less Gilded Future, *The Economist* [Online], 5 May 2011, http://www.economist.com/node/18651114 [accessed 9 September 2012].

Liss, J. and Kelly, A.D. 2002. *ABA Commission on Billable Hours Report 2001– 2002* [Online]. Available at: http://www.judicialaccountability.org/articles/ABABillableHours2002.pdf [accessed 30 January 2012].

McDonough, M. 2005. Demanding Diversity, *ABA Journal* [Online], 28 March. Available at: http://www.abajournal.com/magazine/article/demanding_diversity/ [accessed 30 January 2012].

National Association for Law Placement. 2011. *Class of 2010 National Summary Report* [Online]. Available at: http://www.nalp.org/uploads/Classof2010SelectedFindings.pdf [accessed 4 May 2012].

Newman, J. 2007. Appreciate Your Associates: Make Your Firm a Workplace of Choice, *Legal Management*, March/April, 47–54.

Palmore, R. 2004. *A Call to Action: Diversity in the Legal Profession* [Online]. Available at: http://www.acc.com/vl/public/Article/loader.cfm?csModule=security/getfile&pageid=16074 [accessed 30 January 2012].

Pearce, R. 2005. How Law Firms Can Do Good While Doing Well (and the Answer Is Not Pro Bono), *Fordham Urban Law Journal*, 35(1): 211–16.

Rhode, D. 2005. Profits and Professionalism, *Fordham Urban Law Journal*, 33(1): 49–80.

Ribstein, L.E. 2010. The Death of Big Law, *Wisconsin Law Review*, 2010(3): 749–815.

Schiltz, P.J. 1999. On Being a Happy, Healthy, and Ethical Member of an Unhappy, Unhealthy, and Unethical Profession, *Vanderbilt Law Review*, 52(4): 871–951.

Thies, D. 2010. Rethinking Legal Education in Hard Times: The Recession, Practical Legal Education, and the New Job Market, *Journal of Legal Education*, 59(4): 598–622.

University of Maryland School of Law's Leadership, Ethics and Democracy Initiative Newsletter. 2011. Preparing Students to Be Lawyer-Leaders: An Inspirational Model of Leading a Firm with a Unified Vision of Excellence, Integrity and Diversity, *The Leading Edge* [Online], Spring, 9–10. Available at: http://www.law.umaryland.edu/programs/initiatives/lead/docs/LEAD_SP11_newsletter.pdf [accessed 11 May 2012].

U.S. Department of Labor. 2010–2011. *Occupational Outlook Handbook* [Online]. Available at: http://www.bls.gov/oco/ocos053.htm [accessed 30 January 2012].

Weisul, K. 2011. Why Smart People Make Lousy Teams, *CBS Money Watch* [Online], 11 April. Available at: http://www.cbsnews.com/8301-505125_162-44441284/why-smart-people-make-lousy-teams/?tag=bnetdomain [accessed 30 January 2012].

Williams, J. and Calvert, C.T. 2002. Balanced Hours: Effective Part-Time Policies for Washington Law Firms: The Project for Attorney Retention Final Report Third Ed., *William and Mary Journal of Women and the Law*, 8(3): 357–441.

Zillman, C. 2010. Law Firm Leaders Survey 2010: The New Normal, *American Lawyer*, 32(12): 66.

Chapter 6
Policy and Government Leadership

Mickey Edwards

To serve in government, including as a maker of laws at the local, state, or federal levels, is to engage in one of the most honorable and important undertakings available to an American citizen. And it is a role uniquely suited for men and women who have given themselves over to a mastery of the law, understanding not only what it is, but gaining insight into what it can be. The ultimate purpose of government is to establish justice, and nobody is better prepared for that responsibility—if they are willing to assume it—than the men and women of the legal profession. This chapter explores the form of government developed by the Founders of the United States, the way in which lawyers and law students are uniquely suited to become leaders within that governance framework and how law schools can better prepare them for such leadership roles in public service.

If America is indeed "exceptional," it is not because Americans are inherently different as a people but because the nation operates under a unique system of laws in which the ultimate power of decision rests not with a national "leader" (in fact the United States has no "leader" or "head of government") but with the people themselves through a Constitution that places great authority in the hands of the people's representatives.

In *Henry V*, Shakespeare describes a young British king's actions as he prepares to face an attacking French army at Agincourt. Henry, the ruler, has decreed that any in his band who commit a theft will be executed. One soldier, who happens to be an old friend of his, violates the decree and, at Henry's order, is put to death (Shakespeare 1992). This is top-down government in its rawest form: a leader decides what the law shall be and sees to it that it is carried out. It is precisely that model that this nation's founders rejected.

Even before the United States adopted its Constitution, American colonists had made clear that they would be the arbiters of law. Laws promulgated in England made it a crime to criticize the Crown's appointed colonial governors. To criticize was libel and to libel was to be punished—and the judge who was to preside over the case was to be appointed by the governor who had presumably been libeled, which was very convenient. John Peter Zenger, a New York newspaper publisher, aware of the law, criticized William Cosby, the governor, and was predictably hauled into court to face his punishment. The jury found that he had indeed printed criticisms of the governor—and set him free. They, not the Crown and not the governor, would be the deciders of law (Finkelman

2010). Thus was born freedom of the press. But there, too, was shaped American resistance to arbitrary law.

The Founders placed lawmaking authority in the hands of the people themselves. One little-noted feature of the Constitution is the fact that members of Congress not only retain the sole right to write law ("all legislative powers") but that members of the United States Senate and House of Representatives must be residents of the state from which they are chosen. Lawmakers have, in Edmund Burke's formulation, a responsibility to employ their knowledge and judgment in carrying out their duties, but there is also a clear representational function and, through the election process, accountability (Rush 2005).[1] Legislators must either demonstrate that they faithfully represented the interests and preferences of their constituents or adequately explain why they did not. Or they will be bounced from office and replaced.

What this system has created—a form of government in which the citizens rule—is a breakthrough in civic empowerment. We the People can decide for ourselves what laws we will live under. In such a system, public service and, more directly, government service represent the embodiment of community consciousness. And, as noted above, no one is better suited to assuming leadership in government service than lawyers who have mastered the law during the process of legal education.

In the class on leadership I have taught at the University of Maryland Francis King Carey School of Law, I have also emphasized a second outgrowth of the American emphasis on self-government. While we have the option of long-term careers in official public life, our system, responsive to public will, also allows for targeted and unofficial involvement in public affairs, sometimes for life and sometimes for relatively short periods of time. Men and women with a passion for justice spent long years working in the civil rights movement, the women's movement, the labor movement, the environmental movement. Others jumped into the political battles for a shorter time and for narrower, but important, causes—campaigns to reduce the incidence of drunk driving or to improve the possibility of rescuing abducted children. In some societies, institutional barriers make it difficult for citizen action to be effective; not in America.

Americans are citizens, not subjects, and it is they who determine what laws they will live by, whether they shape government policy from the top down (holding elective or appointive office) or from the bottom up (as policy activists). Both are functions for which lawyers are particularly well suited, bringing from their legal training the necessary combination of passion and dispassion—the quest for justice that should be the hallmark of every lawyer and the ability to objectively analyze the context and challenges the situation presents and to dispassionately devise effective strategies to deal with them. This is not the

---

1   In his famous Speech to the Electors of Bristol, Burke stated: "Your representative owes you, not his industry only, but judgment; and he betrays, instead of serving you, if he sacrifices it to your opinion" (Rush 2005: 61).

typical psychological makeup or the training of an academic, an engineer, a scientist, or simply an average citizen who is sufficiently moved by some event that she is stirred to action. On the one hand, there are the detached observers and objective analyzers; on the other, the angry and determined advocates for change. But neither has the breadth of skills required to effectively lead in shaping public policy.

Enter the lawyer. Lawyers—men and women who, like Thurgood Marshall and Leon Higginbotham, played groundbreaking roles in the American civil rights movement—are ideally suited to be leaders in the creation of a just society. They combine inclination (toward a positive view of the law and its power for good) and training (breaking issues down to their essentials, dispassionate evaluation of strategy options) in ways that are particularly valuable in building persuasive and effective movements for reform.

Unfortunately, most law schools give little or no attention to the task of motivating their students to take on such a role. They offer superb instruction for the provision of important private services—estate planning, criminal defense, tort claims, corporate structure—but little to prepare their charges to step onto the larger stage of devotion to public service or the eradication of injustice.

How, then, can law schools better prepare their students to meet the challenge of service for the public good?

The task can be divided into three distinct parts: the admissions process; curriculum development; and extracurricular activities. In the pages that follow, I examine all three with an eye toward improving the law school's ability to play a pivotal role in directing students toward better and more extensive civic participation.

The Admissions Process

First, consider the ways in which we determine whom to admit to our universities. The most relevant factors—and clearly the most important ones— are academic. A university degree is not easily attained; academic proficiency sufficient to get one admitted to law school is even harder. And doing well enough in law school to receive a degree and eligibility to take—and then to pass—a state bar examination is an even higher hurdle. No law school, and no university, can be cavalier about ensuring that its resources will not be wasted on students incapable of succeeding. Then—because we hope to ensure that our admissions policies do not shut off opportunity—we take into account other factors including financial need, the benefits of a diverse legal community, and whether one's past performance has been such as to generate meaningful letters of recommendation.

What's missing? The short answer is: nothing—if the only goal is to produce lawyers who are able to competently design estates, prosecute criminal activity, argue tort cases, or arrange mergers. Each of those is an important element in a system based on the rule of law and the right of representation. The admissions process described above is well suited to producing lawyers of high quality able to meet these important societal needs.

But it is inadequate for the purposes of developing legally trained activists whose self-appointed mission is to improve society and to eradicate injustice. While the school should not attempt to impose a definition of its own as to what constitutes the problem areas or policy prescriptions that would qualify for a sign of such a commitment, it would nonetheless be beneficial to add to the admissions process a review of the applicant's public activities and interests and a statement of his or her goals for further public service (similar to the standards that were a part of the admissions process in which I participated as vice chairman of the admissions committee at Harvard's Kennedy School of Government). While a law school is not a government school and therefore these "addendums" (history of community involvement, goals for community betterment) cannot be controlling as to admissibility, they can, however, be taken into account to help ensure that applicants who may want to use the law for public good have an opportunity to get legal training even if they fall short of the general academic admission standards for the school.

Lawyers are particularly suited to this task of changing society, whether from a position in public office or operating from within a law firm, advocacy group, or think tank. My own experience in teaching law students and working with practicing attorneys has led me to believe that many of the men and women who enter the legal profession have a decided affinity for autonomy: statute and precedent offer a framework for legal action but many of the best attorneys view those boundaries not as roadblocks but as intellectual challenges, a well-known example being Clarence Darrow's development of a mental incapacity defense. Carving out, or creatively enlarging, exceptions and finding ways to achieve ends, including an expansion of justice, is often a perfect fit with the mindset that leads one into the practice of law.

While there are always lawyers who are imbued with a love for legalism, even some who may confuse law with justice, as the policeman Javert did in *Les Misérables*, the best pursue the practice of law—and the tools of the law—to help shape a better society (Hugo 1992). It should be an important aim of a modern law school to imbue its students with this passion and to offer a curriculum, in the classroom and in the community, that will help those who are so inclined master their ability to contribute to making the world a better place. But how can a school achieve that goal? Let's look at this task, blending the lawyers' proclivities and talents with a more specific look at the strategies a law school can pursue to become a factory that turns out society-changers.

Curriculum Development

The next area to consider is curriculum development. As government has grown larger and more expansive, more Americans have become accustomed to looking to government as the solver of national problems. And it can be. But much of the social progress this country has made has come as a result of citizen involvement, whether in actually bringing about change directly (through organizations, sponsorship of referendums or initiative petitions, or private charitable work) or in serving to increase public awareness of a problem and developing pressure on elected officials to create change by statute or ordinance. How this is done—how problems are identified, short- and long-term goals set, coalitions and alliances created, persuasive messages framed, strategies developed—can be taught. Students can not only have their passions stoked (by speakers, films, activities), they can actually be taught how to channel those passions into effective action. Every law school should have classes aimed at studying the development of society-changing initiatives (such as the environmental movement, the women's movement, the civil rights movement, the labor movement, tax-limitation referendums, and campaigns for veterans' benefits) with a focus on the organization, management, and strategies of such movements, and on the role played by lawyers in bringing about those important advances.

In addition, while a great deal of public policy is generated by men and women who do not hold government positions, it is in almost every case those people who have been elected or appointed to public office who have the final say on such matters. Whether legislating or administering public programs, the various forms of government and quasi-government service—serving in elective office, managing important government agencies and bureaus, or merely becoming active players in the election process—are critical to the functioning of a viable democratic system of governance. While ordinarily relegated to university departments of government, political science, public administration, and the like, there is ample room in a law school curriculum to give sufficient introduction to these career possibilities to motivate our outstanding young men and women to pursue lives of civic engagement and working for the public good. For law schools that teach in "tracks," a "public" track should be an option.

Extracurricular Activities

Then there is the question of what happens in a law school outside the classroom. To repeat an earlier but indispensable point, political involvement—at the level of holding elective office, being engaged in public advocacy, or managing community and government agencies—requires two separate, distinct, and contradictory qualities: passion and dispassion. One needs the psychological commitment to initiate and sustain involvement and, at the same time, the analytical understanding to avoid being blinded by one's passion and thus acting rashly and counterproductively. Dispassion—a framework for strategizing and organizing—can be taught in a classroom. Generating passion—a commitment to noticing, and becoming energized by, injustice—requires something additional.

Thus, extracurricular activities are important elements in moving students toward a greater understanding of their responsibilities in the public sphere and in motivating them to act on those responsibilities. To this end, law schools should regularly schedule visits by speakers who are active in public life, both as classroom guests and for school-wide presentations. As an example, at the law school, I invited to my class the head of pro bono law at a major Washington, D.C., law firm; the assistant United States attorney general in charge of the civil rights division; the lieutenant governor and the attorney general of Maryland; the mayor of Baltimore; and the executive director of the American Society of International Law—each of them an example of an attorney who has chosen to dedicate his or her life to public service. These talks were both pragmatic and inspiring and, with the active support of the administration, were made available to all of the school's students.

Many classes engage students in real public involvement, both in the United States and abroad—working to provide legal representation to the indigent, working with health care and environmental activists, etc. This is an absolutely critical part of the public education of a lawyer and should be pursued actively by any law school interested—as all should be—in seeing America's brightest young lawyers take an energetic role in shaping the societies we live in.

Here, law schools can take lessons from many of the public policy schools that have incorporated specific public involvement tasks into their courses. These "experiential" assignments are not easy to manage: professors must take on the task of building relationships with local nonprofit and advocacy groups that are willing to accept, and direct, students who wish to learn how to engage public issues; and must find an equitable way to measure performance in such activities as a part of the grading process (including making classroom time available for students to report on their activities, evaluate the experience, and incorporate it into their own plans for effecting change). In my classes, students are assigned to study the effectiveness, or lack of effectiveness, of a previous public campaign in terms of message, organization, coalition-building, and other elements of a successful political mobilization activity. Then, as a follow-up activity, they are required to develop a campaign plan for a change they would like to pursue. We have not yet, however, incorporated "externship" opportunities which would require actually giving our students hands-on responsibility under the supervision of local activist groups, nor have we established a protocol for accommodating the out-of-class time these activities would require or the incorporation of those activities into the grading system. Nonetheless, these are essential elements of truly establishing a system for funneling our brightest young legal minds into the various causes that constitute the "public good" in a responsive democratic system of self-government.

While there is a long and successful history of teachers developing in their students higher levels of skill than the teachers themselves possess (thus the truism that those who accomplish the most do so by standing on the shoulders of those who went before them), preparing law students to undertake a career in public service is a more challenging assignment. Telling students to "do as I say, not as I do" has always been problematic, but that is even more true in the attempt to steer students toward a life of commitment to the greater public good, for the simple reason that public service requires levels of passion and motivation that teachers who have not themselves made that same commitment find difficult to impart. Successful teaching invariably requires one to motivate one's students; motivating a student to devote his or her life to a specific career is a difficult assignment for one who has, for other and equally good reasons, chosen a different career path. This is doubly so when trying to inspire a student to enter a public service career, because unless that service is provided through pro bono work supported by an established law firm (a path many lawyers take), one is liable to find the pursuit leads to a lower income (advocacy and nonprofit organizations do not pay at the level one would expect in private legal practice) and higher levels of frustration—private negotiations and courtroom arguments are often frustrating and difficult, but effecting significant change in a nation of 300 million people, with decision-making power widely distributed, is less likely to result in victories than in incremental progress over a period of years. Passion, commitment, and motivation are essential to sustaining one through such an undertaking.

What this challenge suggests is that law schools that wish to undertake a curriculum designed to lead students into public service should be prepared to bring onto the faculty, as associates or adjuncts, lawyers who have made that same leap themselves. In my own teaching, it has been undeniably useful to be able to point to my own career, both in advocacy and as a member of Congress, demonstrating the level of satisfaction and success one can enjoy in this nontraditional form of legal practice. Combined with an effort to provide students with hands-on experience with public officials and policy advocates, and bringing practitioners of public law to address students in their classes and school-wide assemblies, our great law schools can provide the nation with a new stream of bright young men and women ready to take up the task of continuing the protection of freedom and the pursuit of justice that lie at the heart of the American experiment.

Nobody enters the public arena more prepared to exercise leadership than a young man or woman trained in the law school classroom and in the broader law school environment. We have it in our power to infuse American society with new generations of committed fighters for the public good. That is a pursuit that should rank near the very top of every law school's ambitions.

References

Finkelman, P. 2010. *A Brief History of the Case and Tryal of John Peter Zenger: With Related Documents*. 1st edition. Bedford: St. Martin's.

Hugo, V. 1992. *Les Misérables*. New York: Modern Library.

Rush, M. 2005. *Parliament Today*. Manchester: Manchester University Press.

Shakespeare, W. 1992. *Henry V*, edited by A. Gurr. Cambridge: Cambridge University Press.

PART II
Why Leadership Studies in
Law School?

Chapter 7

Why Law Schools Should Emphasize Leadership Theory and Practice

Leary Davis

Sandy D'Alamberte, a true leader within and without the legal profession,[1] has said that people who go to law school already tend to be leaders. He says that they are given little or no purposeful help in leadership development in law school. However, after graduation they assume positions of leadership because of their inherent leadership attributes. As a consequence, he contends, law schools gain an undeserved reputation for educating leaders. D'Alemberte is correct that law faculties don't emphasize leadership theory and practice. I contend they should, for two principal reasons. First, leadership skills are important to law students because they are essential for lawyer competence.[2] Second, leadership theory and practice are important to the academy because they provide interdisciplinary perspectives that help us develop fuller understandings of competence, the legal order, and the processes of legal education; and because the extent of their application determines the state of legal education and the legal profession.

Though philosophized about for centuries, leadership has emerged as an academic discipline only in recent decades. Like law, leadership as a field of study is *multidisciplinary* in that it utilizes perspectives from almost all of the arts and sciences, including cognitive science and management. It is also *interdisciplinary* in that it has melded knowledge and modes of thinking from those disciplines to produce a new art and science. Leadership, like lawyering, is about influence; acts

---

1   D'Alemberte is a former President of the American Bar Association. Before assuming that position, he had been an Eagle Scout, Naval officer, student bar association president, state legislator, chair of the ABA Section of Legal Education and Admissions to the Bar, and President of the American Judicature Society (AJS). He subsequently served as Dean of Florida State University School of Law and President of Florida State University and continues to serve on many significant committees and boards. Among major efforts he has helped lead are establishment of the Central European and Eurasian Law Initiative (CEELI), the establishment of the Florida State University Medical School, and the AJS Center for Forensic Science and Public Policy.

2   Table 7.A1 in the Appendix contains a list of basic and advanced leadership skills described in detail in the US's leading college and graduate school leadership textbook, showing this author's opinion of the relevance of those skills to law practice, leadership of law firms, and civic engagement. The textbook, Hughes, Ginnett and Curphy (2006), is used at several points in this chapter as authority for the current state of leadership theory.

of leadership, like acts of lawyering, originate in the human mind, but become manifest in the world (Gardner 1995: 15). Many definitions of leadership, such as David Campbell's "Actions that focus resources to create desirable opportunities," describe the work of lawyers as well as they do the work of other leaders. It is worth considering the extent to which leadership theory provides a portal, if not for development of a unified theory of law practice and legal education, at least for their improvement.

This chapter examines that portal, first exploring the relevance and potential contributions of leadership theory to our understanding of lawyer competence. I discuss the acquisition of expertise and the roles played by self-awareness, knowledge of others, and assessment for development as one attains competence. I then draw on leadership literature to examine resistance to change in the academy in the face of such calls for reform as the 1992 MacCrate (ABA Section of Legal Education and Admissions to the Bar 1992) and 2007 Carnegie (Sullivan et al. 2007) reports. After noting what some law schools are doing to incorporate leadership into their curricula, I will conclude by examining prospects for the kind of comprehensive, integrative reform advocated by the Carnegie report.

Defining Competence

Competence is best defined as situationally appropriate behavior. What we *do* or *do not do* determines our level of competence. We have come to think of competence as a combination of knowledge and skill, yet lawyers who have good knowledge of legal doctrine and adequate lawyering skills may fail to provide quality legal services in a timely manner. As a 1979 ABA report, later known as the Cramton Report, stated:

> The dimensions of skill and knowledge … will not result in competent lawyering unless they are disciplined and supported by *constructive work habits*, *personal integrity*, and *a complex of attitudes and values*, such as conscientiousness, an understanding of the need to stay abreast of changes in the law, and appreciation of the limits of one's own competence. (ABA Section of Legal Education and Admissions to the Bar 1979: 9, 10, emphasis added)

While knowledge and skill are necessary for competent representation, they are not sufficient. The competent lawyer must possess and employ not only knowledge and skill, but also a host of personal attributes, including the characteristics stated in the Cramton Report. When harnessed by strategy and driven by initiative, these personal attributes combine to serve as a catalyst that transforms knowledge and skill into competent representation. Their development and deployment is what leadership theory and practice are in large part about.

Among these catalytic attributes, in addition to those listed in the Cramton Report, are various forms of intelligence, particularly linguistic, mathematical, intrapersonal, and interpersonal; attitudes such as optimism, self-efficacy, a growth mindset with its sense of becoming, tolerance for ambiguity, and tenacity; physical and mental states such as energy, stress-hardiness and resilience; needs including the need to achieve; value systems that highly prioritize values such as justice; and cognitive and behavioral orientations and preferences that are situationally sensitive to the ways individuals use their personal attributes, such as preferences toward extraversion or introversion.[3] Despite the various ways in which leadership is defined,[4] leadership as a discipline is fairly consistent in its definition of attributes such as needs, values, attitudes, interests, cognitive and behavioral preferences, and the various kinds of intelligence. It also recognizes that these attributes interact in ways that affect their mutual development.

Gaining Competence and Expertise

Nothing I say should diminish in any way the importance of technical knowledge and skill. One cannot succeed in law practice, and one will seldom get opportunities to lead, without first demonstrating technical competence. But, one will not succeed in any but the narrowest of practices, nor will one be likely to succeed once given the opportunity to lead, without possessing the personal attributes needed for success and the generic interpersonal skills of talking, listening, interviewing, counseling, and negotiating that are used in legal contexts.[5]

---

3   I use the terms *extraversion* and *introversion* as defined by their inventor, Carl Jung, and popularized by the Myers-Briggs Type Indicator, or MBTI®, to refer to one's preferred focus of attention and energy, either to the outer world of people and things or the inner world of ideas and reflection. See generally Briggs Myers (1980).

4   Lawyers should not consider the various definitions of leadership as a disqualification of leadership as a discipline. We consider law a discipline despite the fact that its definitions by our leading thinkers are as diverse as Austin's "The command of the sovereign," and Holmes's "The prophecies of what the courts will do in fact." Lawyers are comfortable with contextual theories of meaning, in which words have different meanings in different contexts; for example, a person may be dead for some legal purposes but not for others.

5   Figure 7.A1 in the Appendix, my *Model of the Legal Professionalization Process*, attempts to catalog the technical and interdisciplinary knowledge, technical and interpersonal skills, and some of the personal attributes that are brought into play while learning roles of analyst, advocate, and counselor as one progresses to become a "Stage IV Lawyer": one who exercises good judgment and moves seamlessly between the first three roles as is situationally appropriate.

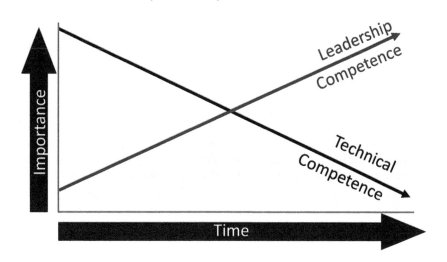

Figure 7.1   Relative importance of technical and leadership competence over time

Source: Adapted from Robert W. Eichinger and Michael M. Lombardo, "Twenty-Two Ways to Develop Leadership in Staff Managers," p. 14. Courtesy of the Center for Creative Leadership: Greensboro, NC.

In its work with well-positioned executives, lawyers, and public officials who have derailed or plateaued in their careers, the Center for Creative Leadership[6] has found that almost invariably those participants will have encountered early success because of either good technical competence or good interpersonal skills, but not both. Later, when a person who was highly skilled technically but lacked interpersonal skills rose to a higher level in an organization, people did not want to work with that person. Likewise, people might have risen in organizations because everyone liked them, but found that they lacked the technical competence to perform at a high level. The key to getting off a plateau or out of a ditch and back on track is to develop the missing ingredient, either technical or interpersonal competence.

This dance between technical and interpersonal or leadership competence is a key theme of leadership theory. Many, if not most, major leadership studies and

---

6   Founded in 1970, the nonprofit Center for Creative Leadership is a global provider of executive education focusing exclusively on leadership education and research. Its stated mission is to advance the understanding, practice and development of leadership for the benefit of society worldwide. It has campuses in Greensboro, North Carolina, Colorado Springs, San Diego, Brussels and Singapore, and outposts in Russia and Africa.

theories explore leadership from these two perspectives.[7] Figure 7.1 shows the relative importance of the two kinds of competence as one continues in one's career. Over time, a lawyer's technical competence becomes a byproduct of technical expertise and does not require the constant monitoring that it did in the lawyer's initial years in practice. But the true legal expert is not merely technically competent; through lessons of experience she has refined her complex of knowledge, skills, and personal attributes by adding operative leadership qualities, which become more important as the breadth and depth of her responsibilities expand.

Expertise

Together, the work of Malcolm Gladwell in his recent book, *Outliers: The Story of Success*, and of Paul Johnson and his colleagues over decades at the University of Minnesota, inform us of the importance of both technical skill and interpersonal skill in gaining expertise, and of the development opportunities needed for their acquisition. After examining the lives of such experts as Bill Gates, the Beatles, and the lawyer Joe Flom, and confirming his observations through the work of other researchers, Gladwell concludes that it takes 10 years, or 10,000 hours, of concentrated work to become an expert, and that it also requires opportunities for development that include the assistance of others (Gladwell 2008: 35–55).

In working with lawyers and accountants in three separate projects, Johnson and his colleagues help us understand the importance of experience in the acquisition of expertise, and how that experience manifests itself in the performance of experts and novices. In their work with trial lawyers (Johnson et al. 1984), they explained the acquisition of expertise as a three-step process:

> Phase I. *Thought (or Cognition)-Instruction*. In this phase novices think about what it is that is being done. They learn what actions are appropriate in which circumstances (and the relationships between action and circumstance) from instruction or from observation and evaluation of their own performance.[8]
>
> Phase II. *Association*. In this phase novices practice the processes about which they obtained knowledge in Phase I, while thinking about the

---

7   Common examples of the interplay of technical and interpersonal aspects are found in the concern for production and concern for people of Blake and Moulton's Leadership Grid®; the task and relationship behaviors of Hersey and Blanchard's Situational Leadership; and the task and relationship motivations of low and high LPC (Least Preferred Co-worker scale) leaders, respectively, in Fiedler's contingency model of leadership.

8   In leadership theory this process of performing, observing, reflecting upon and evaluating one's own performance, then modifying and repeating the performance and observing and reflecting upon that performance, is known as the spiral of experience, discussed later in this chapter.

processes, until they become efficient and proficient in utilization of those processes.

Phase III. *Automaticity*. In this phase proficient practitioners practice processes to the point that they can be done automatically, without thinking.[9]

They concluded that expert trial lawyers are better than novices at analyzing legal situations and anticipating possible future situations, have more adequate implicit psychological theories (Johnson et al. 1984: 141), and are more sensitive to the nuances of particular legal contexts (Johnson et al. 1984: 141–2), and that:

> A key distinguishing characteristic for differentiating expert and non-expert lawyers may be the willingness and ability of the expert to modulate his actions according to the specific situation, and to take a large number of factors into account in deciding on a course of action. (Johnson et al. 1984: 141–2)

Modulating actions so that they are situationally appropriate conforms to our definition of competence as situationally appropriate conduct. The core of this ability is an operative knowledge that consists of two components:

1. Knowledge of law, derived from the lawyer's adaptation to legal training; and,
2. Knowledge of people, derived from adaptation to social situations of all kinds, including those arising in legal environments (Johnson et al. 1984: 138).

In their work with corporate lawyers (Johnson and Pechtel 1985), Johnson and his colleagues once more observed the impact, in a time-limited exercise, of bare technical competence versus the marriage of technical with leadership competence. Both novice (one or two years of practice) and expert (10 or more years of practice) corporate lawyers were presented with an unfolding fact situation and asked to think aloud about each phase of the problem, concluding with a strategy for acquiring a target company. Two-thirds of the novices recommended a hostile takeover, while only one-fourth of the experts did, despite verbal clues suggesting that strategy. The lines of reasoning and approaches of the experts were

---

9   (Johnson et al. 1984: 129). Johnson states that "The result of Phase III learning is that the relationships which form the basis for actions are placed beyond reach of conscious awareness … This state of affairs is not the result of any lack of interest in understanding what they know on the part of experts, but rather the end product of a process of cognitive adaptation. The result of our evolutionary history is a relatively large long-term (unconscious) memory for storing facts, principles, events and knowledge of various sorts, and a severely limited conscious awareness which forces us to automate or place into unconscious memory most of the things that are done with any regularity, and especially those things in which we become highly practiced" (Johnson et al. 1984: 129–30).

varied, as were the extensive experiences that informed them, but because of those experiences the consensus of the experts was that the real value of the target was in its people, and that their client would be unlikely to retain those people in the event of a hostile takeover. This consideration escaped the novices as they related their thoughts about the problem (Johnson and Pechtel 1985).[10]

Finally, in their work with accountants (Grazioli et al. 2006), Johnson and his colleagues revealed two important facts about the limits of competence. The first fact is that high base-rate tasks, in which experts are able to practice processes to the point that they become automatic, are needed for the acquisition of expertise. Low base-rate work consists of tasks that are repeated so seldom or intermittently that they do not lead to such automaticity. In this project, most CPAs, including partners from Big Four accounting firms, were unable to detect the fraud in notorious cases that were presented to them as case studies with the names of the companies changed (Grazioli et al. 2006: 2). The authors concluded that fraud detection is a low base-rate task for most auditors. For them high base-rate work is examining the records of companies that are trying to reveal financial information, not hide it, so they have few opportunities to see financial information being manipulated in ways designed to deceive them (Grazioli et al. 2006: 6, 19).

Reading and analyzing cases, statutes, and regulations are high base-rate tasks for lawyers, who in the process form neuronal pathways that organize knowledge and automate technique. "Thinking like a lawyer" is supposed to be what law school is all about. Our traditional explanation of the value of high base-rate work in helping us think like lawyers is found in Karl Llewellyn's *The Bramble Bush* (1930):

> There was a man in our town,
> and he was wondrous wise:
> he jumped into a BRAMBLE BUSH,
> and scratched out both his eyes –
> and when he saw that he was blind,
> with all his might and main,
> he jumped into another one
> and scratched them in again.

If I understand it correctly, Llewellyn repurposes the old poem as a metaphorical statement of the traditional advice given first-year law students. "I don't know

---

10   Just because the initial thought processes of novices led them to different conclusions than experts within the time constraints of the experiment does not mean that the proper conclusion would have escaped them had they worked through the problem more slowly and completely at the association phase (Phase II) of gaining expertise. A complete creative process includes a verification phase, which would likely have looked at the practical consequences of the proposed strategy and led to replanning by the novices. Cognitive scientists generally look at creativity as a four-step process: preparation or saturation, incubation, illumination or insight, and verification. See, for example, Nyström 1979: 40–41.

exactly how one comes to think like a lawyer, but ... trust me. Work hard. Go blind. Keep working hard. Then you'll see." In fact, Llewellyn's advice to over-practice works for people who follow it. In outlining a path of development from novice to expert lawyer, leadership theory provides a better way for law faculty to explain *why* it works and suggests ways to enhance expert cognition.

The second important fact revealed by Johnson's work with accountants is consistent with other observations about the necessity of marrying technical competence with interpersonal and leadership competence. Around 10% of the auditors were consistently able to detect frauds in the cases presented to them. Johnson and his colleagues concluded that the successful auditors were the ones able to integrate a deep knowledge of others (in this case the knowledge, intentions and preferences of management, a "theory of the mind of the opponent") with an equally deep technical knowledge (of accounting and auditing) (Grazioli et al. 2006: 2, 26).

What we have learned from Johnson and others about the acquisition of competence and expertise suggests that law schools should continue to provide high base-rate work in legal analysis to create technical competence and expertise. Over-practicing these tasks is essential for acquisition of technical skills at which all lawyers should be expert. Knowledge of people being a key component of expert performance in the *application* of doctrinal knowledge, it also suggests that law schools should provide opportunities for students to apply their new knowledge in interpersonal settings—practicing, observing, evaluating, and refining their performances. Students should also be provided a cognitive framework for appreciating what there is to understand about self and others.

Three special kinds of knowledge that do not fall neatly within the concepts of either interdisciplinary knowledge or technical legal knowledge are key among the catalytic personal attributes necessary for competence. The first is knowledge of self, or self-awareness (*intrapersonal intelligence*, in the language of Gardner 1983: 237–76, term defined at 239). Knowledge of self allows lawyers to take advantage of their strengths while alerting them to their weaknesses. Second, they must possess knowledge of other people, both about human nature in general and about the particular people with whom they interact. This knowledge of others (*interpersonal intelligence* in Gardner's language) (Gardner 1983: 239)[11] enables lawyers to build strong teams, alliances and synergies that take advantage of the strengths of collaborators, and to develop sound strategies to protect clients from the strengths of opponents while, when appropriate, exploiting their opponents' weaknesses.

---

11   Johnson's successful auditors possessed a keen interpersonal intelligence. Gardner states that the core capacity of interpersonal intelligence is *"the ability to notice and make distinctions among other individuals* and, in particular, among their moods, temperaments, motivations and intentions ... In an advanced form, interpersonal knowledge permits a skilled adult to read the intentions and desires—even when these have been hidden—of many other individuals and, potentially, to act upon this knowledge ... "* (Gardner 1983: 239, reprinted by permission of Basic Books, a member of the Perseus Book Group).

Figure 7.2   Three special kinds of knowledge
Source: Adapted with the permission of Free Press, a division of Simon & Schuster, Inc., from *Leadership Dynamics: A Practical Guide to Effective Relationships* by Edwin P. Hollander. Copyright © 1978 by The Free Press. All rights reserved.

Third, they possess operative knowledge of relevant external environments (or *situational awareness*). If competence is situationally appropriate behavior, knowledge of the situation is obviously crucial. It is vital to development of sound strategies and, with self-awareness and knowledge of others, generates "street smarts."

The interplay of these three kinds of knowledge is illustrated in a widely accepted description of leadership as a dynamic process involving the interplay of the leader, followers, and the situation (Hollander 1978: 7–9; Hughes et al. 2006: 25–8).

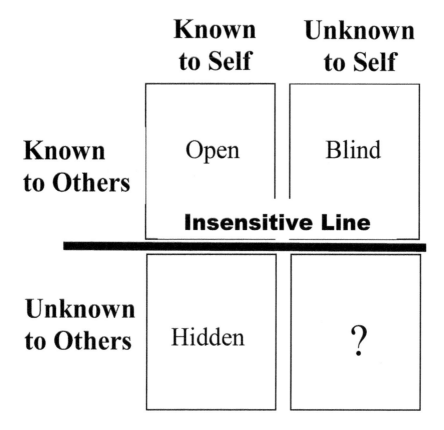

Figure 7.3   Knowledge and the insensitive line
Source: *Group Processes: An Introduction to Group Dynamics*, by Joseph Luft. 1984.
McGraw-Hill. Adapted from "Johari Window" in Luft, J. and Ingham, H. 1969. *Of Human
Interaction*. Palo Alto: National Press Books, p. 13. Courtesy of McGraw-Hill.

Competent lawyering can be seen as a dynamic process involving the same kind
of interplay, if we substitute for the leader the individual lawyer, for followers the
firm's personnel and existing clients, and for the situation an external environment
that includes the law and its instruments of enforcement, potential clients,
competitors, adversaries, allies, decision-makers, and technological, social,
economic and political opportunities and challenges. As the characteristics of
the situation or the followers change, the actions of the lawyer–leader must often
change in order to remain situationally appropriate, or competent. If the lawyer–
leader lacks self-awareness or is otherwise incapable of adapting in ways that are
situationally appropriate, the lawyer–leader is likely to fail. Unfortunately, it is not
always easy to develop self-awareness.

Difficulties in Learning about Self and Others

Michigan law professor Jim White taught the nation's first law school negotiations course. In 1990 I asked him what the most important thing he could teach his students to enhance their negotiation skills would be.[12] His response was, "If I could just tell them some things about themselves, but there's no way they could understand." He was talking about their lack of self-awareness and their tendency to reject information inconsistent with their self-concepts.

Milton Rokeach's book, *The Nature of Human Values* (1973), and the Johari Window are helpful in explaining students' inability, or unwillingness, to understand some information about themselves. The Johari Window[13] is built around two simple facts; that there are some things we know about ourselves and some things we do not know, and that there are some things about us that other people know and some things they do not know. By constructing a matrix using these two dimensions, Joseph Luft and Harry Ingham produced a window with four panes, and gave each pane a name. In healthy organizations and relationships it is helpful for the open pane, what is known by both self and others, to be as large as possible. In other relationships, such as negotiations, it may be situationally appropriate to preserve much of the hidden window, keeping hidden from others, for instance, less favorable terms on which one might be willing to settle. The blind pane, the one that concerned Professor White, is dangerous to the lawyer, for if others know things about a lawyer that she does not know about herself, others might be able to use that information to control the lawyer. The unknown pane, known to neither self nor others, represents an area of untapped growth and potential synergy, once it becomes accessible. Changing the size of any one pane necessarily changes all four panes.

Knowledge of self and others being so crucial to lawyer competence, it behooves us to know as much about ourselves and others as possible, but we face barriers to each sphere of knowledge. The first barrier, our *insensitivity* to others, is more easily overcome than the second, our *sensitivity* to information that is inconsistent with our self-concepts. We tend to have an *insensitive line* between what we know of others and what we do not know of them. That is because we tend to assume that they are like we are. The more we interact with others, the more we understand that they are not necessarily like us, and that they may have different motivations than we have. This experience serves to lower the level of our insensitivity.

The second barrier, the one to which Professor White referred, is our *sensitive line*. Rokeach, Freud, and Carl Rogers all write of the difficulty and even pain of gaining insight into ourselves. So much of our being is tied up in protecting our self-concepts that we tend to reject automatically information that is inconsistent with them, using

---

12   Conversation with James J. White at Speakers' Dinner, 1990 Eastern Bankruptcy Institute, Wilmington, North Carolina.

13   This heuristic device was created by Joseph Luft and Harry Ingham (hence Johari) to explain and improve aspects of interpersonal communication and relationships within organizations (Luft 1969).

such defense mechanisms as denial or repression. Of course, much new information we receive about ourselves *is* consistent with our self-concepts, and that information is relatively easily used to reduce our blind spots. But our ego defense mechanisms may strongly resist information that we fear learning about ourselves. For that reason it is important that such information be objective, be delivered in small bits over time, and be delivered in a supportive environment (Whetten and Cameron 2005: 55–7).[14]

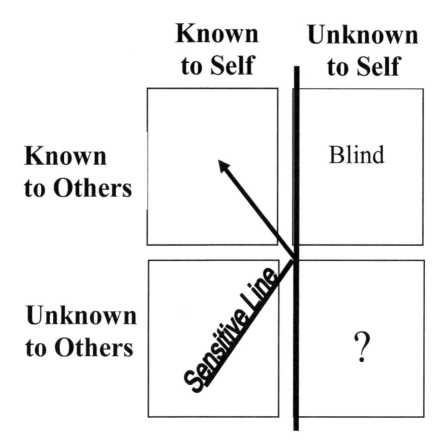

Figure 7.4   Knowledge and the sensitive line

Source: *Group Processes: An Introduction to Group Dynamics*, by Joseph Luft. 1984. McGraw-Hill. Adapted from "Johari Window" in Luft, J. and Ingham, H. 1969. *Of Human Interaction*. Palo Alto: National Press Books, p. 13. Courtesy of McGraw-Hill.

---

14   I was first introduced to the concept of the sensitive line in an earlier version of Whetten and Cameron. The ideas of the insensitive line and using the Johari Window to illustrate them are mine.

Law students who possess a growth mindset and an appreciation of the importance of the interplay between technical and leadership competence will be well positioned to receive, reflect upon, and use that information.

Needs, Values, Attitudes, Interests, and Cognitive and Behavioral Preferences

A good place to begin building one's knowledge of self and others is with regard to several motivators of self and others: needs,[15] values,[16] attitudes,[17] interests,[18] and cognitive and behavioral preferences. Both Rokeach and Edgar Schein view needs, values, attitudes, and interests as primary motivators. Schein says that they provide us with career anchors, attract us to certain careers, and may draw us back to those careers if we leave them (Schein 1978: 124–72).[19]

---

15   Needs are of two kinds, necessities and objects of desire that may not be absolutely essential to survival. The most widely known theory of needs is Abraham Maslow's hierarchy of needs, in which he posited a hierarchy of five types of needs in ascending order (Maslow 1970: 35–8). The needs in ascending order are physiological, safety and security, belongingness and love (social), esteem (status), and self-actualization. Clayton P. Alderfer modified Maslow's hierarchy in his ERG theory of needs by categorizing Maslow's physiological and security needs as Existence needs, his belongingness and esteem (status) needs as Relatedness needs, and self-actualization and self-esteem as Growth needs. Alderfer believes that if higher-level needs are frustrated, one will focus on satisfying lower-level needs (Alderfer 1969). So a lawyer whose self-realization or social needs were being frustrated might focus on compensation at the security need level; money would become a substitute for status and meaning. Unlike Maslow, he did not believe higher-level needs necessarily emerged only as lower-level needs were satisfied. Maslow's theory is widely accepted, and it provides a useful way of categorizing needs, particularly with Alderfer's refinement. Maslow stressed that needs are but one among many types of determinants of behavior, including values.

16   Milton Rokeach has defined values as enduring beliefs that specific modes of conduct (instrumental values) or end-states of existence (terminal values) are personally or socially preferable to opposite or converse modes of conduct or end-states of existence. This conception of values is useful because of its explicitness, which illuminates the interplay of values with needs, attitudes and other contributors to professional behavior. Rokeach sees values in part as the expression of individual needs and societal and institutional demands. Values serve motivational functions by helping people adjust to society, by serving as ego defense mechanisms that enhance self-esteem, and by testing reality in the search for meaning and self-realization. Individuals are distinguished less by the individual values they possess than by their value systems, or the relative priority they assign values (Rokeach 1973: 5–31).

17   Rokeach identifies attitudes as organized groups of beliefs about particular objects or situations (Rokeach 1973: 18).

18   Rokeach says interests resemble attitudes toward specific activities and objects (Rokeach 1973: 22).

19   Schein adds that career anchors also reflect one's discovered talents, work experience being necessary for the development of career anchors (Schein 1978: 171).

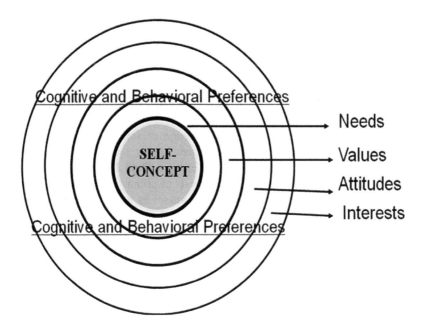

Figure 7.5   Motivators
Source: The author, Leary Davis.

The interactions of these motivators can be profound. For instance, if we are in jobs that meet our needs, allow us to behave consistently with our values, and are interesting, we have good attitudes about work. If not, we do not.

Rokeach believed that one's being is tied up in protecting one's self-concept, and that the relative strength of each of the foregoing motivators is determined by its proximity to the self-concept: needs, values, attitudes, and interests in that order. Therefore, to change someone else's attitudes, one might address their values; and to modify another's values, one should address their needs.

Talents, Abilities, and Cognitive and Behavioral Preferences

No matter how well our needs, values, attitudes, and interests seem to fit with the demands of law practice, we cannot succeed there unless we are sufficiently intelligent and talented. Furthermore, even though we have sufficient latent aptitude for law practice, we may fail to develop our talents completely because we over-rely on situationally inappropriate cognitive and behavioral preferences in order to avoid threat or embarrassment. The introverted lawyer who is a skilled writer may avoid practicing public or extemporaneous speaking and be ineffective when called upon to speak. In order to maintain comfort, control, and the appearance of skillfulness, the expert advocate may maintain an adversarial approach in counseling or other collaborative environments, even though reliance upon adversarial strengths will ultimately prove counterproductive in those situations.

Assessing one's own needs, values, attitudes, interests, and cognitive and behavioral preferences is a good first step in the development of greater self-awareness and knowledge of others, particularly when coupled with assessment of one's knowledge and skill.

Assessment for Development as a Foundation for Development of Technical and Interpersonal Competence

Law schools can learn from other leadership educators in assessing both technical and interpersonal competence. The Center for Creative Leadership has developed effective leadership development programs for executives and high-ranking officials that feature assessment for development. The Center makes this assessment formative by combining it with experiential exercises that require participants to apply what they learn about themselves and others, extensive peer and professional feedback, developmental goal-setting, and extensive follow-up to evaluate progress in achieving those goals. Many of the assessment instruments used provide 360-degree feedback, which includes feedback from superiors, peers, and subordinates as well as self-assessments of both technical performance and personal attributes. Other leading leadership development programs do the same, and their methodologies and materials are relevant to the goals of legal education.

Technical Knowledge

The law school essay examination may be the best assessment for development instrument imaginable for the development of technical knowledge, yet it is seldom used for that purpose. By examining how it is used and imagining how it might be used, one can sense the contributions leadership development practices could make to legal education. At present examinations are used for *summative* evaluation, to reward and punish students and to sort them for potential employers. Development occurs, but usually from what is gathered implicitly and intuitively from taking an examination and receiving a grade, and seldom in an articulated, strategic, efficient manner. Examinations could be used for *formative* evaluation, and often are in undergraduate education. Ask any room full of lawyers how many of them made it a practice to look at their final law school examinations after receiving their grades, and few will raise their hands. Then ask how many reviewed and studied midterm examinations they had taken in undergraduate school when they knew that the same material was going to be covered on their final examinations. Almost all will respond affirmatively. They wanted to make sure they mastered the material for the final examination, relearning the information they used in the past to answer questions correctly, and correcting any areas of deficiency.

Law schools serious about integrating leadership theory and practice into legal education will want to create structures to encourage law students to think of law school exams as they thought of midterm exams in undergraduate school—as part of a spiral of experience in which the examination is viewed as an experience that the student can observe and reflect upon. The student can then use that experience to determine what she could have done differently to achieve better results, and then make plans to cure deficiencies in knowledge and to improve study strategies to better prepare for and perform on future examinations. This strategy would require frequent examinations, feedback, and re-examinations to allow students to practice application of knowledge.

Technical and Interpersonal Skills

The enhanced legal writing and rewriting programs of recent decades provide excellent spiral of experience opportunities in which written assignments become assessment for development instruments. Video of advocacy, interviewing, counseling, and negotiation exercises can serve the same purpose. In all instances the assessment for development processes benefits from, and sometimes requires, collaborators and coaches in the process. The 2006 study, *Best Practices for Legal Education* (Stuckey and Others 2007), is rich with examples of opportunities for formative evaluation that include simulated practice contexts and prompt and constructive feedback.

Personal Attributes and Interpersonal Skills

When most people think of assessment for development, they think of assessment for development instruments to enhance law students' knowledge of themselves and others. There are several valid, reliable self-assessment *instruments* (not tests; they cannot be failed) that can help law students and lawyers expand self-awareness and gain insights into aspects of normal personalities that help explain and predict behavior, both their own and that of others. Instruments are available to assess students' self-perceptions of their needs,[20] values,[21] attitudes,[22]

---

20   The FIRO-B (Fundamental Interpersonal Relations Orientation-Behavior) measures needs for inclusion, control and affection, with scores for each need as expressed toward and desired from others; the DiSC Personal Profile System reveals management styles based upon the relative levels of energy expended in meeting needs for dominance, interaction, stability and compliance with standards of quality.

21   The RVS, or Rokeach Values Survey, allows students to prioritize 18 terminal and 18 instrumental values.

22   The CSI, or Change Style Indicator, and the Kirton Adaption-Innovation Inventory measure attitudes toward change.

interests,[23] cognitive and behavioral preferences,[24] and learning styles.[25] Properly administered, these self-assessment instruments offer the advantages of objective evaluation in a supportive environment. In providing insights, they seldom threaten self-concepts, but rather expand them in a constructive manner.

Law students often find revelations about themselves from the instruments surprisingly powerful. That may be because they already know the most powerful information communicated about them, but only implicitly. Once they hear that information articulated, they are surprised and delighted at what is obvious but had never been explicit for them. Having words for the information, they can use it in a strategic, planful manner, which is what makes it so powerful.[26] Typically, because the instruments reveal little if any information inconsistent with students' self-concepts, they do not implicate the sensitive line.[27]

---

23   The Campbell Interest and Skill Survey (CISS) and Strong Interest Inventory (SII) measure vocational interests and self-confidence.

24   The MBTI, or Myers-Briggs Type Indicator indicates 16 personality types based on four preferences: for introversion or extraversion, for gathering information or *perceiving* by sensing or intuition, for deciding or *judging* by thinking or feeling (a rational process based on valuing), and for living one's outer life perceiving or judging (each of the four preferences has five trait-like facets in the MBTI Step II version).

25   Many, including the Kolb Learning Style Indicator (LSI).

26   Henry Mintzberg describes this process of surprise and delight in "Planning on the Left Side and Managing on the Right" (1976).

27   Diversity program presentations in law firms and other organizations often impinge upon the sensitive lines, sometimes with untoward effects, of both majority participants and those who add diversity to their organizations. A movement toward facilitation in self-assessment and non-threatening self-disclosure can be observed in the use of the Campbell Picture Postcard Deck (CPPD) to examine multicultural awareness and attitudes toward diversity. In this exercise participants view 100 postcards showing groups of people as diverse as women astronauts, Arab horsemen, the family of the King of Sweden, aboriginal tribesmen, a German soccer team, a Billy Graham religious revival, and Chinese acrobats. They might then be asked to pick two or three cards picturing the group that, if they were anthropologists and had a week to study any group, they would most like to be with, and a like number of cards showing the group they would least like to study. Participants are then asked to share in small group settings their choices and the reasons for them. The process is enlightening, as participants discover that while they probably know only 5% of the groups, they have opinions about the other 95%. Early users have been positive about the extent to which the process increases multicultural awareness within a context of psychological safety and freedom, without provoking the resentment that some diversity programs generate.

Using What Is Known about the Law, Oneself, Others, and Situations, and Learning from that Experience

So far, with the exception of classroom analytical and writing skills, we've been talking about assessing and developing attributes that can result in competence, but not competence itself, which we have said is situationally appropriate behavior. Law schools interested in leadership and lawyer competence will provide many opportunities for students to assess their competence in the process of learning by doing. These schools will develop competency models to serve as guides for development, and students will be given opportunities to practice their competencies in clinical situations and well-designed simulations. Students will learn to give and receive prompt, constructive feedback, and faculty members will fulfill practical coaching functions of teaching, modeling, motivating, and inspiring. They will be assisted by practicing lawyers who will engage with students to facilitate their development, including formation of professional identity, in small and large groups and on a one-on-one basis.[28]

Most important, with the guidance of faculty and practicing lawyers, students will learn to learn from their own experience, by themselves. The "spiral of experience" has been referred to as a process for gaining competence in legal analysis and writing. David Kolb, the originator of the Learning Styles Indicator (LSI), has emphasized that experience, without observation and reflection, produces little learning.[29] Repetitious practice of skills without reflection is likely to produce similar results, with cycles of experience modified only by what might have been gained intuitively. But when one critically observes one's own performance (perhaps a class recitation) and its impact on oneself and others, reflects upon why that behavior happened as it did (perhaps because of inadequate preparation or anticipatory stressors), and how performance can be improved (perhaps through more thorough preparation, joining Toastmasters, or taking a public speaking course), one can intentionally re-enter the arena to perform in a more refined way that reflects what was learned from the first experience. In this manner, learning from experience will generate a dynamic, expanding spiral of progressively enhanced performances instead of a constant, repetitive cycle.

Because leadership theory is interdisciplinary and capable of enriching the intellectual life of law schools, and because applied principles of leadership

---

28   Lawyers do this as mentors over a course of three years at St. Thomas and as preceptors in observing and providing feedback to first-year students at Elon. Formal and informal mentors, coaches, preceptors, and gurus play different roles in the development of legal talent (Davis 2008, 2011).

29   Kolb began his exploration of experiential learning and learning styles in an article co-authored with Roger Fry (Kolb and Fry 1975). He elaborated more fully on his theories in Kolb (1984). His cyclical four-part model (concrete experience, observation and reflection, abstract conceptualization, and testing of concepts) has subsequently been adapted and widely used by leadership educators. See, for example, Hughes et al. (2006: 54–60).

development and practice can enhance student competence and help close the gap between law school and law practice, we should examine the extent to which these principles are likely to be applied in law schools.

Why Most Law Schools Will Probably Hesitate to Embrace Leadership Theory and Practice

I have suggested some initiatives that will be undertaken at law schools that embrace leadership theory and practice. However, history suggests that the potential of leadership theory and practice in legal education will not be fulfilled at most law schools in the near term. Over several decades forceful, coherent studies, emanating from powerful organizations, have made realistic recommendations for comprehensive reform of legal education. One result of these studies has been the addition of course offerings at the margins of the traditional core curriculum. Another has been the balkanization of faculty into segregated colonies of traditional (tenured and tenure track) doctrinal scholars, clinicians, legal writing instructors, and interdisciplinary scholars whose disciplines are featured in "Law and [The Discipline]"[30] courses.

These separate colonies and their discrete courses provide the kind of diversity that if integrated rather than segmented should provide greater synergy to legal education.[31] However, diversity that causes synergy does so because it is accompanied by a creative tension that poses the risk, in the absence of interpersonal skill, of becoming synergy-destroying conflict. Generally, diversity will lead to either synergy or conflict—which of the two depends upon the diverse parties and their attitudes. In legal education the parties have for the most part addressed the synergy or conflict issue presented by their diversity by adopting the conflict resolution strategy of avoidance, maintaining the status quo of balkanization rather than risking change.

Leadership theory provides a rational tool for exploring the likelihood of change in legal education with the formula $C = (D \times M \times P) > R$ [amount of Change = (Dissatisfaction x Model of change x Process utilized) > Resistance to

---

30   I recognize that, even with the trend toward hiring J.D.-Ph.D. faculty members, most Law and the Discipline faculty members also teach core curriculum courses. At most schools it is less likely that clinicians will do so.

31   That diversity enhances problem-solving is undeniable. The presence and participation of Thurgood Marshall and Sandra Day O'Connor improved both the quality of decision-making by the United States Supreme Court and the public acceptance of its decisions. Joel Barker (1992: 55–70) argues that most paradigm shifts are initiated by four kinds of people, each of which adds diversity to problem-solving: new entrants to a field, lateral movers, mavericks, and tinkerers. He also explains why their ideas are resisted by insiders.

change].[32] Since D, M, and P are multipliers, if any of these elements is absent, change will not occur. Resistance to change is significant in legal education, triggered by fear of loss of power, status, competence, relationships, identity, and rewards (Beer 2007: 4–5). Yet over the past two decades *U.S. News* magazine has caused tremendous change in the availability and deployment of resources in legal education. It did not generate this vast transfer of wealth to law schools by issuing a call for change, but merely by publishing data and issuing rankings based upon those data. The rankings can threaten the self-concepts of law schools and the esteem needs of individuals affiliated with them, creating substantial dissatisfaction (D in the formula) at most law schools. Given the level of threat and dissatisfaction created by the rankings, the model for change (M) suggested by the *U.S. News* criteria, and faculty governance and university budget processes (P) available, change was easy. Concerns about the affordability of tuition rates provided the only major resistance to those expenditures, and until 2010 law students continued to pay an inflationary going rate with only scattered complaints as the country sank into recession.

The change generated by *U.S. News* data has dwarfed change flowing from repeated calls for reform of legal education. That state of affairs may change, as protests from students and new graduates unable to find jobs in the aftermath of the recent recession have escalated. The number of applicants to ABA-approved law schools in 2012 is expected to decline by over 20,000 from 87,900 applicants in 2010 (and over 100,000 in 2004). If reform is to come, reformers will undoubtedly look to the two most well-known, if little followed, appeals for change in legal education since the Cramton Report.

Both the ABA's MacCrate report (ABA Section of Legal Education and Admissions to the Bar 1992) and the report of the Carnegie Foundation, entitled *Educating Lawyers: Preparation for the Profession of Law* (Sullivan et al. 2007), looked at lawyer competence and the strengths and shortcomings of legal education in closing the gap between law school and law practice. The MacCrate report's goal was stated in its subtitle: *Narrowing the Gap Between Law School and Law Practice*. Its primary contributions were the exploration of ten fundamental lawyering skills and four fundamental values of the profession. It also emphasized that lawyer development is a continuum that begins before law school and continues long after, and recommended enhanced skills training in law school. Unfortunately, it largely ignored the complex of attitudes, values, and other personal attributes that the Cramton Report contended support and discipline knowledge and skill. Indeed, its four fundamental values (the report never defined the term *values*)—Provision of Competent Representation; Striving to Promote Justice, Fairness, and Morality; Striving to Improve the Profession; and Professional Self-Development—might better be designated not as values,

---

32   The statement of the formula is the one favored by Hughes et al. (2006: 614–17). See Beer (2007) for another adaptation from an earlier version attributed to David Gleicher.

but as attitudes or desirable actions that are motivated by values, attitudes, and interests.[33]

An examination of the MacCrate report's 10 skills reveals the relevance of leadership theory and practice. Three of the ten skills were technical legal skills (legal analysis and reasoning, legal research, and litigation and accompanying formal alternative dispute resolution procedures). Seven (not counting informal alternative dispute resolution skills) could be considered generic leadership skills used in a legal context (problem-solving, factual investigation, communication, counseling, negotiation, organization and management of legal work, and recognizing and resolving ethical dilemmas) (ABA Section of Legal Education and Admissions to the Bar 1992: 138–41).

The MacCrate report can be credited as a catalyst in legal education's expansion of training in technical legal skills (analysis, research, litigation and ADR) as well as in counseling, negotiation, and professional responsibility. However, gains were modest with respect to generic leadership skills used in a legal context. This lack of success in the face of demonstrated need is symbolized by the limited extent to which law schools now teach the report's ninth fundamental skill, organization and management of legal work. Jack Mudd, a member of the MacCrate Commission, had led a 1988 Montana study that surveyed levels of competence needed and possessed by new law graduates. That study showed that the greatest difference between the level of competence needed and the level of competence possessed by new lawyers related to "an understanding of the basic business problems of maintaining and operating a private law office" (Mudd and LaTrielle 1988).

Despite this evidence of a high need for practice management skills, a review of the 2009–2010 AALS Directory of Law Teachers reveals that full-time faculty members were teaching practice management courses at only 28 law schools, about half the number of schools offering such courses in the 1980s.[34] These data gain poignancy from the American Bar Foundation's ongoing longitudinal research study, *After the JD—The First 10 Years*, which is tracking the professional lives of more than 5,000 lawyers. Seven years after law school graduation, 60.7% of respondents agreed that they would have benefitted from greater exposure to aspects of business while in law school, a positive response that exceeded their assessment of the helpfulness of specific law school courses (56.6%) and clinical training (52.1%) (Nelson 2011).[35]

The Montana study also found surprisingly low observed competence in areas of substantive law taught in law school for which there was a high reported need for competence. One explanation for the low scores was that the only time students

---

33   See the discussion of needs, values, attitudes, and interests in notes 15–18.

34   I am grateful to my research assistant, Chelsea Glover, for her analysis of practice management courses listed in *The AALS Directory of Law Teachers, 2009–2010*, and for the spreadsheet showing the results of her research, which generated these data.

35   Only instruction in legal writing rated higher in helpfulness, at 63%.

were provided opportunities to apply their knowledge in law school was in taking end of semester examinations, and therefore they did not retain knowledge (Mudd and LaTrielle 1988: 26–7).

More law schools might enjoy more success inculcating substantive knowledge and analytical and other lawyering skills if they positioned courses within thoughtful theories of leadership and law practice. If they did, they would consider the primary motivators of law students: their needs, values, attitudes, and interests. People who study vocational preferences of lawyers know that they are interested in law and politics, public speaking, and leadership,[36] but that they have less than average interest in management.[37] While a main theme of leadership theory is the difference between leadership and management (Hughes et al. 2006: 8–10, 40–45), there is significant overlap and interplay between the two. Leaders have to manage, and leadership theory and practice can provide an engaging portal for development of management skills by law students at the same time they develop substantive knowledge and lawyering skills.

For instance, *The Travis Simulation*, an excellent marital separation and property settlement simulation developed at Columbia Law School, involves students in the application of substantive professional responsibility and family law in the course of planning, interviewing, counseling, and negotiation exercises.[38] Though perhaps labor intensive, it would not otherwise be a complex task to incorporate into the simulation essential basic management tasks and principles that would accompany such a representation in a law firm. The 2007 Carnegie report makes the case for such integration. *Educating Lawyers: Preparation for the Profession of Law* builds upon the MacCrate report and other studies of legal education of the past century, including earlier Carnegie work. This latest Carnegie report calls for comprehensive, integrative reform of legal education.[39]

---

36 With respect to interest in law and politics, none of 58 occupational samples rank higher than lawyers; only five rank higher with respect to their interest in public speaking, and their interest in leadership ranks around the 60th percentile. (Campbell et al. 1992: 105–6). A 1993 survey of law students at Columbia, the University of North Carolina, and Campbell showed that students at all three schools reported a high interest in leadership. Data retained by individual schools. The Campbell data replicated a 1992 survey of that student body (Davis 1993).

37 With respect to the business-oriented interests of sales, advertising/marketing, office practices, and supervision, when compared among 58 occupational samples, lawyers rank 38th, 44th, 46th, and 47th in interest (Davis 1993).

38 *The Travis Simulation*, developed by Carol Liebman and others, can be purchased from the Columbia Law School for a nominal fee.

39 Prior to publication of the Carnegie report Judith Wegner, a Carnegie Foundation senior fellow who directed field work for the project, and the only lawyer and legal educator of the five co-authors, had authored a series of four preliminary papers on the problems and opportunities of legal education. Dean Wegner's work addressed a broader range of issues with a broader range of theory, much of it familiar to leadership scholars, and can fairly be said to be more rigorous than the final report.

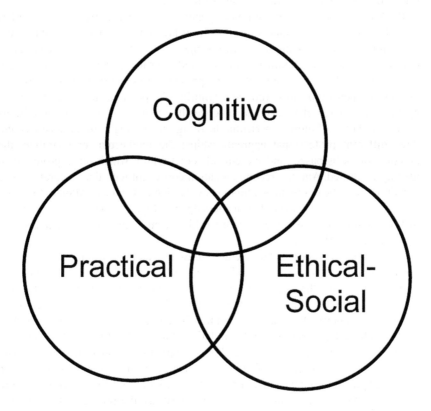

Figure 7.6   Three professional apprenticeships
Source: The author, Leary Davis.

That report, one of a series on professional education, seems to be addressed to higher education generally, and it understandably resolves editorial concerns in favor of that broader audience at the expense of its narrower legal audience. Professor Wegner's four unpublished papers are "Law is Gray: 'Thinking Like a Lawyer' in the Face of Uncertainty"; "Thinking Like A Lawyer: The Lessons of Experience"; "Thinking Like a Lawyer About Law School Assessment"; and "Theory, Practice and the Course of Study: The Problem of the Elephant." She has since published papers expanding on Carnegie's and her own approaches (Wegner 2009) and exploring suggestions to meet student concerns with current crises in legal education, suggesting a bifurcated bar examination, in which a Part I would follow the first year of law school and Part II graduation (Wegner 2010). I would have liked to have seen the Carnegie report consider a broader range of interdisciplinary works, particularly the leadership literature relevant to its task. It seems to me that, like the MacCrate report, though to a lesser extent, the Carnegie report left fallow fertile fields of interdisciplinary research that leadership educators had found fruitful.

It has fostered widespread discussion, mirroring the activity that followed release of the MacCrate report, but with more positive and less negative reaction. It has provided justification for innovation at various law schools, if not much of the kind of comprehensive curriculum reform it proposes. It notes that collective reforms over the years, such as clinical education and interdisciplinary study, have been incremental and additive rather than comprehensive in nature, creating pressures to do too much in too little time and ignoring the potential for synergy offered by the coalescence of theory and practice. Its greatest contribution may be its recommendation of more experiential learning, integrating within the curriculum three different professional apprenticeships: the intellectual or cognitive, the practical or skills-based, and the ethical-social within which one's professional identity is formed. Another recommendation consistent with that integration is to transition from the dominant summative evaluation of legal education to the more formative evaluations favored in leadership development. The report predicted that integration of the three apprenticeships would generate mutual positive transformations of each.

The Carnegie report acknowledges drawing liberally from *Best Practices for Legal Education* (Stuckey and Others 2007) in formulating its approach to integrating the three apprenticeships. *Best Practices* collects constructive responses to the MacCrate report from a network of dedicated law teachers from around the country. It argues for context-based legal education, the problem method, clinical experiences, and simulations tailored to allow students to learn doctrine and to practice professional skills in applying that doctrine. It is rich with examples of opportunities for formative evaluation using the problem method in simulated practice contexts, including the feedback the student gets from the work itself, a staple of leadership education. So what are the prospects for adoption of *Best Practices* and the kind of comprehensive change and synergy Carnegie advocates? The rational change formula, Change = (Dissatisfaction x Model x Process) > Resistance, is not encouraging. Despite turmoil in the profession, with the exception of some students[40] and a scattering of faculty members personified by the *Best Practices* authors, the respective law school colonies continue to be relatively satisfied with the status quo. Student dissatisfaction is more with job prospects and transparency than with the structure of educational programs. Though Carnegie proposes a model for comprehensive change, any process of integration to implement such a model would be hard work for uncertain benefits. In the absence of *U.S. News* deciding to assign law school ranking points for integration of the three apprenticeships,[41] prospects for meaningful change appear dim. Still, leadership theory, the Carnegie report, and *Best Practices* do provide

---

40 As a motivator, students' immediate need for law school success, measured by grades, trumps both their interest in leadership and their distant and contingent needs for interpersonal, business and other practice skills.

41 Since *U.S. News* ceased print publication its rankings have retained their influence in a virtual format.

visions of change. It might be time for a paradigm shift in legal education. Wild cards, what futurists call low probability–high impact events, make it hard to predict the future.

Why It Could Happen

An increased emphasis on leadership theory and practice can occur in two ways. The first follows the current paradigm: in the same way other disciplines and skills have become part of the curriculum, as another addition at the margins of legal education. The second would be part of a new paradigm: as an agent of change at the core of the curriculum, coalescing theory and practice and helping comprehensively integrate the cognitive, practical, and social-ethical apprenticeships. If the present turmoil in the profession proves merely cyclical, change will likely continue at the margins of the curriculum. If, on the other hand, the degree of turbulence represents a true and enduring crisis, more fundamental change is likely. The various colonies and their consumers will expect and even demand great change to resolve the crisis. Many of their members will invest time and energy to find new ways to solve underlying problems, and many more will be willing to accept change at the core of the curriculum as long as the crisis is resolved (Barker 1992: 204–6).

The futurist and leadership theorist Joel Barker says new paradigms emerge when existing paradigms stop solving new problems (Barker 1992: 42–54). We have experienced three different legal education paradigms in the last 120 years. The first was the Apprenticeship Paradigm. In 1890, three-fourths of all new lawyers came to the profession through the apprenticeship system and one-fourth through law school graduation; by 1910, 80% of all new lawyers were law school graduates (Swords and Walwer 1974: 32–3). The apprenticeship system solved neither the demands of a rapidly growing U.S. population nor the problem of what to do with apprentice–scriveners once the typewriter was invented (Swords and Walwer 1974: 32–3). The next paradigm lasted through the 1960s. I'll call it the Competence as Knowledge, or Knowledge Paradigm. Law schools considered it their job to convey knowledge and teach the knowledge-based technical skills of analysis and research, with new lawyers picking up other skills in practice, making modest wages accompanied by modest expectations of productivity in their early years. During the 1960s the Knowledge Paradigm stopped solving new problems in a country with a rapidly expanding economy and an undersupply of lawyers (Davis 1994). With an undersupply of lawyers and an oversupply of work, law firms had to pay associates more and needed them to become productive more quickly. Law schools began teaching skills to students who were eager to learn them, and the Knowledge Paradigm was replaced by what I'll call Competence as Knowledge Plus Skills, or the Knowledge Plus Skills Paradigm. Now, the Knowledge Plus Skills Paradigm, of four decades' duration, may no longer be solving new problems of talent development for a globalized profession in times of economic turmoil. Hinting at the need for a new paradigm, the Carnegie report, published before the beginning of the current recession, stated:

> ... skills training will continue to face an uphill battle unless it is linked with an accepted theory of lawyering that could provide a bridge between theory and practice and perhaps establish a rationale for a more systematic continuing education beyond law school. (Sullivan et al. 2007: 94)

and

> ... the goal of professional education cannot be analytical knowledge alone or, perhaps, even predominantly. Neither can it be analytical knowledge plus merely skillful performance. Rather, the goal has to be holistic: to advance students toward genuine expertise as practitioners who can enact the profession's highest levels of skill in the service of its defining purposes. (Sullivan et al. 2007: 160)

Assuming that the next emerging paradigm is holistic, it could be called the Competence as Integrated Knowledge, Skills, and Personal Attributes Paradigm. Leadership theory and practice may provide the key to moving beyond mere "analytical knowledge plus merely skillful performance" to that paradigm, but the role they play will depend upon the work of paradigm pioneers. Pilot and demonstration projects often lead to broader innovation, and several law schools are developing initiatives and courses integrating law and leadership. The University of Maryland, which has offered a course in leadership development for women since 2002, has created a Leadership, Ethics, and Democracy program ("LEAD") with the assistance of the Fetzer Institute. It has a research component and is developing additional leadership courses and materials.[42] Ohio State has a Program on Law and Leadership that features a Lawyers as Leaders course.[43] The University of St. Thomas in Minneapolis is home of the Holloran Center for Ethical Leadership in the Professions and offers three courses on ethical leadership in the School of Law.[44] Since its founding in 2006, Elon University School of Law has required first- and second-year leadership development courses focusing on leading oneself and leading teams, respectively, and students may elect a third-year capstone leadership experience.[45] Santa Clara also has a

---

42   University of Maryland Francis King Carey School of Law, LEAD Initiative, http://www.law.umaryland.edu/programs/initiatives/lead/.

43   Ohio State University Moritz College of Law, Program on Law and Leadership, http://moritzlaw.osu.edu/pll/initiatives/index.php.

44   University of St. Thomas, Holloran Center for Ethical Leadership, http://www.stthomas.edu/hollorancenter/.

45   Elon University School of Law, The Leadership Program, http://www.elon.edu/e-web/law/leadership/default.xhtml.

Leadership Initiative and has been offering a leadership course since 2005.[46] Its dean, Don Polden, teaches a second course for leaders of student organizations. He also hosts an annual Leadership Roundtable at which law school faculty and staff who are conducting research and developing leadership courses and programs, plus law firm professionals and general counsel who are working in the area of leadership education and development for lawyers, are invited to share their work and perspectives. Law schools that have attended and participated include Maryland, Ohio State, Santa Clara, Elon, Florida Coastal, Golden Gate, Stanford, Georgetown, and Hastings.

At Stanford, Deborah Rhode has produced a book, *Leadership: Law, Policy, & Management*, that should stimulate development of more law school leadership courses. Perhaps the most encouraging recognition of the centrality of leadership theory to law is found in the widely publicized redesign of Harvard's first-year curriculum, which includes a required winter term course in problem-solving, one of the seven MacCrate lawyering skills that is also a leadership skill.

These initiatives tend to extend the reach of the law schools into the rest of the university and its disciplines. They also lead to collaborations with other law schools. Maryland benefitted from the participation of Georgia Sorenson, founder and Distinguished Leadership Scholar at the James MacGregor Burns Academy of Leadership, previously housed at the University of Maryland School of Public Policy. Elon law faculty members have worked with leadership educators from the Center for Creative Leadership and Elon's School of Business and College of Arts and Sciences. Santa Clara has drawn on the expertise of Barry Posner, 12-year dean and professor of leadership at its Leavey School of Business and an internationally renowned leadership scholar and best-selling leadership author. Dean Polden and Dr. Sorenson are collaborating to develop a new journal on leadership education of relevance to law schools.

The courses being taught at these schools can be viewed as additive, at the margins of their curricula, as the Carnegie report described the skills apprenticeship generally. However, when one reads the schools' websites, one sees that the courses are parts of initiatives, and that the movement of the initiatives is holistic, joining law school and law practice. It will be interesting to see if that movement continues.

Another initiative that has the same aim and moves much further in the direction of a comprehensive, integrated curriculum, without consciously focusing on leadership, is Washington and Lee's.[47] In 2011 Washington and Lee began devoting its entire third year to reform. The fall semester begins with an intensive two-week litigation and ADR skills immersion, and the spring semester commences with a similar transactional skills immersion. With the exception of a

---

46   Santa Clara Law, Leadership Initiative, http://law.scu.edu/leadership/index.cfm.

47   Washington and Lee University School of Law, Washington and Lee's New Third Year Reform, http://law.wlu.edu/thirdyear/. I am grateful to Jim Moliterno for the time he took to discuss Washington and Lee's program with me.

full-year professionalism course, the students spend the rest of their third year in a client contact clinic, service learning, and a series of courses built around complex simulations that blend the cognitive and skills apprenticeships. Practicing lawyers are active participants in the simulations. In a typical course a student might learn bankruptcy law while engaged in a complex simulation that requires him to apply the law he learns, as he would in practice if given an assignment in a field he had not studied in law school.[48] Though Washington and Lee's conscious goal was to build a program of experiential learning for legal, and not leadership, competence, the relationship between law and leadership becomes apparent when one realizes that of the six development goals of the reform year, only writing would be considered a purely technical legal skill. Strategic thinking, project management, interpersonal skills, and values are all leadership as well as lawyering subjects. The means for achieving the final development goal of maturity are described as challenge, mentors, feedback, introspection, development and improvement, all elements of leadership development's spiral of experience. As the program matures, it might be informed by leadership theory and practice. Leadership theory and practice can surely be informed and transformed by the program.[49]

Conclusion: What Is Needed

The shift from the Knowledge Paradigm to the Knowledge Plus Skills Paradigm was never at the expense of knowledge, when efforts were made to integrate the two, as is happening at Washington and Lee. Neither will the shift to an Integrated Knowledge, Skills and Personal Attributes Paradigm, or law and leadership paradigm, be at the expense of knowledge or skill. In fact, the new paradigm's more holistic approach enhances knowledge and skill while improving self-awareness and professionalism. However, the new paradigm will require new skill sets within the faculty.

In 1964, when to many the Knowledge Paradigm seemed its strongest, but problems it could not solve were emerging, Walter Gellhorn wrote:

> Law professors are great individualists. Typically each one cultivates his own patch of academic ground to the best of his ability ... [T]he results have by no means been discreditable. But faculties that can plan a genuine team effort may be able to do something more momentous. They may succeed in giving the law school world nothing less than a new model of a legal education, if they can

---

48   It will be interesting to test the extent to which, as Dean Mudd suggested (Mudd and LaTrielle 1988: 26–7), applying the law in simulations will lead Washington and Lee students to improve their knowledge of substantive law.

49   Any reference to schools that integrate the three apprenticeships should not fail to mention Northeastern and its three-year program of structured externships, though, like Washington and Lee, it does not have an explicit leadership agenda.

agree upon the directions of main academic endeavors for the next few years. (Gellhorn 1964: 15)

That it took almost half a century since Gellhorn wrote before a faculty like Washington and Lee's would implement a model that incorporates features that had been extolled for almost a century is evidence of the difficulty of institutional reform. Gellhorn realized that the key to providing a model of a new legal education was a genuine team effort. A true team is not just a group organized to perform a task. It is a group of people who feel about their work and about each other, and who communicate, in special ways. That is what is so encouraging about the initiative at Maryland. All of the faculty and student colonies are represented and integrated in pursuit of its leadership initiative. What is needed to produce another model that might become a paradigm? A big wild card, a low probability–high impact event in the world of legal education that is most likely to occur in a time of crisis: a confluence of acts of leadership.

References

ABA Section of Legal Education and Admissions to the Bar. 1979. *Report and Recommendations of the Task Force on Lawyer Competency: The Role of the Law Schools*. Chicago: American Bar Association.

ABA Section of Legal Education and Admissions to the Bar. 1992. *Report of the Task Force on Law Schools and the Profession: Narrowing the Gap*. Chicago: American Bar Association.

Alderfer, C.P. 1969. An Empirical Test of a New Theory of Human Needs, *Organizational Behavior and Human Performance*, 4(2): 142–75.

Barker, J.A. 1992. *Paradigms: The Business of Discovering the Future*. New York: W. Morrow and Co.

Beer, M. 2007. *Leading Change*. Reprint No. 9-488-037. Boston: Harvard Business School Publishing Division.

Briggs Myers, I. 1980. *Gifts Differing*. Palo Alto, CA: Consulting Psychologists Press.

Campbell, D.P., Hyne, S.A. and Nilsen, D.L. 1992. *Manual for the Campbell Interest and Skill Survey*. Minneapolis, MN: NCS Pearson, Inc.

Davis, L. 1993. *Using the CDSs in the Legal Profession*, 5th Annual Conference, Campbell Development Surveys. Colorado Springs, CO.

Davis, L. 1994. Back to the Future: The Buyer's Market and the Need for Law Firm Leadership, Creativity and Innovation, *Campbell Law Review*, 16(2): 147–90.

Davis, L. 2008. Preceptors, Coaches and Mentors at Today's Law Schools: The Elon and St. Thomas Examples, *The Professional Lawyer*, 18(4): 27–8.

Davis, L. 2011. Building Legal Talent: Mentors, Coaches, Preceptors and Gurus in the Legal Profession, *The Professional Lawyer*, 20(4): 12–16.

Gardner, H. 1983. *Frames of Mind: The Theory of Multiple Intelligences*. New York: Basic Books.

Gardner, H. 1995. *Leading Minds: An Anatomy of Leadership*. New York: Basic Books.

Gellhorn, W. 1964. The Second and Third Years of Law Study, *Journal of Legal Education*, 17(1): 1–15.

Gladwell, M. 2008. *Outliers: The Story of Success*. New York: Little, Brown.

Grazioli, S., Johnson, P.E. and Jamal, K. 2006. *A Cognitive Approach to Fraud Detection*, SSRN [Online], 3 January. Available at: http://papers.ssrn.com/sol3/papers.cfm?abstract_id=920222 [accessed 31 January 2012].

Hollander, E.P. 1978. *Leadership Dynamics: A Practical Guide to Effective Relationships*. New York: Free Press.

Hughes, R., Ginnett, R. and Curphy, G. 2006. *Leadership: Enhancing the Lessons of Experience*, 6th edition. New York: McGraw-Hill.

Johnson, P.E., Johnson, M.G. and Little, R.K. 1984. Expertise in Trial Advocacy: Some Considerations for Inquiry into its Nature and Development, *Campbell Law Review*, 7(2): 119–43.

Johnson, P.E. and Pechtel, B.J. 1985. *Information Overload and the Expert Mind: Dealing with Complexity in Corporate Acquisitions*. Paper presented at the Annual Meeting of the Academy of Management.

Kolb, D.A. 1984. *Experiential Learning: Experience as the Source of Learning and Development*. Englewood Cliffs, New Jersey: Prentice-Hall, Inc.

Kolb, D.A. and Fry, R. 1975. Toward an Applied Theory of Experiential Learning, in *Theories of Group Processes*, edited by C.L. Cooper. New York: John Wiley & Sons, 33–58.

Llewellyn, K. 1930. *The Bramble Bush*. New York: Columbia.

Luft, J. 1969. *Of Human Interaction*. Palo Alto, CA: National Press.

Maslow, A. 1970. *Motivation and Personality*. 2nd edition. New York: Harper and Row.

Mintzberg, H. 1976. Planning on the Left Side and Managing on the Right, *Harvard Business Review*, July–August, 49.

Mudd, J.O. and LaTrielle, J.W. 1988. Professional Competence: A Study of New Lawyers, *Montana Law Review*, 49(1): 11–39.

Nelson, R.L. 2011. The Future(s) of Lawyering: Young Lawyers Assess the Value of Law School, presentation at the American Bar Foundation Fellows CLE Research Seminar, *What Defines Competence? A Debate on the Future(s) of Lawyering*, Atlanta, GA, 12 February.

Nyström, H. 1979. *Creativity and Innovation*. New York: John Wiley & Sons.

Rokeach, M. 1973. *The Nature of Human Values*. New York: Free Press.

Schein, E.H. 1978. *Career Dynamics*. Reading, MA: Addison-Wesley.

Stuckey, R.T. and Others. 2007. *Best Practices for Legal Education*. New York: Clinical Legal Education Association.

Sullivan, W.M., Colby, A., Wegner, J.W., Bond, L. and Shulman, L.S. 2007. *Educating Lawyers: Preparation for the Profession of Law*. San Francisco: Jossey-Bass.

Swords, P.D. and Walwer, F.K. 1974. *The Costs and Resources of Legal Education: A Study in the Management of Educational Resources*. New York: Columbia University Press.

Wegner, J.W. 2009. Reframing Legal Education's Wicked Problems, *Rutgers Law Review*, 61(4): 867–1009.

Wegner, J.W. 2010. Response: More Complicated Than We Think, *Journal of Legal Education*, 59(4): 623.

Whetten, D.A. and Cameron, K.S. 2005. *Developing Management Skills*, 5th edition. Upper Saddle River, NJ: Prentice Hall.

Appendix to Chapter 7

STAGES	SKILLS	
	TECHNICAL SKILLS	**INTERPERSONAL SKILLS**
STAGE I **ANALYST** **Acquisition of Foundation Skills and Knowledge**	Analysis of cases Interpretation of legislation Synthesis of cases and of cases and legislation Modes of argument Basic research Drafting legal memoranda	Oral expression Written communication

STAGE II
 	
ADVOCATE
 	
Development of Advocacy Skills and Knowledge
	Gathering facts from sources
	  other than people
	Marshalling facts
	Trial, administrative, and
	  appellate advocacy
	  Drafting pleadings, briefs, and
	    other advocacy documents
	  Discovery
	  Pretrial and motion practice
	  Administrative hearings
	  Jury and nonjury trials
	  Settlement of case on appeal
	  Preparation of record on appeal
	  Argument of appeal
	  Post-appeal practice
	Application of procedural
	  knowledge
		Gathering facts from individuals
		  and organizations
		Interviewing
		Counseling
		Negotiation
		Persuasive writing
		
		Dispute management and resolution
		  Avoidance
		  Coercion
		  Accommodation
		  Compromise
		  Mediation
		  Conciliation
		  Collaboration

STAGE III
COUNSELOR, PLANNER, AND IMPLEMENTER
Development of Ability to Formulate and Implement Sound Strategies in Complex Environments
	Systems analysis and design
	Planning and taking action
	  Collection and management of
	    information
	  Evaluation of situations
	    and environments
	  Formulation of goals and objectives
	  Analysis and allocation of resources
	  Development of situationally appropriate
	    strategies and tactics
	  Implementation of strategic and
	    tactical plans through creation and
	    utilization of effecting mechanisms
		Implementation of strategic and
		  tactical plans through leadership of
		  people and organizations
		  Involvement of appropriate
		    persons in decision making
		    and implementation
		  Delegation and subsequent monitoring
		  Establishment of credibility through
		    personal example and development
		    of organizational culture
		Management of law offices and
		  other organizations

STAGE IV **INTEGRATED PROFESSIONAL** **Synthesis and Self-Realization**	Synthesis of skills and knowledge of Stages I, II, and III with each other; with life experiences, talents, needs, values, attitudes, interests, cognitive and behavioral preferences and other aspects of personality; and with general knowledge fields beneficial to one's effective work in the legal profession, including Economics, History, Political Science, Literature, Accounting, Information Technology, Philosophy, Religion, Sociology, Psychology, Geography, Anthropology, Sciences, Statistics, Languages, Business, Leadership, Public Administration, the Fine Arts, etc.	

Figure 7.A1   A model of the legal professionalization process
Source: Copyright 1984, 1992, 1995, 2002, 2005, 2006, 2011 Leary Davis. All rights reserved.

CATALYTIC PERSONAL ATTRIBUTES	KNOWLEDGE	
	KNOWLEDGE OF LEGAL DOCTRINE	**INTERDISCIPLINARY KNOWLEDGE**
Talents, needs, values, attitudes, interests and other aspects of personality, the utilization of which may be appropriate in differing professional contexts to help transform knowledge and skill into competent representation, including but not limited to:	Substantive knowledge of doctrine, rationale and trends in basic theoretical or core fields Knowledge of legal procedure: civil, criminal and administrative	General knowledge needed to generate broad perspectives and to comprehend factual situations and legal doctrine in basic theoretical or core fields
	Knowledge of ideas about what law is and of ideas about the operation of law in society	
self-knowledge general intelligence energy situational awareness self-discipline self-efficacy growth mindset	Operative knowledge in functional fields which are subjects of particular cases and transactions	Knowledge in nonlegal fields and disciplines that are the subject of or relevant to particular cases and transactions; knowledge of clients' organizations, industries and environments and their cultures and of relevant situations
interpersonal intelligence integrity initiative tolerance for ambiguity and complexity optimism		
courage assertiveness persuasiveness self-reliance tenacity resilience achievement orientation	Testing and refining, in the contexts of study, practice, action, observation and reflection, ideas about what law is and about the operation of law in society	
dependability openness to new experiences intellectual humility friendliness empathy emotional maturity and stability	Operative knowledge in a large number of interrelated functional fields which may be relevant to the planning process	Knowledge in a large number of nonlegal fields and disciplines that may be relevant to the planning process in general and particularly to individual and organizational behavior and development, leadership, the implementation of plans, and the management of work and personnel; knowledge of clients' organizations, industries and environments and their cultures and of relevant situations
expanded by the lessons of experience, and strengthened by action, observation, reflection, discussion, practice and interaction	Testing and refining, in the contexts of study, practice, action, observation and reflection, ideas about what law is and about the operation of law in society	
Sound judgment	Integrated personal and professional lifestyles consistent with other Stage IV elements	
Professional responsibility	Natural, smooth, efficient, and situationally appropriate behavioral transitions	
Appropriate behavior in differing contexts	Development and continuous refinement of a philosophy of law and of the appropriate roles of law and the legal profession in present and future society	

Table 7.A1   Skills emphasized in Hughes et al., *Leadership: Enhancing the Lessons of Experience*, and their relevance to law practice, law firm management and leadership, and civic engagement

	Law practice	Firm leadership	Civic Engagement		Law practice	Firm leadership	Civic Engagement
Basic leadership skills				Advanced leadership skills			
Learning from experience	x	x	x	Delegating	x	x	x
Communication	x	x	x	Managing conflict	x	x	x
Listening	x	x	x	Negotiation	x	x	x
Assertiveness	x	x	x	Problem-solving	x	x	x
Providing constructive feedback	x	x	x	Improving creativity	x	x	x
Effective stress management	x	x		Team-building for work teams	x	x	x
Building technical competence	x	x		Building high-performance teams		x	
Building effective relationships: peers	x	x	x	Team-building at the top		x	
Setting goals	x	x	x	Development planning	x	x	
Punishment		x		Credibility	x	x	x
Conducting meetings	x	x	x	Coaching		x	x
Building effective relationships: superiors	x	x	x	Diagnosing performance problems in individuals, groups, and organizations	x	x	x
				Empowerment		x	x

Source: Skills emphasized in Hughes, R., Ginnett, R. and Curphy, G. 2006. *Leadership: Enhancing the Lessons of Experience*. 6th edition. New York: McGraw Hill.

Chapter 8

An Argument for Leadership Education in Law Schools

Diane Hoffmann[1]

Courage is the most important attribute of a lawyer. It is more important than competence or vision ... It can never be delimited, dated, or outworn, and it should pervade the heart, the halls of justice, and the chambers of the mind.[2]

Robert F. Kennedy, 1962

What are the essential characteristics of a good lawyer? This question is routinely debated in many law schools accompanied by questions about what we should teach law students in order to best prepare them for legal practice. Most agree that lawyers should be accomplished technicians, that is, experts in the law—or a specific area of law—as well as experts in legal analysis, how the legal system works, and how to accomplish change on behalf of their clients. For the most part, the skills of excellent legal technicians include the ability to analyze a problem and think about it from different perspectives as well as persuasive oral and written advocacy in a variety of forums.

But beyond technical proficiency, there is considerable debate about the additional "traits" of a good lawyer and what law schools can or should do to impart those traits. Among others, traits that have been put forth as essential to a successful lawyer include good judgment, integrity, empathy, detachment, courage, and creativity. Calls for legal education reform that will enhance law school teaching of these and related traits have been made for decades (ABA Section of Legal Education and Admissions to the Bar 1979, ABA Section of Legal Education and Admissions to the Bar 1992), but two recent reports examining the need for legal education reform have energized the debate (Stuckey and Others 2007, Sullivan et al. 2007, Virginia State Bar 2007). Moreover, changes in the practice of law, in the economy, and in how lawyers are perceived by the public due to scandals or questionable moral acts, have further fueled the conversation about what law schools should be teaching (Bennett 2010: 107–19, Fitts 2011: 1545–8, Thies 2010: 610–13).

1   I would like to thank Maura DeMouy for her thoughtful comments (both substantive and editorial) and drafting assistance on earlier versions of this chapter.
2   Speech delivered at the University of San Francisco School of Law. Quoted in Zitrin and Langford 1999: 1.

In the midst of these discussions and in response to the call for reform comes further controversy about whether law schools should train prospective lawyers to be leaders, and, if so, what that might entail (Polden 2008, Rothenberg 2009). Business schools and schools of public policy have included leadership studies for decades, and other professional schools such as schools of medicine and engineering are starting to include leadership courses in their curricula. Law schools have been slow, however, to accept the concept (Cullen 2008: 6–7).

Practicing lawyers—already convinced of the value of leadership training—have not waited for law schools to embrace leadership education. Many large firms have partnered with outside consultants or business schools to develop leadership training for their attorneys (Bradley 2010, Dizik 2009, Jones 2005). For example, Reed Smith is working with the University of Pennsylvania's Wharton School of Business's executive division to create a "Reed Smith University" that focuses on leadership and business development (Reed Smith 2004), and Nixon Peabody and DLA Piper have partnered with Harvard Business School's executive education program to train lawyers in leading the firm successfully (Dizik 2009, Knowles 2006).

An Exploration of the Potential for Leadership Education in Law Schools

In 2007, in the wake of these scholarly calls for educating lawyers in new ways and the rapid changes in law practice itself, the University of Maryland Francis King Carey School of Law partnered with the James MacGregor Burns Academy of Leadership (then housed at the University of Maryland School of Public Policy) and the Center for Law and Renewal, based at the Fetzer Institute, to explore whether there is a need for leadership education in law schools and, if so, how it might become part of the law school experience. The parties convened a Steering Committee, including representatives of each of the participating organizations.

One of the Steering Committee's first endeavors was to conduct a "Delphi"[3] survey on the topic. The survey queried over 50 national experts in the areas of leadership education and legal education as well as national leaders in the legal profession, including managing partners in law firms, judges, heads of advocacy organizations and government agencies (Brown and Allen 2009).[4] Sixty percent (31) of those sent a questionnaire responded.

---

3   A Delphi survey is a structured group survey process that is designed to include several rounds of opinion collection and feedback so that typically initial survey results are shared with all participants and the participants then comment on those results.

4   Allen et al. (n.d.) lists the survey questions and results. The responses to the survey were reported anonymously, although in some cases respondents self-identified based on their position—legal academic, dean, leadership expert, etc. In the published survey results, each respondent was identified by a letter.

After conducting the survey, on February 19, 2008, the school of law hosted a Roundtable on Law School Leadership Education.[5] Attendees at the Roundtable included leadership educators and scholars; current and former law school deans; legal practitioners; heads of law firms; and heads of advocacy organizations such as the Mississippi Center for Justice and the National Women's Law Center.[6]

The results of the Delphi survey suggested that strong support exists for teaching leadership in law schools. In the survey, respondents were asked whether they thought leadership education was an "appropriate" part of law school education. A significant majority of the 31 respondents (87%) said yes (Allen et al. n.d.: 4–8). Six percent said they were unsure and only 6% believed it was not appropriate (Allen et al. n.d.: 4–8).

One Delphi respondent asserted, "[L]eadership education is highly appropriate. I believe we are in something of a leadership crisis nationally. We need good leadership in law firms, civic organizations and in public service. Because lawyers are frequently involved in one or more of these areas, it is critical that we graduate lawyers with more leadership skills." Another commented that "[l]aw students are typically taught to determine whether something can be done—whether it is consistent with the law—rather than whether it should be done, which leaders must constantly do" (Allen et al. n.d.: 5).

Another respondent made a distinction between leadership training for institutional or community leaders who exercise leadership by virtue of their position, and leadership training for lawyers who will be called on to guide their clients in ethical decision-making every day. The latter, he argued, is much more essential for lawyers-to-be: "The profession requires every lawyer to fill a role as a moral leader in that lawyers are expected to fulfill certain ethical standards that are not expected necessarily of others in the community. As a 'gatekeeper' to the justice system, a lawyer necessarily imposes some degree of those ethical standards on his or her clients and, as such, provides a form of ethical 'leadership'" (Allen et al. n.d.: 4).

Another said leadership training was absolutely appropriate because "[l]awyers are leaders in society in both formal and informal ways and many students, while they may think they are leaders, do not practice good leadership" (Allen et al. n.d.: 4). A law school dean said "We encourage students to be individual leaders, i.e., stand up for their rights and live in accordance with their values ... We have found that law students are often 'not connected' to the legal profession in a way that makes it personal to them ... We believe that if they connect their own personal ethics and values to those that are required of lawyers, we will produce more ethical lawyers who lead by doing the right thing at all times" (Allen et al. n.d.: 4).

---

5   http://www.law.umaryland.edu/faculty/conferences/detail.html?conf=63.

6   http://www.law.umaryland.edu/faculty/conferences/conf63/roundtable_participants. pdf.

Although seemingly positive results, this enthusiasm for leadership education was largely expressed by a few law school deans and those external to the legal academy. Most of them were experienced leaders in the profession and could see the benefits of leadership training for lawyers.

Having been a law school associate dean for over a dozen years, I see the value of including leadership education in law schools, but am skeptical about law schools embracing the idea because of the academy's traditional resistance to such efforts. The deans and former deans at the Roundtable who had attempted to incorporate leadership education in their schools shared my perception that law school faculty are largely opposed to adding what they perceive as "soft skills" to the law school curriculum, especially when such courses might take away from the "hard" doctrinal courses they believe are most important for students to take, such as administrative law, criminal procedure, statutory interpretation, business and commercial law, employment, and tax law.

Given the somewhat hostile reaction of law schools to incorporate leadership training into law school course offerings or the law school experience more broadly, advocates of incorporating leadership training into law schools will have to make a persuasive case of the need for it. Proponents will further have to define what they mean by "leadership education," what it would include, and what kind of leaders we hope our law school graduates will become.

Making the Case for Leadership Education in Law Schools

To make the case for leadership education in law schools, advocates first need to determine what it is that most law school graduates do after they graduate. That information should guide what we teach them. For example, only a small minority of lawyers litigate. These lawyers represent one party in criminal or civil trials by presenting evidence and arguing in court to advocate for their client. Other attorneys act as advisors, "counseling their clients about their legal rights and obligations and suggesting particular courses of action in business and personal matters" (U.S. Bureau of Labor Statistics 2011). As advisors, attorneys attempt to ward off disputes by drafting contracts or arranging deals that will prevent future conflicts. Most try to help their clients accomplish certain goals by evaluating various options that the client may have and the legal risks associated with each. Some are deal-makers, negotiators, conflict-resolvers, and creative problem-solvers. Others become judges, elected officials, government administrators, regulators with government agencies, consultants, professors, and heads of law firms, local bar associations or other organizations. Some do more than one of these things; sometimes serially, sometimes concurrently.

No matter which of these types of practice a lawyer engages in, the common denominator is that lawyers are disproportionately in powerful and influential positions, helping their clients strategize and solve problems that will have real and lasting effects on their personal lives, businesses, communities and beyond.

In some cases, such power and influence comes from holding powerful positions, either elected or appointed, in others, from representing and advising powerful clients (Davis 2007: 524).

Indeed, lawyers hold a disproportionately high percentage of leadership positions in our government and a significant number of leadership positions in private business and nonprofit organizations (Hamilton 2009: 361–2). Lawyers in a position of authority such as elected officials or heads of organizations, programs or new initiatives are able to make positive changes in their institution, community, or society by persuading others to work with them to make those changes. Law schools can teach many leadership skills to someone who might become this kind of leader. These skills might include teamwork, effective public speaking and writing, strategic planning, negotiation, conflict resolution, decision theory, project management, and problem-solving.

A second kind of leadership to which many of us hope our students will aspire is broader and much more readily accessible than the kind of positional authority described above. It includes the day-to-day exercise of honesty, integrity, and the ability to put one's own needs and desires aside for the greater good of an institution or group of people. It is the leadership a lawyer exercises when he or she counsels or guides a client toward the resolution of a problem through persuasive influence (Hamilton 2009: 364). This influential leadership does not require the leader to hold a particular title or position. Influence leadership develops over time through demonstrated empathy, trustworthiness, good judgment, and competency. Its impact can be tremendous, however, when one considers the critical problems lawyers weigh in on every day.

Lawyers exercising this second type of leadership become role models for others in an institution or community. They might not be exercising transformative leadership, but in their everyday lives they make choices that take into consideration not only their own interest but also the broader interests of those around them— including people who don't have a voice or who can't effectively express their interests or needs. This type of leadership requires individuals who are clear about their own values and can articulate them thoughtfully and persuasively.

Both of these conceptions of leadership require individuals who understand the implications of various decisions for different parties or constituencies. Arguably, character traits of both types of leaders include a sense of justice and a practice of fair dealing as well as the moral courage to fight injustice.

Leadership Education Trains Lawyers for the Essence of Their Work: Advocates for Justice

If one thinks about fairness or a sense of justice as a necessary trait of both leaders and lawyers, it provides a persuasive argument for why some type of training in leadership would be helpful to law students. Instead of focusing on fairness and justice, however, law schools seem to focus more on training law students to advocate zealously for their clients. This is despite the apparent criticism of lawyers for the actions they take in the name of zealous client advocacy and despite the fact that the American Bar Association Model Rules of Professional Conduct and most state rules of professional responsibility no longer require zealous advocacy (Saunders 2011, Vilardo and Doyle 2011). Perhaps the criticism stems from the ways law schools and the legal profession train lawyers—with too much emphasis on obtaining the maximum for the client paying the bill and relatively little emphasis on whether a result is "just." Such an omission on the part of law schools is shortsighted.

Anthony Kronman, in his seminal book, *The Lost Lawyer*, reminds us that a skilled litigator is not only equipped to make zealous arguments on behalf of his client but also to package those arguments in the broader context of social justice. This is necessary, he asserts, because the lawyer advocate is often appearing before a judge and must "persuade the judge that his client's position is the legally correct one" (Kronman 1993: 149). To do this, he must put himself in the shoes of the judge who must ultimately be concerned with a just result. Kronman explains this dual role of lawyers as advocates *and* counselors as follows:

> An advocate who hopes to make persuasive arguments to judges must thus himself share, to some degree, the civic-minded concerns of the judges before whom he speaks. He must have a judicial temperament of his own. Plato says that an orator who speaks before public assemblies needs a democratic soul, one that shares the interests and ambitions of its audience. My point is that the soul of an advocate who argues before judges requires the ambitions of its audience too—the judicial ambition to preserve and perfect the community of law. (Kronman 1993: 150)[7]

Thus, the lawyer who makes his or her argument "appear to be the one more consistent with justice will triumph" and lawyers who know how to make "justice arguments" are more likely to be successful advocates (Davis 2007: 523). A lawyer should not assume that litigation is a zero sum game unless it really is. Leadership as a lawyer—even in litigation—means looking creatively for win-win solutions. Also, there are limits on what lawyers can and should do to win, not just the proscriptions of the ethics rules, narrowly construed, but also rules of decency. These include limits on processes that might technically not violate a rule but are unfair and undermine the principles of the adversary system, e.g., abusing processes against pro se litigants even though no rule makes that sanctionable.

But, what if a lawyer is not engaging in litigation? Even if the lawyer and his client are not planning to petition a court, a lawyer might be called on at any

---

7   Reprinted by permission of the publisher from *The Lost Lawyer: Failing Ideals of the Legal Profession* by Anthony T. Kronman, p. 150, Cambridge, MA: The Belknap Press of the Harvard University Press, Copyright © 1993 by the President and Fellows of Harvard College.

time to help resolve disputes or provide guidance involving justice. If a client is involved in a dispute, even when parties elect not to take their dispute to court, as a practical matter, they try to negotiate a resolution to the dispute by predicting what a court likely would decide. Similarly, in guiding clients on what action to take, such as how to structure an agreement or whether a proposed action is legal, the lawyer will try to predict what a court would do, which requires the successful advocate to make the best justice arguments she can in favor of the recommended course of action.

Even more important, however, our courts focus on just results because our society and the system of laws it has created want just results. Lawyers must appreciate the important role they play in enhancing or undermining just results and understand that they serve best when they concern themselves with resolving problems fairly, whether in court or out of court. In contrast to society's popular image of the zealous advocate, when possible, lawyers should consider how best to protect their client's *and* the opposing party's interests (Hamilton 2009: 365–8, Simon 1988).

In addition to being an essential trait of lawyering, fairness and justice are essential traits of effective leaders. Leadership scholars point out that the ability of leaders to motivate followers and align follower self-interest with the collective interest of the group or organization is tied to a foundation of trust between the leader and the follower and that "[t]he basis of such trust is the follower's perception that the leader is honest and operates with justice and fairness" (Chemers 2003). Moreover, people who view their leaders as fair "are motivated to give extra effort, make long-term commitments, and to be open to leader influence" (Chemers 2003). Influential leadership scholars have argued that "transformational leaders encourage followers to embrace moral values such as justice, equality, and the interests of the collective, suggesting that transformational leaders 'move followers to higher stages of moral development, by directing their attention to important principles and end values such as justice and equality'" (De Cremer et al. 2011).

If the justification for leadership education in American law schools can be rooted in a justice framework, then the argument that it is a necessary component of legal education may be more persuasive. Such a focus will not only be of benefit to law school graduates who go on to become heads of law firms, government agencies and departments, nonprofit organizations, advocacy groups or to become elected officials, judges, or government regulators, it will also benefit those who are in solo or small practices or associates in law firms. A justice focus arguably will lead to more principled and ethical decision-makers who will command respect from their peers and members of the broader community.

A focus on justice may also have other benefits. For example, it potentially will address some of the unhappiness of many lawyers in private practice, to the extent that such unhappiness stems from a lack of meaning or satisfaction in their work or a lack of clarity about their own values and moral compass. Law schools as currently designed often do little to help students systematically think through ethical dilemmas, identify competing ethical claims, or claims that lack ethical justification. This too may be due to legal education's focus on zealous advocacy and training lawyers to lay out all options to the client who then must decide on one. Under this model, we do not focus on lawyers themselves as decision-makers.

Moreover, a focus on justice for leadership education might also improve lawyers' public image to the extent that it also makes them think about broader justice issues in society. Lawyers are often criticized for being both greedy and self-interested. Disparaging jokes "comparing lawyers to slimy, venomous invertebrates" are common cocktail party fodder (Hogan n.d.). In her book, *In the Interests of Justice: Reforming the Legal Profession*, Stanford Law Professor Deborah Rhode provides some disturbing facts about the profession and its perception by the public:

- Three-fifths of Americans describe lawyers as greedy.
- Only one-fifth feel that lawyers could be described as "honest and ethical."
- Less than one-fifth described lawyers as "caring and compassionate."
- 90–95% of parents do not want their children to become lawyers.
- Two-thirds believe that attorneys are no longer "seekers of justice" (Rhode 2000: 3–4).[8]

A recent Google search of the combined terms "lawyers," "greed," and "self-interest" resulted in 1.63 million hits.[9] While many of the results were not directly on point, among them were several articles detailing the outrageous fees charged by lawyers who worked on the large tobacco settlements on behalf of states against cigarette manufacturers. In Florida, based on a 25% contingency fee, some of these lawyers were charging what amounted to $7,716 an hour. The hourly rate was based on the lawyers working 24 hours a day, 7 days per week for 42 months (Levy 1999). The fees were challenged in court, and the Florida judge hearing the case "denounced the state's 25 percent contingency contract, observing that the fee was $233 million per lawyer, which 'shocks the conscience of the Court'" (Levy 1999).

Not only are lawyers seen as charging outrageous fees, they are also not perceived to be serving those who cannot afford legal services. Unfortunately, this perception might have some basis. In her book, Rhode points out that although many lawyers provide many hours of pro bono legal services or discounted rates to indigent clients, most lawyers provide no services to the poor or for public interest causes. Instead, many lawyers focus exclusively on work that generates income, which itself might affect their decision-making. Law professor Lisa Lerman argues in her article *The Slippery Slope from Ambition to Greed to Dishonesty: Lawyers, Money, and Professional Integrity* (2002), that lawyer greed may lead to ethical lapses in judgment. "Many lawyers," she asserts, "are preoccupied with gaining power within their law firms and with expanding their own incomes …

---

8 Reprinted by permission of Oxford University Press, Inc.
9 Google search on May 29, 2012.

Preoccupation with money tends to have a corrosive effect on integrity." She provides persuasive documentation that lawyer dishonesty is on the rise and concludes that "[i]f many people in our profession have an incessant desire to generate more income, and if that desire leads many lawyers down a slippery slope of dishonesty, we have a problem. This phenomenon threatens serious harm to the ethical culture of our profession and to its reputation."[10]

Law is a privileged profession in which practitioners have significant opportunities to gain power and earn large incomes and acquire valuable assets. Yet, with such opportunities comes the potential for abuse of power and resources. Teaching law students, at a minimum, about the harms related to abuse of power through a lens of justice may improve lawyer standing among the general public.

In writing this chapter, I was influenced by an article titled *Why Not a Justice School? On the Role of Justice in Legal Education and the Construction of a Pedagogy of Justice* by Peter Davis (2007). Davis argues that

> law schools have drifted far from our proper concern, justice, into a deadened and uninspired pragmatism, the only concern of which is law ... cries of injustice and the consequent exploration of moral values are not the currency of the American law school ... our students never confront in any coherent way the great moral issues inherent in law and legal systems. As a result, law schools turn out graduates who practice, function, and even think within very narrow parameters. (Davis 2007: 516–17)

Other legal academics have echoed these concerns. Martha Minow, now Dean of Harvard Law School, wrote in a short piece on "Seeking Justice" that after her students had finished about a month of law school she would ask them "why none of them ever mentions the 'j' word." At first they didn't know what she was talking about, but even after she explained she meant justice, they didn't mention it. Her observation is that "[s]omehow, law school quickly gives the message that law is not about justice. Justice is for the sentimental, the immature, or, in any case, not for lawyers" (Davis 2007, citing Minow 1997).

Others have commented that law schools teach future lawyers to be moral relativists (D'Amato 1990), who "actually come to disdain right-versus-wrong thinking as unprofessional and naïve" (Davis 2007).[11] Leaders, in contrast, must frequently make moral decisions and take moral positions. Training lawyers to be leaders requires that they "be trained in the issues of justice and inequity facing our society; individual rights and the limits of governmental power, economic justice, issues of gender and race, criminal justice issues, and issues of international justice" (Davis 2007: 525). Davis cautions that he is not advocating

---

10 Reprinted with permission of the Hofstra Law Review Association.

11 Davis 2007, citing Nader and Smith 1996: 334, and quoting from a December 1993 interview with Robert Granfield, the author of *Making Elite Lawyers: Visions of Law at Harvard and Beyond* (1992).

that law schools teach what is just or unjust but rather that we teach a concern for justice, and provide students with "philosophical approaches that will help each student decide for herself what is just or unjust" (Davis 2007: 534).

Law schools could easily offer a course based on moral reasoning or theories of justice, but such concepts could also be incorporated into the required legal profession course or other traditional doctrinal courses. There are, in fact, a number of books for the law school market that could be foundational readings for such courses (Lesnick 1992, Luban 1988, Shaffer and Cochran 2009).

Law students should also be reminded that justice comes in a variety of forms: reciprocal, procedural, and distributive.

Law students are exposed regularly to disputes involving reciprocal or corrective justice, which addresses the rights and responsibilities of two parties to one another when one has wronged or harmed the other, for example, breached a contract, committed a tort or a criminal act. That reciprocal justice is only one frame for thinking about justice might not be obvious, however, to most students. Students need more exposure to procedural and distributive justice, the former dealing with the fairness and transparency by which decisions are made; the latter dealing with the fair allocation of benefits, risks, and burdens across multiple groups or constituencies.

Law schools pay some attention to procedural justice in the context of due process in constitutional and administrative law and civil and criminal procedure, but we pay less attention to alternative methods of dispute resolution and the fairness of alternative procedures. Law schools also do relatively little in terms of helping students think about issues of distributive justice. It's not that law schools totally ignore the role of the lawyer in the distributive context—we do train our students to zealously advocate for clients in the context of getting more of the pie or less of the burden or cost associated, most often, with a government program or regulation. However, we do not help our students think much about the kinds of issues that arise for judges, lawyers who are drafting regulations, representing communities or heading organizations. Lawyers in these positions must think deeply about issues of distributive fairness or justice.

In drafting regulations, for example, government attorneys must consider who will be benefitted and harmed by the regulations—will it be the poor, the rich, the well educated, men, women, minorities, small businesses, children, or the elderly? Lawyers representing communities often witness firsthand the consequences of distributive injustice and can be strong leaders in finding the best solutions. In heading organizations, lawyers similarly must think about the impact their decisions will have on various constituencies—the administrative staff, junior professionals or more senior staff, the most or least productive, the lowest paid versus the highest paid, etc. Leadership studies have long supported the concept that successful leaders must understand and consider both procedural and distributive justice, although there is some debate over which is more important (Hoyt et al. 2006).[12]

In addition to content-based curricular reform, law schools must think about using new pedagogy. Davis argues that law school offerings should go further than training in moral philosophy and justice theories; they should also teach students about the dynamics of the legal system and institutions, how to do empirical research assessing the fairness of the legal system, and how to examine "whether our current legal system actually delivers justice and, if not, why and how it might be improved" (Davis 2007: 542).

Davis also suggests an inductive method for teaching justice in law schools as a complement to the traditional case-based teaching method. Under an inductive pedagogy, students would not be given the law first, but rather a set of facts about a dispute. The students would have to write the rule of law that would decide the case. Ideally, that law would be informed by exposure to various theories of justice and approaches to the problem. Such approaches might include comparative law as well as insights from other disciplines, including history, sociology, and psychology.

Davis also confronts the criticism of faculty members who argue that they do not have time to incorporate such justice issues into their classes. His response is that the case-based method adopted by many law school faculty is inefficient and needs to change. By using the case method more sparingly, law professors will have much more time in their classes to devote to ethical and justice issues.

Can Law Schools Teach Moral Courage?

While viewing leadership training in law schools through a justice lens may help law school faculty more readily accept it as a necessary feature of legal education, they are likely to be less receptive to incorporating leadership training in law school that focuses on instilling in students the capacity for moral courage. This may be in large part based on skepticism that moral courage is something that can be taught. While I share that skepticism, I would argue that it is important to share with law students examples of lawyers who have exercised moral courage and why it is often a necessary precursor to achieving significant change.

---

12   Hoyt et al. cite Tyler and Lind, who argue that "more important than followers' specific outcomes are their perceptions of a leader's fairness." In particular, they found that procedural justice is "considerably more important than its counterpart, distributive justice. Leaders and authorities who make decisions fairly gain more voluntary compliance than leaders who simply distribute rewards fairly" (Hoyt et al. 2006: 115, citing Tyler and Lind 1992, reprinted from *Advances in Experimental Social Psychology*, 25(1), Tyler, T.R. and Lind, E.A. *A Relational Model of Authority in Groups*, 115–91, Copyright © 1992, with permission from Elsevier). See Tyler (2004) for more on the importance of procedural justice.

Courage is consistently mentioned as a necessary attribute of leaders, but it is also an important trait for lawyers. As Robert Kennedy said in the quote at the beginning of this chapter, courage is the most important trait of a lawyer. Kennedy made that comment in 1962 when he was Attorney General, at the dedication of Kendrick Hall at the University of San Francisco Law School. His speech was filled with examples of lawyers who demonstrated both physical and moral courage. He started with Andrew Hamilton in 1735, who though ailing and sick, made the long and exhausting trip from Philadelphia to New York to defend an indigent, immigrant printer named John Peter Zenger against charges of seditious libel made by the Governor of New York. He continued with others including Clarence Darrow, who according to Kennedy "gave up a profitable career as attorney for a powerful railroad to defend Socialist Eugene Debs and other officers of the American Railway Union against charges of criminal conspiracy evolving out of the union strike against the railroad for which Darrow was counsel." Kennedy also went on in his speech to express his disappointment at the lack of moral courage displayed by prominent lawyers in the state of Mississippi, who failed to speak out for compliance with federal court orders issued as a result of the Supreme Court's decision in *Brown v. Board of Education* (1954).

Courses can be offered that expose students to case studies of lawyers who have exhibited moral courage. While not a law school course, New York University's Graduate School of Public Service offers a course on Public Leadership and Moral Courage as part of the School's Moral Courage Project. In the project and the course

> "Moral courage" is considered from various perspectives: philosophical, political, literary and psychological. Questions include: What is moral courage? When does it become necessary to speak truth to power and thereby risk the disapproval of your community, your organizational culture, or entrenched interests in "the system"? In times of moral crisis, is there something beyond disapproval that good people fear by going against the grain? Who in our civic and religious traditions best embody moral courage? How did they benefit their communities and not just their individual consciences? (NYU Wagner School of Public Service n.d.)

The course also mentors students and encourages them to practice moral courage in their own lives. A similar course or project could be offered at schools of law, focusing on lawyers who have exercised moral courage.

Concluding Thoughts

In this chapter, I have tried to answer the question of why we need leadership training in law school in large part by answering the question of what we mean by leadership training, what the content of such training would be, and connecting that with the type of lawyer or leader our graduates will become. I make the argument that law school graduates are disproportionately in positions of authority and power, either in the private sector as leaders of institutions (law firms, corporations, nonprofit advocacy groups), or by virtue of serving, guiding, and advising powerful clients, or in the public sector as heads of agencies or as responsible for drafting, interpreting, or enforcing the law. In these positions, they not only are called upon to know what the law is and know the rules of professional responsibility, but they are often in a position where they must make decisions that fall outside the professional responsibility rules or that are outside of the law. They also may have the ability to influence how the law is made or applied. In all of these circumstances, we hope they will consider issues of fairness and have the moral courage necessary to address injustices they see in society, their communities, or workplaces. A conception of leadership training that incorporates decision-making about justice arguably fits clearly within the law school curriculum and may persuade skeptical law school faculty of the place of such training in law schools.

References

ABA Section of Legal Education and Admissions to the Bar. 1979. *Report and Recommendations of the Task Force on Lawyer Competency: The Role of Law Schools*. Chicago: American Bar Association.

ABA Section of Legal Education and Admissions to the Bar. 1992. *Legal Education and Professional Development—An Educational Curriculum: Report of the Task Force on Law Schools and the Profession: Narrowing the Gap*. Chicago: American Bar Association.

Allen, B., Brown, J., Hoffmann, D., Kennedy, T. and Roeper, M. n.d. *Delphi Questionnaire on Leadership Education for Law Students: Context and Responses* [Online]. Available at: http://www.law.umaryland.edu/faculty/conferences/conf63/survey_results.pdf [accessed 1 October 2012].

Bennett, S.C. 2010. When Will Law School Change? *Nebraska Law Review*, 89(1): 87–130.

Bradley, K. 2010. Leadership Development: Should Law Firms Invest in Growing its Leaders?, *Law Practice*, September/October.

Brown, J. and Allen, B. 2009. *Leadership Education in the Legal Academy: Principles, Practices and Possibilities* [Online]. Available at: http://www.law.umaryland.edu/programs/initiatives/lead/docs/LeadershipLawSchoolRpt.pdf [accessed 1 October 2012].

Brown v. Board of Education, 347 US 483 (1954).

Chemers, M.M. 2003. Leadership Effectiveness: Functional, Constructivist and Empirical Perspectives, in *Leadership and Power*, edited by D. van Knippenberg and M.A. Hogg. Thousand Oaks, CA: Sage, 5–17.

Cullen, R.W. 2008. *The Leading Lawyer: A Guide to Practicing Law and Leadership*. St. Paul: Thomson West.

D'Amato, A. 1990. Rethinking Legal Education, *Marquette Law Review*, 74(1): 1–56.

Davis, P.L. 2007. Why Not a Justice School? On the Role of Justice in Legal Education and the Construction of Pedagogy of Justice, *Hamline Law Review*, 30(3): 514–54.

De Cremer, D., Van Dick, R. and Murnighan, J.K. (eds). 2011. *Social Psychology and Organizations*. New York: Routledge.

Dizik, A. 2009. Law Firms Embrace Business 101, *Wall Street Journal* [Online], 20 May. Available at: http://online.wsj.com/article/SB124277243918636539.html [accessed 1 October 2012].

Fitts, M.A. 2011. What Will Our Future Look Like and How Will We Respond?, *Iowa Law Review*, 96(5): 1539–48.

Granfield, R. 1992. *Making Elite Lawyers: Visions of Law at Harvard and Beyond*. New York: Routledge.

Hamilton, N.W. 2009. Ethical Leadership in Professional Life, *University of St. Thomas Law Journal*, 6(2): 358–96.

Hogan, T. Editorial Review for Amazon.com of Zitrin and Langford, *The Moral Compass* [Online]. Available at http://www.amazon.com/Moral-Compass-American-Lawyer-ebook/dp/B005O1BYNC [accessed 8 June 2012].

Hoyt, C.L., Goethals, G.R. and Riggio, R.E. 2006. Leader–Follower Relations: Group Dynamics and the Role of Leadership, in *The Quest for a General Theory of Leadership*, edited by G.R. Goethals and G.L.J. Sorenson. Northampton, MA: Edward Elgar, 96–122.

Jones, L. 2005. Back to School for Partners, *National Law Journal*, 20 July.

Knowles, N. 2006. Nigel Knowles on DLA Piper Rudnick Gray Carey and Harvard Business School. *Adam Smith, Esq.* (blog) [Online], 24 June. Available at: http://www.adamsmithesq.com/2006/06/nigel_knowles_on_dla_pipe/ [accessed 9 September 2012].

Kronman, A. 1993. *The Lost Lawyer: Failing Ideals of the Legal Profession*. Cambridge, MA: Belknap.

Lerman, L.G. 2002. The Slippery Slope from Ambition to Greed to Dishonesty: Lawyers, Money, and Professional Integrity, *Hofstra Law Review*, 30(3): 879–922.

Lesnick, H. 1992. *Being a Lawyer: Individual Choice and Responsibility in the Practice of Law*. St. Paul: West Publishing.

Levy, R.A. 1999. The Great Tobacco Robbery: Lawyers Grab Billions, *Legal Times*, 1 February, 27.

Luban, D. 1988. *Lawyers and Justice: An Ethical Study*. Princeton: Princeton University Press.

Minow, M. 1997. Introduction: Seeking Justice, in *Outside the Law: Narratives on Justice in America*, edited by S.R. Shreve and P. Shreve. Boston: Beacon Press, 1–13.

Nader, R. and Smith, W.J. 1996. *No Contest: Corporate Lawyers and the Perversion of Justice in America*. New York: Random House.

NYU Wagner School of Public Service, Research Center for Leadership in Action. n.d. *Irshad Manji: The Moral Courage Project* [Online]. Available at: http://wagner.nyu.edu/leadership/our_work/moral_courage.php [accessed 9 September 2012].

Polden, D.J. 2008. Educating Law Students for Leadership Roles and Responsibilities, *University of Toledo Law Review*, 39(2): 353–60.

Reed Smith. 2004. *News Release: Innovative Partnership with Wharton School* [Online], 11 August. Available at: http://m.reedsmith.com/innovative-partnership-with-wharton-schoolbrreed-smith-university-launches-this-fall-with-emphasis-on-leadership-development-08-11-2004/ [accessed 9 September 2012].

Rhode, D.L. 2000. *In the Interests of Justice: Reforming the Legal Profession*. New York: Oxford University Press.

Rothenberg, K.H. 2009. Recalibrating the Moral Compass: Expanding "Thinking Like a Lawyer" to "Thinking Like a Leader," *University of Toledo Law Review*, 40(2): 411–20.

Saunders, P.C. 2011. Whatever Happened to "Zealous Advocacy"? *The New York Law Journal* [Online], 245(47) 11 March. Available at: http://www.newyorklawjournal.com/PubArticleNY.jsp?id=1202485578500&slreturn=1 [subscription required] [accessed 9 September 2012].

Shaffer, T.L. and Cochran, R.F. Jr. 2009. *Lawyers, Clients, and Moral Responsibility*, 2nd edition. St. Paul: West Publishing.

Simon, W.H. 1988. Ethical Discretion in Lawyering, *Harvard Law Review*, 101(6): 1083–145.

Stuckey, R.L. and Others. 2007. *Best Practices for Legal Education: A Vision and a Road Map*. Columbia, SC: Clinical Legal Education Association.

Sullivan, W.M., Colby, A., Wegner, J.W., Bond, L. and Shulman, L.S. 2007. *Educating Lawyers: Preparation for the Profession of Law*. San Francisco: John Wiley & Sons.

Thies, D. 2010. Rethinking Legal Education in Hard Times: The Recession, Practical Legal Education, and the New Job Market, *Journal of Legal Education*, 59(4): 598–622.

Tyler, T.R. 2004. Procedural Justice, in *The Blackwell Companion to Law and Society*, edited by A. Sarat. Malden, MA: Blackwell, 435–52.

Tyler, T.R. and Lind, E.A. 1992. A Relational Model of Authority in Groups, *Advances in Experimental Social Psychology*, 25(1): 115–91.

U.S. Bureau of Labor Statistics. 2011. Lawyers, *Occupational Handbook, 2010–2011 Edition*. Washington, D.C.: Government Printing Office [Online]. Available at: http://www.bls.gov/oco/pdf/ocos053.pdf [accessed 30 January 2012].

Vilardo, L.J. and Doyle, V.E. III. 2011. Where Did the Zeal Go? *Litigation* [Online], 38(1). Available at: http://www.americanbar.org/publications/litigation_journal/2011_12/fall/where_did_zeal_go.html [accessed 9 September 2012].

Virginia State Bar. 2007. *News Release: Globalization, Diversity are Conclave Themes*. [Online]. Available at: http://www.vsb.org/site/news/item/globalization-diversity-are-conclave-themes/ [accessed 9 September 2012].

Zitrin, R. and Langford, C.M. 1999. *The Moral Compass of the American Lawyer: Truth, Justice, Power, and Greed.* New York: Ballantine.

Chapter 9
Thinking Like a Lawyer versus Thinking Like a Leader[1]

Michael Kelly

I argue in this chapter that this preposterously abstract subject has useful practical implications. Even if I fail to convince my audience, I hope at least to make progress by offending and riling them up, and thereby stimulating people to think like good readers.

My larger purpose is to contribute constructively to understanding and answering a question of some consequence: should the educational mission of a law school encompass the subject of leadership? The premise of this chapter is that advocates for enlarging the function of legal education to include leadership[2] need first to consider what might be described (my title says it more simply) as the relative cognitive dimensions of law and of leadership. I want to explore whether law and leadership fit together or promise to connect well as a coherent learning experience. Before reaching the main question about amplification of the role of legal education, we need to address questions of whether there are distinctive ways of thinking about problems and decisions that are emblematic of lawyers and of leaders. If lawyers and leaders take characteristically different approaches to addressing fundamental issues in their work, the "versus" of my title signals further questions like: How much of a difference is there? Are the two in opposition? Are there some similarities between the two that may shed insights into the respective roles of lawyer and leader? Is the relationship, if any, between lawyering and leadership fruitful enough to be worth exploring in more depth than I propose to do here?

After exploring these questions, I briefly take up the issue of whether there are characteristics of lawyers and law students—the people for whom leadership training might be designed to benefit—that ought to be taken into account in answering the question of teaching leadership in law school. Then, I speculate on whether law faculty, the people in charge of curriculum change at most schools, are likely to consider leadership a discipline that should play a significant role in the legal academy (other than as an unobjectionable trinket in the upper class

---

1 This chapter is a substantial expansion of a talk delivered on February 19, 2008, at the Roundtable on Law School Leadership Education at the University of Maryland School of Law. Michael Kelly © 2010.

2 See, for example, Heineman (2007), Rhode and Packel (2011).

curriculum). Finally, I state my case for a particular approach to teaching leadership in American law schools.

We should begin by acknowledging and addressing a major complication that deeply affects our topic. The whole idea of thinking has been revolutionized during the last few decades by the cadre of cognitive psychologists who have begun mapping out new territory, new concepts of thinking about thinking. As one analyst sums it up, "There is an immense gulf between the way we think and the way we think we think" (Hanson and Yosifon 2004: 37). As for the way we actually think, cognitive scientists describe a fundamental feature of what goes on in our minds as an innate capacity to use shortcuts to simplify and make parsimonious the work of the mind. The easiest way to grasp this insight may be to imagine the power of stereotypes. Our minds are organized to assemble an immediately plausible mental package, a kind of syntax of the situation or a familiar short story that connects and condenses perceptions and insights and predictions drawn from our actual or virtual experiences. As best the brain scientists can describe it, these connections or stories are structured densely and are directly accessible. They are incomparably useful mental facilities, invaluable to anyone who wants to get anything done.

Daniel Kahneman, one of the premier cognitive scientists of our era, describes all of this as "fast" thinking (Kahneman 2011).[3] Memory storage sites in the mind condense a "read" of a situation, a grasp of relevant associations and experiences, the people and the situation and learned or inherent "takes" that are easily reached, quickly intelligible and thus utterly indispensable. These are the proverbial "gut instincts" that are formidable and often unconscious resources of the human mind, always at the ready with an opinion, an emotional reaction, and a prediction regardless of the quality of evidence on which it is based. Naturally, there is risk of getting things wrong, of mistaken, irrational thinking. (Recall our initial description of these mental sites: fast thinking encompasses valid as well as unfounded stereotypes—even pernicious stereotypes.) This conception of our mind at work is at once the glory and the bane of humans, and academic psychologists have assembled a long list of the inherent pitfalls of human thinking that arise from fast thinking. If there is one theme of the huge array of snags or potential drawbacks of human cognition scientists have assembled over the last several decades, it is how vulnerable humans are to the demands of a decision- or estimate-making situation. Our fast thinking instincts that surface immediate reactions can lead us astray by drawing too heavily, for example, on recent experience or vivid and emotional memory (availability bias), first impressions (anchoring[4]), what we believe friends or associates or others are thinking or doing

---

3   Academics label the cerebral capacity for fast thinking with various terms of reification such as packets, schema or scripts. Kahneman's primary label for fast thinking is "System I," something that he repeatedly describes as a "fictional" creation representing this particular facility of the brain. He labels slow thinking as "System II."

4   Anchoring is also a feature of "slow" thinking (Kahneman 2011: 120).

(conformity, an enormously powerful force), eagerness to decide (closure bias), what people either want to have happen or expect to happen (confirmation bias), and a host of other common distortions built into human thinking. Thinking—in the bias-plagued world described by cognitive scientists—sometimes seems akin to walking along an ill-lit, poorly maintained path, negotiating roots, rocks, ruts and potholes, many of which we cannot even see.

It is here that "the way we think we think" can and does perform an important function, enabling a walker on a tricky path to move forward and minimize or avoid obstacles. Let us characterize the way we think we think as the engaged mind, concentrating, reasoning, working and assembling facts and drawing on memory and knowledge, developing preferences and then informing a conclusion or making a decision. Cognitive scientists acknowledge that we do sometimes, sometimes even often, think this way. Daniel Kahneman calls this "slow" thinking, but perhaps a better term for it is "hard" thinking because we tend to avoid it and are lazy about using it when fast thinking is always available with an instant conclusion and estimation. In fact, reluctance to engage and work the mind in a slow/hard thinking mode often means that fast thinking significantly influences, impacts, or distorts our slow thinking. While it may be naïve to assume we typically engage in hard thinking, it remains, nevertheless, our great resource for understanding and making headway through some of the potential pitfalls of the path offered by fast thinking.

"Thinking like" a leader or a lawyer or a person in almost any role or position that requires skill in an activity framed with goals and conventions or rules, e.g., a shortstop, is inevitably dominated by fast thinking, informed and enriched by learned experience in the role. Expertise is, in important respects, hard or slow thinking that matures through experience into fast thinking. One key feature of the condensed story lines of fast thinking described above that makes them so useful is that they are immediately accessible, instantly at hand. People typically (but not always) come to think so fast that it can seem inseparable from action. Donald Schön calls it "thought in action" (Schön 1988, quoted in Groopman 2007: 35). As Jerome Groopman describes it in relation to the decision-making of physicians, it is not evident that any reasoning is being used at all when a doctor makes a diagnosis because it all happens too fast for the actor to describe. "An immediacy of perception" occurs through the experience of practice, pattern recognition, and mental resources. Fast thinking connects immediate decisions and longer-term objectives, almost unconsciously combining a series of perceptions and projected implications. Hypotheses surface immediately about how best to approach solution of a problem, typically first presented in terms of incomplete information. Sorting this out—as more information and pattern recognition comes into play to arrive at a relatively firmer set of hypotheses for action—occurs almost instantly, an amalgam of thought and action, "fast and frugal," the core of flesh-and-blood decision-making (Groopman 2007: 34–5).[5] By and large it is this kind of action or fast thinking—action that is almost a subspecies of thinking—that we will be examining in looking at leaders and lawyers.

The good news about these insights about thinking is that they represent something of a needed antidote to a phenomenon called the "fundamental attribution error," a term that psychologists use to describe the (admittedly typically American) penchant to ascribe and explain most group or organizational behavior and results in terms of the personal skills, characteristics, dispositions, and actions of individual leaders. The errors identified with focusing on the individual leader include the short shrift given to the absolutely crucial importance of the group being led, ignoring external (to the group) factors such as luck, and failure to take into account reactive, derivative fast thinking shaped by the situation of the group or organization, including erroneous biases in decision-making. The bad news is that many brain scientists and their followers go much too far (in my opinion) to overstate what they call the fundamental "situationalist" structure of thinking. Instead of focusing on the crucial importance of analysis of the perils and opportunities of particular circumstances, groups, or organizations, they seem to deny altogether the possibility of corrective slow or hard thinking and the personal coherence, character and integrity of an actor. This overreaching tends to ignore the counter-factual examples of the legions of people (including leaders and lawyers) who address and transcend their mental biases and situational challenges to make a positive difference in the lives of their customers, followers, or clients.[6]

Thinking Like a Lawyer

Although it represents but a thimbleful compared to the ocean of material on leadership, a fair amount of ink has been spilt on the matter of thinking like a lawyer. It might be useful to begin with some skepticism about the term. Lon Fuller, a brilliant law teacher and legal philosopher, called it an "innocent and tautological assertion" devoid of insight that should not be taken too seriously. Fuller, however, went on to try to rehabilitate the idea by suggesting a replacement

---

5   For a good review of the enormous literature drawn from cognitive science on this topic, see Blasi (1995). Chen and Hanson (2004) contains a review of the relevant scientific literature (as applied to law and legal theory, not explicitly to lawyers' practical thinking/action for clients).

6   Despite occasional acknowledgement of the possibility of an individual engaging in "de-biasing" (Chen and Hanson 2004: 1228–35), the trajectory of the "situationalist" argument appears to be deeply skeptical of the possibility of law (described as an illusion 1244–5) and of the coherence or integrity of the human person. This chapter is written from a moderate or weak situationalist perspective, believing as I do in the coherence of the human person and that the crucial attribute of a leader or lawyer is the capacity for situational analytical thinking.

synonym, "intellectual discipline," on condition that the term does not imply fixed procedures or routine methods of attacking problems and is something that "grows from within"—not a constraint, but a form of freedom and insight offering "release from the routines of thought and habits of prejudgment" that keeps people from "really thinking" (Fuller 1950: 37–8). If we were to frame Fuller's skepticism about "thinking like a lawyer" anachronistically in a modern cognitive science framework developed decades after his death, he seems to be calling for aggressive slow/hard thinking efforts to understand and, if appropriate, carefully use, constrain or even purge fast thinking, the built-into-our-mind stereotypes and biases that are so characteristic of the way we think.

Keeping in mind Fuller's caveat, it may be helpful to identify a crude distinction between two major capabilities lawyers deploy when they think and work:

- an analytic capacity or skill typically called "legal reasoning" related to developing an understanding of what the law is, and
- "problem-solving" related to a more situational (and common) role of the lawyer representing, advising and helping a client pursue a course of action.

Both are deeply jurisprudential (i.e. deeply related to lawmaking). The first is focused almost entirely on interpreting lawmaking generated by crucial authorities like courts, legislatures and regulatory entities. The second represents a vastly larger and more pervasive form of lawmaking (in the aggregate), namely advice from lawyers to clients about norms of conduct they should observe and courses of action they can or should take, and specific activities by the lawyer to support the client's decisions.

Both of these kinds of thinking, depending on the situation, may call upon fast and/or slow thinking. Law school pedagogy is heavily oriented to inculcating slow thinking skills in their students, largely in the realm of legal reasoning.[7] Despite a significant presence of clinical programs in the curricula of many schools and so-called "skills" courses, relatively little law school pedagogy focuses on client problem-solving or the development of pedagogy focused on the inculcation of slow thinking skills to prepare students for more disciplined forms of fast thinking expertise in solving client problems. In fact, the mark of a highly skilled lawyer may be her ability to recognize anomalies in what she is getting from understanding the law, or hearing from the client, or coming to terms with the facts of a situation. Anomalies become a trigger to deploy slow thinking—to recognize when she needs to probe deeper and more critically, literally slow down and enrich her fast thinking instincts.

Legal reasoning and problem-solving are distinct but closely related. The client learns the law through the problem-solving of the lawyer, who deploys her legal reasoning (obtained fast from memory or slow by study and analysis) to establish

---

7   For a discussion of the complexity and implications of how the teaching of legal reasoning actually operates in American law schools, see Mertz (2007).

the legal framework for consideration of the client's conduct or future action. Law, whether legislation, regulation or court decisions, is in turn affected directly (e.g. lobbying and litigation) and indirectly (by public opinion) through individuals and entities often informed by problem-solving advice from a lawyer.

The typical distinction made between "thinking like a lawyer" and lawyer "skills," a term rampant in the world of law and legal education, is utterly baseless. What are commonly called skills are forms of problem-solving that predominantly entail (in an experienced lawyer) fast thinking, thinking-in-action—e.g. interviewing, negotiating, cross-examination, assembling and framing facts, short and long forms of persuasive writing or drafting, arguing before a judge or regulatory decision-maker or adversary, persuading a client of a strategy or course of action. The quality of these and countless other forms of "skills" deployed by experienced lawyers are typically fast thinking addressing the relevance, relationship and fusion of several categories of information: interpreting the law, the facts or reality of the situation, the client's needs and purposes, and the larger context of the industry or field in which the client operates or finds herself. Such work can range widely in quality from the lousy to the superb. But skills in the practice of law are a fundamental species of thinking like a lawyer.

Legal reasoning is, of course, also a fundamental skill essential to practicing law. It is predominantly a skill of slow thinking that can be learned and practiced— unlike other practice skills—oblivious of context. It is what a lawyer first learns to do in law school, and appellate courts do in reviewing a predetermined record or set of facts and law established by a lower court. One should avoid the temptation to label this a form of deductive reasoning (law applied to facts = result) but rather acknowledge a certain deductive trajectory to legal reasoning. Edward Levi's *Introduction to Legal Reasoning* (1949) argues that the concept that the law is a system of known rules to be applied by a judge or advising lawyer is only a pretense. The reality—informed by the reality of the interests and situation of a client—is closer to indeterminacy of facts as well as applicable law drawn from court decisions and unclear language of legislation and constitutional provisions related to unanticipated situations. Much of contract or deal-making, particularly the common forms that suffuse our everyday activities, is an effort to throttle uncertainty and create facts and rules that can simply be applied—to convert indeterminacy and the affectation that it isn't there into something approaching hard, sharp-edged rules that lend themselves to something more like simple deduction from rule to facts to result.

Problem-solving, on the other hand, can be more clearly identified as a species of inductive reasoning because it entails a wider angle perspective of understanding the client's needs, goals, situation and potential moves to resolve a problem or achieve a goal. The lawyer reads, interprets, and shapes facts in connection with reasoning about the law—all seen or conceived in the context of the client's intentions or interests.

The lawyer marries the legal reasoning thinking skill with problem-solving thinking by creating or characterizing the facts to corral the indeterminacy of the law through arguments and thinking strategies—deploying analogies, principles, policies, rules—to predict what the law is and advise a client how best to proceed within the boundaries of possibilities that the lawyer represents as the law for the situation. Problem-solving is suffused with thought-in-action performance: convincing the client of a suitable strategy for the situation, persuading or challenging adversaries, drafting documents, arguing on behalf of a client before (and adapting to projections of decisions from) a wide variety of law-authoritative forums.

Thinking Like a Leader

People who practice law are rather clearly defined by dint of their special education and (at least in this country) certification or license and focus of work that entitles them to hold themselves out as a lawyer. No such clarity applies to leaders. Although we tend to reference authorized heads of corporate, nonprofit, or governmental organizations as "leaders," anyone can function as a leader regardless of their education, their field of endeavor, formal authority, or even their title or place within an organization or an informal group. We need to be wary of comparing an extremely fluid and malleable activity like leadership with a relatively more circumscribed or defined practice like acting as a lawyer.

The literal meaning or etymology of "leader," an Anglo-Saxon word, is the person who finds the path (and, of course, draws or enables others to follow the path). So the term leader, as it is commonly used today, is itself a metaphor. And if we extend the metaphor from the person doing it to the activity of "leading" or "leadership," we enlarge the framework of the metaphor beyond the individual pathfinder and focus on closely related details and questions that form the context, the immediate frame for slow or fast and frugal flesh-and-blood decision-making:

> What's the terrain of the path? What is the field or activity that requires path-finding? To what extent is competition involved and, if so, how does it affect the enterprise and pressures of path selection?

> A path for whom or what? Individuals? A group, organization, or state? What are the capacities and inclinations of the potential followers to take the path? Do they care whether they need to move? Are they in good shape? What do they think of the leader?

> What kind of path? Path of least resistance? Path well-trodden? Path with what immediate and near-term obstacles? Path headed in what direction?

What's the destination and why? Are there critical interim stages? And would failure to reach these points significantly diminish the resources and ability to proceed?

Leadership is always contextual in terms of the particular landscape being traversed, the difficulties of the path chosen, the goal as well as the hiking capacities, expectations, and willingness of people to follow. The intellectual core of leadership entails analysis and understanding of the group or organization being led, its aptitude, its weaknesses, its short- and long-term needs, its chances of responding to interventions to move it, and discernment of an appropriate direction or destination in light of the challenges the group faces. One of the reasons to be skeptical of identifying a particular set of skills or qualities or styles of leadership germane to leaders is that leadership is an enterprise fundamentally determined by context—by discerning and answering the path-related questions listed above. The questions can be addressed through slow thinking, involving multiple frames of understanding, or answered by fast thinking stereotypes, either of which can lead to strong performance as a leader. The peculiar alchemy of successful leadership is the ability to transform the analysis of these questions into a communal force that incorporates the distributed knowledge, motivations, and trust of its individual members.

Like politics, all leadership is local (i.e. often best understood in terms of a particular constituency being led). It applies to an almost unimaginable array of different groups, subunits or organizations (where there may be scores of distributed leaders), fields or markets, histories and challenges and goals or understandings of the meaning of success. Skills and character traits and techniques of leading are only relevant to the extent they directly serve efforts of a particular individual to move a particular group (or organization or nation) along a particular path. Without an implicit analytical framework of thinking about the group or entity and figuring out where and how to move it, skills and character traits can turn out to be merely the pretense of leadership.[8]

The work of leadership, of course, extends well beyond analysis because leadership is basically performance, or a variety of different performances, constituting the kind of thinking-in-action we've been discussing. The leader's first challenge is to take into account the character of the group she is leading, assess how to enlist and marshal allies and followers, and use her judgment about how best to discern the right direction for her group or organization. In important respects, the group makes, or is a primary element in the formation of, a leader.

---

8 Selznick (1957) and Heifetz (1994) are, as best as I can identify, the primary sources or inspiration for this brief, highly metaphorical account of leadership thinking. Like virtually all the literature on leadership, mine is an effort to generalize about a subject so inherently particularized to context, situation and immediate challenge that it tends to resist coherent analysis.

It enables the leader to devise an understanding of the environment[9] in which her group operates, as well as a sense of the opportunities and strategies the group or entity can muster to succeed in that environment. The leader's second great challenge is to act on these analyses, assessments, and judgments and to perform by evincing understanding, dedication, and determination that persuades others and gains their trust and support, or by challenging or negotiating with adversaries or rivals. As we pointed out earlier in introducing the subject of thinking, analysis and action are often telescoped into what is virtually a single move, informed by structures of thinking that coalesce a wide range of vicarious and personal experiences into readily accessible packages that underwrite action. The third great challenge is to adapt performance to thinking, thinking to performance, and alter both as circumstances change and new thinking and performances become necessary as the leader and followers proceed along a path (Schön 1983).

Similarities

Framing Reality

One of my favorite truisms from the leadership literature is Max DePree's "The first responsibility of a leader is to define reality" (DePree 1989: 1). Another way to express this is the lawyer/judge Jerome Frank's allusion to the pain and anguish of giving birth to the facts—of creating a story that is plausible, operational and does justice to essential specifics. Lon Fuller also underscores how crucial surfacing and understanding and communicating facts—realities—is to a lawyer: "One of the most perilous of human operations is attempting to transmit intact a set of facts from one human head to another" (Fuller 1948: 194). One could say that framing reality—describing the facts—is the first responsibility of a lawyer as well as a leader. Discerning reality for a group or a client is a creative endeavor, an intellectual and moral challenge not unlike that facing a writer of nonfiction seeking to construct a coherent and engaging account of the circumstances facing an individual or institution. The lawyer and the leader must master the art of nonfiction. One of the characteristics of fast thinking is that it always comes with a storyline, including projected causes and consequences. Fast thinking is a resource for people who need to construct reality for followers and clients and adversaries who, as fast thinkers themselves, have an insatiable appetite for stories. Since reality is a story to be conveyed, the shape and relevance of the story comes, in effect, from astute choice by both lawyer and leader of the problems or challenges to be confronted and their sequencing within the plot of the story. These critical, all-too-changeable, choices entail operating within the critical constraints

---

9   A good grasp of the field or industry or larger institutional context in which the group or organization operates is a particularly important strategy for understanding any group or organization. See DiMaggio and Powell (1991).

of various kinds of slow thinking, e.g., a commitment to accurate information, including statistics, appreciation of the complexities and nuances of context (of the person, industry, or group including threats, opportunities and alternative ways of moving ahead), and a sense of the expectations of readers, clients, employees and a larger audience, particularly their ear for detecting a phony story.

Agency

Clients hire lawyers to be a special kind of leader, an expert pathfinder guiding individuals and organizations in the terrain of the law. Lawyers and certain types of leaders operate within the formal constraints of the law of agency. The lawyer acts as the agent of the client—on behalf of the client. Agency is in some sense the answer to the questions: To whom do I owe my allegiance? To whom am I accountable? Leaders in some organizations are also in many respects formal agents and must act on behalf of or be the agent of an authoritative segment of the organization like a partnership or board of directors, department or subsidiary or stockholders of a corporation. The idea of agency, in effect, creates a crucial frame of understanding, whether in fast or slow mode of thinking. For the lawyer, it has important consequences for establishing the confines of the client relationship, its attendant obligations and the focus on problems being addressed. And even within the borders of agency, contradictions or confusions about the leadership role of the lawyer as agent have spawned a rich literature on the complexities of the lawyer–client relationship, primarily driven by how both lawyer and client work out an understanding of the lawyer's role in representation (technician or commodity producer? counselor? collaborator? hired gun? diplomat? etc.).[10] A different, but no less powerful, set of contradictions adheres to the role of leaders like a CEO, executive director, or managing partner who are treated as agents under by-laws or partnership agreements or norms of corporate law—or act under a leader's own sense of her accountability priorities. A formal or informal agency frame can markedly affect the actions of management and its relationships with particular stakeholders, ranging from stockholders, to partners, suppliers, employees, regulators, alumni, fans, customers, etc.

---

10   See, for example, a compendium and review of some of the vast literature on the lawyer–client relationship in Condlin (2003). See also Sarat and Felstiner (1995: 142), alluding to the opposition between assumptions of agency and assumptions of lawyer "professionalism," with the result that "… lawyer–client relations are sites of conflict and negotiation in which the conditions of power change from moment to moment and in which both parties are as calculating and strategic in their relations with each other as they are in their dealings with their formal adversaries." Kritzer (1990: 165–8) articulates the tension between the lawyer as "broker" (tracking the business relationship with clients) and "professional" (reflecting the autonomy of lawyer decision-making).

Problem-solving Capacities

Lawyers and leaders share certain problem-solving capacities. Fast or slow, they think as *synthesizers* of disparate elements, ranging from the current circumstances and the goals or interests of the client or the group, to the framework of applicable law, understanding of the industry or arena of operations, predicted behavior of customers or target audiences, and capacities of the people and resources required for needed performance. They are *persuaders* attending to disparate audiences to persuade legal authorities, adversaries, allies, vendors, financing sources, and the public or their own people, clients themselves. They use a potpourri of argumentative resources or tools, including rules, analogies, policies, principles, precedent, customs, practices, scenarios of the future, and competitive threats.

Lawyer and leader problem-solvers are inherently *strategic* thinkers/actors. A problem is a question, or a bundle of closely related questions. An important finding of cognitive scientists is the enormous impact of how questions are framed (Kahneman 2011: 367–74).[11] We have alluded to framing as a matter of consequence both for lawyer and leader in their construction of factual stories or reality setting, and in the formal or informal sense of agency. Even more crucial is setting the appropriate frame of problems.

Problem-solver strategists approach their work with an experimental and controlled, skeptical, slow-thinking temperament. They shift actions and interpretations to shape relatively indeterminate situations in order to achieve results, sometimes engaging in larger, more informative framing to ameliorate the effect of short-term fast thinking.[12] The best among them see how a complicated problem must be seen whole or broken into serial segments or stages, completion of each of which is essential to ultimate resolution of the problem or a successful result.

Differences

Framing

A lawyer's role with a client is what might be termed a limited or "special purpose" leadership. A leader's context is much less tightly framed, if only because the extraordinary range of leadership roles within all kinds of formal and informal groups and organizations—even when the bottom line is of paramount importance.

---

11   A popular text addressing framing is Russo and Schoemaker (1989: 15–63).

12   Chief culprits may be priming and anchoring. Priming is thinking or behavior excessively, often unconsciously, influenced by the environment of the moment. Anchoring (identifying a particular value for an unknown quantity before estimating that quantity) guides and constrains thinking because of a failure to imagine how one could think if there were no anchor or a different anchor (Kahneman 2011: 119, 128).

A leader must demonstrate a more capacious perspective, what might be termed a communal state of mind.

Thus, it is no exaggeration to state that lawyers and leaders of groups or organizations more often than not think differently. One aspect of this difference between lawyers and leaders (although, of course, some people can excel at both) is the wide range of subjects and constituencies and variety of techniques or styles needed to operate and move a group or organization. Leaders typically deploy a much broader set of frames of analysis than a lawyer. Another way of describing this difference is that the leader's fundamental task is to identify the crucial problems her group or organization needs to solve, array them in some sequence for solution and constantly adjust them. The array of problems, their relative priority, and their interrelationships may change quickly. The lawyer, on the other hand, does problem-solving directly connected to legal reasoning and the lawmaking responsibilities of the lawyer, as a result of her commitment to guide appropriate client conduct within an interpretation of the meaning and confines of the law. Leadership may require action and understanding of the interrelationships of diverse fields such as finance, operations, the law, human resources, competitive environment, political environment, internal culture, industry or field norms, marketing, etc. Lawyers, as leaders of their clients, must focus primarily on problem-solving arising from the client's short- and long-term needs and actions that affect or are affected by the law.

Biases

If we take seriously the enormous variety of traps or unconscious biases that affect thinking as identified by cognitive scientists, lawyers and leaders may be prone to different cognitive mistakes. Let me simply mention a couple of possibilities out of the enormous variety of traps or unconscious biases identified by brain scientists. Leaders are vulnerable to overconfidence and tend to suppress doubt and neglect ambiguity or limitations of factual data on which they base their decisions. Lawyers have a justified reputation for being risk averse and (assuming an entirely plausible "bread and butter" bias) neglect to restrain and provide a balanced perspective to excessively overconfident or highly risk-averse clients in order to extend and pile up costs of lawyers' representation.

Success

One distinctive element of leadership that distinguishes it from law is what constitutes success. A leader's destination is often derived from the views and analytical frames of various constituencies—members of the group, colleagues, employees, stockholders, customers, a board of directors, journalists, the public at large or competitors and other entities and people who are wise heads in the same field. The interim stages of the path can be evaluated by a variety of measures— from financial strength, to political or social effectiveness, growth, market share, rank in some pecking order of prestige, or satisfaction of employees and onlookers. The success of a leader can vary enormously over time, depending on circumstances of the group or organization and the perspective of the evaluator. A classic bias of leaders is to overvalue indicators of short-term success of an organization at the cost of long-term sustainability. Success is something of an unstable phenomenon—in important respects a function of perceptions in a variety of communities affected by the leader.

Thinking and acting like a lawyer, on the other hand, is more circumscribed, if only because lawyers not only represent clients' interests but must account for a larger frame of thinking, something more than clients. The lawyer, through litigation and advice-giving and contract-drawing, actually participates in lawmaking, which can be considered the core of the lawyer's role as thinker and actor—a form of retail or situational making of law conceived of as establishing more or less authoritative guidance that people or institutions follow. And in law—despite the many changes in the profession in recent decades driven by fierce competition, massive consolidation, and obsession with compensation by owners of private firms—success as a lawyer still turns on fulfilling criteria internal to the profession as a community of shared standards of excellence (Brown 1992). The success of a lawyer is not necessarily affected by a client's opinion, or losing a case, but is still in large measure a matter of the reputation of the lawyer as a skilled lawmaker in the judgment of peers in the profession.

Agency

We have alluded earlier to the role of lawyer as agent of the client, a special form of authority and leadership. The situation of leader is entirely different because there is a distinction between leadership and legal authority. Informal groups and many varieties of small organizations are characterized by amorphous or vague or nonexistent authority structures.[13] But they still can be well or poorly led. Even in

---

13   Eisold (2004: 299–302) asks "How does one take up the task of leadership with an awareness that it is a function of the group, that is, a task beyond what you as an individual can or should hope to accomplish alone, and that the group has to create your authority to function on its behalf? ... One needs to keep in mind the fact that there are no rules; every task and every group is sufficiently different to require a fresh approach ... [I]n oneself, one does not know enough both about the objective problems that are faced by the group but perhaps, more importantly, about the resources in the group that are available to deal with it. In other words, one has to keep in mind that one is a member of the group ... You have to keep in mind that though you may have formal authorization by virtue of the position you occupy in your organization, you have to generate and sustain the informal authorization of those with whom you work ... [T]he leader has to share the risk. The group has to know and understand that they all participate and share the risk of the enterprise. The leader does not purchase immunity by virtue of his position as evaluator ... He is accountable above to his superiors, vulnerable directly because of the ability of those with whom he is working to function effectively ... [H]e is, in fact, being continually evaluated or judged

large organizations, leadership "without authority" is not unusual as people step up to leadership roles by dint of their energy, risk-taking and ability to engender the trust and support of their colleagues. In fact, a key strategy of many successful heads of entities is to identify and ally with those natural leaders in the ranks in order to unleash existing energy or new ideas, build support, and demonstrate that the leader at the top understands the real sources of strength and initiative in the organization. Heads of firms can exhibit leadership despite their authority spelled out in partnership or corporate documents by moving an organization to action without having to play the heavy hand of their formal powers. Or they can be described as using their authority well, or skillfully, as if authority is just one of many mechanisms to deploy in effective leadership. Leaders may be said to reverse the agency relationship characteristic of the lawyer–client relationship. They become, in effect, principals who attract other parts of the group or constituencies of the organization to act as agents—a contradiction that, at least in corporate theory, spelling out the status of the leader as agent of the board of directors and stockholders complicates and befuddles corporate governance.

Risk

Another major difference between a lawyer and a leader is setting direction, a function critical for both the lawyer (as the leader of the client) and the leader. For a lawyer, direction often focuses on assessing and helping manage risk that a client has run afoul of or is entertaining. For leaders, taking calculated risks is the core of their work. One could argue that a leader using larger, more capacious frames devised through slow thinking may be the perfect antidote to a lawyer who offers only a narrowly focused legal frame to solve a problem. This is the argument of executives who complain constantly about lawyers interpreting the law as an unavoidable obstacle and lawyers' failure to grasp the larger goals and needs of the client enterprise. On the other hand, a lawyer might be the perfect antidote to leaders who suffer the typical cognitive bias of overconfidence (Kahneman 2011: 255–65). A lawyer's slow-thinking exposition of a variety of complications the leader failed to take into consideration or deeper evaluation of the evidence on which a decision is based can be invaluable. The lawyer manages the client relationship by identifying more or less authoritative guidance with respect to the law in conversation with the client and making sure that there is convergence on how to proceed between the client/principal and the lawyer/agent.

---

by members of the group ... Not all problems can be solved. But at least they can be faced and understood ... The most entrenched myth we have in our culture, more entrenched even than that of the heroic leader—is the myth of the individual person, whether or not he or she is highly effective. It is an up-hill battle to remind ourselves day after day and task after task that we are members of groups, and that we derive our meaning and our effectiveness from those groups" (A.K. Rice Institute, www.akriceinstitute.org and www. grouprelationsarticlesonline.com).

Increasingly, some clients are sophisticated enough to question expertise through their own experience or via legal and other departments in the organization.

Reliance on Expertise

The premise of the lawyer/client relationship is usually an acknowledgement of the client's reliance on the lawyer's expertise and guidance. A leader's relationship with his followers is typically more challenging because followers are not necessarily interested in or moved by a leader's expert knowledge. Followers, in fact, often represent reservoirs of expertise available to a leader. A leader in important respects is a function of, may even literally follow the followers, or enlist and earn her followers in order to build trust essential to engaging people to move in a certain direction. Trust-building is an enormously complex subject, but it at least includes persuading people of the circumstances of the organization and its alternative futures, and describing what actions are plausibly necessary to bring about a desirable future for the group or organization. Much of this may be drawn from the "followers." If followers are to accept a leader's risk-taking, there is in trust-building an important element (and necessity) of establishing solidarity as well as the competence and credibility of the leader. David Maister talks about how revealing the etymology of terms related to heading any organization is. The word *leader*, as we have indicated, derives from the Anglo-Saxon meaning the person who discovers the path. *Manager* originates from the medieval French family of words like ménage and literally means the person who keeps the beasts. *Administrator* comes from Latin, meaning to minister to or serve. In my experience, in large or small organizations, if the head of the organization cannot serve or perform or make sure surrogates perform service tasks well, and cannot manage (or have some capacity in place to manage) relationships that keep the beasts calm or at least productive and working in harness,[14] he or she will not be able to build the trust or cohesion that authorizes the leader to find the right path or direction for the organization.

Lawyers and Organizations

Thus far my argument has been rather formal. Let me now turn to what can probably best be labeled as a slightly-more-than-off-the-cuff argument about the character of lawyers and law students.

One of the key premises of advocates for teaching leadership in law schools is that the leadership role of lawyers is significant, if not pervasive, in government and for-profit and nonprofit sectors in the United States. With all the budding, unhatched leaders attending law school, the argument goes, legal educators ought

---

14   A common perception that there is a sharp distinction between management and leadership is, in my opinion, largely mistaken.

to undertake to improve the general quality of leadership of lawyers in our society. Of course, we do not fully understand why some lawyers tend to assume leadership positions (assuming this is an accurate reading of the current profession and that lawyers are more successful as leaders than ordinary mortals). The emergence of law-trained leaders may be the result of the analytical skills developed in law school. It may be the fact that people with strong cognitive abilities and ambitions to excel are attracted to law school. It may be a combination of these plus opportunities and access lawyers have in practice to associate with leaders in politics, business, and the nonprofit world.

And it may be that lawyers need to unlearn aspects of their training to become leaders. Earlier in this chapter, I described the requisite mentality of a leader as "communal." It may be no exaggeration to portray lawyers as anti-communal. Managing partners of law firms would acknowledge some validity to the crude generalization that lawyers are people who might be called "organizationally challenged."

A number of different reasons might account for this tendency of lawyers not to participate very effectively in group or organizational life.

1. One factor may simply be the structure of law practices, namely that the work of lawyers for clients is in large measure a decentralized, relatively autonomous activity that does not lend itself to much hierarchical oversight or group decision-making. (This traditional structure may be changing significantly in some forms of practice.) Many lawyers consider practice organizations as something of a marriage of convenience rather than a necessity bearing on their service to clients (Kelly 2007: 264–73). Although the examples of self-effacing team players in the law must be legion, the desire for autonomy runs deep in most lawyers' psyche.

2. Another explanation offered by some lawyers is the dominant role of law school in professional training, which attends almost entirely to developing legal reasoning. Critics of law schools point out that the client—absolutely fundamental to thinking and acting like a lawyer—is (despite the addition in recent years of clinics and some courses involving virtual clients) largely missing from legal education. The "case method" tends to be based on appellate court decisions, not on cases/stories of clients presenting ambiguous factual situations and needing help with a problem. Also missing in law schools is study or experience of collective activities that pose issues of compromise that are a day-to-day necessity of group life. Law school tends to take autonomy-seeking personalities and train them firmly to stay that way.

3. Some observers emphasize the self-selection that goes into becoming a lawyer (reinforced by the nature of legal education) and point to personality tests that suggest that lawyers compared to the general population show disproportionately more:

    a. skepticism (including cynicism and being judgmental, questioning and argumentative),

    b. urgency (impatience, brusqueness, and poor listening habits),

    c. autonomy (resistance to being managed, bridling at being told what to do, and prizing independence),
and disproportionately less:

    d. sociability (they are disinclined to interact with others), and

    e. resilience (they are defensive, resistant to feedback, and hypersensitive to criticism) (Richard 1993, 2002).

4. A psychological explanation of the lawyer's situation suggests

> [P]rofessionals resist group life, with all its opportunities and dangers, in order to skirt the issues of rivalry, authority, and mutuality in groups and they do so by creating an ideology of collegiality ... . [Lawyers] learn to be aggressive in their professional work because they feel that it is objectively deployed and is independent of their actual character and feelings. Thus in their professional work they are not faced with the dilemma of integrating mutuality and aggression, the good and the bad [of organizational life], because these are not their feelings ... By contrast general managers [of law practices] ... must draw on their own personal and emotional resources to shape their thinking and acting ... and come to appreciate the complex and often hopelessly contradictory character of group life ... (Hirschhorn 1989: 235)

This crude collective character sketch of lawyers suggests proclivities for slow/hard thinking (questioning, prizing independence) as well as fast thinking (impatience, resilience). But the important point to emphasize is lawyers' general discomfort with group and organizational life may pose challenges to anyone hoping that leadership learning will gain serious traction with law students.

The Subject of Leadership

If there is one premise or pretension of law school faculty, it is commitment to a rigorous and intellectually demanding educational program. The question for the professoriate will be whether leadership education is a worthy academic partner that matches the seriousness of legal education.

A fundamental problem at the outset is the difficulty of defining leadership and identifying an academic discipline that legal educators might find adds value to law school programs. As Deborah Ancona, a faculty member teaching leadership at the Sloan School of Management at MIT puts it, "We all hunger to know what leadership is, yet the concept remains amorphous" (Ancona 2005). "A search through the leadership research does not add clarity, because it yields almost as many definitions as there are scholars to propose them" (Ancona n.d.).

Joseph Rost in his book, *Leadership in the Twenty-first Century*, puts the point more sharply when he argues that leadership is "anything anyone wants to say it is" and, as a subject, "does not add up because leadership scholars and practitioners have no definition of leadership to hold on to" (Rost 1991: 14, 8, quoted in Khurana 2007: 357). A teacher in a major university leadership program characterizes most leadership literature as "a Christmas tree of platitudes."

Rakesh Khurana,[15] in his survey of the history of the American business school, concludes that "leadership as a body of knowledge, after decades of scholarly attention under the social science research lens ... remains without either a widely accepted theoretical framework or a cumulative empirical understanding leading to a usable body of knowledge" (Khurana 2007: 357).[16] Khurana describes in some detail three major approaches taken by most contemporary business schools:

1. explicit theories and knowledge about the general business environment or the modern corporation and decision-making,
2. the development of interpersonal skills and their application to small-group situations, and
3. personal growth and self-discovery, including taking advantage of opportunities for personal development.

He sees these differences as symptoms of confusion: "... [T]he history of leadership scholarship and pedagogy within business schools to date suggests that, at the very least, business schools will find the task of creating a professional knowledge base around leadership no easier than previous [unfulfilled] efforts to establish firm intellectual foundations for the study and teaching of management" (Khurana 2007: 356).[17]

This picture of conceptual disarray in graduate business education, the intellectual center of leadership research and teaching, contrasts sharply with the massive scale of the educational industry in leadership in this country. United States businesses are reported to spend $50 billion yearly on leadership training (Gomez 2007).[18] Leadership education is featured in most graduate business schools, public administration schools, and undergraduate education in the U.S.,

---

15   Khurana is the author of two books, *Searching for a Corporate Savior: The Irrational Quest for Charismatic CEOs* (2002) and *From Higher Aims to Hired Hands* (2007). The latter book received the American Sociological Association's Max Weber Book Award in 2008 for most outstanding contribution to scholarship in the past two years. The book was also the Winner of the 2007 Best Professional/Scholarly Publishing Book in Business, Finance and Management, Association of American Publishers.

16   The stakes in business education are now higher, as the schools try to address—in part by rethinking leadership training—the current economic crisis and the role of business schools in the formation of business leaders. See Holland (2009).

17   Copyright © 2007, Princeton University Press.

18   The $50 billion is probably a significant underestimate since the date of the estimate is 1997.

not to mention the 37 master's degree programs in leadership at U.S. universities (Crawford et al. 2002). We are a culture drenched in leadership, whether it is the yields (in January 2012) on Amazon.com of 84,880 current titles on the subject, or 503,000,000 results on Google. Leadership education is the most flattering of all subjects, invariably popular with students and others exposed to it, in part because it is a Rorschach test with invariably favorable resonance. People read into "leadership" what they want to believe it to be. It is a cultural phenomenon, a strand in the American DNA. It is the story of individual success to which almost everyone should aspire and can, with concerted effort, achieve.[19]

Leadership occurs in a bewildering variety of contexts within almost any organization of any size. It is distributed up and down the ranks, in people with managerial and supervisory authority and those without it—people of different skills and inclinations, educational backgrounds and experiences who contribute to what might be called the orchestration of many instruments of leadership in an organization. In addition to the extraordinary distribution of leadership within formal organizations, there is the matter of leadership in more or less informal groups and organizations: PTAs, Alcoholics Anonymous meetings, storefront churches, neighborhood softball teams, neighborhood opponents to developers, study groups in college, etc. This suggests that leadership, whatever it is, must express itself in profoundly different ways depending on the task at hand, or the location of the individual in the group or organization. If leadership is conceived of as certain skills, it must require identifying a handful of Ur-skills that apply to the infinite range of leadership situations or it becomes an almost meaningless wish list, the myopic product of some current organizational operating ideas/fashions reflecting particular types of organizations of particular size that may have little or no relevance to the varied experiences of leadership to be found in other organizations.

If the requisite skills for a leader are so dependent on the situation of the leader and the demands of the group or organization, it would follow that the first priority should be to understand the organization or situation and assess where and how to move it along a particular path or direction. Relevant skills follow, and can be acquired by necessity through learning on the job, adapting, collaborating, hiring or allying to attain them.

---

19   Gladwell (2008) argues that for every great success celebrated by a culture such as ours that is enthralled with the tale of an individual achiever, there is a powerful (hidden) parallel narrative of the unheralded family or institutional support system, fortuitous timing, sheer luck, and opportunity to practice relevant work that lies behind individual success. The "real" story of success, argues Gladwell, is the context that made success or leadership possible. Gladwell's "real" stories of success appear to support validity of The Fundamental Attribution Error—the tendency we all have to over-value dispositional or personality-based (or I would add, skill-based) explanations for the behaviors of people we identify as leaders and under-value explanations based on situations that induce or enable actions.

Teaching Leadership in Law Schools

The lesson I draw from this exploration of the relationship between lawyer thinking and leadership thinking is that the best way to teach leadership in law school is to pursue an arena of thinking like a lawyer in which lawyers and leaders most resemble each other—problem-solving. Both lawyers and leaders engage in sizing up the context of a problem, identifying and addressing key questions and challenges, adopting frames of analysis, building stories from facts as they evolve, keeping attuned to the role of biases and potential mistakes in thinking, synthesizing different understandings of the realities of the situation, and strategizing how to move forward and persuade others to follow their lead.

To take such an approach is to question the usefulness of the dominant form of leadership training in the U.S. outside of legal education, namely teaching focused on the skills and character development of "leaders." This skills-and-character orientation, which addresses what particular or paradigmatic leaders do or should think, affects most higher education and in-house corporate and nonprofit leadership training, highlights the leader and minimizes the crucial analytical framework or context for any form of leadership—the field and/or market or organizational or group setting that makes leadership intelligible. It is also unlikely to command respect from law school faculty as a coherent discipline that strengthens legal education. Leadership only makes sense within the boundaries or constraints of the group or organization being led, the problems requiring attention, and realistic and perhaps sobering options of strategies for change and goals capable of being achieved. Leadership training works best within that very rare group or organization that actually operates the way it says it does, and where leadership skills are deemed essential to the survival and thriving of both the organization and the leadership trainee—for example, the U.S. Marine Corps.

Law students, if I have accurately described tendencies of being organizationally challenged, are in no position usefully to absorb generic leadership skills, a situation not unlike the futility of teaching journalism students how to run a newspaper or TV station. Problem-solving inevitably must introduce the context and character of a particular group or organization. Organizational learning of this kind is particularly useful for beginning lawyers who can, through slow thinking instruction, develop fast thinking instincts helpful in sizing up how different forms of client and adversary organizations operate (Kelly 2011). Most lawyers will represent organizations of various kinds—nonprofits and small and large business enterprises. Knowing something about the challenges facing these organizations, how the overall industry or field in which they are located affects their operations, and how leaders and lawyers representing them think through difficult issues is crucial to understanding organizational clients and representing them well.

Although many law schools have invested in client-facing problem-solving through clinical programs and some forms of skills courses and externship programs, it is no exaggeration to say that problem-solving has only a tangential foothold in American law school curricula. Seeing the law (or making law retail in the public or private law office) in terms of serving clients, their needs and goals, is by and large missing in American legal education. There are many ways to address this gap, but for the purposes of the limited frame of this chapter let me simply suggest that problem-solving can be taught in the classic low-cost large classroom setting through well-designed cases or simulations that make it possible to help students:

- assess situations of clients facing problems, including gathering a quick read (not deep research) or understanding of the range of law relevant to the situation and identifying what, if any, are the client's legal problems,
- appreciate how to unearth, or create, or manage and frame relevant information and respond to indeterminate or changing facts,
- evaluate strategies for solving the client's problem(s) and arguments for persuading the client of the wisdom of following guidance relating to a particular strategy,
- grasp, by placing them in a wide variety of practice settings, the extraordinarily wide range of organizational pressures, resources and ethical issues that arise in the American legal profession, and
- take practical first steps for the client, including slow thinking exercises of interviewing, negotiating, and drafting documents to anticipate or protect against litigation and/or to establish forms of collaboration (Fuller 1948: 195).[20]

This form of teaching is the polar opposite of the appellate case, the staple of so many law school classrooms focused on legal reasoning, where facts have been hewn into stone by serial litigation. Training in lawmaking through client problem-solving is a practical and theoretical jurisprudence comparable in importance to legal reasoning. And unlike the standard forms of leadership training, it is likely to be directly helpful to students emerging as newly minted lawyers in almost any form of law practice.

Despite the many ways clinical legal education and skills courses strengthen legal education and benefit law students, legal education is still centered on preparing people to think like an appellate lawyer, one of the rarest of experiences in the practice of law. Success as a lawyer depends fundamentally on postgraduate experience—the way law graduates make use of their training and build their skills, knowledge, judgment, and the respect of clients and legal forums to become accomplished lawyers. The best law school can do is to insist in its own practice that students fully grasp—think intelligently and deeply about—the reality that being a lawyer is work dominated by representing, advocating against, and practicing in organizations. A strong slow-thinking introduction to the client

---

20   Materials co-authored by Joe Singer and Todd Rakoff that meet most of these specifications are currently in use for a required first year course at Harvard Law School entitled Problem Solving Workshop.

problem-solving experience will prepare law students better for acting and fast thinking as a lawyer, and in turn affect positively their future careers in the law and possibly their success as leaders in communities within which they practice. The challenge of being a leader in a postgraduate world ultimately depends on the myriad contingencies and opportunities of the law, discernment of the nature of organizations, and negotiation of a career in a world of organizations that thirst for sound leadership.

References

Ancona, D. n.d. Leadership in an Age of Uncertainty, in *Class Note*, M14-8.

Ancona, D. 2005. Leadership in an Age of Uncertainty, *Center for eBusiness Research Brief* [Online], 6(1). Available at: http://ebusiness.mit.edu/research/Briefs/Ancona_Leadership_Final_VI.pdf [accessed 31 January 2012].

Blasi, G.L. 1995. What Lawyers Know: Lawyering Expertise, Cognitive Science, and the Functions of Theory, *Journal of Legal Education*, 45(3): 313–97.

Brown, J. 1992. *The Definition of a Profession: The Authority of Metaphor in the History of Intelligence Testing, 1890–1930*. Princeton: Princeton University Press.

Chen, R. and Hanson, J. 2004. Categorically Biased: The Influence of Knowledge Structures on Law and Legal Theory, *Southern California Law Review*, 77(6): 1103–254.

Condlin, R.J. 2003. What's Love Got to Do with It—It's Not like They're Your Friends for Christ's Sake: The Complicated Relationship between Lawyer and Client, *Nebraska Law Review*, 82(2): 211–311.

Crawford, C.B., Brungardt, C.L., Scott, R.F. and Gould, L.V. 2002. Graduate Programs in Organizational Leadership: A Review of Programs, Faculty, Costs and Delivery Methods, *Journal of Leadership Studies*, 8(4): 64–74.

DePree, Max. 1989. *Leadership is an Art.* New York: Dell Publishing.

DiMaggio, P.J. and Powell, W.W. 1991. *The New Institutionalism in Organizational Analysis.* Chicago: Chicago University Press.

Eisold, K. 2004. Leadership and the Creation of Authority, in *Group Dynamics, Organizational Irrationality and Social Complexity: Group Relations Reader 3*, edited by S. Cytrynbaum and D.A. Noumair. Jupiter, FL: A.K. Rice Institute, 289–302.

Fuller, L. 1948. What the Law Schools Can Contribute to the Making of Lawyers, *Journal of Legal Education*, 1(2): 189–204.

Fuller, L. 1950. On Teaching Law, *Stanford Law Review*, 3(1): 35–48.

Gladwell, M. 2008. *Outliers: The Story of Success.* New York: Little, Brown and Co.

Gomez, D. 2007. The Leader as Learner, *International Journal of Leadership Studies*, 2(3): 280–84.

Groopman, J. 2007. *How Doctors Think*. New York: Houghton Mifflin.

Hanson, J. and Yosifon, D. 2004. The Situational Character: A Critical Realist Perspective on the Human Animal, *Georgetown Law Journal*, 93(1): 1–179.

Heifetz, R.A. 1994. *Leadership Without Easy Answers*. Cambridge, MA: Belknap.

Heineman, B.W., Jr. 2007. Lawyers as Leaders, *Yale Law Journal Pocket Part* [Online], 116: 266–71. Available at: http://yalelawjournal.org/the-yale-law-journal-pocket-part/professional-responsibility/lawyers-as-leaders/ [accessed 9 September 2012].

Hirschhorn, L. 1989. Professionals, Authority, and Group Life: A Case Study of a Law Firm, *Human Resource Management*, 28(2): 235–52.

Holland, K. 2009. Is It Time to Retrain B-Schools?, *New York Times*, 15 March, Sunday Business Section, 1–2.

Kahneman, D. 2011. *Thinking, Fast and Slow*. New York: Farrar, Straus and Giroux.

Kelly, M.J. 2007. *Lives of Lawyers Revisited: Transformation and Resilience in the Organizations of Practice*. Ann Arbor: University of Michigan Press.

Kelly, M. 2011. A Gaping Hole in American Legal Education, *Maryland Law Review*, 70(2): 440–50.

Khurana, R. 2002. *Searching for a Corporate Savior: The Irrational Quest for Charismatic CEOs*. Princeton: Princeton University Press.

Khurana, R. 2007. *From Higher Aims to Hired Hands, The Social Transformation of American Business Schools and the Unfulfilled Promise of Management as a Profession*. Princeton: Princeton University Press.

Kritzer, H.M. 1990. *The Justice Broker, Lawyers and Ordinary Litigation*. New York: Oxford University Press.

Levi, E.H. 1949. *Introduction to Legal Reasoning*. Chicago: University of Chicago Press.

Mertz, E. 2007. *The Language of Law School, Learning to "Think like a Lawyer."* New York: Oxford University Press.

Rhode, D.L. and Packel, A.K. 2011. *Leadership, Law, Policy, and Management*. New York: Aspen.

Richard, L. 1993. The Lawyer Types, *American Bar Association Journal*, 79(7): 74–81.

Richard, L. 2002. Herding Cats: The Lawyer Personality Revealed, *AltmanWeil Report to Management*, 29(11): 1–4, 9–12.

Rost, J.C. 1991. *Leadership for the Twenty-first Century*. New York: Praeger.

Russo, J.E. and Schoemaker, P.J.H. 1989. *Decision Traps: Ten Barriers to Brilliant Decision-Making and How to Overcome Them*. New York: Doubleday.

Sarat, A. and Felstiner, W.L. 1995. *Divorce Lawyers and Their Clients, Power and Meaning in the Legal Process*. New York: Oxford University Press.

Schön, D.A. 1983. *The Reflective Practitioner: How Professionals Think in Action*. New York: Basic Books.

Schön, D.A. 1988. From Technical Rationality to Reflection-in-Action, in *Professional Judgment: A Reader in Clinical Decision Making*, edited by J. Dowie and A.S. Elstein. Cambridge, UK: Cambridge University Press, 60–77.

Selznick, P. 1957. *Leadership in Administration: A Sociological Interpretation.* Evanston, IL: Row, Peterson.

PART III
Developing a Curriculum:
An Interdisciplinary Approach

Chapter 10

Charting a New Professional Responsibility Course in a Post-Carnegie World

Brenda Bratton Blom, Lydia Nussbaum and Bonnie Allen

This chapter describes what the clinical law faculty at one institution, the University of Maryland Francis King Carey School of Law, has done to enhance its curriculum with an experimental seminar: *Professional Responsibility and Practice: The Rules and Reality*. The course was developed as part of a broader initiative, which was born out of a partnership between the law school and the Fetzer Institute, launched in 2008 to focus on "Leadership, Ethics and Democracy-Building" (LEAD Initiative). The LEAD Initiative is designed to help law students realize their leadership potential, build good ethical and moral judgment, develop cross-cultural competence, and discover how they can use law to reinforce democracy, achieve justice, and engage in fulfilling careers.[1] The curricular innovations that comprise the LEAD Initiative serve as one way the school of law is working to respond to the calls for reform in legal education that the Carnegie Report on Legal Education articulated so powerfully.

The Rules and Reality course aims to create opportunities for law students to explore establishing their own professional identities as lawyers and, as part of that process, to develop a greater understanding of ethical leadership. Using the Rules of Professional Conduct as a starting point, the course then engages in several different types of learning about professional responsibility: readings and discussions on lawyers' ethical responsibilities to each other, the profession, and the whole of society; talking about live client ethical dilemmas among themselves and with larger Professional Responsibility classes; panel discussions with seasoned professionals about topics affecting the legal profession; reflection on

---

1   For a full description of the LEAD Initiative, see the LEAD Initiative Home Page, http://www.law.umaryland.edu/programs/initiatives/lead/ and "Funding Proposal to the Fetzer Institute: University of Maryland School of Law, Leadership, & Professionalism Initiative" (on file with the authors). The school of law has long been committed to providing a legal education that focuses on public service. This commitment continues under the leadership of the current Dean Phoebe A. Haddon, who has written about the importance of teaching young lawyers about their professional responsibility to promote social justice. See Haddon (1994).

the importance of personal ethical foundations; and significant discussion about the choice to be leaders and communicators in a democracy.

In this chapter, the authors discuss the origins and impetus for the seminar, what we have learned during the years the course has been offered, the changes to format and content we have made based on student feedback, what our students have shared about their experience taking the course, and our hopes for taking this kind of teaching to scale in other areas of Maryland's curriculum and in the broader legal academy.

I. Law Schools Need to Help Their Students Develop Professional Self-awareness

The moral and ethical challenges of twenty-first-century lawyering are no secret to lawyers and judges who operate in the day-to-day trenches or who supervise law students or young lawyers. Increasingly, it is recognized that the integrity of lawyers too often becomes compromised in client relationships, institutional roles, and community life.[2] Many observers of the profession describe the challenge as a crisis in values and morale.[3] Skyrocketing student loan debt drives many law students to make career choices inconsistent with their deepest vocational goals (Erlanger et al. 1996: 851–4). The demands of law firm culture, with its ultimate emphasis on billable hours and business development, leave lawyers little time for family life, personal health, pro bono work, or civic engagement (Fortney 2000: 284). Cutthroat business competition among lawyers and declining civility create enormous strains on lawyers, their relationships with clients, and case outcomes (Rhode 2000: 7). With the recent financial crisis, many law school graduates are facing unemployment or accepting jobs that pay far less than they expected when entering law school, thus exacerbating the student loan debt problem (Koppel 2010).

The personal and public consequences of these pressures are real. An estimated one-third of American lawyers suffers from depression or substance addictions, a rate that is two to three times higher than that of the general public (Rhode 2000). A majority of lawyers reports that they would choose another career if they

---

2   For an insightful discussion of what it means to practice integrity, see Luban (2007a). Luban defines integrity as "wholeness or unity of person, an inner consistency between deed and principle. 'Integrity' shares etymology with other unity-words—integer, integral, integrate, integration. All derive from the Latin *integrare*, to make whole. And the person of integrity is the person whose conduct and principles operate in happy harmony" (Luban 2007a: 267, reprinted with the permission of Cambridge University Press).

3   In *The Professionalism Problem*, Rhode captures many observers' commentary on the crisis of professionalism among lawyers. Rhode specifically identifies a trade-off that lawyers must make between moral independence and their expectations of "worldly rewards, such as power, wealth, and prominence" (Rhode 1998: 303–15, 311).

could make the decision again and three-quarters would not want their children to become lawyers (Rhode 1998: 296–7, citing Glendon 1994: 257–8). Eighty percent do not believe that the law lives up to their expectations in contributing to the social good (Rhode 1998: 11). Plummeting public confidence, respect for, and trust in lawyers and the legal system seem to reinforce this self-perception.[4]

Many members of the profession and the legal academy are voicing concerns that legal education falls short in equipping lawyers with the full range of competencies needed to practice law effectively and compassionately. These concerns were articulated compellingly in the Carnegie Foundation Report, *Educating Lawyers: Preparation for the Profession of Law* (Sullivan et al. 2007: 22), and a multiyear study on legal education, *Best Practices in Legal Education* (Stuckey and Others 2007).

The Carnegie Foundation Report identified a common goal among "otherwise disparate-seeming educational experiences" of professional education: "to initiate novice practitioners to think, to perform, and conduct themselves (that is, to act morally and ethically) like professionals" (Sullivan et al. 2007: 22). Furthermore, the Report continues, this initiation should comprise three "apprenticeships": 1) the cognitive or intellectual apprenticeship that provides students with the academic knowledge base, 2) the apprenticeship that forms expert practice, and 3) the apprenticeship of identity and purpose (Sullivan et al. 2007: 28). The Carnegie Foundation reported that this third apprenticeship of identity and purpose poses the greatest challenge for law schools and is the portion of legal education in most need of augmentation.[5] Finally, the Report emphasized the importance of bridging the gap in the law school educational experience "between the formal skills of legal analysis and the more fluid expertise needed in much professional work" (Sullivan et al. 2007: 88). By "teaching for practice," law schools can motivate students to engage in the "moral dimensions of professional life" and initiate young lawyers into "the wisdom of practice" (Sullivan et al. 2007: 91, 88, 95).

The Carnegie Report went on to say that law schools fail to equip students with the ethical and social skills they need to "engage the moral imagination" (Sullivan et al. 2007: 188). The Carnegie Report attributes much of the shortcoming of legal education to its heavy reliance on a single form of teaching, the case-dialogue method, and on the limitations of that one form. This methodology involves abstracting the legally relevant aspects of situations and persons from their real-

---

4 For a clear discussion of public perspectives on the legal profession, see Rhode 1998: 285–96.

5 "Today's law school experience is severely unbalanced. The difficulty, as we see it, lies in the relentless focus, in many law school courses, on the procedural and formal qualities of legal thinking. This focus is sometimes to the deliberate exclusion of the moral and social dimensions and often abstracted from the fuller contexts of actual legal practice. It is this one-sided emphasis on an academic apprenticeship insulated from considerations of ethical engagement or public responsibility that undercuts the principal aims of the ethical-social apprenticeship" (Sullivan et al. 2007: 145).

world situations. Consideration of the social or ethical consequences of legal conclusions is left out of the analysis.[6] Students are warned to set aside their concerns for justice, moral consequences, or compassion (Sullivan et al. 2007: 187). Columbia Law School Professor William H. Simon attributes this phenomenon to the tendency of the dominant conception in legal theory to define the lawyer's role in terms of formalistic, categorical, and mechanical forms (Simon 1998: 3). He adds: "The profession has promulgated an ideology, backed by disciplinary rules and sanctions[,] that mandates unreflective, mechanical, categorical judgment rather than practical reason" (Simon 1998: 23).[7]

The *Best Practices in Legal Education* study also found that law schools need to do more "to expand their educational objectives to more completely serve the needs of their students and to provide instruction about the knowledge, skills, and values that will enable their students to become effective, responsible lawyers" (Stuckey and Others 2007: 17–18). One "notable gap" in legal education identified by the study relates to students' understanding of the legal profession and their role as future lawyers. According to the study, students received neither a "systematic grounding in the roles and responsibilities of lawyers" nor an understanding of "the broader intellectual and social context[s] in which law operates" (Stuckey and Others 2007: 16). As a result, today's "law schools are not producing graduates who provide access to justice, are adequately competent, and practice in a professional manner" (Stuckey and Others 2007: 18, 18–21).

While other fields of graduate professional education, including business and public policy, have diversified learning methodologies, encouraged in part by the work on multiple intelligences by Howard Gardner (2006), most law schools have not followed that trend. In his best-selling book, *The Soul of the Law*, Benjamin Sells, a Chicago-based trial lawyer and psychologist, describes the perils of legal education and the process of "becoming a lawyer" as acculturating the legal mind. Somewhere along the way, law students undergo a subtle, though radical, change. Their very perceptions begin to be structured by assumptions provided by legal education (Sells 1996: 35). Sells points to the example of a law professor telling first year students: "You are not here to find truth and justice, you are here to learn the Law" (Sells 1996: 36). Sells observes that the Law does not know what to do with grand ideas of the heart that escape analytic definition. Over time, the Law's

---

6   As the Carnegie Report authors noted: "Overall, however, we came away from our campus visits with the strong impression that in most law schools, the apprenticeship of professionalism and purpose is subordinated to the cognitive, academic apprenticeship. In fact, in the minds of many faculty, ethical and social values are subjective and indeterminate and, for that reason, can potentially conflict with the all-important values of the academy—values that underlie the cognitive apprenticeship: rigor, skepticism, intellectual distance, and objectivity" (Sullivan et al. 2007: 133).

7   Reprinted by permission of the publisher, from *The Practice of Justice: A Theory of Lawyer's Ethics*, by William H. Simon, p. 23, Cambridge, MA: Harvard University Press, Copyright © 1998 by the President and Fellows of Harvard College.

reluctance to engage these grand ideas can limit and restrict the imagination (Sells 1996: 37). These mental habits include objectification by the lawyer of people and situations, and the resulting detachment from self and others. Lawyers, Sells asserts, have become abstracted from the world of experience (Sells 1996: 175). This poses an enormous problem for practicing lawyers who are called upon to make difficult decisions in the messiness and complexity of their own lives, the organizations in which they operate, and the clients that they serve.

Most law schools have not taken seriously the critical role of the legal academy in equipping law students with the self-awareness and practices needed to create an enduring moral framework that will help them navigate the moral minefields of practicing law.[8] While Ethics and Professional Responsibility has long been a required course for all law students in accredited American law schools, most institutions have taught this course in large classes that combine lectures on the Rules with case study reviews, leaving students little time or encouragement for personal and group reflection on the intersection of personal values and professional expectations.[9] The good news is that a growing number of law schools are attempting to address these questions through new pedagogies and curricula, experiential learning opportunities such as legal clinics, as well as other institution-wide innovations.[10] Faculty are introducing reflective and

---

8   This is not to say that the legal profession has not voiced concerns about ethics and professionalism and the failure of law schools to instill moral practice in students; to the contrary, lawyers' criticism of their colleagues' ethics and of legal education appears to have been around for as long as the profession itself (Brest 1995, Galanter 1996, Lerman 1998, Luban and Millemann 1996). But when it comes to the *legal academy* and the extent it has changed its teaching to respond to the profession's concerns about its members' ethics, there are few examples of across-the-board changes in legal pedagogy. The best example of change that American law schools have made to the way they teach their students is the development of clinical education, which is a relatively recent phenomenon of the past three decades (see Grossman 1974), but still is not a requirement for accreditation under the American Bar Association (Chapter 3, Interpretation 302-5 of the 2010–2011 Standards and Rules of Procedure for Approval of Law Schools). As the results of the Carnegie Report show, the core of law school pedagogy, with its emphasis on appellate case law, remains unchanged even when it comes to teaching law students about professionalism and ethics in practice.

9   Indeed, it has been noted that many law students (and their professors) view courses on Professional Responsibility as "add-ons," given that they frequently count toward fewer credit hours and focus solely on the law of professional ethics. See Bundy (1995: 27–8), Pipkin (1979).

10   The Committee on Curriculum of the Association of American Law Schools (AALS) conducted a survey of current curriculum reform efforts and received responses from 96 law schools. A number of schools reported developing special programs for teaching ethics to law students as well as overhauling the first-year curriculum to provide, among other things, more opportunities for self-evaluation and critique. The complete results of the survey as well as postings from schools detailing their curricular innovations are available at http://www.aals.org/services_curriculum_committee_survey.php [accessed

interdisciplinary approaches to teaching ethics and professional responsibility that incorporate novels, films, journaling, student interviews of practitioners, guest speakers, and candid class discussions about the gap between the Rules and reality of practicing law.

II. Building a New Course

The school of law has a tradition of developing curriculum that teaches students not only the rules, doctrine, policy, and procedure of legal systems, but also what it means to practice responsibly within such legal systems.[11] Most recently, the school of law began conversations with the Center for Law & Renewal[12] about improving how lawyers learn and practice the law as well as ways to ground the practice of law in an "ethic of care" for clients and community by emphasizing leadership and professionalism.[13] These conversations culminated in the Center's recommendation to its funder, the Fetzer Institute, to make a significant financial investment in the school of law so that Maryland could develop its curriculum to advance these values; the result was the Leadership, Ethics and Democracy Building Initiative. The subject of this chapter, the course "Professional Responsibility and Practice: the Rules and Reality," is one of the curricular programs in LEAD's Ethics and Professionalism component.

The background for the course included a three-day gathering of 20 legal educators and practitioners at The Crossings, a beautiful retreat center in the Texas hill country outside of Austin. Two people from the school of law attended the retreat: Professor Barbara Bezdek and Rebecca Saybolt Bainum, then the

---

31 January 2012]. For a more detailed discussion of innovations undertaken at Stanford Law School, Indiana University Maurer School of Law, and Washington & Lee School of Law, see Cunningham and Alexander (2011), Schultz (1995). After 130 years of following the Langdell model for law school curriculum, Harvard Law School decided to reform its first year curriculum in order to better prepare its students for practice (McArdle 2008).

11   The University of Maryland School of Law began its Clinical Law Program with the aim of "afford[ing] students the opportunity to begin the transition from law school to law practice; from learning to be a lawyer to being a lawyer" (Bezdek 1991: 112). The School of Law also created Legal Theory and Practice courses in order to provide students "an alternative vision of professional role and the possibilities of law" (Boldt and Feldman 1992: 1112–13). See also Bezdek (1992a, 1992b).

12   The Center operated for seven years as a nonprofit organization based in Kalamazoo, Michigan. The Center was dissolved after its board and staff made the decision to migrate its mission to the new "Leadership, Ethics and Democracy Building" initiative based at the University of Maryland School of Law.

13   The concept of teaching professional responsibility as an "ethic of care," a term originally used by Carol Gilligan, is not new at the University of Maryland. See Glennon (1992).

Managing Director of the Clinical Law Program.[14] Bonnie Allen, then Executive Director of the Center for Law and Renewal, who later became an adjunct professor at the school of law, convened the gathering. The purpose was to share models of experiential teaching that members of the law faculty are using to encourage law students to examine their professional goals and moral identity as they move toward law practice. Then housed at the Fetzer Institute, the Center was a hub for convening different groups of legal professionals to discuss and discern how best to advance reforms in the profession that will foster a relationship-centered ethic of lawyering. Center-sponsored programs included *Courage to Lead* retreats for law professionals based on the *Circles of Trust™* model,[15] *Leadership, Ethics and Innovation* workshops for leaders in private sector law, and democracy-building work through *Spirit of Justice* retreats and community lawyering training programs in post-Hurricane Katrina Mississippi.

The Center's hope in sponsoring the Texas retreat was to create a relaxed, open, and affirming space where educators could share classroom-based curriculum and action-learning programs that prepare students to examine ethics and professional responsibility "beyond the rules" as they make important decisions in their lives.[16] These decisions include discernment about vocational direction, understanding the different models of lawyering and the ethical implications associated with each, relating to clients in roles that extend beyond amoral "hired guns" or legal technicians, and becoming good stewards in advancing democracy and justice through the law.[17] The Center also sought to encourage: 1) building a stronger

---

14   Ms. Saybolt Bainum is now the Director of Academic Services at the University of Baltimore School of Law in Baltimore, Maryland.

15   Based on the work of Parker J. Palmer and the Center for Courage and Renewal, www.couragerenewal.org, this cross-professional model uses reflective practices to focus on the rejoining of "soul and role," and reconnecting who we are with what we do.

16   Facilitated by Washington, D.C. attorney, educator and group facilitator Cait Clarke, the agenda was designed to create opportunities for participants to engage in deep reflection on their own values, professional identities and vocational paths, as well as to generate group dialogue about using law school courses to encourage this kind of reflection by students. The retreat also featured a "fishbowl" exercise where several practitioners sat in the middle of a circle, surrounded by legal educators who listened to the practitioners discuss what they wish they had learned in law school about coping with ethical and moral challenges. One of the evening sessions included a sample of a *Circles of Trust™* retreat, and discussion with Patti Gearhart Turner, Assistant Dean for Student Affairs at Texas Wesleyan University School of Law, and Roland Johnson, Fort Worth attorney and 2009–2010 President of the Texas Bar, about how they were able to persuade the administration to include a retreat approach to Ethics and Professional Responsibility in the curriculum. They stressed the importance of taking the students off campus into a retreat setting, and the very positive reviews that students gave of their experience.

17   David Hall, then professor at Northeastern University School of Law and current President of the University of the Virgin Islands, addressed the group on the topic of the spiritual challenges in the law. Recognized as a leading teacher and scholar in the areas

network of educators and practitioners interested in these matters and kinds of teaching; 2) exposure to new teaching models and ideas; 3) identification of common goals, themes, and practices across curriculum and institutions; and 4) a clearer sense of how to take this kind of teaching to scale in the legal academy.

The participants from the school of law returned from the retreat newly inspired to answer the critiques of legal education in the Carnegie Report and *Best Practices* study. Cognizant of the need to provide more meaningful instruction about professionalism and legal ethics, Allen, Saybolt Bainum, and Professor Brenda Bratton Blom began crafting a proposal in the spring of 2007. In May of that year, the Clinical Faculty at the school of law passed a resolution to support a course that would expand and systematize the time and space when clinical students might reflect on their developing identities as legal professionals, thereby extending the clinical program's mission of linking theory and practice into the realm of ethical development.[18] The Clinical Faculty tasked Blom and Saybolt Bainum, along with Bonnie Allen, to carry out this resolution.

This new course, as approved by the Curriculum Committee, was a seminar available only to students concurrently enrolled in the clinical program[19] and

---

of Ethics and Professional Responsibility, Professor Hall acknowledged the difficulty— but importance—of integrating the rules, personal values, reflective practices, and vision into law school teaching. He also stressed the need to develop teaching materials that systematically demonstrate how to achieve these goals, and a casebook that brings validity to this kind of teaching. Professor Hall cautioned the academy to avoid operating in isolation, but rather to work consistently with the profession and bar associations to reposition the Rules. Finally, he stated that the legal profession must be able to assess and measure what these approaches achieve; otherwise, the skeptics will marginalize them as "soft stuff." At the end of the retreat, participants voiced strong interest in staying connected as a network, exchanging curriculum and syllabi, developing a Table of Contents for a casebook, and collectively identifying levers of power that could move this work forward nationally.

18   The School of Law at Maryland has a nationally recognized Clinical Law Program, consistently ranked among the top 10 programs in the country. Each full-time day student is required to take an experience- or practice-based course in order to graduate. This requirement, called the Cardin Requirement after U.S. Senator Ben Cardin '67, includes any course of at least five credits that provides students with an experience of how the law operates in practice and that also includes a discussion of race, class, and the structure of our legal service delivery system. Almost every student satisfies this requirement by working in a clinic or taking a Legal Theory and Practice (LTP) course. The clinics cover a wide range of topics but all involve providing legal services to the poor, to those without access to justice, or to the organizations that represent these groups. Each year, over 250 students enroll in one of the more than 20 clinics or LTP seminars offered. These students must have completed at least a third of their graduation requirements in order to represent clients, so most students are in their second or third year of law school.

19   "Clinical program" for the purposes of this chapter includes all courses involved in live client and legal advocacy activities, whether clinical courses or those under the Legal Theory and Practice description.

provided students with an opportunity to explore the ethical issues of practice as they made their first foray into practice. Faculty believed that creating a course of study that was both complementary to, yet distinct from, specific and concentrated clinical work would help deepen students' facility with complex philosophical dimensions of lawyering. A fundamental premise of the course was that the Rules of Professional Conduct, though important for defining acceptable practices for the legal profession, operate as a floor and not a ceiling. The Rules do not always provide clear guidance or proposed courses of action to lawyers, nor do they adequately explore what is ethical conduct in different contexts.

There were several core principles that drove the course development. The first was that "significant attention would be paid to the discussion of lawyers as leaders and communicators in a democracy."[20] The second was to maintain a fundamental commitment to support each student as they worked to link their personal code of conduct with the Rules of Professional Responsibility. And the third was to create a safe space, a step away from the general competitive drive that has been built into law school and legal practice, where students could reflect upon their experiences and struggle with the complex issues facing the legal professional in ways that would allow integration into their own core personal codes of conduct.

The course also aimed to provide many different opportunities for clinical students to use their developing knowledge about the legal profession in a variety of modalities. The value in taking a multifaceted approach to student course work in law school is clearly articulated in Robin Boyle's article "Employing Active-Learning Techniques and Metacognition in Law School: Shifting Energy from Professor to Student" (Boyle 2003), in which she reviews the literature about teaching and learning both inside the legal profession and beyond. Boyle explains that enhancing law students' metacognition, a term originating in the field of psychology that refers to individuals' ability to play an active role in guiding their learning processes and to apply what and how they learn across different settings, will maximize their "ability to absorb both the doctrine and the skills necessary for the practice of law" (Boyle 2003: 5, 8, quoting Gavelek and Raphael 1985). To accomplish this, teachers should employ a variety of teaching techniques in order to engage with the varied learning styles (visual, tactual, kinesthetic, analytic, and global) of their students (Boyle 2003: 8–12). Thus, because the Rules and Reality seminar's primary purpose was to build a particular kind of metacognition—an ability for students to actively integrate doctrinal rules of professional responsibility into their experience as practicing student attorneys in the clinic, and vice versa—among students with varied learning styles, the course used a variety of texts and assignments.

---

20   Course Proposal to Curriculum Committee. On file with author Blom.

III. Organizing the Learning Activities:
The Nuts and Bolts of the First Three Years of Teaching

"Professional Responsibility and Practice: The Rules and Reality" began with eight articulated goals: 1) Students should understand and be able to articulate the primary stressors within the profession; 2) Students should develop the ability to think critically about the profession; 3) Students should understand the variety of forms of practice, and choices that they have, including using their degree not to practice but in other ways; 4) Students should understand that lawyers can be agents of change, and have the opportunity to reflect on themselves as agents of change; 5) Students should understand the Rules of Professional Responsibility (both Model and Maryland), Codes of Civility, specialty rules for specialty bars, and other statutory and advisory locations for the ethical boundaries and advices of the profession; 6) Students should understand these rules as a floor, not a ceiling; 7) Students should have some appreciation for the history of the development of our professional rules and codes of conduct; and 8) Students should be able to pass the Multistate Professional Responsibility Examination (MPRE).

Although the course began with these eight goals, in the first three years that the course was offered, three distinct foci emerged: 1) what are the Model Rules of Professional Conduct and how are they applied; 2) what are the philosophical underpinnings of legal ethics; and 3) how do legal practitioners incorporate both the Model Rules and theories of ethics into their day-to-day practice, personal and professional identity? These foci are, of course, not dissimilar to every professional responsibility course offered in every law school. But our goal was to make this adventure personal and grounded in students' own practice in law clinics. In this section, we present the teaching methods we used and the adjustments made along the way.

A. Studying the Model Rules

Rules by the book, but which book?   There was a continuing struggle to find the book that captured what and how we were attempting to teach the Model Rules of Professional Conduct (the Rules). Teaching the course three times, we used a different text and compendium each year. Each text approached the Rules differently, so we developed assignments that complemented the readings and made the students think critically about the Rules and their application.

The first year, using the text *Professional Responsibility: Ethics by the Pervasive Method* by Deborah Rhode (1994), students were responsible for answering the problems within the readings, with each student responsible for leading at least one class during the semester. The assignments asked the student to identify which Rules were invoked by the problem, to solve the problem using the Rules as the basis for the answer, and then to discuss any additional considerations beyond the Rules that influenced the students' conclusion. All students would post their answers on Blackboard at least 90 minutes before each Monday class (the day we worked from the Rhode book), and then come prepared to participate in the discussion during the class period. Having each student work independently to solve the ethics problem and then submit an answer before class ensured that everyone was prepared to have an informed conversation; each had taken the time to read the Rule, think about what it says and does not say, and then see how the Rule applied to the problem. The challenge was to make sure that conversation about the problem did not lapse into whether the student "got the right answer" or "got the wrong answer" and instead to engage the students in thinking critically about whether the Rules adequately addressed the problem.

The second year, we used *Ethics of the Lawyer's Work*, by James Moliterno (2003). Each student was assigned to a group (A or B), and the group was responsible for presenting the problem and answer, which then was worked through collectively in class on Mondays. Answers were, again, posted on Blackboard. This approach worked well because it required students to work together in groups to resolve the ethics problem presented in the text and craft an ethics opinion on which the entire group agreed. The unexpected downside was that much of the rich debate and discussion that went into resolving the ethics problem occurred outside of class and was lost when the students made their presentations in class. The rest of the class (including the professors) missed hearing the varying viewpoints on how to apply the Rules to the problem at hand.

In the third year, we did not choose a "problem-based" text. At the beginning of the class, each student was assigned a Rule to read and present to the rest of the class. The student had to include some of the key cases that shed light on how the rule should be interpreted, as well as the core ethical debates surrounding each rule. The purpose of the assignment was for students to grasp not only the content of the Rules, but also to have an appreciation for grey areas in the Rules. It was made clear at the beginning of the course that the aim of studying the Rules was not to prepare students for the standardized Multistate Professional Responsibility Examination (MPRE).[21]

Students reacted positively to this open approach to discussing the Rules. In fact, it was so successful that we could not keep to our scheduled time. One alternative approach to discussing the Rules that allowed for a more effective use of class time was to have students use an online discussion board to post their comments about the Rule before coming to class. Having the students read a Rule

---

21 The goal of preparing students to take the MPRE was a continuing and vexing problem. The first year, the mid-term exam was a practice MPRE. The scores for the MPRE were not counted but became a "bump up or down" in the grading process. The second year, the mid-term was graded, but we strongly suggested that students enroll in an MPRE preparation course. The MPRE is not required for bar membership in Maryland, and in year three, it was decided to delete MPRE preparation as a goal for the course, though one class was spent on the conundrum of taking an "ethics by the bubble method" approach in the field of law. We worked through a series of MPRE practice questions together, after having the students take a practice exam for an assignment. The conversation was rich.

and a short summary of the ethical debates surrounding the Rule made for a more controlled, but lively, class discussion.

Each year, we have used a compendium of the Rules. There are many examples that are available, each with strengths and weaknesses. We have used *The Law Governing Lawyers* by Martyn and Fox, and Rotunda and Dzienkowski's *Professional Responsibility, A Student's Guide*. Each of these was supplemented by the Maryland Code of Civility and a comparative analysis of the Maryland Rules and Model Rules when appropriate.

Attorney Grievance Commission cases: reading about practice   Occasionally, in the first two years, we would circulate a particularly interesting or disturbing ruling by a court about alleged or found attorney misconduct. This became a staple of the course during the third year. Each student had an assignment to research a Maryland attorney disciplinary case and briefly present that case to the rest of the class. During the first 10 minutes of class, the students had to explain the underlying facts of the case, the claims brought by the Attorney Grievance Commission, the Rules of Professional Conduct allegedly violated (as well as any additional laws violated), and the ultimate decision of the Court of Appeals, the highest court in Maryland and the forum responsible for making final decisions about petitions for attorney discipline. The purpose of the assignment was two-fold. First, students learned about the process of professional discipline in a self-regulated profession like the practice of law.[22] Second, students began to see that many of the lawyers were disciplined for making the same mistakes, mishandling client funds and failing to communicate properly. The existence of these patterns of misconduct opened up conversations about the pressures of practice and ways to fortify against those pressures.[23]

Application to student practice in-class clinic case rounds   In the first year, we regularly asked students to reflect on their work in their journals. We scheduled one day during the term where students were asked to come to class prepared to present ethical issues from their clinics. The second year, we created three days for case rounds. All students from a particular clinic were asked to work together to prepare to present ethical issues/challenges from their clinic. For the third year, we continued the three case rounds days, but did not suggest that clinical students from each clinic work together to prepare. It became a more free-flowing

---

22   The ABA Survey on Lawyer Discipline Systems (SOLD) provides a wonderful look at lawyer discipline systems in jurisdictions across the United States and serves as a great starting point for discussions of how and why the legal profession regulates itself (ABA Standing Commission on Professional Discipline 2009).

23   As an aside, the *ABA Journal* noted that 20% of the cases decided in the October 2009 term of the U.S. Supreme Court were on attorney misconduct. This astounding percentage of the docket makes for an interesting set of discussions in and of itself (Weiss 2010).

discussion. Students were invited to talk about their client work and any concerns arising from their practice.

Because all of the students and the professors were in the clinic "law firm," confidentiality was not a problem. Some students shared feelings of apprehension about the clients they worked with, sometimes clients who the students did not like personally, and asked whether they were really serving the greater social good by advocating for their clients' interests. Students discussed the challenges of professionalism they faced, either in dealing with student colleagues in the clinic or with other lawyers they met during the course of handling client matters. The clinic case rounds gave students an opportunity to talk to each other about their professional experiences, to provide feedback and alternative perspectives— learning how to be good colleagues by practicing in a seminar setting.[24]

Another benefit came from the fact that the class draws from a variety of clinics in which students do different kinds of legal work—criminal defense, community advocacy, public health legislation, mediation. The clinic case rounds allowed students to hear from each other about the variety of forms of legal practice, the different roles lawyers take on, and the special challenges included in those roles.

Reflection—journal entries   Students wrote journal entries at various points during the semester. The journals were reflective pieces responding to questions about the materials students were reading, the discussions that were unfolding in the classroom, as well as their personal thoughts on practicing in the clinic and becoming a lawyer. In the first year, these journal entries were due weekly and were tied to a particular reading, though we asked students also to tie their reflections to their clinic work. In the second year, the journal entries were more targeted to readings and reflections about what visiting practitioners were saying. In the third year, we asked students to reflect on their learning in response to general questions five times during the term.[25]

Through trial and error, the professors found that there needs to be a substantial period of time between journal entries to allow students to build up a wealth of experiences upon which they can reflect. Minimally, students would write three

---

24   For more on theory and best practices of clinic case rounds, see Bryant and Milstein (2007).

25   Journal questions included: 1) reflection on an excerpt from Parker J. Palmer's book, *A Hidden Wholeness: Journey Toward an Undivided Life* (2004), which poses questions about one's greatest fears about "getting lost in the storm" as a lawyer and what the law student will use as a rope to "find his or her way home" when the blizzards strike; 2) Are you afraid or excited about the changes in the profession? Why? Do you view these changes as good changes or bad? Why?; 3) What are your thoughts about the importance of integrity in the profession? How should the profession ensure lawyer integrity? Does the MPRE provide any indication about the integrity of the practitioners in the professions? What tools might be more helpful?; 4) Do the Rules provide sufficient guidance for our profession? Could we do better? What other tools will you use?; and 5) How has this discussion challenged, changed, or affirmed your thinking about our profession and your place in it?

journal entries, one at the beginning of the semester about their personal ethics, one at the semester mid-point, and one at the end of the semester.

B. Philosophy and Ethics

Readings were selected with the hope that they would address the philosophy of lawyering: the role of lawyers in society and the personal challenges of lawyering. The objective was to have students read about lawyers as agents of change and to think critically about the legal profession and their role in it. This meant attempting both to provide a historical appreciation of the development of legal and professional ethics and identity, as well as some ways to understand the current dialogues about the role of ethics in the profession.

In the first year, we used Susan Carle's book, *Lawyers' Ethics and the Pursuit of Social Justice* (2005). In the second year, we used the Rhode and Luban book, *Legal Ethics: Law Stories* (2006). In the third year, we used Luban's *Legal Ethics and Human Dignity* (2007b). Each text has strengths and weaknesses. The Luban book has a much more complete history of legal ethics and is much more philosophical (and therefore more challenging for some law students). We found that the students who liked it the most were equal in number to those who liked it the least. The discussion about legal ethics was, for teaching faculty, some of the richest and most difficult to lead.

Lawyers and ethical engagement—stories and practitioners   For the first two years, the final project for the class was to interview practitioners about their real-world ethical challenges and to present the results of their finding to the class in a format that would produce discussion and meaningful learning.[26] The first year presentations included: a charrette comparing and illustrating the common and distinct characteristics between an estate attorney and a public defender that resulted in more similarities than differences; a highly sophisticated distillation of four practitioners' profiles and attributes in which the rest of the class had to guess which feature fit which profile (which, interestingly, challenged most of our assumptions of the profiles); and a dramatic presentation of real-life ethical dilemmas that illustrated the complexities and "gray areas" of the rules.

The second year continued presentations on the results of practitioner interviews with a mix of media. There were some videotaped interviews of practitioners and there were PowerPoint presentations that deleted specific identifiers, as the

---

26   Other law school professional responsibility courses integrate practitioner interviews into the course curriculum. For example, John Conley and Paul Haskell used interviewing in their course, "The Law Firm," for students at the University of North Carolina School of Law and Duke University School of Law. The course centered on an ethnographic interviewing project that provided an empirical study of legal professionals while simultaneously allowing students to learn about the culture of the legal profession and better understand what it means to be a practicing lawyer (Conley 2003: 1956–62).

practitioner made clear that his ability to honestly answer the questions was linked to anonymity. That, in and of itself, was an eye-opener for students.

We did not use this final project in the third year, though this exercise was reintroduced into the teaching model for the fifth year of teaching. Students find it to be an extraordinarily rich "capstone" experience for the class.

Students and ethical engagement—the blizzard   Each year, we used exercises that were targeted at getting students to experience ethics questions in a nonlinear way. Drawing on the Circles of Trust™ model developed by Parker Palmer and the Center for Courage and Renewal, we used the "Touchstones" exercise, which asks students to work with art materials to create a visual map that traces their own moral development and vocational journeys. We also used the "Temple" exercise developed by Professor David Hall at Northeastern University School of Law to explore the Rules as a "floor," accompanied by values, experiences, reflection, and vision, to shape moral and professional judgment. These vehicles for exploring the moral foundation of students' understanding of ethics and professionalism were both disorienting and challenging. Students reported learning about themselves and others in ways they had not in law school. Former students have shared that they refer back to these exercises as critical to internalizing their own story of moral development.

Reflection—personal mission statement   Each year, at the end of the semester, each student drafted a mission statement concisely articulating his or her professional purpose and how he or she would realize that purpose in the future. We worked to find ways to teach writing mission statements and ultimately developed a series of questions to pose in order to help students develop a mission statement. We asked students to reflect on why they want to be lawyers, what opportunities or needs they will address as lawyers, and what principles or beliefs will guide their work. These statements were collected, along with envelopes with permanent addresses, with the intention of mailing these statements to students after they have been practicing for two or three years. The thought was that, by that time, they may be ready for a check-in about whether they are practicing consistent with the mission they created for themselves.

C. Practice—What are the Parameters of the Profession and What am I Doing Here?

Readings and panel discussions with experienced practitioners   Each year, the seminar included guest speakers invited to talk about their experience in legal practice. During the first two years, speakers were invited to talk with the class around some particular reading or topic. In the first year, the conversations were about the way their practice developed and how they understand their personal responsibility for leadership and professionalism. Speakers came from big firms, academia, solo firms, criminal and civil practice areas, public interest, and profit-making settings. In the second year, we invited a practitioner almost every week, and they co-presented readings from the Rhode and Luban reader, using their own experience as a reference point in the conversations with students.

In the third year, we assembled a panel of attorneys who agreed to come to the class four times during the semester.[27] They took the lead in a discussion of Richard Susskind's book, *The End of Lawyers?* (Susskind 2008). Having the same panel of practitioners return to the class proved rewarding. The speakers had a chance to bounce ideas off one another, to agree and disagree, and to share their individual perspectives on student questions. As the semester continued, they felt more comfortable sharing their personal, not just professional, insights.

In addition to speaking about their personal experiences, the panel of returning guests discussed the future of the legal profession and how it is changing. The panelists and the students read the same assignments from Susskind's book, allowing us to incorporate a mini "book club" in which the practitioners and students discussed their reactions to the book. The discussion about the future of the profession, technology, and ethics was a wide-ranging conversation that revealed both the fears of students graduating in the midst of a legal (and larger economic) recession as well as the hopes by these experienced practitioners and students that this crisis presents opportunities for the profession to change for the better. There was a lively debate about the power of technology to usher in positive change and what would make the profession "better." While there was fairly uniform agreement that the structure of the profession and client expectations of legal professionals are in rapid transition, the vision of where the profession is headed was not at all clear or uniform. This ambivalence was both unsettling and interesting for the students.

Presentations   In the third year, students in the seminar were assigned to research live ethical dilemmas arising in the clinic and then make group presentations to the Professional Responsibility lecture courses. Some of the topics came out of the seminar students' own clinic work and other topics were tagged by the larger Clinical Faculty and recommended as presentation topics for the seminar students to use. Sharing students' clinical experience was intended to give faculty with different academic interests the ability to include current, live topics of professionalism in their teaching. Rather than relying on imaginary hypothetical situations or the outlier cases that make it into a Professional Responsibility casebook, professors could use these real ethics problems to give students in the

---

27   In the end, they actually came only three times, as the first scheduled panel was snowed out in the great "Snowmageddon" of 2010 in Baltimore. This panel included one African-American solo practitioner, one senior Jewish male partner in a small, boutique (and highly successful) civil rights firm, one Latina working on issues of access to the courts as an employee of the court system, and one white female partner from a mega-firm with offices around the world.

Professional Responsibility lecture courses an understanding of why a critical engagement with the Rules is extremely important for practice.

The seminar students took on the role of guest teachers, visiting the lecture class for a discussion of the ethical challenges of their practice with colleagues. In order to prepare for their presentations, the seminar students gathered information about the clinic matter by talking with the clinical professor and students. They wrote and distributed to the lecture class a general statement of facts that gave the background to the ethics problem without revealing any confidential details relating to the clinic's representation. The seminar students then developed a series of discussion questions that asked the members of the lecture class to talk about how they would respond to the situation and what Rules of Professional Responsibility would guide their decision-making.

The first group presented a legal ethics problem that arose from work that involves partnering with organizational clients, such as community organizations, service providers, other University of Maryland graduate schools, and legal service providers, in order to craft new policies. The Clinic had joined a coalition of organizations to work on one such policy that entailed drafting legislation. After two unsuccessful attempts to implement the policy, a federal lawsuit was brought by the U.S. Department of Justice against the Mayor and City Council of Baltimore City. The coalition members decided as a group to intervene in the litigation and chose the Clinic as their legal representative.

It was the Clinic's new role as the coalition's legal representative that stimulated the conversation about legal ethics and professional responsibility. The seminar students developed questions that sought to define the relationship between the Clinic, the coalition, and the individual groups comprising the coalition. The students explored the special responsibilities of communication that come with representing organizational clients and the unique conflict-of-interest problems that arise for lawyers when representing a coalition to which they belong.

The second group's presentation developed out of a case in the Immigration Clinic. In this case, the Immigration Clinic agreed to represent a woman seeking asylum in the United States from ethnic persecution in her home country. When the Immigration Clinic decided to take her case, the client had already filed her asylum application, been denied, and was waiting for trial before an administrative asylum judge. The Immigration Clinic students conducted a thorough background investigation of the client's story, checked facts with witnesses in the home country, ran the client's story by an expert witness, and had the client attend more than 20 counseling sessions with a local nonprofit organization that specialized in this particular type of asylum case. Other than a minor discrepancy involving the issue date of the client's birth certificate, a discrepancy for which the client provided a reasonable explanation, the client's story was credible and the Immigration Clinic prepared for trial. A few days before trial, the opposing counsel from the Department of Homeland Security (DHS) notified the Immigration Clinic student attorneys that she believed the client's story to be fraudulent; the DHS attorney did not elaborate and gave no further explanation. At trial, following the Immigration

Clinic students' presentation of their case, the DHS attorney confronted the client with asylum applications from two individuals who had identical asylum stories—same family members, names, dates, and format. The DHS attorney explained that all three people, including the Immigration Clinic's client, had employed an independent paralegal service to help prepare and file their asylum application and the preparer was the subject of a year-long investigation by DHS for selling and filing fake asylum applications. The client denied the accusation at the proceeding but, afterwards, eventually did confess to the Immigration Clinic students that she bought the story because she believed her own was not sufficient to gain asylum in the United States.

For their presentation, the seminar students presented the case and then asked the lecture class to talk about whether the Immigration Clinic could be found liable for the client's misrepresentations. They explored whether the DHS attorney had a duty to disclose to the Immigration Clinic students that she knew their client's story was false prior to the beginning of the trial and to provide specific information about the general allegation that had been made. And finally, the students asked the lecture class to decide what the Immigration Clinic should do about continuing representation of the client—should the Immigration Clinic continue to assist the client, should it advise the client to cooperate as a witness in the DHS investigation, should it withdraw entirely from all representation, and what, if anything, should it say to the Administrative Law Judge?

The third and final group of seminar students to present to a Professional Responsibility lecture class looked at the JustAdvice® service, a brief advice program run by the Community Justice Clinic. For a JustAdvice® session, customers pay $10 for 30 minutes of brief advice from an attorney. The purpose of the JustAdvice® service is to fill the gap in legal services between those who qualify for Legal Aid assistance and those who have the means to hire a private attorney. The customers seeking a JustAdvice® session are primarily working poor who have legal questions and need guidance in developing a plan for their own *pro se* representation. The attorneys are volunteers, either retired members of the Maryland bar or members of the lo-bono network, Civil Justice, Inc. In order to protect its volunteer attorneys from allegations of malpractice, the JustAdvice® service had the customers sign a Disclaimer of Representation. The Disclaimer explained that the conversation with the attorney was *not* intended to "render a definitive legal opinion" and that the attorney does not represent the customer as a result of the conversation they have in a JustAdvice® session.

The seminar students used the Disclaimer of Representation as the basis for their presentation. They asked the students in the lecture class to explain why such a disclaimer was important to the lawyers and then asked whether the lawyers could in fact disclaim representation in instances where they provided customers with more than plain legal information. Students were asked to assess whether the language of the Disclaimer accomplished that task and to propose redrafted language if they found the language problematic. The entire conversation was framed by a larger discussion about the importance of making limited representation and unbundled legal services available, and in so doing protecting both the interests of lawyers and their customer-clients.

Overall, an unexpected and positive outcome of these presentations was that the research the seminar students conducted on the ethical dilemmas increased the clinical firm's capacity to find resolution on current ethical issues. An unexpected challenge of this presentation assignment was that it proved difficult for the seminar students to teach their peers in a way that used discussion, rather than a top-down presentation style.[28] Ultimately, the presentations of ethics problems from the Clinical program sought to add real-life practice to the instruction of professional responsibility, to broaden the sense of collegiality, and to create interdependence among law students and law professors around the topic of what ethical practice means.

IV. Lessons Learned: Effective Ways to Engage Law Students in Legal Ethics and Professional Identity Formation

The first lesson, of course, in every class, is that no matter the syllabus and intent, how the class develops is influenced greatly by the students that register to take the class. The first year we offered the class, 17 students enrolled: 12 women, 5 men, 2 African Americans, 1 Asian American, and 1 Orthodox Jew. The diversity of projected practice settings was wide—from large firms to public interest or government—and from defense and prosecution to in-house lawyers. Several were headed to clerkships and then firms. The second year, 13 students enrolled: 7 women and 6 men; 1 African American student, 1 Asian American student, and 1 student not born in the United States. Slightly over half were in their last semester of law school. Again, the practice settings where students were headed were diverse, both in content and structure. The third year, we had 14 students enroll: 6 women and 8 men; 9 second-year law students, and 5 students in their last semester of law school. Four students were African American, 2 Asian Americans, and 1 student born outside of the United States. The practice settings where people were headed included an even wider range of prospects, including business and entrepreneurship interests, the military JAG Corps and a range of big firm, small firm, government, and nonprofit practice areas. In each year, there were a few students who had experiences in the work world before entering law school as well as part-time students who worked full-time jobs during the day. This "leavening" experience was always an interesting addition to the conversation.

Several things that we expected happened. We expected that students would be a little uncomfortable with some of the more "nonacademic" exercises. We also

---

28   We have clearly modeled the lecture style in most of their legal education. It was what they were, then, playing back to their fellow students. They are not skilled as Socratic teachers, and we had not really thought through how to teach them to teach, perhaps undervaluing a skill that we have developed over years of teaching.

expected them to be a little bit resistant to journaling. We expected that they would not have a very expansive language to talk about complex ethical issues. Further, we expected that they would worry obsessively about their grades. For each of our teaching years, generally, these expectations turned out to be correct. Each year, there were, of course, outliers. Always, there were some generally deep thinkers (and over-thinkers). All of the students learned to use their journaling over time, but there were some who were deeply expressive from day one. And every year, we had a student or two who had been philosophy majors in undergraduate school. And in the third year, we had a student who had graduated from Yale Divinity School.

After the first year, we summed up three things that we had not expected to happen in the course. Some of these discoveries led us to change how we structured the following years. Some of these things just continued to be seemingly unsolvable.

The first thing that we were not really prepared for was how hungry the students were for this conversation. Sometimes, this was because of the clinical work itself, as they were struggling to inhabit a lawyer identity for the first time, balancing and juggling the many different aspects of creating a relationship with a client, managing time, finding and arguing the appropriate law, forging (or not forging) appropriate relationships with supervising attorneys, attorneys for the opposing side, witnesses, and experts, not to mention court clerks and judges. They jumped into the discussion with vigor and, sometimes, rancor. They debated hot-button issues of the profession as if they were members of the profession!

The second thing we did not anticipate was the level of judgment they carried about different kinds of practice settings. "Public Interest" and "Big Firm" were both set up as polar opposites in value-laden (value-dripping!) terms. We professors were taken aback by the prevailing—and overly simplistic—perceptions among many law students about different practice settings and we used class discussion with guest speakers as an opportunity to model and articulate an alternative view. Because of the feedback we received in the mid-term meetings, we immediately delivered a lecture on the structure of the legal profession and the need to understand how to move between types of practice organizations (big firm, medium-sized firm, government, solo firm, clinics) and the ways in which lawyers in all practice settings can serve those who lack access to justice (public interest, public service, pro bono, cause lawyering, community lawyering, etc.).[29] Finally, the discussion

---

29 We agree with Elizabeth Chambliss's argument that law schools have an institutional duty to communicate to students about the structures of the legal profession and to help students develop a vision of where, and how, they will fit into the profession (Chambliss 2012). Indeed, other law schools have taken steps to incorporate recent research on the profession into the first-year pedagogy. At the Indiana University Maurer School of Law, first-year law students take a special course, "The Legal Profession," on the economic and socio-legal structure and substance of the modern legal profession, incorporating current research from its Center on the Global Legal Profession. Students learn about

focused on what is needed for democracy to thrive—a vibrant civil society. This lecture de-polarized the class, and established a more professional attitude toward colleagues for the duration of the class.

Beginning with the second year, we decided to open the course with this depolarizing and informative lecture about the organizational structures within the profession and the multitude of ways that lawyers work within those structures to maximize access to justice. Summing up now, our expectation was that this lecture would encourage a more sophisticated discussion about the professional pressures and opportunities for engaging in ethical practice. It might, however, have dampened the frank nature of early discussions that were very rich sources of learning for the students. It was top-down information rather than bottom-up discovery.

The third thing we did not expect was how easy it is to assign too much to do! This could have been a five-credit course, rather than a three-credit course, and we still might have assigned too much to do. This conundrum holds true. Those of us who teach the course continue to struggle to match the readings to the time commitments expected. We have a better understanding at this point of how long some assignments will take and juggle between them. But the first half of the semester is heavy work for all of us.

In spite of making adjustments after the first year, second year brought another unexpected twist. There were two clinics that were over-represented: the community justice clinic and the mediation clinic. In the second year, the mediation students provided mediation services but never represented anyone in mediation. This over-representation of people who were *not* struggling with the lawyer-client relationship actually dampened the discussions within the class.

So, the things we learned that we cannot control are: who shows up, the diversity of student experiences both before law school and within the clinic, and whether students will be willing to stake out a position for debate and discussion. The things that we can control have to do with the syllabus, the guests, how often we have students to lead class, and the timing of their exposure to active and reflective practices.

It is also worth mentioning that hiring within the profession was still strong in year one, but the economy had been in major crisis for a year by the time we taught this course for the third time. Offering the reading and conversation on the restructuring of the legal profession seemed to tap into a discussion that the students desperately needed to have about their own future career options. Having that discussion within the context of the ethical obligation of the profession and the people within the profession proved both timely and provocative.

---

their new profession so that they can evaluate their own interests, abilities, and values in order to create a personal career path. Southwestern Law School also enhanced its Legal Analysis, Writing and Skills course, one of the first year required courses, to include a greater emphasis on the realities of legal practice, how to construct a legal career, and the ethical and social responsibilities of lawyers.

Certainly, we as educators, whose careers are relatively stable (not to dismiss or minimize the furloughs and budget cuts at law schools) need to pay attention to the stressors that we are not directly feeling but that our students are feeling acutely.

V. Student Evaluations: What They Told Us

We asked for student evaluation and feedback about the course each of the years that it has been offered. As discussed earlier, during the three years this course has been offered, three primary objectives emerged. Students were to learn about: 1) the Model Rules of Professional Conduct and how are they applied; 2) the philosophical underpinnings of legal ethics; and 3) how legal practitioners incorporate both the Model Rules and theories of ethics into their day-to-day practice, and personal and professional identities; *and* students would learn these components as part of a personal adventure that was grounded in their own clinic practice. Given that we had specific elements we wanted to accomplish through the course, we have, to a greater or lesser degree, tried to have students reflect on each of these elements.

Furthermore, the students have known from the beginning that the course was created as part of the LEAD Initiative and that we were deeply interested in their evaluation and input as to whether the course had any impact on their personal development as ethical leaders and socially conscious practitioners. To encourage candor, all evaluation questionnaires were filled out anonymously and students were made to understand that the contents of the questionnaires would not be reviewed until after grades had been entered.

With regard to the Model Rules and their application to legal practice, students gave very positive feedback. First, many students wrote in their evaluations that they specifically sought out a seminar setting for learning Professional Responsibility because they thought the topic was better suited to discussions in a small class rather than large podium lectures. As one student from the third year wrote, "I wanted to engage in meaningful discussion about various ethical topics. I was hoping for the smaller class environment where it would be easier to participate and interact with the rest of the class. Also, I wanted to more than just to be lectured on the rules." Another remarked, "This course was valuable to me, and I enjoyed my experience. It allowed me to take the time and think about legal ethics, and it did not threaten my learning by suggesting that I had to memorize the rules for an exam." Also, students found valuable the connection between the seminar discussions and their work practicing in the clinic: "Another thing that I have learned, which has been reinforced by my clinical experience, is the level of responsibility that you carry as a lawyer. And indeed, as someone mentioned in class, I am grateful to be entrusted with the responsibility BUT there are significant risks that accompany accepting this sort of responsibility and I think that I have a clearer idea of some of these risk factors now that I have taken our course."

Second, students wrote that working to apply the Rules to real, live ethics problems proved valuable. If anything, they wanted more time to discuss the Rules: "[I] have enjoyed learning more about the rules themselves and how they have been applied in a real-life context. Also, I highly enjoyed the presentations [of live clinic ethics problems] as I felt more involved and was able to learn a lot, in-depth of a few rules." Students from the first year responded: "I think the assigned problems forced me to wrangle with the Rules of Professional Responsibility and to ask myself where I would draw the line in ethically gray situations" (Last Journal Entry). Another wrote, "I think critical thinking about professional responsibility issues in real practice is far more helpful and beneficial than rote memorization and application of the professional rules." Similarly, another student said, "The rules were easily the most important thing I learned, but I think the need to look back at the rules and go over them were just as, if not more, important to remember. Just like any other kind of law, it is important to go back and look up the rule." Other students said that their biggest learning about the Rules occurred outside the classroom, in the clinic or at their student clerkships, when they applied what they had discussed in class to their own practice.

As to the teaching of the philosophical underpinnings of legal ethics, students returned mixed reviews. About half the students loved having an opportunity to sink their teeth into fleshy, philosophical questions of Law while others found the philosophy inaccessible and a digression away from real, practical concerns. For example, one student wrote, "I came into the course thinking that the rules do not, and cannot, provide zero-sum right or wrong answers in any given situation. They simply provide boundaries and, with exceptions, [serve] more as a guidance document than anything else. Ultimately, the rules allow behavior that I personally would feel uncomfortable engaging in. That is why the philosophical/ethical discussions are critical and far more important than simply analyzing the text of the rules—one must be introspective and analyze [his] personal framework and then compare that to the rules." While another student, from the same class, wrote: "This course helped me to realize many things that I like and dislike. For example, it made me realize that I enjoy teaching and perhaps I would like to enter legal academia. It also made me realize that I dislike philosophical/intangible discussions. I am someone who gets a lot more out of practical situations. The more words and fluff, the further I distance myself from the discussion."

Interacting with practitioners around issues of legal ethics and professionalism was well received by students. One student noted that it was "through the panel discussions [that] I was able to see how current practicing attorneys deal with the Rules that govern the legal profession … It was also interesting to learn about the legal profession through a 'popular' medium—not a legal journal or casebook." Some enjoyed hearing about the different career paths the practitioners took after law school. One student said s/he "found the panel discussions to be most effective in distilling the realities of the profession." Another noted that hearing from a variety of practitioners "made me realize that the term 'lawyer' does not mean one type of person. There are many types of lawyers. Similarly, there is no one set way to 'practice law.' This is what makes the legal profession challenging and, perhaps, the reason why the professional rules of ethical conduct exist. Everyone has a different view on what it means to be a 'lawyer' and what it means to 'practice law.' In order for our profession to function, we need a common thread. The ethical rules act as this common thread."

Perhaps the most reaffirming of all the comments received are those that describe the personal impact the course had on students. Students talked about how the course affected their views on the practice of law: "The course was valuable in that it introduced us to some lawyers and we spent a lot of time discussing what it will be like to be a lawyer. I am not sure if I had imagined myself in the role of a lawyer before this class;" and "At times during this course I felt more cynical about lawyers and the practice of law because it seems as though we separate ourselves and make assumptions about the profession based on what kind of practice the individual lawyer does. At other times, I felt optimistic that there are a number of talented lawyers trying to solve major problems facing our country and the world. I am not sure that this course has changed my views, so much as it has opened me up to thinking about problems from multiple views." Another talked about how the course affected his or her opinion of where the profession is going: "I agree with [Richard] Susskind that the traditional lawyer will dwindle as technology makes huge leaps. I think that lawyers just like any other profession will need to keep adapting to stay on top of the times."

When asked about whether the course impacted their personal values, many students said that they learned the importance of identifying boundaries across which they will not go, what Luban calls the professional equivalent of the canary in the mine (Luban 2007a: 295).[30] For example, one student wrote, "I appreciate [Luban's] idea of writing down my ethical 'canaries' so that when I encounter tough ethical problems in the future I am able to recognize what my limits are." And another: "I think this course helped me to realize that there are certain types of law that I would be completely incompatible with. Further, I feel that I learned that it may be necessary to draw a proverbial line in the sand regarding my ethical norms and values." Other students talked about how the course reinforced their own internal value system: "This course reminded me that I will remain true to my values by the same ways that I have stayed true to [them] over time. Mainly, by regularly assessing what I have done and why I do it, also by holding myself to a higher standard than is required by our profession, to my own standard." And another wrote, "I think this class reaffirmed my confidence in my own personal decision-making. Through our debates I learned to trust my own instincts more in

---

30   "My advice is to choose your canary carefully, understanding that before you enter a role your ideas about what ethical demands it entails may well be naïve. But, once you've selected the canary, never ignore it. If necessary, write down the 'I will never, ever' formula. Put it in an envelope, keep it in a drawer, and pull it out sometimes to remind yourself what it says. And, the moment the canary dies, get out of the mineshaft" (Luban 2007a: 295, reprinted with permission of Cambridge University Press).

regards to considering legal and ethical issues. I determined that I am very good at thinking logically but that I must learn to be a bit better at 'going with the flow,' when I cannot control things I am working on."

Conclusion

The LEAD Initiative at the school of law began as one way to address the challenge made by the Carnegie Foundation Report to legal educators. As the Carnegie Report identified, legal education lacks one of the fundamental components of professional training: an opportunity for students to develop their own professional identity and purpose. "Professional Responsibility and Practice: The Rules and Reality" sought to provide that opportunity in combination with the other two apprenticeships the Carnegie Report discusses, the cognitive or intellectual apprenticeship that provides students with an academic knowledge base and the apprenticeship that forms expert practice. The cognitive apprenticeship took shape around studying and analyzing the Model Rules of Professional Responsibility, learning about the systems in place that allow for the legal profession to self-regulate, as well as understanding the many different kinds of organizations and legal practitioners comprising the legal profession.

The expert practice apprenticeship occurred in a variety of settings. An essential part of the course was the application of the Rules of Professional Responsibility to real practice. The use of problem-based texts in the first two years and then the live clinic problems pushed students to work through the kinds of ethical dilemmas they will certainly face in real practice. In addition, the journaling requirement had students practice self-reflection and professional awareness, both of which are essential to being an expert legal practitioner. And the discussions during the Clinic Rounds had students practice the skills of reaching out to colleagues for advice, listening, and giving professional feedback. Finally, the continued presence in the classroom of expert practitioners, who interacted with students and shared their own experiences and insights into the profession, gave students additional exposure to the processes that seasoned legal practitioners employ to resolve questions of professional and legal ethics.

The course also created an environment in which students could develop their own professional identity, purpose, and definition of ethical leadership. The seminar was open only to students concurrently enrolled in clinic and who were having their first experience as legal practitioners. The exercises that asked students to trace the development of their own value system and the readings on legal ethics led to class discussions in which these new members of the profession could share their ideas about lawyers' roles in a democratic society. Students used their journal entries to discuss which of those roles they might, or might not, feel comfortable fitting into and to explore the reasons why. And the activity of writing a mission statement allowed students to verbalize what kind of a lawyer they wanted to become and to identify the personal values that would guide their work.

The class became an opportunity for these law students to think carefully about their personal and professional limitations, strengths and weaknesses.

We believe that the class provides an essential forum for law students to interact with each other as members of the legal profession as well as a workspace in which they can begin to articulate a professional ethos. The next challenge will be to determine whether this learning experience can be expanded to include more second and third year students.

If we were to envision taking this course "to scale" (i.e., making it a requirement concurrent with students' clinical experience), there would be several challenges. The first, an enduring and difficult one for any requirement, would be the issues related to faculty coverage. Teaching small sections for writing and reasoning requires a complex assembly of full-time faculty and adjunct professors. For our clinical program, to be able to provide enough slots for students to meet their Cardin requirement, we must make sure that we have sufficient numbers of faculty. This has created an ecosystem of tenured/tenure track, long-term contract, short-term contract, adjuncts, and visitors. To now add another requirement for professionalism that must be staffed to accommodate every student in a small section setting (no more than 25) seems unrealistic, given the financial constraints on legal education institutions.

We could envision a more robust relationship between the seminar (which might be offered every semester, rather than once a year), and the more traditional podium sections of professional responsibility. Clinic students from the seminar would be more involved in presenting live ethics material from the clinic to the lecture classes. This would require modifications to the seminar syllabus in order to include a more robust preparation for the teaching component of the seminar. Having a dialogue between the clinic and the lecture courses would insert the reality of practice back into the core professionalism curriculum. It could also anchor an ongoing role for students to become "ethics counsel" for the clinical program in a more sophisticated way. We could actively recruit students for this seminar and this function. The challenge for this is that it requires sophisticated and ongoing collaboration between those faculty members who teach more traditional professional responsibility classes and those who teach in the clinic, and also requires a commitment to coordinate curricular choices. Additionally, as it is nearly impossible to anticipate what ethical issues will arise in the clinic, it is hard for podium lecture classes to match issues from the clinic with the topic areas preset in the syllabus. We would want to be sure to preserve a sense of responsiveness and immediacy between the clinic and the lecture classes when dealing with live client matters. Part of what the students face in creating a professional identity is linked to the task of responding to the immediacy of these real-world challenges.[31]

---

31   The richness of learning when students needed to prepare an opinion on the "lying client" issue when they knew that their colleagues needed to be prepared to respond to the judge and the state within a short time window was invaluable. It provided the adrenaline to

The LEAD Initiative has long contemplated using live client experiences to create hypothetical situations for use by podium faculty who teach subject matter specific classes. This could become another option for the class. The final exam might become the creation of a hypothetical situation involving ethics to be used in a subject matter specific classroom. These could be made available for all faculty through a bank of hypothetical scenarios based on the real-world experience of students who are practicing and studying professionalism simultaneously. The development of this bank has the capacity to drive the ethics conversations and learning back into the first and second year curriculum in a way that might be more lively and useful.

Whatever the next steps might be, the Rules and Reality course has been a significant learning experience for both students and faculty at the school of law. The quest to provide places for the development of professional identity and ethical leadership in law schools is not an impossible dream. It is a journey that, if we open ourselves to the challenge, will be transformative for students and faculty alike. It means that we will need to change the ways we teach to model the professionalism that we ask of our students. We will need to open our classes and our curricula to analysis and evaluation by our colleagues, and to see professionalism in light of what the Model Rules require and what our ethical framework suggests. We will be asked to model a reflective ethical practice with our colleagues, engaging their choices and our own. We will ask ourselves and our colleagues to engage Luban's "antidote for integrity"—"a stance of perpetual doubt toward one's own pretensions as well as the pretensions of others ... by trying to make a habit of doubting one's own righteousness, of questioning one's own moral beliefs, of scrutinizing one's own behavior—'Know thyself'—with a certain ruthless irony" (Luban 2007a: 297).

Little in our professional relationships prepares us for this engagement. This "new frontier" stance of collegial engagement is part of the fun of it. It is definitely part of the importance of it. We will need to learn to teach and also to learn to learn from each other, from our students, from our alumni, from Bar Counsel, from judges who preside over the cases where lawyers have lost their moral compass, and from our clients. We are in new waters, charting our way on a journey critical to the education of young lawyers and critical to the profession itself. We have lessons to learn and lessons to share. The school of law community will continue to explore pedagogies and experiences that provide students with opportunities to develop their own professional ethics and sense of themselves as leaders. In so doing, we hope to broaden our reach through dialogue and collaboration with colleagues in other law schools who also seek to address the moral and ethical challenges of the legal profession.

---

move the issue from an intellectual endeavor to that murky ground of advice that uncovers your moral/ethical propensities.

References

ABA Standing Commission on Professional Discipline. 2009. *2009 Survey on Lawyer Discipline Systems* [Online]. Available at: http://www.americanbar.org/content/dam/aba/migrated/cpr/discipline/2009sold.pdf [accessed 31 January 2012].

Bezdek, B.L. 1991. Clinical Programs of the University of Maryland School of Law, *Journal of Professional Legal Education*, 9(2): 111–20.

Bezdek, B.L. 1992a. Reconstructing a Pedagogy of Responsibility, *Hastings Law Journal*, 43(4): 1159–73.

Bezdek, B.L. 1992b. "Legal Theory and Practice" Development at the University of Maryland: One Teacher's Experience in Programmatic Context, *Washington University Journal of Urban and Contemporary Law*, 42(1): 127–46.

Boldt, R. and Feldman, M. 1992. The Faces of Law in Theory and Practice: Doctrine, Rhetoric, and Social Context, *Hastings Law Journal*, 43(4): 1111–46.

Boyle, R.A. 2003. Employing Active-Learning Techniques and Metacognition in Law School: Shifting Energy from Professor to Student, *University of Detroit Mercy Law Review*, 81(1): 1–30.

Brest, P. 1995. The Responsibility of Law Schools: Educating Lawyers as Counselors and Problem Solvers, *Law and Contemporary Problems*, 58(3–4): 5–19.

Bryant, S. and Milstein, E.S. 2007. Rounds: A "Signature Pedagogy" for Clinical Education?, *Clinical Law Review*, 14(1): 195–252.

Bundy, S.M. 1995. Ethics Education in the First Year: An Experiment, *Law and Contemporary Problems*, 19(3–4): 19–36.

Carle, S.D. 2005. *Lawyers' Ethics and the Pursuit of Social Justice: A Critical Reader*. New York: New York University Press.

Chambliss, E. 2012. Two Questions for Law Schools About the Future Boundaries of the Legal Profession, *Journal of the Legal Profession*, 36: 329–52.

Conley, J.M. 2003. How Bad Is It Out There?: Teaching and Learning About the State of the Legal Profession in North Carolina, *North Carolina Law Review*, 82(6): 1943, 1956–62.

Cunningham, C.D. and Alexander, C. 2011. Developing Professional Judgment: Law School Innovations in Response to the Carnegie Foundation's Critique of American Legal Education, in *The Ethics Project in Legal Education*, edited by M. Robertson et al. New York: Routledge.

Erlanger, H.S., Epp, C.R., Cahill, M. and Haines, K.M. 1996. Law Student Idealism and Job Choice: Some New Data on an Old Question, *Law and Society Review*, 30(4): 851–64.

Fortney, S.S. 2000. Soul for Sale: An Empirical Study of Associate Satisfaction, Law Firm Culture, and the Effects of Billable Hour Requirements, *UMKC Law Review*, 69(2): 239–310.

Galanter, M. 1996. Lawyers in the Mist: The Golden Age of Legal Nostalgia, *Dickinson Law Review*, 100(3): 549–62.

Gardner, H. 2006. *Multiple Intelligences: New Horizons*. New York: Basic Books.

Gavelek, J.R. and Raphael, T.E. 1985. Metacognition, Instruction, and the Role of Questioning Activities, in *Metacognition, Cognition, and Human Performance: Instructional Practices*, edited by D. Forrest-Pressley, G. MacKinnon and T.G. Waller. Orlando: Academic Press, 103–36.

Glendon, M.A. 1994. *A Nation Under Lawyers*. New York: Farrar, Straus, and Giroux.

Glennon, T. 1992. Lawyers and Caring: Building an Ethic of Care into Professional Responsibility, *Hastings Law Journal*, 43(4): 1175–86.

Grossman, G.S. 1974. Clinical Legal Education: History and Diagnosis, *Journal of Legal Education*, 26(2): 162–93.

Haddon, P.A. 1994. Education for a Public Calling in the 21st Century, *Washington Law Review*, 69(3): 573–86.

Koppel, N. 2010. Bar Raised for Law-Grad Jobs: Employment Prospects Dim as Firms Retrench, Derailing Career Paths for Many, *Wall Street Journal*, 5 May, A1.

Lerman, L.G. 1998. Teaching Moral Perception and Moral Judgment in Legal Ethics Courses: A Dialogue About Goals, *William and Mary Law Review*, 39(2): 457–88.

Luban, D. 2007a. Integrity: Its Causes and Cures, in Luban, D. *Legal Ethics and Human Dignity*, 267–98. Reprinted with permission of Cambridge University Press.

Luban, D. 2007b. *Legal Ethics and Human Dignity*. New York: Cambridge University Press.

Luban, D. and Millemann, M. 1996. Good Judgment: Ethics Teaching in Dark Times, *Georgetown Journal of Legal Ethics*, 9(1): 31–88.

Martyn, S.R., Fox, L.J. and Wendel, W.B. 2006. *The Law Governing Lawyers: National Rules, Standards, Statutes, and State Lawyer Codes*. New York: Aspen.

McArdle, E. 2008. A Curriculum of New Realities, *Harvard Law Bulletin* [Online], Winter. Available at: http://www.law.harvard.edu/news/bulletin/2008/winter/feature_1.php [accessed 4 May 2012].

Moliterno, J.E. 2003. *Ethics of the Lawyer's Work*. 2nd edition. St. Paul: Thomson West.

Palmer, P.J. 2004. *A Hidden Wholeness: Journey Toward an Undivided Life*. San Francisco: Jossey-Bass.

Pipkin, R.M. 1979. Law School Instruction in Professional Responsibility: A Curricular Paradox, *American Bar Foundation Research Journal*, 4(2): 247–76.

Rhode, D.L. 1994. *Professional Responsibility: Ethics by the Pervasive Method*. Boston: Little, Brown.

Rhode, D.L. 1998. The Professionalism Problem, *William and Mary Law Review*, 39(2): 283–326.

Rhode, D.L. 2000. *In the Interests of Justice: Reforming the Legal Profession*. New York: Oxford University Press.

Rhode, D.L. and Luban, D. 2006. *Legal Ethics: Law Stories*. New York: Foundation Press.

Rotunda, R.D. and Dzienkowski, J.S. 2001. *Professional Responsibility: A Student's Guide*. St. Paul: West.

Schultz, F.M. 1995. Teaching "Lawyering" to First-Year Law Students: An Experiment in Constructing Legal Competence, *Washington and Lee Law Review*, 52(5): 1643–66.

Sells, B. 1996. *The Soul of the Law: Understanding Lawyers and the Law*. Shaftesbury: Element.

Simon, W.H. 1998. *The Practice of Justice: A Theory of Lawyers' Ethics*. Cambridge, MA: Harvard University Press.

Stuckey, R.T. and Others. 2007. *Best Practices for Legal Education: A Vision and a Road Map*. New York: Clinical Legal Education Association.

Sullivan, W.M., Colby, A., Wegner, J.W., Bond, L. and Shulman, L.S. 2007. *Educating Lawyers: Preparation for the Profession of Law*. San Francisco: Jossey-Bass.

Susskind, R.E. 2008. *The End of Lawyers?: Rethinking the Nature of Legal Services*. New York: Oxford University Press.

Weiss, D.C. 2010. 20% of Supreme Court Docket Involved Lawyering Cases in Legal Ethics "Revolution," *ABA Journal* [Online], 12 July. Available at: http://www.abajournal.com/news/article/20_of_supreme_court_docket_involved_lawyering_cases_in_legal_ethics_revolut/ [accessed 31 January 2012].

Chapter 11

Developing Leadership through Discussion and Passion: A Law Student's Perspective

Avery M. Blank

Leadership education should be integrated into the law school curriculum. While some believe leadership is something more innate than learned, the principles of leadership certainly can be researched and discussed. However, this is made more difficult in law school due to the use of the Socratic Method, in which professors ask students questions and lead the lecture. Not only does the Socratic Method deny students the opportunity to assume leadership in the classroom, but it also precludes discussion, another way to nurture leadership. The Socratic Method involves structured dialogue led by the teacher; the student speaks only after the teacher asks a question. Fortunately for the students at the University of Maryland Francis King Carey School of Law, a course entitled "Foundations of Leadership Seminar: Theory and Praxis" ("Foundations of Leadership"), which is part of the law school's Leadership, Ethics and Democracy (LEAD) Initiative, provides its students with the opportunity to research and discuss leadership. After taking the "Foundations of Leadership" class, I came to believe that leadership education should be integrated into the law school curriculum generally. I am a recent law graduate, who just completed my J.D. at the school of law, and in this chapter I share my perspective on the benefits of the kind of leadership training I received during my legal education.

The act of leadership—or what I call the "doing" part of leadership—is very important. But perhaps the most effective way of preparing to act in roles of leadership is to first understand the concept of leadership—what I call the "thinking" part of leadership. The "Foundations of Leadership" class provides a framework for how students might (better) lead in the future.

We read works by Plato, Mahatma Gandhi, and James MacGregor Burns, a prominent scholar in the field of leadership. We learned about trait theory and the concept of leadership-followership—an idea that suggests that the emergence of a leader is based on the existence of followers. We met and listened to leaders in their respective professions. We wrote about leadership.

One discussion we had was about how society sees lawyers as natural leaders. When there is a problem, people look to lawyers because they believe that lawyers have the capacity to solve the problem. This raises the following question:

if the public sees lawyers as leaders, why doesn't the legal community see the importance of including leadership theory in the law school curriculum? Perhaps it is because some lawyers believe it is an inherent part of our profession and, thus, we do not need to teach leadership to prospective attorneys. This dismissive attitude is of concern because it would seem that just about anyone could benefit from the discussion and study of leadership theory. The study of leadership helps to identify your strengths and weaknesses, which you can use to improve your leadership skills for your own benefit and the benefit of those around you.

Leadership theory can also teach you more about yourself and about your relationships with others. As part of the course, we each participated in a leadership assessment known as the Leadership Practices Inventory (LPI).[1] The LPI assesses individuals on the following five "practices": (1) encourage the heart,[2] (2) enable others to act,[3] (3) model the way,[4] (4) inspire a shared vision,[5] and (5) challenge the process.[6] This tool helps an individual better understand his or her leadership style and, in turn, become a more effective leader.

In 2009, at the beginning of my second year of law school, my highest LPI score was in "enable" and my lowest LPI score was in "encourage." I scored higher on "enable" because I value determination to engage in future actions. According to the LPI, the behavior of "encourage" involves an outward or overt expression of some sort. I, however, manifest encouragement through more indirect ways like support or listening, which are both behaviors identified by the LPI under the practice of "enable." This suggests that encouragement can manifest itself in different ways.

I was surprised that I manifest my encouragement through more indirect ways because I think of myself as a very direct person. I like being direct with someone

---

1   The LPI was developed by James M. Kouzes and Barry Z. Posner. The LPI assessment is based on 25 years of research. It has been applied in many organizational settings and is highly regarded in both the academic and practitioner world. The LPI was developed through a triangulation of qualitative and quantitative research methods and studies. In-depth interviews and case studies generated the framework. ("Common Questions About LPI Online." *LPI Online*, http://www.lpionline.com/lpi_about.html.) One reviewer of the LPI assessment concluded: "The LPI is one of the most extensively researched management development tools I have encountered. It is a model of sound research design from its initial development and refinement through subsequent concurrent validity studies. The instrument and instructions are easy to read and follow and the trainer's guide is logical and clear. I highly recommend it as a development tool ..." (Lewis 1995: 557).

2   Encourage the heart is to recognize, show appreciation for, and celebrate contributions and victories.

3   Enable others to act is to build relationships with others and, in turn, support others by increasing self-determination and developing competence.

4   Model the way is to set an example by aligning actions with shared values.

5   Inspire a shared vision is to help others share an exciting, aspiring vision.

6   Challenge the process is to look for opportunities and take risks, as well as learning from experience.

because I do not like wasting time. Unsurprisingly, this directness highlights the value I place on efficiency. When I looked at the behaviors in which I scored myself the highest, these behaviors also suggest that I value efficiency. I scored myself a "10" on the following three behaviors: develops cooperative relationships; follows through on promises and commitments; and treats others with dignity and respect. Cooperation allows for easy forward movement. Following through means that you do not have to regress and re-address an issue. Respect for others eliminates discord and, consequently, allows the group to focus on the issue itself as opposed to how to work within the group dynamic to solve the issue.

The LPI revealed that my behaviors are geared more towards the product than the process. I value efficiency because it gets me to the product (the "end") in the fastest way (the "means") possible. Unfortunately, based on a variety of literature I have read over the years, it seems that society generally holds product-driven people in a negative light (see Cartwright 2001, Topolski 2005: 31–6). I think there is a tendency to see product-driven people as individuals who lack morals or values because people think that product-driven people do not care *how* they reach the end result. Society views product-driven people and process-driven people differently because these people have different sets of values, both of which are valid and crucial to the success of any venture. Just like leaders need followers, so too do process-driven people need product-driven people.

My scores on the practices "model," "inspire," and "challenge" fell in between "enable" and "encourage." I scored the highest on "model" and "inspire" in comparison with the several thousand people who have taken this version of the LPI. Namely, compared with others, I scored higher on "model" and "inspire" than on "enable." This illustrates two things: (1) although my best practice is "enable," most others believe they are better enablers than I am, and (2) my actual best practices might be "model" and "inspire." This suggests that there is a difference between how you view yourself and how others view you and, consequently, you cannot identify your best (or worst) practice without comparing it with others.

In 2010, when I took the LPI assessment a second time, I scored the highest on the "challenge" practice, which I scored second lowest on in my first assessment. This shows that I changed over the course of one year of law school. Now more confident in myself and my interests, I am more willing to seek challenging opportunities to test my skills.

To summarize, my LPI assessments have helped me to realize my leadership style; they have helped me recognize that I am, among other things, direct, supportive, and a risk-taker. Discussing my results in class and comparing them with the results of my classmates helped us all to realize that many styles of leadership exist.

In addition, "Foundations of Leadership" allowed me to research, write, and present on an area that greatly interests me: female leadership in the law. The time is ripe for research and discussion of leadership in the law, in general, and of female professional development within the law, specifically. The legal field needs leadership to determine how it will cope with the changing economy and, in turn, how it will survive as a viable, even flourishing, profession. Although women have made great strides in many career fields, the fact that men hold most of the senior executive positions within private companies, including law firms, and the campaigns of Hillary Clinton and Sarah Palin, which were ultimately unsuccessful, suggest that women still have a difficult time attaining top leadership positions (Catalyst 2012).

I completed original research on the current status of female leadership in private law firms. For this research, I carried out 16 interviews with lawyers from a range of law firms of varying size and practice areas.[7] Many lawyers and members of law firm management told me that this subject holds great interest for them and their firms. These conversations indicate that my research is meaningful and useful to the legal field.

My study reveals that "Women's Initiative" programs of private law firms are ineffective in helping female attorneys assume leadership in the firm (i.e., become partner). The statistics at the firms I researched reveal that the number of female partners has remained constant over the last 20 years. If these programs do not help female attorneys become leaders, another way we might be able to achieve the same goal is to strengthen legal education by incorporating leadership study. Many female attorneys that I interviewed believe that learning leadership skills would improve their chances of becoming a partner in a private law firm.

The research I conducted, my introspection, and the discussions I had—all as part of the "Foundations of Leadership" course—have helped me to become a passionate leader in the field of women and the law. The "thinking" I have done as part of this course has led to my "doing" (i.e., my becoming a leader). This made me realize that passion can naturally generate leadership; the key to producing a leader is giving a person the opportunity to pursue his or her passion. With the inclusion of leadership training into law school curriculums, law schools will be on their way to nurturing many future leading lawyers.

References

Blank, A.M. 2012. Women's Initiatives in Private Law Firms: Their Contribution to and Impact on Female Leadership in the Legal Profession, in *Leadership and Law Journal* (forthcoming).

---

7   My study focused on three private law firms that had "Women's Initiative" programs: (1) Holland & Knight LLP, a national and general practice firm of over 900 attorneys, (2) Miles & Stockbridge PC, a regional and general practice firm of over 200 attorneys, and (3) Howrey LLP, a now-dissolved global firm of over 500 attorneys focused on intellectual property. At all three law firms studied, the percentage (%) of female partners was at or close to the national average of 17% (Women's Bar Association of the District of Columbia 2006).

Cartwright, S. 2001. Why Promote Process over Product? Why Process Emphasis Supports Learning, *Child Care Information Exchange*, March/April.

Catalyst. 2012. *Statistical Overview of Women in the Workplace* [Online]. Available at: http://www.catalyst.org/file/672/qt_statistical_overview_of_women_in_the_workplace.pdf [accessed 10 September 2012].

Cronin, T.E. 1995. Leadership and Democracy, in *The Leader's Companion*, edited by J.T. Wren. New York: The Free Press, 303–9.

Kouzes, J.M. and Posner, B.Z. 2009. *Leadership Practices Inventory: Feedback Report for Avery Blank*.

Kouzes, J.M. and Posner, B.Z. 2010. *Leadership Practices Inventory: Feedback Report for Avery Blank*.

Lewis, M.A. 1995. Review of the Leadership Practices Inventory, in *The Twelfth Mental Measurements Yearbook*, edited by J.C. Conoley and J.C. Impara. Lincoln: University of Nebraska Press.

Topolski, A.C. 2005. *Teaching Art: Process over Product.* Rochester, NY: University of Rochester.

Women's Bar Association of the District of Columbia, Initiative on Advancement and Retention of Women. 2006. *Creating Pathways to Success: Advancing and Retaining Women in Today's Law Firms* [Online], May. Available at: http://wba.timberlakepublishing.com/files/Advocacy%20&%20Endorsements%20Files/Initiative%20Reports/Creating_Pathways_to_Success-May_2006.PDF [accessed 10 September 2012].

Wren, J.R. 2006. A Quest for a Grand Theory of Leadership, in *The Quest for a Grand Theory of Leadership*, edited by G.R. Goethals and G.L.J. Sorenson. Northampton, MA: Edward Elgar, 1–38.

Chapter 12

Recovering Relational Lawyering: Building Ethical Leaders through Mentorship

Brenda Bratton Blom and Dorcas R. Gilmore

I. Lawyers as Leaders

Lawyers lead. President Obama is a lawyer.[1] Vice President Biden is a lawyer.[2] While the exact numbers have varied slightly from election cycle to election cycle, and the percentage has declined since 1930,[3] nearly half of all members of Congress continue to be attorneys.[4] Why might that be? And why is that true, when research shows that as a profession, lawyers are introverts and not natural leaders?

Legal education uniquely prepares people to understand the structure of government and law. After three (or more) years of intensive study of the development of law and the structure of both law and enforcement of the law, law graduates are often well prepared to articulate the rights and responsibilities of citizens and government bodies with a force and eloquence that is compelling to non-lawyers. Further, powerful networks are created and maintained by lawyers, beginning in law school and maintained throughout their careers. Although lawyers' knowledge, networks, and skills make them well positioned for leadership positions, are they enough to provide the skills to be a good leader? Can legal educators train people to be leaders?

---

1   Barack Obama, J.D., Magna Cum Laude, Harvard Law School, 1991.

2   Joseph Biden, J.D, Syracuse University School of Law, 1968.

3   In the 71st Congress, 1929–1930, 70 out of 109 (64%) Senators had a law background. Senator biographies on file with author (search conducted by Senate Librarian Melanie Jacobs of the Biographical Directory of the United States Congress, April 23, 2012). From the 67th to the 71st Congresses (1921–1930), 58.0% of Representatives reported "law" as an occupational background (Bogue et al. 1976: 284).

In the 79th Congress (1945–1946), 41.61% of Representatives and 43.75% of Senators reported an occupation in "law." In the 112th Congress (2011–2012), 23.91% of Representatives and 37% of Senators reported an occupation in "law" (Petersen 2012: 22).

4   In 2008, 179 Members of the House (41%) and 57 Senators held law degrees (57%) (Amer 2008).

There is one strand of research and theory that suggests that leaders are born, i.e. genetically determined (Arvey et al. 2006). However, "[t]he accumulated research clearly suggests that genetics accounts for only some 30% of the variance in leadership ratings and leadership role occupancy. Another 10–15% of the variance appears to be attributable to work and broader life events, whereas the remaining 50% is as yet undiscovered" (Arvey et al. 2007: 704). Whether you agree or disagree that any of the core elements of being a leader are genetically determined, even according to Arvey and others, at least 65% of why a person is a leader is due to reasons unaffiliated with genetically determined tendencies (Arvey et al. 2007: 704).

A second theory is that parenting styles and early life experiences about rule-breaking might be the best predictor about whether people will assume leadership roles as adults. Avolio has studied parenting styles related to leadership and is currently publishing about the positive results associated with "modest rule-breaking behaviour" (Avolio et al. 2009).

Another theory asserts that leaders emerge because of a combination of traits and attributes: "… a number of studies have linked personality variables and other stable personal attributes to leader effectiveness, providing a substantial empirical foundation for the argument that traits do matter in the prediction of leader effectiveness" (Zaccaro 2007: 6). This set of theories expands the traits of leaders beyond genetic traits to traits that can be "defined as relatively coherent and integrated patterns of personal characteristics, reflecting a range of individual differences, that foster consistent leadership across a variety of group and organizational situations" (Zaccaro 2007: 7). These theories open the door to another set of theories that begin to speak about leaders and leadership as two distinct but connected frameworks. Zaccaro refers to the traits of leaders as "distal attributes": those of Cognitive Abilities, Personality, and Motives or Values (Zaccaro 2007: 11). These distal attributes (more like those of heredity) combine with what he refers to as "proximal attributes": Social Appraisal Skills, Problem Solving Skills, and Expertise/Tacit Knowledge (Zaccaro 2007: 11). These traits are more like the learned social skills that combine to underscore the preparedness to lead. Proximal attributes are more closely aligned with the theories about leadership development, or skills sets that can be built.

But the emergent theories of leadership development research offer some of the most promising and engaging ideas for those studying the legal profession. These theories give the authors ways to both describe our experience and leverage it to make predictions about how to train ethical lawyers and good leaders in the future. These theories distinguish between "born" leaders and the development of leadership.

Leadership development is defined as expanding the collective capacity of organizational members to engage effectively in leadership roles and processes ... with or without formal authority ... [and] ... involves building the capacity for groups of people to learn their way out of problems that could not have been predicted, (Dixon 1993) or that arise from the disintegration of traditional organizational structures and the associated loss of sensemaking (Weick 1993). (Day 2000: 582)[5]

For several reasons, this captures the experiences of lawyers in practice and lawyers in training. First, while much of the law is about applying statute and case law to the facts of the matter, there is no lack of variety of facts. The likelihood that a lawyer will spend his or her days with "problems that could not have been predicted" is high. The "disintegration of traditional organizational structures and the associated loss of sensemaking" place us in the right universe of thought in two distinct ways. First, for law students, just the realities of becoming a lawyer, putting aside all your previous views of the world, and relearning the world as you "learn to think like a lawyer," creates a loss of sensemaking. There are few law students who do not experience this phenomenon their first year of law school, spending the next two (or more) years working their way back to a new sense of order. But currently, in the fast-paced and fast-changing world in which lawyers find themselves, the entire profession is trying to find its feet in a world where we are learning our way out of problems not predicted in a profession where traditional organizational structures are disintegrating around us. Books like *The End of Lawyers? Rethinking the Nature of Legal Services* (Susskind 2008), and *Avoiding Extinction: Reimagining Legal Services for the 21st Century* (Kowalski 2012) cry out this reality. In this context, those who are becoming lawyers, those who are lawyers, and those who teach about becoming lawyers are uniquely situated to engage in the dialogue on how to effectively provide leadership and train for leadership in law and in society.

"*Leader* development is based on a traditional, individualistic, conceptualization of leadership ... [, while] *leadership* development has its origins in a more contemporary, relational model of leadership ... [that] ... assumes that leadership is a function of the social resources that are embedded in relationships" [emphasis added] (Day 2000: 605). This relational component is critical to the authors' experience and argument: Good lawyering is, at its core, relational. To build good and ethical lawyers, legal training must include modeling and engaging both the core legal competencies and the leadership training necessary to be a good and ethical lawyer. For this chapter, we will rely on the definition of leadership suggested by Vroom and Jago: "We see leadership as a process of motivating people to work together collaboratively to accomplish great things" (Vroom and

---

5 Reprinted from *The Leadership Quarterly*, 11(4), Day, D.V., Leadership Development: A Review in Context, 582, 605, Copyright 2000, with permission of Elsevier.

Jago 2007: 18). The leadership process that drives the collaboration to "accomplish great things" can occur through mentoring relationships.

II. Building the Mentoring Relationship

A. Mentoring: What We Know and What We Don't Know

Mentoring may be the most widely used and vaguely defined term used in the literature about support and development of young people or novices to a profession. It means different things within different professions. Maryann Jacobi's literature review of studies about mentoring and undergraduate academic success yields at least 15 different definitions of mentoring, spanning three different career areas: higher education, management/organizational behavior, and psychology (Jacobi 1991: Table 1). But, as she concludes, "mentoring provides any, or all, of 15 different diverse functions ... [that] ... reflect three components of the mentoring relationship: (a) emotional and psychological support, (b) direct assistance with career and professional development, and (c) role modeling" (Jacobi 1991: 510). And, she points out, although few researchers are able to measure the rewards for the mentor that arise from the relationship, "The recognition that mentoring provides benefits to both mentors and protégés has given rise to programs in which members of a target population assume the role of mentor to other, generally younger, individuals" (Jacobi 1991: 512).[6]

Upon further examination, it appears there are different types of mentoring: developmental and instrumental. "Developmental mentoring, in which the primary focus is on facilitating the relationship between mentor and mentee as a way of promoting the youth's development, reflects the assumption that mentoring influences social, emotional and academic development through the creation of supportive relationships" (Karcher et al. 2006: 714). This type of mentoring focuses on activities that draw the youth into social interchanges with the mentor. "Instrumental mentoring differs ... in that the primary goal is the learning of skills or the achievement of specific goals" (Karcher et al. 2006: 714). Activities would then focus on achieving the particular goal, whether it is finishing high school, or effectively launching a new product in a company. There is also a set of research about mentoring relationships within clinical educational practice. This will become important as the authors share our story. There are lessons that might apply:

> Leadership mentoring during clinical practice thus provides three important outcomes. First, it stimulates role socialization for aspiring and novice principals (Crow and Matthews 1998, Matthews and Crow 2003). Second, veteran principals serving as mentors have opportunities for their own professional

---

6 Copyright © 1991 by American Educational Research Association. Reprinted by permission of SAGE Publications.

development (Gordon 2004, Hansen and Matthews 2002). Finally, leadership mentoring during clinical practice increases the capacity of both new and veteran administrators to meet the demands of school leadership (Lane 1984, Mullen, Gordon, Greenlee and Anderson 2002, Ortiz 1982, Wenger 1998). (Browne-Ferrigno and Muth 2004: 470)[7]

Mentoring within the framework of leadership, where both mentors and mentees are solving their way out of problems, also "requires the replacement of traditional power roles ... with collegial–peer relationships that rely on 'conditions of trust, openness, risk-taking, problem identification, problem solving, and goal setting' (Hansen and Matthews 2002: 34)" (Browne-Ferrigno and Muth 2004: 470).

Our story: an example of leadership mentoring   The relationship between the co-authors started and grew in an environment of shared values and interests with the opportunity to observe and interact with one another in practice. In this section, we use our own relationship as an example of how leadership mentoring can work. From the beginning of our professional relationship, we knew we shared values around public service, community economic development, and the law as a tool for social change. We were brought together by the University of Maryland Francis King Carey School of Law's inaugural Leadership Scholars interview process. Brenda, then Director of the Clinical Law Program, was one of the faculty and staff that interviewed Dorcas, a prospective Leadership Scholar. In this exchange, we learned about each other's mutual interest in community economic development and passion for public interest law. This initial meeting was the beginning of a mentorship relationship that took root in the Public Interest Mentoring Program that the law school's Career Development Office facilitated.[8]

Through the faculty–student matching in the Public Interest Mentoring Program, Brenda was selected as Dorcas's public interest mentor. In our initial official meeting, we talked about our respective career paths, professional goals, and Dorcas's experiences so far in law school. Our first conversation led to developing a plan for the continuation of the mentoring relationship through regularly scheduled meetings. During the course of these meetings, we developed a sense of trust and camaraderie that served as the foundation for our continued work together.

As Dorcas's first year of law school progressed, she sought out Brenda for advice about navigating law school and maintaining her vision of herself as a racial justice lawyer. These conversations about the challenges Dorcas faced as a Black woman dedicated to serving low-income communities and communities of color helped Dorcas to find her place in the law. In these conversations, Dorcas was able to identify her own motivation to continue her legal education—not only because

---

7   Copyright © 2004 by the University Council for Educational Administration, reprinted by permission of SAGE Publications.

8   Unfortunately, this program has been discontinued by the School of Law.

of Brenda's advice, but also because of Brenda's willingness to trust Dorcas as a colleague. Brenda shared her own experiences of being a White woman and a nontraditional law student who was committed to public interest lawyering. The mentorship provided an invaluable space in law school that affirmed the importance of Dorcas's prior experiences, both professional and personal, to her future legal practice. This mentorship helped to combat the multiple forces in law school that alienate students from their former selves and undermine a commitment to public service. As a result of these conversations, Dorcas decided to fulfill her clinical requirement her second year of law school in Brenda's new clinic, the Community Justice Clinic.

The clinic was the place where the relationship grew from one of advice and sharing of law school war stories to one that was rooted in a common vision of law and justice and renewed commitment to community lawyering. Through watching Brenda interact with clients and connect the importance of liability protection, governance, and well-crafted contracts to community empowerment, Dorcas saw her own place in the practice of law and how she might create a space and a community of her own in the legal profession. Through common action and reflection, the cornerstones of a lifelong professional relationship were laid. The clinical experience provided this unique pedagogical and mentoring opportunity for two years, in which we worked on diverse issues with a wealth of new challenges to work with clients to identify and address. In the process of problem-solving together we saw each other's strengths, challenges, commitments, and values reflected in the work. From this practical and relevant vantage point, the traditional roles of teacher and student were still present, though not as prominent as the roles of colleague and team member. In the clinical experience, we also were able to see each other grow professionally. As the clinic unfolded in its first and second years, we worked together to gain fluency with the subject matter and the structure of the course.

Brenda also supervised Dorcas's advanced legal writing requirement (Certification Paper). This theoretical inquiry is a place where Dorcas's long-term interests and prior experiences began to meld into a more theoretically sophisticated articulation of law and policy endeavors that would shape the next several years of her work, and open new areas of interest and inquiry for Brenda. Dorcas's work on youth entrepreneurship created new areas where Dorcas would provide both theoretical and practical leadership inside the mentoring relationship, adding to the complex and wonderful conversations and work the two shared on racial justice inside the law, both in structure and policy implementation.

Since Dorcas's graduation from law school, the mentorship has continued through deliberate and regular discussions about Dorcas's career path, professional collaborations, and the future of community economic development. We have identified areas where we can work together professionally and have developed friendships with others that continue and expand our professional and personal circles of connection. Mentorship worked for us because of our own interests in mentorship, institutional opportunities for intergenerational collaboration, similarity of personalities and world views, and the creation of a "collegial-peer" relationship. Our experiences of mutual respect, growth, trust, and problem-solving laid the foundation for a long-term mentoring relationship.

B. Leadership Mentoring and the Colleague Relationship

Our story highlights the key elements of successful leadership mentoring. First, a clear commitment to the importance of leadership and cultivating new leaders in the legal profession is a vital starting point. We originally met through the Leadership Scholars' interview process, which profiled leadership as necessary to the profession. The second element is the opportunity for both the veteran and novice to self-identify as having shared values or interests. In our case, the Public Interest Mentoring Program was a means for Dorcas to express an interest in being mentored, Brenda to express an interest in mentoring, and both of us to express our shared value of commitment to public service. Third, the cultivation of mutual trust was the foundation of our relationship. This trust resulted from becoming colleagues, which meant authentic listening, sharing, valuing each other's strengths, and growing from our work together. Lastly, the clinic provided the opportunity to problem-solve together in a meaningful way through client work and to reflect on the theory and practice of law. This foundation of shared values, mutual trust and respect, commitment to maintaining our mentoring relationship, and joint problem-solving has enabled us to have discussions about a range of difficult subjects, including our racial and social class privileges and their impacts on our work. Our experience underscores "that strength and competence grow in context with ongoing encouragement and support" and that resilience and courage are generated in community (Jordan 2004: 24).

Our relationship has qualities that have been instrumental to sustaining the mentorship and making it valuable to the novice lawyer and the veteran lawyer. These qualities include mutual respect, commitment to intergenerational mentorship, creativity, risk-taking, collaboration, joint problem-solving, and shared power. Whether writing together or working together in professional organizations, we both give and receive something of value in the mentorship. Our experience of mentorship has been very positive without the tensions of some mentoring relationships due to our similarities in approach to problem-solving, means of open communication, sense of professional purpose, commitment to community lawyering and community economic development, respect for one another, and time devoted to cultivating the relationship.

III. Leadership Mentoring and Developing Ethical Lawyers

Leadership mentoring in law school and beyond is essential to the profession, and it must be rooted in the practice of ethical lawyering (Dolovich 2002). Lawyers are leaders in many areas of public life; however, lawyers must choose to be ethical leaders. The choice of being an ethical leader requires learning how to integrate one's personal moral framework with the Rules of Professional Responsibility and what it means to "think like a lawyer" in a practice setting. Through leadership mentoring, the novice lawyer sees how the veteran lawyer goes about integrating her own moral views and personal experiences into the practice of law. This integration is central to increasing lawyers' satisfaction in the profession and to improving the public's perception of lawyers.

Despite the importance of leadership mentoring as an effective means of training legal professionals, enhancing satisfaction in the profession and improving the public image of lawyers, the history of legal training shows a shift from a more integrated, relational approach to a more decontextualized method of study. Modern legal training began with the apprenticeship model, where aspiring lawyers worked side-by-side with veteran lawyers to learn the law and the art of lawyering (Friedman 1985: 318–19). When the case study method was adopted by Harvard Law School, it changed the thinking about how to train young legal minds (Friedman 1985: 612–13). Slowly, it became the core teaching method of the legal academy (Friedman 1985: 617–18), severely reducing practice from the training of young lawyers. It was assumed that the firms that employed young lawyers would create apprenticeships for them. The academy began to be mainly populated by theoreticians rather than practitioners (Friedman 1985: 615–16). Not until clinical education seeped into the academy did this decoupling of theory and practice face greater challenges within the academy and the profession.

Traditional legal education emphasizes "abstracting the legally relevant aspects of situations and persons from their real-world situations. Consideration of the social or ethical consequences of legal conclusions is left out of the analysis" (Brown and Allen 2009: 6). The current model not only plays a role in the level of lawyer dissatisfaction in the profession, but also affects the negative public image of lawyers. This model of legal education is both highly individualistic, as opposed to relational, and minimizes the importance of building professional competence through veteran and novice solving problems together. The traditional case-dialogue method does not provide the opportunity for multiple approaches to problem-solving or the ability to gain experience with creative and strategic thinking (Sullivan et al. 2007). In addition, the lack of opportunity for the novice and veteran lawyer to practice skill-building together is a critical loss. In practicing law side-by-side with the veteran lawyer, the novice lawyer begins to gain competence, which "depends on being in a context that is responsive to one's voice and actions" (Jordan 2004: 16).

Clinical education plays a central role in recovering relational lawyering through leadership mentoring. By providing opportunities to work as co-counsel in representational and problem-solving situations, clinical education opens possibilities for co-mentoring: Law professors/attorneys are able to provide on-the-ground evaluation, assessment and feedback to students about their practice choices; students/attorneys are able to challenge assumptions of the professors due to their own presumptions about the world and legal theory that might be outdated or underinclusive. This exchange is much more difficult without concrete problem-solving that challenges and engages both the professor and the student on behalf of a client. The client strips the professor-student relationship down to the core shoulder-to-shoulder "in the trenches" relationship. It allows mentor and mentee to value each other's contribution to an activity that holds a joint success or failure dynamic that binds them in the project and creates opportunities to explore values, leadership, and ethical choices not present in a merely intellectual or self-serving encounter.

The recovery of relational lawyering is not only necessary for the growth of the profession, it is important to growing the diversity within the profession. For those historically excluded, particularly people of color and women, leadership mentoring is essential for building the skills and relationships to carve out a space to thrive in the profession (American Bar Association 2010). Lawyers being well equipped to practice in the twenty-first century depends on their ability to adapt to changing circumstances and gain greater satisfaction in their professional lives. The legal profession's ability to rise to this challenge will depend heavily on rethinking how lawyers lead, the training they have to lead, and the relationships that support their leadership. Recovering relational lawyering through leadership mentoring allows us to reach back, and reach forward, linking past and future in a common quest that focuses us all on justice. Leadership forged with this focus promises to improve not just the lives of those who are immediately touched, but the larger project of democracy and justice as well.

References

Amer, M. 2008. *U.S. Congressional Research Service Report No. RS22555: Membership of the 110th Congress: A Profile.* Washington, D.C.: Government Printing Office.

American Bar Association. 2010. *Diversity in the Profession: The Next Steps* [Online]. Available at: http://www.americanbar.org/content/dam/aba/migrated/2011_build/diversity/next_steps_final_virtua_accessible_042010.pdf [accessed 30 January 2012].

Arvey, R.D., Rotundo, M., Johnson, W., Zhang, Z. and McGue, M. 2006. The Determinants of Leadership Role Occupancy: Genetic and Personality Factors, *Leadership Quarterly*, 17(1): 1–20.

Arvey, R.D., Zhang, Z., Avolio, B.J. and Krueger, R.F. 2007. Developmental and Genetic Determinants of Leadership Role Occupancy Among Women, *Journal of Applied Psychology*, 92(3): 693–706.

Avolio, B.J., Rotundo, M. and Walumba, F.O. 2009. Early Experiences as Determinants of Leadership Role Occupancy: The Importance of Parental Influence and Rule Breaking Behavior, *Leadership Quarterly*, 20(3): 329–42.

Biographical Directory of the United States Congress. [Online]. Available at: http://bioguide.congress.gov/biosearch/biosearch.asp [accessed 9 September 2012].

Bogue, A.G., Clubb, J.M., McKibbin, C.R. and Traugott, S.A. 1976. Members of the House of Representatives and the Processes of Modernization, 1789–1960, *Journal of American History*, 63(2): 275–302.

Brown, J. and Allen, B. 2009. *Leadership Education in the Legal Academy* [Online]. Available at: http://cuttingedgelaw.com/content/leadership-education-legal-academy-principles-practices-and-possibilities [accessed 31 January 2012].

Browne-Ferrigno, T. and Muth, R. 2004. Leadership Mentoring in Clinical Practice: Role Socialization, Professional Development, and Capacity Building, *Educational Administration Quarterly*, 40(4): 468–94.

Day, D.V. 2000. Leadership Development: A Review in Context, *Leadership Quarterly*, 11(4): 581–613.

Dolovich, S. 2002. Ethical Lawyering and the Possibility of Integrity, *Fordham Law Review*, 70(5): 1629–88.

Friedman, L.M. 1985. *A History of American Law*, 2nd edition. New York: Simon and Schuster.

Jacobi, M. 1991. Mentoring and Undergraduate Academic Success: A Literature Review, *Review of Education Research*, 61(4): 505–32.

Jordan, J.V. 2004. Towards Competence and Connection, in *The Complexity of Connection*, edited by J.V. Jordan, M. Walker and L.M. Hartling. New York: Guilford Press, 11–27.

Karcher, M.J., Kuperminc, G.P., Portwood, S.G., Sipe, C.L. and Taylor, A.S. 2006. Mentoring Programs: A Framework to Inform Program Development, Research, and Evaluation, *Journal of Community Psychology*, 34(6): 709–25.

Kowalski, M. 2012. *Avoiding Extinction: Reimagining Legal Services for the 21st Century*. Chicago: ABA Publishing.

Petersen, R.E., Congressional Research Service. 2012. *R42365: Representatives and Senators: Trends in Member Characteristics Since 1945*. Washington, D.C.: Government Printing Office.

Sullivan, W.M., Colby, A., Wegner, J.W., Bond, L. and Shulman, L.S. 2007. *Educating Lawyers: Preparation for the Profession of Law*. San Francisco: Jossey-Bass.

Susskind, R. 2008. *The End of Lawyers? Rethinking the Nature of Legal Services*. Oxford: Oxford University Press.

Vroom, V.H. and Jago, A.G. 2007. The Role of the Situation in Leadership, *American Psychologist*, 62(1): 17–24.

Zaccaro, S.J. 2007. Trait-Based Perspectives of Leadership, *American Psychologist*, 62(1): 6–16.

Chapter 13
Reflections on Team Production in Professional Schools and the Workplace

Robert J. Rhee

Leadership is a broad, amorphous topic, but it can be discussed in concrete terms. When I think about leadership, I do not view it in the romantic sense—the view of the leader who inspires others to follow through force of personality, brilliance, or authority.[1] My view is more functional and instrumental. In the world of Robinson Crusoe, the concept of leadership is meaningless.[2] Leadership is only relevant in team production, and the first step toward being a leader is having the ability to work effectively within a team environment. Let's stay with this minimum concept. There are two essential attributes: effectiveness and teamwork. It is unclear to me whether great leaders are born or made, but certainly the minimum attributes of better leadership can be taught and encouraged in a formal educational environment. In this chapter, I draw lessons from my past educational and professional experiences, and discuss ways in which law schools can better integrate the concepts of leadership and team production into the academic curriculum.

I am fortunate to have attended two fine professional schools, and to have put my training to the test in the workplace in two different professions. I trained to be a lawyer at George Washington University, and thereafter proved my mettle as a law clerk on the Third Circuit and as a trial attorney at the U.S. Department of Justice. Intellectual curiosity then took me on a detour and I went back to professional school again. At the University of Pennsylvania, I studied finance, and thereafter spent several years working as an investment banker in London and New York. These educational and professional experiences inform much of my thinking on professionalism, leadership, and educational pedagogy.

In a word, I would characterize my law school experience as *nondescript*. The study of law was a solitary pursuit. In the first year, every class except legal writing and moot court had one final exam worth the entire grade. Outside of moot court and my "study group" (friends who studied together more than an

---

1   The dictionary definition of leadership emphasizes the qualities of guiding, directing, and taking charge (Merriam-Webster 2008: 707).

2   I borrow this turn of phrase from Harold Demsetz, who provides the correct frame of reference: "In the world of Robinson Crusoe property rights play no role" (Demsetz 1967: 347).

organized affair), the only opportunities for interaction with fellow students were the occasional social gatherings and school functions. In the second and third years, I took trial advocacy, which required a co-counsel, and I enjoyed the collaborative experience. For me, law school was a series of doctrinal courses with no rhyme or reason other than intellectual interest (and there were many) coupled with scheduling feasibility: so I took antitrust, immigration, corporations, law and economics, conflicts of law, and international law, just to name a few.[3] Truth be told, I acquired enough knowledge and skill after the second year to pass the bar exam. To this day, I still question whether law school *really* should require three years of school under the current pedagogical structure of classroom emphasis (Rhee 2007a).[4] My comments here should not be construed as specific criticism of my alma mater, for I suspect that my law school experience is not so unique.

In law school, each student individually pursues the quest for knowledge and achievement.[5] Of course, this is far from the reality after law school. In truth, the best trials are the product of collaborative effort. The intimacy of a judge's chamber requires an understanding of teamwork and collegiality. In-house counsels manage the business of outside lawyers as much as they practice law. And, sophisticated clients understand that the "best lawyer" is shorthand for the lawyer who can best leverage the human resources of the firm. More broadly, the labor market today is such that law school graduates frequently pursue business and other nonlegal

---

3   I suspect that I'm not the only law student who chose courses in this manner. I did not particularly seek out opportunities in the clinic or externships. They were not mandatory or emphasized in any way, and my experience was that I didn't know what they were about and so let inertia (laziness) set in during course registration.

4   The legal academy and the profession are increasingly alarmed by the cost of legal education and growing debt levels carried by students. See, for example, Henderson and Morriss (2008), McGill (2006), Romano (2003), Sebert (2002), Wilder (2007), Wroth (2004). Given the cost of legal education and the opportunity cost of not working for a year, the total cost of a third year of law is a rather large sum of money, perhaps as much as $100,000 in after-tax money (Rhee 2011: 331). This raises a serious question for law schools and the American Bar Association: what is so compelling about a third year of law school that justifies such enormous cost expenditure? To put this in perspective, after two years of business school and a few months of in-house training at UBS Warburg, I was ready to execute a £97 million corporate acquisition and to advise directly the senior management team of a major American corporation as a junior investment banker. In the medical field, medical school is four years, but only the first two years constitute classroom work and the last two years are reserved for clinical rotations. See, for example, http:// dms.dartmouth.edu/ed_programs/mdprog.shtml (describing Dartmouth's M.D. academic program). One wonders whether the legal analysis or the bar exam are so inherently difficult that they require three full years of coursework to acquire a basic level of competency. See Butler (2006: 56), quoting Professor George Shepherd, Emory Law School: "Right now, we require everybody to get a sophisticated, expensive legal education—to buy the Lexus training, when most people would be content with a Corolla education."

5   This aspect of legal education is famously embodied in the film *The Paper Chase* and Scott Turow's memoir *One-L*.

professions. Success in any professional endeavor has as much to do with team production as with an individual's knowledge acquisition and dissemination. Yet, the law school experience diminishes the former, and emphasizes the latter. Most law students, even at the most elite institutions, do not go on to become judges and academics, but instead pursue careers in the marketplace, whether they practice law or not. We teach them sophisticated legal analytic skills—the ability to think like judges or law professors—but delegate the training of "soft" and "fuzzy" concepts like teamwork and leadership to the marketplace. Yet, the marketplace has been increasingly critical of legal education and the ability of law school graduates to add value, and have increasingly balked at subsidizing professional training on the client's dime (Rhee 2011: 316–24). The ability to think about the law and policy to the *N*th dimension, or to make the connection to some other academic discipline, is not the sole skill or tool required by practicing lawyers, even for lawyers in sophisticated practices. One wonders whether there is an overemphasis on the academic aspects of a student's legal study, at the cost of professional training in skills such as problem-solving, teamwork, leadership, and project management.[6] The issue is one of balance. The curriculum should also focus on professional training of law students that typically costs well over $100,000 in direct costs and perhaps an equal amount in opportunity cost as well. It is no exaggeration to suggest that the undertaking of legal education requires a financial commitment in savings and loans akin to the cash purchase of an average middle-class house, and the typical twenty-something student leaves law school already saddled with an education mortgage. In this mandatory three-year program, law schools should deliver more than just teaching how to think like a judge or a law professor. With a command of technical legal analytic skills to read cases and statutes as a given, transactional and organizational awareness, problem-solving skills, and teamwork are other important value-added skills in the workplace. Yet, with respect to developing teamwork and leadership skills which coincide with a certain minimum level of maturity, law schools as collective enterprise have made too little effort to develop as yet.

Although culture in legal institutions changes at a glacial pace, law schools have changed since I was a student. Experiential learning, such as externships

---

6   I believe that research mission is a primary and necessary function of law schools which are a part of research universities (Rhee 2011: 312). In this respect, law schools should embrace highly theoretical research, and there is no reason why research should be "practical" in the sense that it caters to the needs of judges and clients (Rhee 2011: 312). My quibble here is whether there is a perfect correlation between the law faculty's research efforts and the curriculum where most law students, including students from the most elite law schools, will end up practicing the profession. I have previously argued that some law schools may benefit from having a self-funding affiliated law firm as a part of the law school enterprise to better connect law schools to the practice of law (Borden and Rhee 2011).

and skills training, has taken greater prominence in the curriculum.[7] But legal education still lags in developing leadership and teamwork skills. There is a hole in the professional training of lawyers in the law school curriculum. My experience as a business school student, after graduating from law school, confirms this point.

If law school was nondescript, then in a word my business school experience was *balanced*. Like law school, the first year was a fixed curriculum of required courses in assigned sections. One would think that subject matter would have been the biggest difference between law and business schools: proximate cause versus portfolio theory, civil procedure versus financial modeling, due process versus arbitrage, etc. Not so, in my view. The subject matters used different academic languages, but they were equally interesting and rigorous. Instead, the most pronounced difference was the academic programming.

From the beginning, business was taught as a team endeavor. Every student was assigned to a "Learning Team," composed of four to five randomly assigned students.[8] During the entire first year, each Learning Team submitted assignments constituting a substantial portion of a student's grade. This taught us that individual success was intertwined with group effort. Accordingly, teamwork and leadership development were stressed and woven into the fabric of the curriculum.[9] Importantly, I never heard a complaint concerning the fairness of group accountability or randomness of the process. To be sure, there were many complaints about such and such underperforming or difficult person, but never a complaint about the concept of group work. Indeed, since becoming a law professor, I have also taught corporate social responsibility at the University of Maryland Robert H. Smith School of Business. In these courses, a part of a student's final grade is allocated to group projects, and I have never had a complaint about this arrangement (group work is just understood as a part of the curriculum).

The curriculum sets the incentive structure. There were high-performing groups as well as dysfunctional ones and everything in between. I suspect that success, failure, and everything in between offered vital lessons in leadership and professionalism. My group worked hard to be efficient, spending time on assessing each other's strengths and weaknesses, developing personal bonds, delegating and monitoring assignments, and performing internal reviews of each other's performance. Some of this was mandated by the curriculum, including a

---

7   A few law schools, most prominently Northeastern University, make this aspect a hallmark of their education. See http://www.slaw.neu.edu/coop/default.htm (describing its "Cooperative Legal Education Program"). Other schools, like Drexel University, have followed this example. See http://www.drexel.edu/law/coop-home.asp (describing its "Co-Op" program). The incorporation of externships and experiential learning into the core academic program is more the exception than the general practice.

8   See http://www.wharton.upenn.edu/mba/academics/learnteam/index.cfm (describing the integration of "Learning Teams" into the core curriculum).

9   See http://www.wharton.upenn.edu/mba/academics/leadership/index.cfm (describing how leadership training is an essential aspect of the education).

facilitator-led 360° evaluation of each member, written critiques of team members, and regular evaluation meetings. Much of figuring things out was left to us: What did we do well? Who is strong in what? How should the work be assigned? In the end, we performed because we worked well together. Accountability, respect, and friendship bonded the group. We remained close friends after graduation, and we have become a critical support network during our careers.

Group work was not just limited to classroom assignments. Learning teams also had to integrate classroom and experiential learning. Groups were required to execute a real consulting project done on a pro bono basis. Each team had to originate an idea, secure the assignment, and execute a consulting project. This required independent work by individuals and groups with very little guidance from the professor. In the end, we found a radio component manufacturer in Illinois. We pitched the idea of a pro bono project. The company flew us to its headquarters. We quickly learned the business, and provided a presentation to the senior management of our findings and recommendations. This complex task would have been impossible without strong teamwork and leadership by each member.

Business schools must teach effective team production because the profession of running a business requires teamwork.[10] Ultimately, such effectiveness is a core measurement of professional success. Although it is hardly "tested" in the traditional academic sense of an exam and a grade, the "soft" skills learned in the group meetings were as important as the "hard" knowledge learned in the lecture halls.

That business school emphasized teamwork and leadership in the core program did not make it any less intellectually rigorous than law school. I found the program at the University of Pennsylvania challenging and intellectually stimulating. The faculty was world-class in terms of scholarship and academic accomplishments, and there was no sense that there was any institutional inferiority complex in terms of its academic bona fide. Nevertheless, I never got the sense that there was a disconnect between classroom learning and professional development. The chance of such a disconnect occurring is probably reduced significantly by the fact that all students already have significant real-world experience, which is a core

---

10 For example, the Wharton School's MBA program heavily emphasizes leadership and teamwork in its first year curriculum. See http://www.wharton.upenn.edu/mba/academics/core.cfm. The program requires two courses in the area of "Leadership Essentials" as well as a pre-term Learning Team Retreat, which is described as a two-day, off-campus retreat designed to begin the process of team formation and to learn to lead in a peer environment. We can see that instituting leadership and teamwork skills into the curriculum is a significant commitment of resources on the part of the Wharton School. Other top business schools have similar commitment of resources to developing leadership and teamwork skills. The Harvard Business School requires courses in "Leadership and Organizational Behavior" and "Leadership and Corporate Accountability" as well as a program called "Field Immersion Experiences for Leadership Development." See http://www.hbs.edu/mba/academics/required.html.

requirement of the admission process, and their participation and feedback are a crucial part of the learning and academic experience.

In sum, the commonality in legal and business education was the intellectual rigor of the subject matters. But the educational experiences were starkly different. Business schools integrate a variety of pedagogical methods, including lecture, case study,[11] group work, and experiential learning. The traditional law school classroom experience is the Socratic method, by which I mean some form of a classroom dialogue between teacher and students. These differences in educational experiences are not attributable to different needs of the legal and business professions. Quite to the contrary, the professions were more alike than dissimilar.

Litigation and investment banking are different in subject matter, but they are remarkably similar in requiring a set of common skills. Beyond the capacity to analyze the problem and think through the solutions, the professional must also have "execution" skills. In a trial or a deal, the professional must turn desktop analysis into transaction execution. As a trial attorney, this meant managing the entire trial production: managing assistants and paralegals on research, filings, and exhibits; procuring experts and guiding their production; interfacing with opposing counsel and client; organizing and preparing documentation and schedules; communicating complex information to courts and attorneys; and managing organizational bureaucracy. As an investment banker, managing the deal required the following tasks: managing analysts on financial modeling; procuring accountants and lawyers and coordinating their workflow; interfacing with opposing banker and client; organizing and preparing information memoranda, offering circulars, financial models, fairness opinions, presentations to the board, and due diligence documents; communicating complex information to boards and management; and managing organizational bureaucracy. The nature of the transaction was different, but the job functions were very similar. In retrospect, my experience as a trial attorney served me well as an investment banker, and

---

11   The case study is different from the case method of law schools. In business school, there are a number of case studies, written by business school professors, on actual business events and problems. The Harvard Business School has a large repository of case studies. See http://harvardbusinessonline.hbsp.harvard.edu/hbsp/case_studies.jsp. These case studies typically present complex, fact-intensive, open-ended problems that form the basis of classroom discussion. On the other hand, the law school case method is centered on the study of appellate opinions. The facts and much of the history of the case have been sanitized in the opinion, which present only the material facts that are needed to decide the precise legal issue. Legal cases and transactions are not presented in such tidy packages. The focus on case opinions emphasizes the intellectual aspect of the rule of law, whereas frequently the far more difficult challenges in professional settings involve solving problems in whatever form and context they arise and leading or working within a team or organization. The case study method better trains a lawyer to think in terms of a complex set of facts or circumstances. I have suggested previously that law schools should incorporate more case study approach to augment the pedagogical methods used (Rhee 2007b, 2011).

this should not be a surprise since each job is part of a highly educated and skilled profession.

The business school academic program better balanced desktop analysis and execution skills. The curriculum was more attuned to market needs, and graduates were better prepared for complex tasking in a professional setting. This is not the case with legal education. The study of law is typically a monastic, intellectual pursuit, and it does not emphasize enough a broad range of problem-solving skills. The concepts of leadership and team production are not incorporated into the curriculum. This is regrettable, for complex problems in the professional world typically require both desktop analysis and execution.

Young lawyers working on complex endeavors in institutional settings will confront several problems early in their careers. I have every confidence that they can research and analyze discrete legal issues and problems (after all, they just spent three years doing the same in law school). It is no surprise that such projects constitute the bulk of a junior attorney's work. Instead, the problems they confront are of the "softer" kind. They may experience culture shock as a result of transition from the solitary pursuit of legal study to the professional world of team production. Without close supervision, they may have difficulties integrating their work product into a more complex endeavor. They may not appreciate the human and organizational dynamics of a professional enterprise. They may lack an understanding of "the bigger picture" of how business and legal transactions get done. They may lack the confidence to ask questions and understand their limitations. They may lack the understanding that in most settings the practice of law is a complex enterprise, requiring all the different sets of skills necessary to successfully participate in a complex enterprise. These are real challenges of the workplace, and law schools should provide some training in this regard.

So, should law schools adopt the business school model? No. Although the idea is not without merit, there are practical impediments. First, the makeup of student bodies is different. Business schools draw older, more experienced students, who come to school already accepting the fact that professional advancement entails success in leadership and team production. Second, law faculties tend to be conservative in their approach to curricular changes, and this conservatism tends to avoid academic fads and to maintain a rigid emphasis on analytics. Lastly, one can argue that leadership skills are needed more immediately for the typical business school graduate than a law graduate, whose first task is to learn the application of theory to practice. Many business school graduates go immediately into leadership positions, or at least positions where the "train up" period is short.

With that said, there are ways to introduce concepts of teamwork and leadership into the law school curriculum without doing violence to it. Consider, for example, the following modest steps.

- In the introductory week of first year, place incoming students into randomly assigned groups and give them a manageable project. For example, we can imagine an assignment that asks them to cull the relevant facts of a hypothetical case given a short package of case opinions, deposition testimonies, client interview notes, other documents and evidence.

- In the first year courses, assign a group midterm or project. For the teacher, this means additional grading, but only an incremental fraction of the regular grading load (e.g., 60 students divided into groups of 4 is an additional grading burden of 15 papers).

- In the first year writing courses, assign students into editing teams, each of whom are responsible for editing and critiquing the work of their team members. Assign partial accountability and responsibility for the work product of others.

- Provide opportunities for group projects in externships. Such projects would include personal journals and 360° evaluations of team members, and a portion of the evaluation would be a group review or grade.

- Provide a lecture series that emphasizes the importance of "soft" skills, with a mix of practitioner and academic perspectives.

- Provide a menu of one-credit practicum courses revolving around problem-solving in various contexts: for example, in the area of business law (my field of teaching and research), setting up a business organization from beginning to a full draft of the operating or partnership agreement, or fully working through a corporation's capital needs and financing options within a team or organizational contexts. These courses would emphasize an integration of desktop analysis and transaction execution and would develop teamwork and leadership skills.

These are modest proposals, superficial perhaps. But even minimal efforts to incorporate teamwork and socialization into the curriculum should have tangible impact on attitudes and culture. At the least, such efforts can plant the seeds of further reflection. What would a student take away if a group effort produced positive output? What would she learn from a negative experience? In my experience, at least, the best lessons come from failures and losses.[12]

Fortunately, there are law schools that swim against this tide, and today legal education is increasingly changing to integrate new kinds of training (Borden and Rhee 2011: 2). These are positive developments. My comments here stem from my experience as a student with the added perspective of an academic. Law schools have three years to train students—too much time *if* the goal is just to teach them to think like judges or professors, or to pass the bar exam. Two years,

---

12   Indeed, I typically include a group midterm in my first year Torts class. Like my business school experience, I assign the groups randomly and the project is graded. Without exception, I've always had some students tell me that they learned from their poor results. Indeed, I think that students who do poorly are the ones who learn the most. Some past student observations include: (1) failure to take initiative, (2) failure to organize, (3) failure to listen to others, (4) failure to allocate assignment properly, (5) failure to manage personalities.

I think, would suffice to teach students how to competently read cases and statutes, particularly when one considers the enormous cost to the student associated with the third year.

We increasingly hear complaints from the marketplace that graduates are not "market ready" (Rhee 2011). This criticism is directed in part at the perceived emphasis on abstract thinking without framing in concrete problems (Rhee 2007b). But I wish to note another aspect of the criticism. Law students graduate without the socialization and broader perspective on professional life that are necessary for long-term success. I question whether the "culture" of law school is one that provides the best model of professional life, career development, and incentive structures, and whether we teach them the subtle skills of maximizing individual output through team production. In my experience as a student, law school was not so good at integrating aspects of socialization and culture while business school made them a core part of the curriculum. After the first few years of climbing the learning curve on "hard" skills, the knowledge and competence in a particular subject matter, the "soft" skills like leadership skills assume greater importance, and the rate of professional development may depend on how fast one acquires them. In the final analysis, law schools can import, modestly, some aspects of the business school model to provide a richer learning experience.

References

Borden, B.T. and Rhee, R.J. 2011. The Law School Firm, *South Carolina Law Review*, 63(1): 1–12.

Butler, C.K. 2006. Rethinking Law School, *U.S. News and World Report*, 10 April, 54–7.

Demsetz, H. 1967. Towards a Theory of Property Rights, *American Economic Review*, 57(2): 347–59.

Henderson, W.D. and Morriss, A.P. 2008. What Rankings Don't Say About Costly Choices, *National Law Journal*, 14 April, S1.

McGill, C. 2006. Educational Debt and Law Student Failure to Enter Public Service Careers: Bringing Empirical Data to Bear, *Law and Social Inquiry*, 31(3): 677–710.

Merriam-Webster, Inc. 2008. *Webster's Collegiate Dictionary*, 11th edition. Springfield, MA: Merriam-Webster.

Rhee, R.J. 2007a. Follow the M.B.A. Model, *National Law Journal*, 28 May, 22.

Rhee, R.J. 2007b. The Socratic Method and the Mathematical Heuristic of George Pólya, *St. John's Law Review*, 81(4): 881–98.

Rhee, R.J. 2011. On Legal Education and Reform: One View Formed from Diverse Perspectives, *Maryland Law Review*, 70(2): 310–40.

Romano, V.A. 2003. Law School Debt Hampers Public Interest Employment, *Michigan Bar Journal*, 82(11): 26–7.

Sebert, J.A. 2002. The Cost of Financing of Legal Education, *Journal of Legal Education*, 52(4): 516–27.

Wilder, G.Z. 2007. Law School Debt and the Urban Law School, *Southwestern University Law Review*, 36(3): 509–28.

Wroth, L.K. 2004. Access to Justice: The Problem of Law Student Debt, *Vermont Bar Journal*, 30(1): 28–9.

Chapter 14

Law, Leadership, and the Literary Canon

Alan D. Hornstein

Several years ago, the University of Maryland Medical System dedicated a new wing of its hospital. As is common on such occasions, there was a ceremony to mark the event. The platform party at that ceremony, as at most such festivities, included medical professionals, philanthropists, public officials, business executives and other community leaders. But what was striking about the platform party—and this too is typical—was how many of the participants held law degrees. Whether practicing law or not, the legally educated are disproportionately represented in leadership positions—local, state, national and even international.

Legal education is leadership education. In part—but only in part—this is attributable to the recruits; successful applicants to law schools are among the intellectual elite of their college generation. But medical school applicants, too, are intellectually gifted. And intellect alone is hardly sufficient to assure the qualities of leadership. Among the many qualities important to sound leadership are courage, tenacity, knowledge, and intelligence. But central to sound leadership—and too often lacking—are judgment and wisdom.

The skills and habits of mind inculcated by legal education have much to do with the leadership qualities of law graduates. Former Dean of the Yale Law School, Anthony Kronman, among others, has recognized the ideal of the "lawyer-statesman" and has also recognized that, despite the often well-deserved criticism of traditional legal education, its materials and methods have contributed much to developing the problem-solving skills and the judgment essential to assuming leadership roles in society. In large measure, the focus on the particular facts of cases out of which legal principles are to be drawn grounds judgment in a way that focusing on abstract ideas alone is unlikely to do—at least to the extent that the individuals involved in these cases are treated as more than mere stick-figure components of a purely intellectual problem.

Wisdom can be developed through reflective experience, and the best law school clinical programs strive for that. When students represent real clients they can use those experiences as the tools for reflective learning in much the same way they use casebooks as the tools for learning in the classroom. But while experience—direct or vicarious—is essential, it is not sufficient. The vicarious experience of the classroom and the personal experience of the clinic can contribute to the judgment-making that is essential to good legal practice and to leadership by grounding judgment in the particularity that is the stuff of life. But it can do so only if accompanied by guided reflection on those experiences.

The intellectual skill of manipulating abstract ideas is an important part of legal education. So, too, however, is the development of the affective dimension, the ability to understand and appreciate others' needs and positions. In combination, they make for good lawyers—and good leaders.

And yet, if law schools are to serve as an incubator for tomorrow's leaders, more is required. For while cases, whether appellate opinions in casebooks or live cases in clinic, permit reflection on lawyers' work, there is absent from the law school curriculum opportunities to reflect on leaders' work. Where are we to find opportunities to reflect on the qualities of mind and character—the wisdom— demanded by leadership, not just as an abstract matter, but grounded in the same sort of particularity that cases provide in legal training?

Martha Nussbaum, in her book *Poetic Justice* (Boston: Beacon Press 1995), encourages judges to engage with great literature as a way of informing their decision-making with wisdom that cannot be achieved through more didactic means. Among others, Robin West and James Boyd White (in a decades-long series of books and articles) make a similar point. Reflecting on works of literature can be an important part of lawyers' education in wisdom by providing material on which to reflect on the human condition.

When it comes to education in leadership, however, reflecting on such material assumes a more important function. For there are no legal cases that address directly what is required for leadership. Reflection on the qualities of wisdom so essential to leadership in particular can be supported through the study of the lives of individual leaders through history or through the study and discussion of biography or through case studies developed for that purpose. But great works of literature can distill and illustrate the requirements and pitfalls of leadership in a more nuanced and fully fleshed out context than most other available materials permit. Reflection on such works allows leadership itself and as it is practiced to be the subject of study.

Not surprisingly, Shakespeare had more to offer on these matters than most in the Western canon, though he was by no means the only one with something to say. In *Measure for Measure*, for example, Shakespeare illustrates the interplay between individual personality and the role of leadership. When the good, but apparently weak, Duke of Venice decides that a stronger hand is necessary to keep good order in the city, he pretends to leave the city and turns over the reins of leadership to the strict and moralistic Lord Angelo. The Duke describes Angelo as "precise ... [, one who] scarce confesses that his blood flows or that his appetite is more to bread than stone." The Duke then goes on to raise one of the central questions of the drama: "Hence shall we see, if power change purpose, what our seemers be" (Shakespeare 1997: 589). Will the Angelo put in charge of the city be the same as the private Angelo?

Angelo begins his rule as the same strict moralist he has always seemed to be, imposing a death sentence on Claudio for the crime of fornication, in this case with his fiancée. When the beautiful and pure Isabella comes to plead with Angelo for her brother's life, Angelo seems to lose his bearings. The once (self)righteous Angelo offers Isabella her brother's life in exchange for her chastity, that is, if she agrees to an assignation with him—a bargain that Angelo has no intention of honoring once he achieves his aim. Thus, Angelo exhibits a devastating flaw in leadership: in modern parlance, what we have come to call the arrogance of power. After the impersonations, twists and turns we have come to expect in Shakespearean comedy, all turns out well. The Duke (who has been the *deus ex machina* for most of the plot's developments) reappears, reasserts his authority and makes things right. Angelo, now relieved of his leadership role, returns to his strict moralism. Applying its strictures to his own behavior, he calls for a sentence of death upon himself—a sentence the Duke does not impose.

Thus, over the course of the play, Angelo has gone from a private man of unflinching righteousness to a public leader marked by evil and hypocrisy and back to being a private and (self)righteous man. The play provides an opportunity—richly contextualized and concrete—to examine, discuss and reflect upon the effect of leadership on leaders. Was Angelo's evil always a part of his character, and did leadership simply open a window of opportunity for its exercise, or is there something about the assumption of leadership that changes the personality? That is, does leadership's effect on the personality function more like a magnifying glass or more like a catalyst? Does the effect of assuming a leadership position depend upon what sort of private person one is; is the strictness of Angelo's private personality in adhering to authority related to his degeneration when he becomes the authority? Does *Measure for Measure* have anything to suggest about the qualities we should look for in a private person who seeks to lead?

Shakespeare's *Henry V* provides different grist for considerations of leadership. King Henry, having been transformed from the ne'er-do-well Prince of Wales of the three parts of *Henry IV*, to the heroic king of his own play, suggests the importance of the ability to inspire those one would lead. The English army at Agincourt, riven by disease and badly outnumbered by a French force five times its size, was badly in need of inspiration. The battle to be fought the following day, St. Crispin's Day, seemed near hopeless for the English. On the eve of battle, Henry walked among his troops as one of their number, and through his words—one of Shakespeare's most stirring speeches—inspired a desultory force to victory:

> This story shall the good man teach his son;
> And Crispin Crispian shall ne'er go by,
> From this day to the ending of the world,
> But we in it shall be remembered—
> We few, we happy few, we band of brothers;
> For he to-day that sheds his blood with me
> Shall be my brother; be he ne'er so vile,
> This day shall gentle his condition;
> And gentlemen in England now-a-bed
> Shall think themselves accurs'd they were not here,
> And hold their manhoods cheap whiles any speaks
> That fought with us upon Saint Crispin's day. (Shakespeare 1992: 167–8)

Lest the role of rhetorical inspiration be thought significant only in fictional accounts of leadership, one need only recall a more contemporary historical parallel. Churchill's leadership of the British Empire during the Second World War depended in large measure on his rhetorical ability to inspire. Facing an overwhelming Nazi assault, Churchill called his countrymen to arms in language that recalls Henry's speech at Agincourt:

> We shall not flag nor fail. We shall go on to the end. We shall fight in France and on the seas and oceans; we shall fight with growing confidence and growing strength in the air. We shall defend our island whatever the cost may be; we shall fight on beaches, landing grounds, in fields, in streets and on the hills. We shall never surrender ... (Speech before House of Commons, 4 June 1940)[1]

And a few days later: "Let us therefore brace ourselves to our duties, and so bear ourselves that if the British Empire and its Commonwealth last for a thousand years, men will still say, 'This was their finest hour'" (June 18, 1940).

A study of inspirational rhetoric in the context in which it was delivered, whether fictional or historical, can be an important component of explorations of leadership. It is an importantly different rhetorical inquiry from that typically undertaken in law schools: why a particular argument is or is not persuasive. Consideration of the reasons that a particular rhetorical piece inspires to action is essential to a complete understanding of the requirements of leadership.

As compelling as Henry or Churchill, though in a different sort of battle, is the inspirational rhetoric of Dr. Martin Luther King's leadership. Dr. King's *Letter from Birmingham Jail* and, of course, his "I Have a Dream" speech on the steps of the Lincoln Memorial helped to awaken the conscience of a people. But the rhetorical inspiration to be found there might have had far less influence without

---

1 Churchill, W.S. 1940. Speech before the House of Commons. Reproduced with permission of Curtis Brown, London, on behalf of the Estate of Sir Winston Churchill. Copyright © Winston S. Churchill.

the actions that it reflected. King's leadership was not just in what he said, but also in what he did, each reinforcing the other. And this sort of relationship of word and deed makes for more effective leadership than either might alone. Henry, after all, was to fight at the head of his army, rather than simply inspiring it. So, too, Dr. King.

Others of Shakespeare's plays also raise issues pertinent to reflections on leadership. *Richard II* can furnish the basis for an inquiry whether it is possible to be a good person and a good leader, or whether the qualities of one make assuming the role of the other problematic. Similarly, *Henry VI, Part III* can be a useful vehicle for considering whether one who seeks contentment and tranquility is suited to leadership.

Shakespeare, of course, is hardly the only participant in the Western canon to whom one can turn for enlightenment on leadership. Questions of leadership were central even at the birth of the Western tradition.

Central to Sophocles' *Antigone* (Green and Lattimore 1954) is the question of the legitimacy of the decree issued by the new King of Thebes. Having just prevailed in a civil war in which Oedipus's son/brother, Polyneices, attacked his own city, Creon decrees that Polyneices shall remain unburied, fodder for carrion. Antigone, the sister of Polyneices, resists the decree and seeks to bury her brother, claiming the edict violates the law of the gods: "Nor did I think your orders were so strong that you, a mortal man, could over-run the gods' unwritten and unfailing laws" (Green and Lattimore 1954: 173–4). *Antigone* has provided a perpetual source of inquiry over the tension between natural and positive law, but the tragedy is also a fruitful vehicle for considering the relationship between leadership and authority. Creon was the undisputed King of Thebes, with the authority to rule that position entailed, and, apart from any conflict with divine law, his decree was, at least arguably, a reasonable response in the aftermath of civil war. His stubborn— or depending on one's point of view, strong-minded—refusal to bend to the pleas of his son, his citizens, his seer, until it was too late led to disaster. Was this a failure of leadership? And if it was, what lessons can be learned from it? To say that one should not disobey the law of the gods may be true, but is not particularly helpful. Was Creon's failure a failure of judgment or a failure of character?

Oedipus Tyrannus (Sophocles 2005) written by Sophocles after *Antigone*, though set earlier in time, is generally considered the model of tragedy. Aristotle so regarded it. Oedipus possessed the qualities of leadership: He was brilliant—he solved the riddle of the sphinx to become King.[2] He was relentless in the pursuit of justice and the good of his city, seeking to cleanse Thebes of the plague caused by the murder of the old king. He was resourceful, leaving his home to avoid the curse of the gods that he would kill his father and marry his mother. Insofar as it

---

2   "What walks on four legs in the morning, two in the afternoon, and three at evening? Man, for he crawls as an infant, walks erect as an adult and uses a cane in old age" (Sophocles 2005: 65).

was in his power to cultivate the qualities of leadership, he was masterly. Alas, his destiny, his fate, dictated an otherwise undeserved end.

Although it is a fashionable conceit of modern thought that character determines destiny, *Oedipus Tyrannus* raises the uncomfortable possibility that destiny may be beyond our power to control. No consideration of the realities of leadership can afford to ignore the place of fate—what we moderns might call "luck"—in the life of the individual and the polity. Even Aristotle considered good fortune to be essential to a happy life. The tribulations of Oedipus provide an especially rich basis for considering the place of fortune in leadership.

A more recent account of leadership, actually the failure of leadership, is given us by Henrik Ibsen in *An Enemy of the People* (Ibsen 2001), an especially salient—one might say prescient—tale in light of today's environmental concerns. The problem confronted by Ibsen's characters is surprisingly contemporaneous. Dr. Stockmann has discovered that the town's health baths, the development of which has rejuvenated the town's otherwise failing economy, are hopelessly polluted. The baths are more likely to cause illness than cure it. Stockmann believes he will be hailed as a hero by the town for making this discovery. And, at first, he appears to have been correct. His many friends and allies have resisted the established authority in the town, represented by the mayor, who happens to be Stockmann's brother. As they come to recognize that their self-interest would be put at risk by the disclosure of problems with the baths, they turn on Stockmann, finally declaring him to be "an enemy of the people" (Ibsen 2001: 195).

Throughout the drama, it is unclear whether Stockmann's primary interest is in the town's welfare or whether he simply wishes to be recognized as the town's hero, the leader who saved the town from the pollution of the baths and the political pollution of his brother's corrupt leadership. Whether it is the good of the town or his own glory that propels him on, he seems utterly naïve about what leadership requires. It is not enough merely to be right, even courageously right. As Stockmann discovers, the assumption that others will follow, and if they do not, the failure is theirs, is hardly a recipe for leadership. As Plutarch suggests in *Life of Lycurgus* (Plutarch 2009), people do not follow unless leaders know how to lead. Stockmann is the opposite of the apocryphal politician who asks which way his supporters are marching so that he may rush to the head of the crowd. Stockmann will march even if the streets behind him are empty or the citizens are moving in the opposite direction. He seems to believe he can change their course by the simple expedient of uttering the truth. Stockmann may be leading in the right direction, but nobody is following.

His brother the mayor, on the other hand, is able to manipulate the citizenry for his own purposes. Whether this counts as "leadership" is a question worth pondering. Assuming that being right is not a sufficient basis on which to found leadership, is it even necessary?

A different and even more complete failure of leadership, whatever the criteria, is portrayed in George Orwell's short memoir of his experiences as a colonial policeman in Burma (Orwell 2003). The policeman is called out because an elephant has gone into must—essentially has become mad—and is rampaging through the town. The policeman takes up his rifle, but by the time he has arrived on the scene, the must has passed and the elephant, a valuable resource to its owner, has calmed. Nevertheless, the crowd of Burmese, despised by the policeman and despising him in return, are expecting the policeman to provide a spectacle by killing the elephant.

Knowing he is acting badly and acting for the empire he has come to regard as illegitimate, the policeman follows the expectations of the crowd and shoots the elephant. The beast dies a long painful death in a symbolic recreation of the death of empire itself.

It would be fruitful to inquire about the relationship between acting for an organization one despises on behalf of a people one despises and the failure of leadership exemplified by Orwell's policeman. Can one truly lead in the absence of respect for the cause to be pursued and people on whose behalf one is acting? What is the relationship between professional satisfaction (or its lack) and professional leadership?

One might explore all these questions of leadership—and more—through a close reading of Plutarch's *Lives of the Noble Greeks and Romans.* Plutarch provides myriad opportunities for the study of leadership. In example after example, Plutarch allows us to explore the requirements, successes and failures of leadership in democracies, aristocracies and monarchies, in war and peace, in turbulent times and pacific ones, in the development of social order and in well-established regimes. His presentations of these *Lives* permit us to examine, in a richly contextual framework, how leadership works and why it might fail. It raises questions of definition: do we mean by "leadership" the ability to move a people in a particular direction or should we be concerned as well with the ends sought to be achieved? He raises questions of character later echoed by others in the Western tradition: What is the relationship, if any, between being a good person and a good leader? Do the qualities required for leadership depend upon the particular characteristics of those who are to follow?

What Plutarch gives us through examples, Machiavelli purports to provide didactically. No exploration of what leadership entails in the Western tradition would be complete without reference to Machiavelli's instruction manual of political leadership, *The Prince* (Machiavelli 1992). Ostensibly written as a leadership guide for Lorenzo Medici, *The Prince* has been a rich source of controversy and conversation. It raises and purports to resolve many questions of leadership we have already addressed and others space has not permitted us to address—the roles, for example of reason or virtue on the one hand and force or its threat on the other. In almost all cases Machiavelli provides examples to illustrate his points.

A close reading of Machiavelli and Plutarch might alone provide sufficient material for a comprehensive exploration of leadership. But there is so much that is so rich in the Western literary canon that touches on the notion of leadership, its requirements, its limitations, its responsibilities, that it would be foolish to limit our perspective. The opportunity to reflect on problems of leadership by exploring its exercise in particular contexts is not unlike the opportunity to enhance our understanding of legal doctrine through clinical experiences that can provide the rich real-world context that is beyond the power of appellate opinions to convey. The law school clinic can provide the experiences essential to the development of the sort of practical wisdom that lies beyond the theories and doctrines that are the typical fare of the law school classroom and that is possessed by the best lawyers. Similarly, the vicarious experience of leadership made possible by the best that the Western literary canon has to offer enables the development of wisdom, without which leadership can descend to demagoguery and power to destruction.

References

Green, D. and Lattimore, R. 1954. *The Complete Greek Tragedies: Sophocles I*. Chicago: University of Chicago Press.

Ibsen, H. 2001. Enemy of the People, in *Four Major Plays, Volume II: Ghosts; and Enemy of the People; the Lady from the Sea*, translated by R. Fjelde. New York: Signet Classics, 115–222.

Machiavelli, N. 1992. *The Prince*. 2nd edition, edited and translated by H.C. Mansfield. Chicago: University of Chicago Press.

Orwell, G. 2003. *Shooting an Elephant and Other Essays*. Introduction by J. Paxman. New York: Penguin.

Plutarch. 2009. *Lives of Noble Grecians and Romans*. The Dryden translation, edited and revised by A.H. Clough. Digireads.

Shakespeare, W. 1992. *Henry V*, edited by A. Gurr. Cambridge: Cambridge University Press.

Shakespeare, W. 1994. *Henry IV, Part 1*, edited by B.A. Mowat and P. Werstine. New York: Washington Square Press.

Shakespeare, W. 1997. Measure for Measure, in *The Riverside Shakespeare*. 2nd edition, edited by G.B. Evans et al. Boston: Houghton Mifflin.

Shakespeare, W. 1999. *Henry IV, Part 2*, edited by B.A. Mowat and P. Werstine. New York: Washington Square Press.

Shakespeare, W. 2002. *Henry IV, Part 3: The Oxford Shakespeare*, edited by R. Martin. Oxford: Oxford University Press.

Shakespeare, W. 2003. *King Richard II*, edited by A. Gurr and A.R. Braunmuller. Cambridge: Cambridge University Press.

Shakespeare, William. 2008. *Henry VI, Part 3: The Oxford Shakespeare*, edited by R. Martin. Oxford: Oxford University Press.

Sophocles. 2005. *Oedipus Rex*, translated by J.E. Thomas, edited by E.O. Clayton. Delaware: Prestwick House.

West, R. 2000. Are There Nothing but Texts in this Class? Interpreting the Interpretive Turns in Legal Thought, *Chicago-Kent Law Review*, 76(2): 1125–69.

West, R. 2007. Speech, Silence, and Ethical Lives in the Law, *Michigan Law Review*, 105(7): 1397–401.

White, J.B. 1982. Law as Language: Reading Law and Reading Literature, *Texas Law Review*, 60(2): 415–46.

White, J.B. 1984. *When Words Lose Their Meaning: Constitutions and Reconstitutions of Language, Character, and Community*. Chicago: University of Chicago Press.

White, J.B. 1985. *Heracles' Bow: Essays on the Rhetoric and Poetics of the Law*. Madison: University of Wisconsin Press.

White, J.B. 1989. What Can a Lawyer Learn From Literature? *Harvard Law Review*, 102(8): 2014–47.

White, J.B. 1990. *Justice as Translation: An Essay in Cultural and Legal Criticism*. Chicago: University of Chicago Press.

White, J.B. 1994. *Acts of Hope: Creating Authority in Literature, Law, and Politics*. Chicago: University of Chicago Press.

Chapter 15

Acknowledging Uncommon Relationships: Changing How We Teach Students to be Leaders

Susan Leviton, Kerry Cooperman and Jeremy Grant-Skinner

Introduction

In January 2008, on the first day of a new semester at Baltimore Freedom Academy (BFA), a small, social-justice themed charter high school and middle school in East Baltimore, a tenth-grader named Corey stood on his chair: "This is so boring!" he announced to his classmates, referring to the "Forming the Legal Argument" class that was about to begin.[1] "I'm cancelling school for the day." The result was immediate. Some students erupted in laughter and screaming; others darted into the hallway to chat with friends; others took out their headphones; one or two buried their heads in their arms. In the next class, which focused on the structure of legal argument, Corey gave the following oral presentation: "I am Corey. Me and my partner will argue this class is boring. Three people have laid their heads down. A couple have not shown much in the class. My team believes this class is boring." This triggered other predictable reactions: running into the hallway, laughing, chatting, throwing assignment packets. The third and fourth classes had similar disruptions, similar beginnings, and similar endings.

In the fifth class, however, something changed, and it caught the class and the law student instructor by surprise. A pair of students sitting in the second-to-last row placed their sneakers on their desks to interrupt a lesson called "Hip Hop Music in Society." Immediately and inexplicably, Corey interjected: "Don't do that today. We're trying to have a discussion here. Let him teach," he said, pointing to the second-year law student in the front of the room who was struggling to jump-start a discussion about the NAACP's campaign against the use of racist language in the media. Many students laughed and chatted. Some cursed at Corey, reminding him that he was not their teacher. But the disruptive students placed

---

1 This class was taught to all tenth grade BFA students by members of the Juvenile Law, Children's Issues and Legislative Advocacy Clinic (Juvenile Law Clinic). The Juvenile Law Clinic at the University of Maryland Francis King Carey School of Law enrolls approximately 10 law students per year to teach a law and policy-related course at BFA's high school and to form and run social-justice projects for BFA's tenth-graders.

their sneakers back on the floor and were comparatively quiet for the rest of class. By the seventh class, about the scope of the Second Amendment right to keep and bear arms, Corey played an active role in keeping his classmates focused. He voluntarily sat beside one of the more disruptive students to keep him on track; he explained the writing assignment to another student who arrived late; he volunteered to read passages aloud and asked his classmates questions about the readings.

After the first day of class, Corey wrote the following on his weekly feedback form, which the law-student instructors at BFA use to track the successes and failures of each lesson: "Class was bad and didn't work well." After the second class, Corey wrote: "This is boring." After the third class, he wrote: "Class be fine. I don't mind and actually enjoy." After the fifth class, he wrote: "Better classes. More production. Minor behavior with some students. We'll fix." After the sixth class, he wrote: "Classes way improve. I enjoy being involved and hope class keeps going this way." After the eighth class, Corey wrote: "Thanks for the support. I liked watching your moot trial competition. I prefer this class than others. I will continue to do what I can to help."

This informal catalog of reactions reveals more than just one student's adjustment to a new classroom. In under three months, Corey had changed from a deliberately disruptive force to a deliberately constructive leader—one who motivated his classmates by example and showed all of us, including his instructor, some of the steps and risks we must take to become better leaders in our families, our jobs, and our communities. To a measurable degree, Corey had made a decision to "buy in" not only to our classroom lessons, our commitment to professionalism, and our rules of mutual respect, but more importantly, to himself and the people around him. He had chosen to buy into his own capabilities, to the competence of his classmates, and to the possibility that his own leadership would somehow matter in ways that were not immediately clear. He had not found or signed up for or been assigned his role in our classroom. Corey created his role; almost spontaneously, he summoned the skills to make that role valuable and dependable to those around him, and in so doing reminded all of us that to lead is not merely to organize and manage resources. To lead is to inspire those around you to care about one another's success, to depend on one another's support, to believe in yourself and one another's abilities and ideas, and to work together to solve problems.

By example, Corey showed both his BFA classmates and the members of the Juvenile Law Clinic that we can learn to become better leaders in unlikely settings, in unexpected ways, and in spite of challenging circumstances. Through his conduct, he reminded his classmates that the classroom can be a place in which we build the relationships, the self-awareness, and the caring to enable those around us to trust one another, to buy into a shared goal, and to work together to develop and follow through on a plan.

Since partnering with BFA's high school in 2002, members of the Juvenile Law Clinic have worked to achieve one mission: to make Corey's story replicable by using our experiences in BFA's classrooms, in our law school seminar, and in our social-justice projects to learn and teach leadership more successfully. This chapter seeks to identify ways to teach leadership to high school and law students through the use of problem-solving-based learning and building relationships based on acknowledging and understanding what makes each of us different but valued. Moreover, we have found that by teaching adolescents to form a shared goal, to motivate one another to buy into that goal, and to work together constructively to see the plan through to its end, law students and high school students learn to become better leaders and more effective teachers.[2]

I. Origins of the Partnership Between BFA and the Juvenile Law Clinic

The Juvenile Law Clinic has for the past 25 years worked with children in crisis trying to get them better educational programs, nurturing homes after they have been abused or neglected, and appropriate services once they become involved in the juvenile justice system. After many years of having law students work with

---

2   What is a leader? Are leaders defined by what they accomplish, their personal characteristics, or the circumstances of their environment? What aspects of social reproduction make it difficult for lower-class students to become leaders? How do socioeconomic differences impact what leadership means to each of us and the manner by which we pursue it? Certain leadership theories, e.g. great man theory, trait theory and contingency theory, are based on assumptions that we think are incompatible with our goal of leadership development. The premise of these theories is that leadership cannot be learned and/or that each of us is capable of leadership only in a narrow and fixed set of circumstances. For example, Thomas Carlyle, thought to be the founding father of leadership theory, sought to identify the talent, skills, and physical characteristics of men who successfully rose to power. Specifically, he sought to "explain history through the impact of great men." Carlyle believed that men shaped history through their "personal attributes" and "divine inspirations" (Hirsch 2002, Stogdill 1974).

Similarly, trait theory is founded on three basic assumptions. First, people are born with certain inherited traits. Second, certain attributes and characteristics are particularly suited to leadership. Third, a good leader must have a specific combination of the traits that are designated as suited for leadership (Straker 2008).

Finally, contingency theory is based on the assumption that certain people have a particular set of traits and skills that make them strong leaders in certain situations.

Whether true or false, these premises do not promote (and potentially harm) efforts to teach and learn leadership in the BFA setting. Consequently, we ascribe to a more developmental theory of leadership that is based on an assumption articulated by psychologists Blau and Mallery, who advocate that:

"[E]veryone has the capacity to demonstrate and exhibit leadership. This does not mean that one must command a brigade, supervise hundreds of employees or give speeches to an audience of thousands. Rather, it means that, in everyday activities, every person has the ability to act and behave in ways that are goal oriented and can encourage others to do the same" (Blau and Mallery 2010: 7–8).

children in crisis, we began a discussion of how we could do our work better. One student talked about how she was saddened that much of the primary work of dealing with children in the clinic was at a stage when so many things were broken in their lives. It was extremely frustrating to represent children when they had already suffered a long history of abuse, violence, and criminal activity and were at a point where it was unlikely they could escape the cycle of arrest, incarceration, and drug abuse.

We discussed how many of the clients we represented in juvenile court were totally unable to make eye contact with the judge or to use language to explain why they hadn't seen their probation officer or that the probation officer, when they went to the office, had never shown up. We then had a discussion about how, for many people, the use of language and the ability to use it to negotiate life's problems were inculcated from their early experiences. However, for many of our clients, this was not true. We then realized that it would be an exciting experience if we could work with youngsters in a school setting before they got in trouble—to help them see that they could use language to negotiate for themselves and others and to resolve many of the problems within their families and their communities.

Because we were interested in producing leaders for the community, we delved into research on what leads certain individuals to help while others turn their backs. Much research shows that it is important to have compassionate values, but that simply espousing those values is not enough. Rather, those individuals who were willing to help were distinguished by a sense of confidence. Because they saw themselves as being able to make a difference, they were willing to take risks. Each saw himself as a leader.[3] To develop students as leaders requires more than implanting facts and figures in young children's minds. One principal's letter to her teachers at the beginning of each school year makes a similar point:

> Dear Teacher: I am a survivor of a concentration camp. My eyes saw what no man should witness: gas chambers built by learned engineers. Children poisoned by educated physicians. Infants killed by trained nurses. Women and babies shot and burned by high school and college graduates. So I am suspicious of education.

---

3   Helping students gain confidence, take risks and become leaders is based on the concept of transformational leadership theory. This theory focuses on inspiring and helping every member of the group to believe in their capabilities, change their expectations, buy into the leader's goal and cooperate in achieving that goal. Leadership expert James MacGregor Burns, who originated this theory, explained that transformational leadership occurs when "leaders and followers make each other advance to a higher level of morale and motivation" (Burns 1978). Later, leadership scholar Bernard Bass noted that transformational leaders "garner trust, respect and admiration from their followers" (Bass 1985). Bass added that there are four components of transformational leadership: (1) intellectual stimulation (encouraging creativity), (2) individualized consideration (supporting each follower), (3) inspirational motivation (clearly, enthusiastically articulating a vision); and (4) idealized influence (followers trust and respect the leader and thus want to emulate her and internalize her goals) (Riggio 2009).

My request is: help your students become more human. Your efforts must never produce learned monsters, skilled psychopaths, educated Eichmanns. Reading, writing, arithmetic are important only if they serve to make our children more human. (Ginott 1972: 317)

Consequently, in 2002, the school of law began a partnership with the proposed Baltimore Freedom Academy (BFA). Conceived as a small, innovative high school with funding from the Bill and Melinda Gates Foundation and local foundations, BFA then opened in the fall of 2003 with a focus on law-related education, leadership, and problem-solving.[4] Since then, law students participating in the Juvenile Law Clinic have taught law and advocacy related courses and worked on various other projects at BFA, receiving an opportunity to explore educational policy issues through direct experience in a school. Through the BFA partnership, we sought to add an innovative component to clinic work, which would benefit young people in Baltimore and law students at the same time.

This partnership was especially appropriate because the goals of the clinic for law students and of BFA for high school students are very similar. The ultimate aim of both programs is, essentially, to cultivate advocates for positive social change. A major component of this cultivation was to build both students' confidence in and commitment to effecting change and their belief that one can make a difference and ensure justice in a world many see as unjust. For many students at BFA, the institutions that are supposed to work for them (e.g., schools, police, courts) have not been effective in helping them achieve success. Both they and law students need to develop the confidence that they can overcome the obstacles that everyday experiences present.

In order to accomplish this, we have discovered that both groups of students indeed require quite similar skills and tools to be successful. In both programs, which emphasize learning by doing, we focus on the importance of hard work, how to build relationships, and the role law plays in different communities and our society overall. Our teaching emphasis has been mostly on teaching students to think critically and to question, as well as how to persuasively use language—both oral and written—to express their needs and to advocate for others.

Additionally, from our experiences at BFA, we believe that clinic classes and BFA classes must both explore issues beyond these topics. In particular, it is necessary to explore the significance of identity, confronting issues of race and class and feelings of being an outsider; and to investigate ways to develop leadership abilities. Along with this, we try to broaden the perspective of both

---

4   Founded in 2003 through grants from the Bill and Melinda Gates Foundation, the Baltimore City Public School System (BCPSS), and other local charitable foundations, the Baltimore Freedom Academy was one of Baltimore's first "innovation" high schools. The innovation high schools were created to provide small high schools designed around three principles: (1) academic rigor, (2) small supportive structures, and (3) effective, accountable leadership and instruction (Baltimore City Public School System 2004).

law students and BFA students and to teach each how to get out of their comfort zone and live in a complex and often chaotic world. In the end, to be successful, students must have not only the traditional skills advocacy requires, but also the commitment, confidence, and cultural competency to allow them to successfully utilize those skills to push for social change.

We then engaged in discussion of how to foster leadership among ourselves and high school students as well as maximizing their academic achievement. Like the story of Kitty Genovese (Dowd 1984), in which a woman was murdered and the majority of people turned their backs, research shows that relationships and a strong sense of identity are required in order for one to step forward and make a difference.[5] Thus, educational materials that focus on helping students examine their own identity are required in order to develop strong leaders. Also, in order for students to become leaders, they must believe that they have the ability to succeed without compromising themselves.[6] Often students believe that intelligence is fixed—and poor and/or Black students are more likely to feel that they are less smart than others. To get students to work hard—and eventually to be leaders— teachers must discuss academic progress and its relationship to hard work (as opposed to fixed abilities).

Despite the similar goals of the law school and BFA, their respective students often come from very different places. BFA serves poor students from Baltimore City, while the law school's students represent more than half of the 50 states plus five other countries, along with over 125 undergraduate institutions.[7] Although the law school is quite racially diverse compared with many law schools, with 28% of the students identifying themselves as persons of color, more than 70% of its students are white.[8] In contrast, over 95% of BFA students are black (Education Policy Center 2007: 6). Also, at least 75% of BFA students qualify for free or reduced price lunches,[9] while law students are often the children of the middle class (Sander 2011: 632, 637). Finally, while there are no admissions criteria to enter BFA—admissions are by lottery—the law school is very selective.

---

5   Kohl (1992) discussed the importance of developing the right relationships; Brown and Posner (2001) noted the importance of "relationships that are supportive and trusting"; Stables (2003) evaluated classroom teaching that associates learning with positive identity development.

6   Bandura (1993: 117) noted that "[s]tudents' beliefs in their efficacy to regulate their own learning and to master academic activities determine their aspirations, level of motivation, and academic accomplishments."

7   http://www.law.umaryland.edu/aboutus/student_profile.asp.

8   http://www.law.umaryland.edu/about/facts.html.

9   Like many urban communities around the nation, Baltimore City educates the most poor children in Maryland with the poorest physical facilities and the least qualified teachers. The number of Baltimore City students who qualify for free or reduced meals ("FARMS") is 84% among elementary school students, 82% among middle school students, and 69% among high school students (Maryland State Department of Education 2011).

The 2009 entering class had a median undergraduate GPA of 3.6 and a median LSAT score of 162.[10]

Society has very different expectations for these two groups of students. Options abound for graduates of the law school; 40% of them entered private practice after graduation, another 14% entered the government or other public service work, and 15% of them entered prestigious judicial clerkships.[11] Quite the opposite, students at an open-admissions urban high school such as BFA seldom meet much success. When one researcher examined test scores at high-poverty, high-minority schools across the entire nation, he found only 23 "high-flying" schools—a term used for schools which meet success despite high numbers of poor, minority students (Tough 2006).

II. Acknowledging Identity and Building Relationships

Every student at every level of education brings into school each day quite a profound question: "Who in the world am I? Or who am I in the world?" (Ayers 2004: 32). This dual question influences every aspect of teaching and learning in the classroom, from whether students enjoy a class and how much they participate, to whether they plan to go to college and what they hope to become. To be effective, teachers must help students confront this question—and, indeed, must confront the question themselves as well. For teachers with a progressive vision for education, teachers fighting against the achievement gap, and teachers who differ in significant ways from their students, issues of identity are even more important. Because clinic students who teach at Baltimore Freedom Academy (BFA) fit two or three of these criteria, they must commit to learning about identity and applying this knowledge to their classrooms in order to maximize their impact on students.

Events and interactions in daily life constantly demonstrate the significance of identity to all people, as individuals and as members of one or more groups. On April 4, 2007, radio host Don Imus used a racist and sexist phrase to refer to the players on the Rutgers University women's basketball team (Prunty 2007). This event occurred within a year of Academy Award winner Mel Gibson blaming Jews for all the wars in the world (Booth 2006), actor Isaiah Washington calling his television co-star an anti-gay slur (Puente 2007), comedian and former sitcom star Michael Richards repeatedly shouting the N-word during his stand-up act at a comedy club (Farhi 2006), and now-former NBA basketball player Tim Hardaway saying he "hates" gay people (Winderman 2007).

In classrooms, the respective identities of students and teachers become relevant in many ways. First, teachers who have examined their own identities and others' identities (and respective privileges) are less likely to carry biases

---

10   These numbers are based on a profile of the Fall 2009 entering class, http://www. law.umaryland.edu/about/facts.html.

11   http://www.law.umaryland.edu/about/facts.html.

into classrooms that will prevent them from maintaining high expectations, understanding and responding appropriately to student behaviors, or remaining motivated, among other things. Second, students who feel that their identities are acknowledged and respected are more likely to engage more fully in classroom goals and activities. Third, classrooms in which the teacher and students discuss identity and its relationship to academic content—even just by relating topics and activities to students' interests—can help students continue to form their identities and become empowered to serve as leaders and advocates for social progress.

Students at BFA come from a homogeneous swath of society; often poor, overwhelmingly African American, and often disserved by "the system": the justice system, the law enforcement system, and even the educational system. Schools have long operated on a Eurocentric system of education, functioning from a point of view that represents that of the majority, often at the expense of the achievements of minorities and dissenting opinion. History and humanities classes, among others, have long marginalized the innovations of minorities and Eastern culture, and as such, many minorities do not relate to conventional approaches to instruction. The students at BFA have responded to Afrocentric approaches to the study of law that involve a critical look at the justice system and the constitution, with a special focus on institutional racism and the way it affects modern jurisprudence. The students see this exchange as refreshing, because it gives them a chance to tie their life in their communities to the theoretical underpinnings of the law. Simply attempting to teach a dry interpretation of the law as the majority sees and benefits from it is just not enough in the urban classroom.

Identity and the Classroom

> The concept of identity is a complex one shaped by individual characteristics, family dynamics, historical factors, and social and political contexts. Who am I? The answer depends in large part on who the world around me says I am. (Tatum 2003: 18)[12]

Furthermore, this phenomenon links closely to privilege. Usually, in groups in which people are asked to identify themselves, people point out the part of their identity that stands out among the group. That is, in a group of mostly White people, a Black person is likely to identify by his or her race, while a White person is more likely to not even "see" his or her race (Stout 2006). In the context of race or ethnicity, gender, religion, sexual orientation, socioeconomic status, age, or physical or mental ability, Tatum explains, "It is the targeted identities that hold our attention and the dominant identities that often go unexamined" (Tatum 2003: 22).

---

12 Copyright © 1997 Tatum, Beverly Daniel. Reprinted by permission of Basic Books, a member of the Perseus Book Group.

Indeed, BFA students do strongly identify themselves according to race.[13] For clinic students, Tatum's arguments can explain why discussions about race (along with class, perhaps) are necessary both among teachers and within classrooms.

The consequences of ignoring identity in the classroom—or attempting to impose another identity on students—are described by Ayers in his book *Teaching Toward Freedom* (2004). He describes several classrooms in which identity was mostly or completely ignored and the dehumanization that this disregard entailed. First, in Toni Morrison's *Beloved*, Schoolteacher exhibits "cold brutality, abominable sadism, towering arrogance linked to profound ignorance" with his slave students (Ayers 2004: x). Similarly, in the 2002 film *Rabbit-Proof Fence*, which offers a glimpse of schools established for aboriginal children by the Australian government, teaching is unconnected to identity. Indeed, these schools were designed to strip aboriginal children of their identity. Ayers writes:

> *Destroying* their identities, beating culture, knowledge, language, and memory out of the skins of native kids, emptying them completely in order to fill them up with better stuff, breathing "whiteness" into them—all of this was "for their own good." (Ayers 2004: 2, emphasis added)[14]

Lastly, the 2002 film *The Magdalene Sisters* depicts the life stories of several young Irish women sent to an asylum. There, Ayers writes,

> [W]e experience the denial of thought, of expression, and of choice, the denial of the right to question and to decide for oneself, to make up one's own mind—the repudiation of the essential humanity of students ... [W]e witness the horrifying process of human subjects being treated like inanimate objects.

In these classrooms, where obedience and conformity are paramount, students are not seen, appreciated, or respected as individuals. Ayers provocatively (but perhaps not inaccurately) calls this "the classroom as slave galley" (Ayers 2004: 8). To instead "teach toward freedom," teachers must confront both their own identities and the identities of their students.

---

13 Similarly, White teachers at a mostly Black school such as BFA will, perhaps in a rare occurrence for many (usually being in the majority), *feel* their race very profoundly when they first step in front of a class.

14 Republished with permission of William Ayers, from *Teaching Toward Freedom: Moral Commitment and Ethical Action in the Classroom* (2007); permission conveyed through the Copyright Clearance Center, Inc.

The Teacher's Identity

Almost without exception, clinic students teaching at BFA will be different in some ways from their students. First, almost all BFA students, but a minority of law students and sometimes a minority of law students teaching at BFA, are African American. Second, many law students, but few BFA students, have parents or other older family members who went to college (or beyond). Third, BFA students mostly are poor or live in poor neighborhoods, while far fewer law students have that experience. Each of these examples emphasizes that, when teaching at a school in an underserved district, every teacher will confront some "otherness" on a regular basis (Teach for America 2011).[15]

This does not mean that clinic students will not find common ground with students at BFA or that only individuals who share common backgrounds can relate to each other. Surely, clinic students and BFA students will share some similarities, but even individuals who identify themselves similarly often find that they have very different experiences and beliefs. Additionally, the differences— namely, those of race and class—will be more profound because they are linked to different levels of privilege, which in turn are linked to very different life experiences and opportunities.

> For teachers, understanding privilege is important because it is closely related to bias:
>
> In a manner of speaking, [bias and privilege] are corollaries of one another. If one carries a bias, he or she has some unfounded assumptions that shape expectations of the targeted group's behavior or abilities. On the other hand, if one enjoys a "privilege" … one likely has some unfounded assumptions about one's own contribution to his or her success in the world. That is, "privilege" is closely related to "bias" in that "privilege" involves unquestioned assumptions about *one's self*. In both cases, the process of "uncovering" or "unpacking" that bias or privilege is a process of replacing those assumptions with a more nuanced and real vision of one's interactions with others. In the context of teaching, this quest for a more nuanced and realistic view of the world is particularly important and has direct implications for a teacher's interactions with and leadership of students. (Teach for America 2011: 66)[16]

---

15   As Teach For America (2011: 49) states: "No matter what your background and identities, … you are likely to encounter dynamics of difference and sameness in ways you may not have before." "Dynamics of difference and sameness" refers to, according to the text, "the complex—often unspoken or even unrealized—dynamics of power or bias that can arise in any human interaction."

16   Copyright 2011 Teach for America. Diversity, Community & Achievement. Available at http://www.teachingasleadership.org/sites/default/files/Related-Readings/ DCA_2011.pdf.

In *The Corner*, David Simon and Edward Burns provide a more vivid illustration of the link between privilege and bias. They offer an oration from what they perceive to be the perspective of many middle class (and usually White) individuals on the experiences of people living in concentrated poverty. With great sarcasm, they write:

> If it was us, if it was our lonesome ass shuffling past the corner of Monroe and Fayette every day, we'd get out, wouldn't we? We'd endure. Succeed. Thrive. No matter what, no matter how, we'd find the fucking exit. If it was our fathers firing dope and our mothers smoking coke, we'd pull ourselves past it. We'd raise ourselves, discipline ourselves, teach ourselves the essentials of self-denial and delayed gratification that no one in our universe ever demonstrated. And if home was the rear room of some rancid, three-story shooting gallery, we'd rise above that too. We'd shuffle up the stairs past nodding friends and sullen dealers, shut the bedroom door, turn off the television, and do our schoolwork. Algebra amid the stench of burning rock; American history between police raids. (Simon and Burns 1998: 477–8)

The authors make a clear statement that these attitudes are rooted in ignorance of privilege. They describe that outlook as a "myth" and a "lie that allows us to render our judgments" (Simon and Burns 1998: 478). Furthermore, they say it "becomes a possibility only through the arrogance and certainty that so easily accompany a well-planned and well-tended life" (Simon and Burns 1998: 478–9).[17]

---

17 At a very early age, so many White middle class adolescents learn that they can get much of what they need. Furthermore, these White students know that if they don't have direct access to something that they may need, they can get access to it through their networks—which often include their well-connected parents, their parents' associations and so many others. This is a foreign notion to most minority poor students. Minority students often do not have a network of people that they can reach out to. If they do have a network, it is often not as influential as that of their White peers. Although some people may not see this as a disadvantage because it has no part in an individual's personal skill and ability, it is by far an influential factor because it is the way that so many people operate today. An example is when a young person gets a job through a "family friend." These connections are common in today's society and it is something that minority students miss out on.

In addition to the setback that minority students face through White privilege connections, minority students also face the stigma of being outside of the White privilege circle. Minority students have accepted the fact that the majority students have an upper hand in many different areas. It is clear to them that these "privileges" are basically inherent to the White race. Consequently, many minority students often don't even understand that they can have a place where majority students are. Minority students don't think that they have a place at "their" universities. Minority students don't believe that they can be a part of "their" networks. Minority students don't even understand the influences that they can gain by penetrating these groups. As a result, most minority students don't even attempt to come out of their comfort zones where they have presence, influence, and value.

In order to develop the "more nuanced and realistic" worldview, teachers must spend time getting to know their students and the communities where they live. However, we are all vulnerable to the views around us in society. As B.D. Tatum states in *Why Are All the Black Kids Sitting Together in the Cafeteria?*, "Prejudice is one of the inescapable consequences of living in a racist society. Cultural racism … is like a smog in the air" (Tatum 2003: 6). In a sense, we have been conditioned to believe certain things about certain groups of people—even when the group is one to which we belong.[18]

Several activities are particularly helpful for discussing and reflecting upon privilege. In the Juvenile Law Clinic class, after reading parts of *The Corner* showing a typical day in a particular area with very concentrated poverty, law students were asked to reflect and share reflections on the activities and pace of a typical day in their lives. Because most Americans who do not live in concentrated poverty avoid most interaction with those who do, accurate depictions of the "other world" such as that provided by Simon and Burns are extremely helpful as springboards for reflection on privilege. Looking at a much longer time period than one's typical day, law students are asked to draw a line graph to show the highs and lows of their lives so far. Comparing these with each other is often informative; drawing such a line graph for someone like DeAndre McCulloch[19] makes the comparison even more graphic.

Finally, like those of *The Corner*, discussions of Tatum's book itself served as a great catalyst for unpacking privilege and confronting issues of identity. Any of these activities help individuals better understand others and can therefore help prevent or stop bias. "Exploring one's own beliefs, perspectives, and privilege is a means to effective teaching, not an end unto itself" (Tatum 2003: 56). That is, these activities should all come back to the question of how it affects what we do with students.

The Student's Identity

Both positive and negative events often relate to the treatment of identity in any classroom, but this is particularly true in middle and high schools and when students represent subservient groups in society. Identity is acutely significant to adolescents because they are in the midst of major transformations, which include the shaping and refining of their identities. Tatum states, "Choices made in adolescence ripple throughout the lifespan" (Tatum 2003: 20). Then, identity is also especially important for society's "others" because schools—most of which perpetuate dominance—present special challenges for them. "All the structures of privilege and oppression apparent in the larger society are mirrored in our schools" (Ayers and Ford 1996: 88).

---

18   See Tatum (2003) for a short explanation of internalized racism.
19   DeAndre McCulloch is the central character in *The Corner*.

For members of a subordinate group, such as Black adolescents—who make up most of BFA's student population—schools and classrooms that do not value their identity pose a threat to their integrity. Herbert Kohl calls the common outcome "not-learning." He writes,

> Not-learning tends to take place when someone has to deal with unavoidable challenges to her or his personal and familial loyalties, integrity, and identity. In such situations, there are forced choices and no apparent middle ground. To agree to learn from a stranger who does not respect your integrity causes a major loss of self. The only alternative is to not-learn and reject the stranger's world. (Kohl 1994: 6)[20]

The result for students is oppositional behavior, incomplete assignments, apparent disrespect, and other actions that threaten academic success.

Law students in their classrooms must build, for each student, a "place to stand"—a social, physical, and intellectual space to feel confident, to trust the people around you, to care about the people you rely on, to be involved, experience achievement, and get genuinely positive feedback from people who are genuinely excited for you.

A place to stand, which allows students to more comfortably summon their leadership skills and to feel like they are part of a small community to which they matter, is what poor urban teenagers lack and it is what teachers ought to challenge themselves to create. In most of the tenth grade classes at BFA, very few students feel like they have a valuable place to stand in the world. One tenth-grader repeatedly complained to his "Forming the Legal Argument" teacher that writing mock letters to the *Washington Post* or to the BCPSS Superintendent were stupid because "these people don't give a shit about what we have to say. They don't care about us at all, so what's the point?" Another student pointed out that there is no reason for him to care about this class if the school district does not care enough to have air conditioning, a sports program, and unbroken desks.

In their neighborhoods and in their homes, many BFA students, literally and figuratively, have almost no place to stand—no community that deems them vital, no relationships that make them feel needed, nobody to impress, no big or small entity to give them a sense of confidence, security, and purpose. The challenge that schools face in building meaningful relationships is that traditional classrooms are designed to teach math and reading, not to build leaders. When the authors of this chapter surveyed a group of 15 BFA tenth-graders, 14 of the 15 stated that the classroom is a particularly poor setting to teach leadership. One tenth-grader explained that the classroom is a place that students "dread" coming to; another stated that she associates the classroom with "worksheets and boring lessons";

---

20   Herbert Kohl, from *I Won't Learn From You* (Minneapolis: Milkweed Editions, 1994). Copyright © 1994 by Herbert Kohl. Reprinted with permission from Milkweed Editions. www.milkweed.org.

another stated that classroom experiences always feel like "appointments" and that she "counts the minutes until the end"; another explained that you can't learn leadership by "sitting at a desk and reading papers"; another stated that if teachers wanted to teach leadership in the classroom, they would not simply "bark out orders" and "tell us what to do every minute."

Given that classrooms are inevitably the core spaces of learning in schools throughout the country, how can educators build relationships with students by closing communications gaps, effort gaps, identity gaps, and trust gaps? When 15 BFA tenth-graders were asked why teachers were not able to connect to them in a useful way, nearly every student pointed to the failures of most teachers to acknowledge students' identities. One student said, "They just don't get us. They don't respect us." Another said, "They don't respect how we communicate." Another said, "I always do the work, but it's never what they want." Another said, "White teachers really can't know us."

In the tenth grade law classes at BFA, one law-student instructor explains how communication and cultural gaps make it implicitly difficult for teachers to adequately respect a student's identity. When the law students tell a story in a BFA classroom, they tend to do so in a topical and chronological order, using transition words and varied vocabulary. When tenth-graders tell a story in a BFA classroom, they do so "in the episodic, random manner of the casual-register story structure."[21] They generally do not have the vocabulary or knowledge of sentence structure and most of the meaning comes not from the word choices, but from the nonverbal assists. As Payne explains, "to be asked to communicate in writing without the non-verbal assist is an overwhelming and formidable task, which most of them try to avoid" (Payne 2008: 43).

Because most BFA teachers are unfamiliar with the communication structures of their students and because most BFA students are largely unfamiliar with the communication structures of their teachers, all of us struggle to converse and to acknowledge one another's identity. The law students tend to get right to the point, and speak in outline form (e.g. "First ... Second ... Third"), whereas the BFA students tend to use a compilation of narrative fragments, rather than a topic-centered structure, to tell their stories.[22] These communication gaps, and a

---

21   (Payne 2008). Payne talks about how most minority and poor students do not have access to "formal register" at home, which is the language used in all job interviews, SAT and school tests (Payne 2008: 42–3).

22   There is a significant body of anthropological and educational literature concerning the different narrative styles used by people of different racial, ethnic, class, and cultural backgrounds. One scholar observes that the discourse style of teachers tends to be topic-centered, i.e., "tightly organized, centering on a single, identifiable topic," whereas the discourse style of African American students tends to be "topic-associating," i.e., consisting of a "series of implicitly associated personal anecdotes" and without an "explicit statement of an overall theme or point." "Research indicates that children from different racial, ethnic, class, and cultural backgrounds bring to the classroom different styles for organizing

failure to understand the reasons for those gaps,[23] are in part what cause teachers to undermine their students' identities and are what cause students to mistrust and push away their teachers. Building relationships in this context, and in the span of a one- or two-hour class, becomes increasingly difficult.

How might we close the identity and communications gaps to make meaningful relationships possible? How might we communicate with our students and create settings for relationship-building?

One strategy that has helped many members of the Juvenile Law Clinic to close the identity gap in their classrooms is to use subject matter and teaching strategies that allow students to explore their own identities. In our "Forming the Legal Argument" course, for example, we teach linguistic, organizational, and problem-solving skills through formal debates about race relations, school resources, affirmative action, urban violence, and historically Black colleges—topics that help our students not only to connect to each other, but to learn new skills through material with which they are already confident and familiar. When the law students bring their computers to class to play YouTube clips of Chris Rock or Barack Obama, the BFA students tend to be more open to practicing argument and problem-solving skills. When one law student created a program that allowed students to learn leadership by organizing and performing in their own spoken word show—through rap, dance, and vocal skills—the students summoned their leadership in incredibly successful ways. When we created an environment in which students' views, identities, and communication methods were acknowledged and accepted in a real way, students responded and discourse improved. When we failed to do so—when we failed to honor and acknowledge our students' identities by assigning projects that plainly required formal register and middle-class experience—we made little progress.

One crucial element of building relationships that inspire episodes of leadership is the ability of a class to motivate students to care about each other's success. Whereas relationships of trust and respect generate good results, relationships of caring generate the kind of leadership that encourages students to work hard. Teachers play an important role in triggering this process. During the first week of BFA classes, one law student calls each student's home to introduce himself and to encourage parents to call the law student if they think of ways to improve the class. Another law student appoints certain tenth-graders as "teacher assistants" early in the semester, and encourages their leadership in weekly feedback comments. After week three of the spring semester, for example, one law-student instructor wrote the following to one of his BFA students: "I would like you to

---

narratives" (Méndez Barletta 2008: 2–4). We have observed this precise phenomenon in BFA classrooms.

23   Paul (1989) analyzed the different narrative structures used by an 11-year-old underprivileged Black girl and an 11-year-old middle-class White girl and observed that the former style is "often misunderstood in the school context" whereas the latter style is "highly compatible with school-based values."

be my assistant throughout the semester and to encourage your classmates to follow your outstanding example." After week four, the teacher wrote: "I deeply appreciate your constant leadership and your helping to keep everyone in control. You are certainly the student-teacher." After week five, the teacher wrote: "I have noticed your excellent ability to keep your classmates focused and on track. I truly appreciate all of this. You were an exceptionally successful leader last week."

Feedback, especially positive feedback, matters immensely. After being asked to serve as the teacher's assistant for the semester and to encourage other classmates by example, the BFA tenth-grader embraced his leadership role—voluntarily sitting beside disruptive students to keep them on task, asking students who interrupted the lesson to stop doing so, leading class discussions, and explaining assignments to students who arrived late or had been absent. Because the teacher's weekly notes to the student referred to him as a teacher's "assistant," a "successful leader," and a "student-teacher," the student came to view himself as such, to carry out leadership tasks without being asked, and to assist his classmates in spite of their ridicule. He took pride in his leadership responsibilities and in the results of his efforts, reporting to the teacher, "Minor behavior with some students. We'll fix" and, "Classes way improve. I enjoy being involved and hope class keeps going this way." To give students a place to stand, a role of importance in a professional setting, and reasons to know that they matter have a significant effect on their willingness to become and act as leaders.

Demonstrations of caring during class time show students that they have an immediate reason to be leaders and that their contributions have value—a message that many lower-income students from lower-income neighborhoods do not receive at home or elsewhere. During the last 30 minutes of each class, one law student deliberately initiates conversations with every BFA student individually: the teacher moves a chair around the room to sit next to each student, asks how each student's week has been, asks what the student has planned for that weekend, and tells the student about law school. Most students are utterly uncomfortable with respectful, non-contentious one-on-one dialogues with authority figures who sit next to them, make eye contact, smile at them, and ask them about their lives. They are not used to this kind of interaction, and they initially dislike it. Authority figures in many lower-income neighborhoods, including teachers, parents, police officers, and judges, more often than not have one-on-one discussions with adolescents only to reprimand them or talk at them—almost never to genuinely ask them how their lives are. But the law student who tried this kept it up, and the behavior of his students improved. When one student had fits of anger, the law-student teacher would sit next to him and ask him, "Are you ok? Is there anything I can do right now to make this class better for you?" the student always said "No," but seemed surprised by this gesture and kept himself generally calm for the rest of class. When other students put their heads down on their desks during writing assignments, the law student would sit next to them to guide them through the writing process. This emphasis on positive reinforcement and caring relationships always produced far better results than reprimands.

Conclusion

There is no formula for teaching leadership. There is no formula for building productive relationships between struggling African American tenth-graders and more privileged law-student instructors. There is no formula for creating a school culture—in a high school or a law school—in which students buy into a social-justice mission, care about one another's progress, and trust that their commitments to teamwork and professionalism will be rewarded. There are, however, a series of leadership objectives that all schools should prioritize and a series of pedagogical strategies that all educators ought to consider to make both students and faculty more capable, self-confident, and civic-minded citizens. We have found that teachers who rely on experiential problem-solving-based lessons, treat their students with respect and care, demonstrate the same level of commitment that they require of their students, and honor their students' identities by recognizing differences often succeed in building the relationships of trust that are the basis of good leadership.

References

Ayers, W. 2004. *Teaching Toward Freedom: Moral Commitment and Ethical Action in the Classroom*. Boston: Beacon Press.

Ayers, W. and Ford, P. 1996. Introduction: Chaos and Opportunity, in *City Kids, City Teachers: Reports from the Front Row*, edited by W. Ayers and P. Ford. New York: New Press, 81–90.

Baltimore City Public School System. 2004. *2004 Innovative High School Planning and Implementation Guidelines.*

Bandura, A. 1993. Perceived Self-Efficacy in Cognitive Development and Functioning, *Educational Psychologist*, 28(2): 117–48.

Bass, B.M. 1985. *Leadership and Performance*. New York: Free Press.

Blau, G.M. and Mallery, C. 2010. Personal Vision and Leadership in *The Leadership Equation: Strategies for Individuals Who are Champions for Children, Youth, and Families*, edited by G.M. Blau and P.R. Magrab. Baltimore: Paul H. Brookes Pub. Co., 7–17.

Booth, W. 2006. Mel Gibson's Latest Drama Stars Himself, *Washington Post*, 30 July, D1.

Brown, L.M. and Posner, B.Z. 2001. Exploring the Relationship Between Learning and Leadership, *The Leadership & Organizational Development Journal*, 22(6): 274–80.

Burns, J.M. 1978. *Leadership*. New York: Harper and Row.

Dowd, M. 1984. 20 Years After the Murder of Kelly Genovese, the Question Remains: Why? *New York Times*, 12 March, B1.

Education Policy Center, The Urban Institute. 2007. *Baltimore City's High School Reform Initiative: Schools, Students, and Outcomes* [Online]. Available at: http://www.urban.org/UploadedPDF/411590_baltimoreschools.pdf [accessed 10 September 2012].

Farhi, P. 2006. "Seinfeld" Comic Richards Apologizes for Racist Rant, *Washington Post*, 21 November, C1.

Ginott, H.G. 1972. *Teacher and Child*. New York: MacMillan.

Hirsch, E.D. 2002. *The New Dictionary of Cultural Literacy*, 3rd edition. Boston: Houghton Mifflin Co.

Kohl, H. 1992. "I Won't Learn From You": Thoughts on the Role of Assent in Learning, *Rethinking Schools*, 7(1): 16–17, 19.

Kohl, H. 1994. *"I Won't Learn from You": And Other Thoughts on Creative Maladjustment*. New York: New Press.

Maryland State Department of Education 2011. *2011 Maryland Report Card: Baltimore City Demographics* [Online]. Available at: http://www.mdreportcard.org/Demographics.aspx?K=30AAAA&WDATA=Local+School+System [accessed 31 January 2012].

Méndez Barletta, L. 2008. Teachers' Differential Treatment of Culturally and Linguistically Diverse Students During Sharing Time, *Colorado Research in Linguistics*, 21(1): 1–21.

Paul, J.G. 1989. Two Styles of Narrative Construction and Their Linguistic and Educational Implications, *Journal of Education*, 171(1): 97–115.

Payne, R.K. 2008. *A Framework for Understanding Poverty*, 3rd revised edition. Highlands, TX: Aha! Process.

Prunty, B. 2007. Remarks by Imus Infuriate Rutgers, *New Jersey Star-Ledger*, 7 April, 3.

Puente, M. 2007. Here's the Dirt on Using This "F" Word, *USA Today*, 30 January, 2D.

Riggio, R.E. 2009. Are You a Transformational Leader?, *Psychology Today* [Online], 24 March. Available at: http://blogs.psychologytoday.com/blog/cutting-edge-leadership/200903/are-you-transformational-leader [accessed: 31 January 2012].

Sander, R.H. 2011. Class in American Legal Education, *Denver University Law Review*, 88(4): 631–82.

Simon, D. and Burns, E. 1998. *The Corner*. New York: Broadway.

Stables, A. 2003. Learning, Identity and Classroom Dialogue, *Journal of Educational Enquiry*, 4(1): 1–18.

Stogdill, R.M. 1974. *Handbook of Leadership: A Survey of the Literature*. New York: Free Press.

Stout, D. 2006. Senator Says He Meant No Insult By Remark, *Washington Post*, 16 August, A14.

Straker, D. 2008. *Changing Minds: In Detail*. London: Syque Press.

Tatum, B.D. 2003. *Why Are All the Black Kids Sitting Together in the Cafeteria?* 5th anniversary edition. New York: Basic.

Teach for America. 2011. *Diversity, Community, and Achievement* [Online]. Available at: http://teachingasleadership.org/sites/default/files/Related-Readings/DCA_2011.pdf [accessed 10 September 2012].

Tough, P. 2006. What It Takes to Make a Student, *New York Times* [Online], 26 November. Available at: http://www.nytimes.com/2006/11/26/magazine/26tough.html?pagewanted=all [accessed 31 January 2012].

Winderman, I. 2007. Hardaway: I Hate Gays, *Florida Sun-Sentinel*, 17 February, 1C.

Chapter 16

Teaching Gender and Leadership

Paula A. Monopoli

Therefore it is
We must assist the cause of order; this
Forbids concession to a feminine will;
Better be outcast, if we must, of men,
Than have it said a woman worsted us ...
Foul spotted heart-a woman's follower.

From Sophocles' *Antigone*

In a previous chapter, Alan Hornstein eloquently describes the rich source of material available for law students in the Western literary canon. Sophocles' ancient play *Antigone* is replete with images of leadership and followership embodied in the characters of Creon, Antigone, Ismene, and Haemon. The play also explores the relationship between the state and its citizens and the relationship between men and women. The idea that it is out of the natural order of things for women to lead men and for women to lead the state is deeply embedded in *Antigone* and in our Western canon generally. Chaos will presumably reign if women are allowed to lead men and the natural order is upset.

In *Antigone*, Sophocles (1993) also draws sharp distinctions between fear and courage. Upsetting the natural order requires Antigone to overcome fear. Women are associated with courage when it comes to protecting their children and families. But the kind of courage needed to lead in the public sphere is associated with men. The ability to act with agency and passion in defense of the state is a decidedly male attribute in Western culture. These insights into gender and leadership form the core of a curricular program I designed for my students over the past decade. This chapter describes the path I have taken to understanding gender, power, and leadership and the program I designed to disrupt my students' understanding of gender and revise their definitions of leadership.[1]

The seeds of this program began 25 years ago when, after two years as young lawyers on Wall Street, my husband, Marin Scordato, and I moved to Tallahassee, Florida. Marin joined the faculty at Florida State University and I joined what was then a predominantly Florida-based law firm, Holland & Knight, where I chose to

---

1   This sentence is paraphrased from the title of a chapter in Deborah Rhode and Barbara Kellerman's book, *Women and Leadership: The State of Play and Strategies for Change* (San Francisco: Jossey-Bass, 2007). The title of Chapter 17 is "Disrupting Gender, Revising Leadership," by Debra Myerson, Robin Ely and Laura Wernick.

work with Martha Walters Barnett, the first woman partner at the firm. Martha had built the legislative practice in Tallahassee into an integral part of the multi-office firm. She was fearless; working with her was a powerful lesson for me on how women can lead.

Holland & Knight is now a global firm and I have long since joined the world of legal academia. But the lessons I learned at Martha's side have never left me. Her courage to take on unpopular causes and her skill in persuading legislators to support them was something to behold. Martha encouraged me to go out and speak at conferences when I would have preferred to stay in the safety of my office. She encouraged my pro bono work in child advocacy and helped me join state and national bar committees that brought me into contact with other lawyers doing similar work. We took on the case of a Miami woman serving a minimum mandatory 25 years to life sentence. She was a victim of emotional abuse, and she had killed her abuser. Martha took me with her when she traveled to Miami to meet with then-State's Attorney (and later first female U.S. Attorney General) Janet Reno to ask for her support in the clemency proceeding we planned to initiate. Martha sent me to lobby the Governor and his cabinet and to persuade these tremendously powerful men to give clemency to our client, a non-English-speaking mother of two young boys. We succeeded and, in the process, Martha had given me the opportunity to do the most important lawyering I would ever do.

Several years later I moved from practice to academia—a path I may well not have taken if Martha had not given me opportunities to develop confidence in my own legal voice. She eventually became president of the American Bar Association. Under Martha's leadership, the ABA's office of the President, the ABA Commission on Women in the Profession, the American Association of Law Schools, and the Center for Public Leadership at the Kennedy School of Government convened a remarkable Women's Leadership Summit at Harvard in 2001. Martha invited me to participate. At the Summit I met other academics like Judith Resnik from Yale Law School and Deborah Rhode from Stanford Law School with whom I was able to exchange ideas about what law schools could do to better develop women leaders. After the Summit, Deborah published a series of essays by the participants entitled *The Difference Difference Makes: Women and Leadership* (Rhode 2003). In 2003, I designed a two-course sequence in gender and leadership and used *The Difference Difference Makes* in my first seminar. That curricular sequence is now called the Women, Leadership & Equality (WLE) Program and it is supported by a generous endowment from the Marjorie Cook Foundation. Ten years later, Deborah Rhode's work in gender and leadership and in the nascent field of leadership studies in the law school curriculum continues to inspire me.[2]

---

2   Most recently, Deborah Rhode has co-authored the first casebook in the field, targeted at leadership courses in law schools (Rhode and Packel 2011).

Course One: The Theory Seminar

When I taught my first course in gender and leadership in 2003, my goal was to design a curriculum that would be instructive and provocative for my students. I aimed to deconstruct their understanding of women as leaders and to spark in them the courage to lead—not only in traditional ways as informal leaders but to take on formal leadership roles often denied to women. I shared with my students my own definition of leadership—the ability to persuade others to embrace your ideas and implement them. I thus made my understanding of the nexus between legal education and leadership clear to them. The art of persuasion is an essential lawyerly skill that we spend a significant amount of time developing in our students. I asked them to focus on the power that comes with being able to deploy that skill effectively and make the link to leadership—sometimes formal and sometimes informal; sometimes in private institutions like law firms and other times in the public sphere as a judge or legislator.

My approach to course design was interdisciplinary. Readings included law, political science, social psychology, philosophy, gender studies and leadership theory as it relates to barriers to women assuming leadership roles in society. In addition to reading *Antigone*, we looked at the work of Karin Klenke, whose empirical approach is developed in her book, *Women and Leadership, A Contextual Perspective* (Klenke 1996). We read social psychologist Virginia Valian's book, *Why So Slow? The Advancement of Women* (Valian 1998), to explore the role gender schemas play in holding women back from leadership positions. We initially read Deborah Rhode's *The Difference Difference Makes* (Rhode 2003), described above, and we now read Rhode and Barbara Kellerman's book, *Women and Leadership: The State of Play and Strategies for Change* (Kellerman and Rhode 2007). We also explore the intersection of race and gender and grapple with identity. My students of color and my LGBT students have taught me more than I could ever have imagined about the malleability of gender and the power of racial and gender schemas, the toll they take, and the courage it requires to persevere in our profession despite them.

Course Two: The Applied Workshop

Early in my career as a law professor, I was faced with the dilemma of educating young women to think like lawyers but watching them unable to stay long enough in their law firms to deploy that skill. Law firms are important because they are the organizational structures within which approximately 70% of law school graduates begin their careers (Dinovitzer et al. 2004). Moreover, the skills that those graduates use to navigate barriers in law firms are transferable to other sectors,[3] including government, the judiciary, and the nonprofit sector. Those realities led me to develop an applied workshop as a second course in the WLE programmatic sequence. It was clearly important to equip students not only with an intellectual understanding of the structural barriers to ascending to leadership but to provide professional skills training in those areas of competence (in addition to substantive legal analysis) that allow women to be successful in legal workplaces. If students were armed with both the intellectual understanding that the difficulties they encountered in the workplace were not their fault—that schemas about all women as lawyers and leaders were the reason they were finding it difficult to stay—and the specific skills training to overcome those schemas, more of them would be able to stay long enough to ascend to formal leadership positions in their legal workplaces. In that way, they could acquire the power to alter the structural barriers that held women back.

The applied workshop focuses on the development of professional skills that the research demonstrates women either find difficult to deploy or for which they receive more negative pushback than men. For example, negotiating for salary increases is difficult for women, according to the research, but even when trained to do so they have to be equipped to weather the negative feedback that comes with violating gender norms in this regard (Babcock and Laschever 2003).[4] I developed a series of workshops that helped students hone those skills in the specific context of law practice, including communication, personal negotiation, self-promotion, business development, and management skills. I also added sessions that exposed students to academic disciplines that had not traditionally been included in the law school curriculum, such as organizational behavior and dynamics.

For example, if law students had instead attended a graduate business school program, they would be exposed to a course in organizational behavior and dynamics during their first semester. These skills are just as essential in the field of law. The fundamentals of organizational behavior prepare the students to recognize, for example, who holds informal power in the firm and who has the power to decide who is promoted to partner. If one is in a general counsel's office in a corporation, one should understand the organizational structure of the company and who holds what kind of power at each level.

Management skills are also essential to young lawyers, especially women lawyers. Many students start law school immediately after graduating from an undergraduate institution, with no experience in managing people. Research demonstrates that it is difficult for women to manage within an organization

---

3   In addition, 9.8% of 2007 graduates accepted judicial clerkships, 11.8% accepted jobs in the government, and 14.1% accepted jobs in the field of business, with the others accepting jobs in public interest, academia, and other fields (Dinovitzer et al. 2004).

4   Babcock noted that 20% of women self-report that they never negotiate (Babcock and Laschever 2003: 10).

because there are particular gender issues associated with managing others.[5] In the applied workshop, students develop an understanding of those issues. They are thus less likely to internalize a negative reaction if their authority is questioned when they have to manage staff or younger lawyers on a team. The unique curriculum helps them to understand that these are structural barriers and that the barriers exist in large part because of their gender, not their competence. That information steels them and allows them to be more persistent, thus allowing them to stay longer in the profession and ascend to leadership positions.

The applied workshop also includes an exploration of fear as an emotion that inhibits leadership. My early experiences as a young lawyer grounded me in the reality that one cannot lead until one overcomes fear. Students are led through a series of exercises by Jenn Stillings,[6] a graduate of the United States Naval Academy, an institution with a highly developed four-year leadership curriculum. This retired officer was trained as a fighter pilot and she explores with students the relationship between a thought, and fear as an emotion triggered by that thought. It is a powerful skill-building exercise that moves students through a series of contextual scenarios in which they are taught to alter their thought process in order to reduce fear.

Alumni like Sandy Gohn, partner at DLA Piper, and adjunct professor Maura DeMouy often return to the law school to work with students in the seminar and the workshop. Laura Black, founder of the temporary legal staffing company now known as Special Counsel, works with students on "rainmaking," i.e., client development skills. Partners in law firms now must bring in a minimum of $1 million a year in revenue (and often more) in order to achieve full equity partner status. Thus, specific training in this skill by our women alumni who are entrepreneurs and equity partners has been invaluable to the students in the program. They begin to understand the economic realities of law firm practice in today's world as well as to acquire a different vision of how to develop business. They learn that traditionally masculine strategies, like playing golf with potential clients, are not the only way to develop business. Many of their natural networks as young women and eventually as mothers may yield connections to potential clients that they had never imagined. Alumni have been an integral part of the program because they can talk about the realities of practicing law as women. In addition to preparing students to engage in the substantive practice of law and do excellent work, students are taught to understand how to navigate through legal organizations in a way that allows their value and merit to be recognized and rewarded. This kind of mentoring teaches students about leadership in a new way. And it has the additional benefit of binding our alumni back to us as an institution.

---

5   Schein (2001) examined managerial sex typing as a major psychological barrier to the advancement of women.

6   http://www.transitiongroup.net/jenniferstillings.

The Optional Practicum

Finally, I integrated theory and practice in a third way by offering a practicum component that allows students to intern for women leaders like Joanne Pollak, general counsel of Johns Hopkins Health System, and at organizations, like the National Women's Law Center that work on women's policy issues. This optional component allows students to see women lawyers leading these organizations and being instrumental in creating policy changes that benefit women. Students are given an experience similar to that which I had so many years ago working alongside Martha Barnett at Holland & Knight. There is no substitute for observing leadership skills modeled in the field. These placements offer students the opportunity to see women hold meetings, manage staff, and run an organization. They have the chance to hear about the variety of paths women take to leadership positions in law and about the hurdles they faced along the way.

The two-course sequence plus practicum program framework is consistent with other substantive programs at the law school in environmental law and health law. This model of integrating theory and practice is a core part of our pedagogic philosophy at Maryland. I also submitted the program courses for approval by the faculty curriculum committee. Thus, the program is embedded in the academic curriculum at the heart of the intellectual enterprise. Conferring academic credit on the courses signals to the law school community the significance of the courses and the centrality of these issues to a student's legal education.

The curricular sequence teaches students about long-entrenched cultural norms and structural barriers to women assuming leadership roles and the more practical issues that face them when they assume those positions. The curriculum has helped the more than 70 students who have completed it since 2003 become more effective lawyers, because they are better able to communicate their ideas so that those ideas are heard and implemented in their organizations.[7] In the end, this is what binds people to an organization. If young lawyers feel that their contributions are valued and that colleagues will embrace their ideas, then they feel invested in that organization and they will stay. In addition, the students who have completed the WLE program have formed strong bonds and provide support to each other well beyond graduation. This was an unforeseen but very significant benefit of the program. My hope is that this network will also help these women stay long enough in the profession to ascend to formal leadership in private legal

----

7   See Romer (2009: 10): "[WLE Fellow] Alexina Jackson, JD '07, is now thriving in her new environment and credits the program with honing her skills. 'When I started at the law firm, I quickly diagnosed the dynamics in which I am operating and thought about how to maximize my opportunities in that environment,' says the 31-year-old associate at Crowell & Moring LLP in Washington, D.C. 'I was aware of what I wanted and the compromises I was willing to make, and so I now spend more of my time executing my goals rather than trying to understand them.'"

workplaces as well as branching out to assume public leadership roles as judges, legislators, or in the executive branch.

As we approach the tenth anniversary of our program, I have reflected on how Martha Barnett taught me how to lead and how Deborah Rhode's groundbreaking work has taught me why it is so important to expose our law students—particularly our women students—to leadership studies in the law school curriculum. More than 10 years after the Summit, we are still grappling with the same questions about why there are so few women in formal leadership positions in law.[8] Progress continues to be slow.[9] Even though women have been at least 40% of law school graduating classes since the mid-1980s, there are still few women partners, judges, and general counsel of major companies in the United States (Chanow et al. 2006). Since the Summit, the number of women enrolled in law schools has actually declined (Chen 2011).[10]

The women who graduated from law school in the 1950s and 1960s, like former law professor and current U.S. Supreme Court Associate Justice Ruth Bader Ginsburg, focused their efforts on achieving formal equality. They developed theories of gender-based discrimination through litigation, and they lobbied for statutes that were aimed at eliminating intentional discrimination (Franklin 2010: 85). However, while building a framework of formal equality is necessary to women's ascension to formal leadership positions in society and in our profession, it has proven insufficient. So, subsequent generations have been faced with the task of dismantling what some might consider even more intractable barriers—like the fact that women still bear the largest share of the family caregiving, that law firms are structured in ways which are completely unforgiving in terms of a balanced

---

8   For the status of women in the profession as of the time of the Summit in 2001, see Rhode (2001). "Women now account for almost 30% of the profession, but only about 15% of federal judges and law firm partners, 10% of law school deans and general counsels, and 5% of managing partners of large firms ... However, what data are available reflect significant disparities in pay and promotion for lawyers of color, as well as for members of other identifiable groups such as lesbian and disabled lawyers" (Rhode 2001: 14).

9   "Women constitute just a third of all lawyers, 22 percent of the federal judiciary and 26 percent of state judges. In law firms, 45 percent of associates are women but just 15 percent have reached equity partnership. At the largest 200 law firms, the numbers are even more dismal. Female lawyers too often earn 75 percent or less of what male counterparts earn for doing the same job ... For the first time since 2006, there has been a decline in the number of women entering big-firm practice, according to a National Association of Women Lawyers study. The survey found that female lawyers are more likely to hold nonpartner-track positions, and that female equity partners earn just 86 percent of what their male peers earn" (Robinson 2012: 8).

10   "But what's surprising is that women's enrollment at law schools overall has been on a steady decline since 2002, when women constituted about 49.05 percent of law students. The ABA's newest statistics show that women made up about 47 percent of all first-year law students for 2009 to 2010, and 45.9 percent of all law school graduates" (Chen 2011).

life and, finally, that gender schemas about women's competence or lack thereof still pervade the culture (Rhode 2001: 14–20).

Our program encourages students to work on parallel tracks and to consider both structural barriers, like balancing work and family and the organization of legal workplaces, and individual barriers that may arise due to implicit bias and gender schemas. Breaking down both types of barriers is essential to integrating women more fully into all levels of the profession. By helping students acquire the theoretical knowledge and practical skills to stay in their organizations long enough to obtain leadership positions, women will then have the power to be change-agents within their own organizations and the legal profession. An integrated approach to teaching gender and leadership, which encourages both individual and collective strategies, is essential to resolving the gender gap in leadership that exists within our profession and society as a whole.

References

Babcock, L. and Laschever, S. 2003. *Women Don't Ask: Negotiation and the Gender Divide*. Princeton: Princeton University Press.

Chanow, L.B. et al. 2006. *Creating Pathways to Success: Advancing and Retaining Women in Today's Law Firms*. Washington, D.C.: Women's Bar Association of the District of Columbia.

Chen, V. 2011. Women Spurn Law Schools, *The Careerist* [Online], 16 May. Available at: http://thecareerist.typepad.com/thecareerist/2011/05/fewer-women-at-nations-law-schools.html [accessed 10 September 2012].

Dinovitzer, R., Garth, B.G., Sander, R., Sterling, J. and Wilder, G.Z. 2004. *After the JD: First Results of a National Study of Legal Careers*. The NALP Foundation for Law Career Research and Education and the American Bar Foundation. Overland Park, KS: NALP and Chicago: American Bar Foundation.

Franklin, C. 2010. The Anti-Stereotyping Principle in Constitutional Sex Discrimination Law, *New York University Law Review*, 85(1): 83.

Kellerman, B. and Rhode, D.L. 2007. *Women and Leadership: The State of Play and Strategies for Change*. San Francisco: Jossey-Bass.

Klenke, K. 1996. *Women and Leadership: A Contextual Perspective*. New York: Springer.

Myerson, D., Ely, R. and Wernick, L. 2007. Disrupting Gender, Revising Leadership, in *Women and Leadership: The State of Play and Strategies for Change*. San Francisco: Jossey-Bass, 453–73.

Rhode, D.L. 2001. *The Unfinished Agenda: Women and the Legal Profession*. Chicago: ABA Commission on Women in the Profession.

Rhode, D.L. 2003. *The Difference Difference Makes: Women and Leadership*. Palo Alto: Stanford University Press.

Rhode, D.L. and Packel, A.K. 2011. *Leadership, Law, Policy, and Management*. Boston: Aspen.

Robinson, W.T. 2012. Advancement of Women Lawyers. *ABA Journal*, January, 8.

Romer, L. 2009. Raising a Gavel for Women's Equality, *University of Maryland Baltimore: Research and Scholarship 2009* [Online]. Available at: http://www.oea.umaryland.edu/Files/2009MarylandMagazine.pdf [accessed 10 September 2012].

Schein, V.E. 2001. A Global Look at Psychological Barriers to Women's Progress in Management, *Journal of Social Issues*, 57(4): 675–88.

Sophocles. 1993. *Antigone*, translated by Sir George Young. New York: Dover.

University of Maryland Francis King Carey School of Law. 2012. *Women, Leadership and Equality Program* [Online]. Available at: http://www.law.umaryland.edu/programs/wle/index.html [accessed 10 September 2012].

Valian, V. 1998. *Why So Slow? The Advancement of Women.* Cambridge, MA: MIT Press.

Appendix

Leadership Education in the Legal Academy: Principles, Practices and Possibilities
A Report from the James MacGregor Burns Academy of Leadership— University of Maryland[1]

Co-Authored by Judy Sorum Brown, Ph.D. and Bonnie Allen, J.D.

Contributing Authors:

Georgia Sorenson, Ph.D.
Carol Pearson, Ph.D.
Richard Couto, Ph.D.
Nina Harris, Ph.D.

May 4, 2009

Table of Contents

I. Introduction and Context
II. The Leadership Challenge in the Legal Profession
III. Inquiry and Perspectives on Leadership in the Legal Profession
IV. Findings
V. Recommendations for Next Steps

I. Introduction and Context

In 2007 and 2008, the James MacGregor Burns Academy of Leadership at the University of Maryland (Burns Academy), the Center for Law & Renewal,[2] and the University of Maryland School of Law (School of Law) undertook a collaborative process of inquiry into the purpose of leadership education in the legal academy. This report describes that process and the findings it revealed.

---

1   Full Report available at http://www.law.umaryland.edu/programs/initiatives/lead/docs/LeadershipLawSchoolRpt.pdf.

2   A nonprofit organization based at the Fetzer Institute, an operating foundation located in Kalamazoo, Michigan.

The authors make the case for leadership in the legal academy and provide guidelines for introducing it, fully recognizing the institutional challenges that exist. This document is intended to be a vehicle for stimulating reflection and discussion in the legal academy and the broader profession. It highlights trends and provides examples, but it is by no means a comprehensive description of current curricula and programs. The authors welcome comments from readers, in the hope that it will produce an expanding national and international dialogue in the academy and broader legal profession.

The academic study of leadership is one of the fastest growing interdisciplinary endeavors in American higher education. 2003 data documented more than 1,800 leadership programs in U.S. universities (Sorenson, Goethals and J.M. Burns 2004). These efforts range from undergraduate certificates, minors and majors to graduate and doctoral degree programs in leadership studies. Leadership programs are embedded in every discipline. While the social sciences and business schools remain the most likely in which to find leadership studies, there is tremendous growth in these programs within liberal arts, history, agriculture, literature, and philosophy. In the last few years, a plethora of programs has emerged in the professional schools, notably MBA programs, schools of public policy, public administration, and medicine, in the United States, Europe, and elsewhere (Sorenson, Goethals and J.M. Burns 2004).

In the spirit of the best professional education, leadership studies teach critical thinking, effective communications through writing and speaking, creativity and problem-solving, human diversity as an asset, social responsibility, history as a source of knowledge for understanding the present and planning for the future, collaboration and empowerment, conflict resolution, negotiation, and group and organizational development. Moral development and ethics are integrated into many leadership studies programs. By its very nature, leadership studies teach the importance of engaging firsthand with contemporary issues and problems of policy, the law, power-sharing, conflict, and collaboration (Sorenson and Goethals 2006).

It is important to consider leadership education in the legal academy in the broader context of higher education for professionals. While each profession has its particular educational goals and challenges and may differ on substantive knowledge and technical skills, the professions share the common goal of developing the character and skill set needed to create "professionalism."[3] In many professions, leadership studies and programs have been an effective vehicle for pursuing this goal.

Interestingly, legal education has been slow to embrace leadership studies. While several American law schools have added leadership courses to their curriculum, developed leadership scholars programs, or made explicit commitments

---

3   William F. May discusses the "marks of the professional" in *The Beleaguered Rulers: The Public Obligation of the Professional* (Louisville, KY, Westminster John Knox Press, 2001: 7), as "intellectual, moral and organizational"—with "correlative virtues."

in their missions to prepare lawyers to be leaders, the legal academy has yet to integrate leadership teaching into the mainstream of its pedagogy.[4] The dearth of leadership studies in legal education presents a paradoxical challenge. Lawyers comprise a significant number of leaders in government, business and community, yet law schools do not formally prepare lawyers to be leaders. As a result, many practicing lawyers lack grounding in the intellectual and practical leadership disciplines that are fundamental to exercising sound professional judgment, helping clients solve problems, communicating effectively, managing self and others, and navigating the increasing complexity of organizational cultures.

To address this challenge, the Center for Law & Renewal engaged the Burns Academy to develop an inquiry into the need, purpose and methodologies for introducing leadership education into the legal academy. Housed in the School of Public Policy at the University of Maryland, College Park, the Burns Academy is internationally recognized for its broad range of initiatives focusing on leadership education, public service and scholarship. Currently led by renowned scholar Carol Pearson, the Burns Academy features the work of recognized leadership luminaries including presidential biographer James MacGregor Burns and founder Georgia Sorenson.

This inquiry grew out of the work of the Center for Law and Renewal, a nonprofit organization created by the Fetzer Institute that examined the tensions between personal values and moral codes of lawyers and the demands of the profession and legal institutions. The Fetzer Institute has a history of supporting similar inquiries in the fields of medicine, higher education, business, and politics. The Center developed a framework to advance a "relationship-centered ethic of lawyering" by offering programs that equip lawyers with self-awareness, skills, and tools they need to practice ethics and professionalism beyond the technical rules, serve as leaders and change agents in their institutions, and operate as democracy-builders in their communities. Now dissolved as an entity, the Center for Law and Renewal's mission continues through a partnership between the Fetzer Institute and the University of Maryland School of Law that created the Leadership, Ethics and Democracy-Building Initiative (LEAD) led by Professor Michael Millemann ... The Fetzer Institute's partnership with Maryland School of Law builds on the law school's nationally recognized clinical law program and its Women's Leadership Program directed by Professor Paula Monopoli, who also oversees the leadership components of the new initiative.

The Burns Academy's inquiry into leadership education in law schools included a review of relevant literature, a survey of the field and a roundtable dialogue among leaders in law and leadership studies. This report reflects perspectives of leaders in the legal academy and broader profession, as well as scholars in the field of leadership studies. The report also documents the Burns Academy's findings

---

4   Santa Clara University School of Law, University of Maryland School of Law, Duke University School of Law, Ohio State University College of Law, Elon University School of Law, St. Thomas Law School, and Harvard Law School are among these institutions.

and recommendations regarding the goals and methodologies for integrating leadership studies and programs into law schools, based on experiences and models drawn from other fields of professional education. We preface our discussion of the inquiry by describing the context and challenges in the legal profession that law school-based legal education could address.

II. The Leadership Challenge in the Legal Profession

Lawyers play an essential role in American democracy. They are the guardians and gatekeepers of the rule of law, a cornerstone of a civil society. Lawyers control our judicial systems, are significantly represented in the halls of Congress and state legislatures, and advise corporate executives in business decisions that have far-reaching consequences for stockholders and consumers. They also serve in important public leadership roles as elected officials and high-ranking government agency staff, and often are the chief architects of public policy.

The American legal profession and legal institutions face enormous challenges in the twenty-first century. Public confidence, respect for and trust in lawyers and legal systems have eroded significantly in the past few decades. Many civil courts are unable to effectively manage overwhelming caseloads and demand, and matters frequently are disposed of in bureaucratic ways that leave all parties dissatisfied. The criminal justice system is widely viewed as broken and without the means or power to reduce crime or help victims and perpetrators heal their lives. Bar-sponsored studies indicate that eighty percent of the civil legal needs of low-income people and thirty percent of those of moderate-income people are not met, due in part to a legal services delivery system that grossly underfunds legal aid programs. The United States spends far less than other Western industrial societies on subsidizing legal representation (Rhode 2000: 7).

Alongside these "systems failures" is a significant crisis in morale for individual lawyers. Skyrocketing student loan debt drives many law students to make career choices inconsistent with their values and vocational goals. The demands of law firm culture, with its ultimate emphasis on billable hours and business development, leave lawyers little time for family life, personal health, pro bono work, or civic engagement. An estimated one-third of American attorneys suffer from depression or substance addictions, a rate that is two to three times higher than the general public (Rhode 2000: 8). A majority of lawyers report that they would choose another career if they could make the decision again, and three-quarters would not want their children to become lawyers. Eighty percent do not believe that the law lives up to their expectations in contributing to the social good (Rhode 2000: 8).

Legal education plays a key role in precipitating this crisis in the legal profession and legal systems. The Carnegie Report on *Educating Lawyers: Preparation for the Profession of Law*, published in 2007, found that law schools fail to equip students with the moral and social skills they need to "engage the moral imagination"

(Sullivan et al. 2007). The Carnegie Report attributes much of the shortcoming of legal education to its heavy reliance on a single form of teaching, the case-dialogue method, and on the limitations of that one form. This methodology involves abstracting the legally relevant aspects of situations and persons from their real-world situations. Consideration of the social or ethical consequences of legal conclusions is left out of the analysis. Students are warned to set aside their concerns for justice, moral consequences or compassion (Sullivan et al. 2007: 146). Stanford Law Professor William H. Simon attributes this phenomenon to the tendency of the dominant conception in legal theory to define the lawyer's role in terms of formalistic, categorical and mechanical forms (1998: 3). He adds "the profession has promulgated an ideology, backed by disciplinary rules and sanctions that mandates unreflective, mechanical, categorical judgment rather than practical reason" (Simon 1998: 23).[5]

While other fields of graduate professional education, including business, public policy, and the military, have diversified learning methodologies, encouraged in part by the work on multiple intelligences by Howard Gardner, law schools have not followed that trend. In his best-selling book, *The Soul of the Law*, Benjamin Sells, a Chicago-based trial lawyer and psychologist, describes the perils of legal education and the process of "becoming a lawyer" as acculturating the legal mind. Somewhere along the way, law students undergo a subtle, though radical, change. Their very perceptions begin to be structured by assumptions provided by legal education (Sells 1996: 35). Sells points to the example of a law professor telling first year students: "You are not here to find truth and justice, you are here to learn the Law" (1996: 36). Sells observes that the Law does not know what to do with big grand ideas that escape analytic definition. Over time, the Law's reluctance to engage the grand ideas of the heart can limit and restrict the range of its imagination (Sells 1996: 37).

These mental habits include objectification by the lawyer of people and situations, and the resulting detachment from self and others. Lawyers, Sells asserts, have become abstracted from the world of actual experience (1996: 175). This poses an enormous problem for practicing lawyers who are called upon to make difficult decisions in the messiness and complexity of their own lives, the organizations in which they operate, and the clients that they serve.

The Carnegie Report recognizes that some law schools are attempting to address the increasingly apparent shortcomings of legal education. Many law schools are introducing forms of experiential learning, including stronger clinical programs and discussion-oriented seminars. The University of Maryland School of Law, Northeastern School of Law, Fordham University School of Law, Marquette University Law School, Georgetown University Law School, Hamline University School of Law, and the University of Southern California Law School are just

---

5   Reprinted by permission of the publisher from *The Practice of Justice: A Theory of Lawyers' Ethics* by William H. Simon, p. 23, Cambridge, Mass.: Harvard University Press, Copyright © 1998 by the President and Fellows of Harvard College.

some of the institutions now offering reflective and interdisciplinary approaches to teaching the required course of Ethics and Professional Responsibility that incorporate novels, personal essays, student interviews of practitioners, guest speakers from the profession, and class discussion about the gap between the rules and reality of practicing law.[6] Law school Student Affairs offices are presenting workshops on work-life balance and related topics. One new entrant into the field, Elon University School of Law, was founded in 2006 with an explicit mission of preparing lawyers to be leaders as well as problem-solvers.

The Carnegie Report goes on to observe, however, that the tendency of law schools is to address inadequacies in legal education in an additive, rather than integrative way. This incremental—rather than comprehensive—approach to reform fails to generate the desired results. The Carnegie Report includes a strong recommendation that legal educators respond to the needs of our time and recent knowledge about how learning takes place by combining the elements of legal professionalism—conceptual knowledge, skills, and moral discernment—into the capacity for judgment guided by a sense of professional responsibility. Thus, there is a compelling call for an integrated curriculum that includes doctrine and analysis, practice, and the exploration of the identity, values, and dispositions consistent with the fundamental purpose of the legal profession (Sullivan et al. 2007: 194).

Since its publication, there has been tremendous response by law schools and bar associations to the Carnegie Report, as evidenced by a proliferation of conferences and writings on the topic in the past two years. Highly significant among these responses is the American Bar Association's decision to undertake a process of revising law school accreditation standards to include professionalism competencies.

A. Making the Case

Recognizing the compelling need for cultural change in the profession, legal educators and leaders in the practicing bar themselves have begun to build a case for the integration of leadership studies into law school curricula. Increasingly, lawyers are speaking and writing of a "crisis in values" in the profession and legal systems that can be addressed only by courageous leaders who are willing to create and act upon a new vision. Ben W. Heineman, Jr., former General Counsel at General Electric Company, spoke on "Law and Leadership" at Yale Law School in 2006, advancing the thesis that law schools should more candidly recognize the importance of leadership and more directly prepare and inspire young lawyers to seek roles of ultimate responsibility and accountability (2007: 266).

---

6   In 2006, the Center for Law and Renewal convened a group of 20 legal educators to exchange ideas and curriculum for teaching the required law school course of Ethics and Professional Responsibility in ways that challenge students to "think beyond the rules" and to explore the ethical rules in the context of their own values and moral codes.

"Graduates of law schools should aspire not just to be wise counselors but wise leaders; not just to dispense 'practical wisdom' but be practical visionaries" (Heineman 2007: 266). Heineman supports his claim by arguing first that our society is suffering from a leadership deficit in public, private and nonprofit spheres. Second, he asserts that the legal profession is experiencing a crisis of morale arising out of a disconnect between personal values and professional life. Providing leadership can affirm and test our vision and core values. Third, he observes that other professional schools have as their explicit mission the training of leaders for the various sectors. The core competencies of law provide as solid a foundation for leadership as do those of other professions. Law schools need a similar vision to enhance the education and careers of their graduates, thus serving society and addressing the values crisis affecting so many in the profession (Heineman 2007: 266).

Heineman argues for an interdisciplinary approach to legal education that not only teaches core legal capacities, but also "complementary capacities" that will prepare lawyers for the real world demands of law practice, business and public leadership roles (Heineman 2007: 266). These capacities will engender "breadth of mind" and instill the skills needed for lawyers to employ creativity, vision, values, and strategies to maximize human and other resources as they build and lead law firms, businesses, government agencies, and nonprofit organizations (Heineman 2007: 266).

Donald J. Polden, Dean of the Santa Clara University School of Law, echoes Heineman's sentiments in his article "Educating Law Students for Leadership Roles and Responsibilities" (2008: 353–60). Dean Polden asserts that leaders emerge in organizations and situations in which they are called upon to create change. To do so, leaders rely on their skills, relationships and insights through a leadership process (Polden 2008: 355). Fundamental leadership skills are necessary for lawyers, whose role often includes persuading and influencing others. Lawyers operate out of a vision or solution that involves problem-solving, team building, motivation of others, and collaboration. Emphasizing that leadership education for law students is values-based, Polden asserts that practicing leadership requires the definition and creation of a vision or solution that results in positive and ethical change (2008: 355).

While wholeheartedly supporting the integration of leadership studies into legal education, Northeastern University School of Law Professor David Hall candidly observes the challenges inherent in this endeavor. In his book, *The Spiritual Revitalization of the Legal Profession*, Professor Hall (2005) asserts that the culture and values of the legal profession and legal education are not conducive to developing authentic leaders. True leadership, he says, does not relate to what we do, or the role we occupy in an organization. Leadership relates to the person we are and the values we manifest. It is more about being than doing. Leadership grows from a deep well of self-reflection and self-realization as we attempt to transform the world around us. Hall adds that the leadership traits of vision, compassion, creativity, courage, humility, faith, determination, and love do not emanate from an intellectual well alone but also come from the spirit. It is the synergistic combination of mind and spirit that enables lawyers to transform institutions and their own lives (2005: 175–6). Professor Hall notes that lawyers are confronted with leadership opportunities and challenges every day (2005: 180).

B. The Practicing Bar as a Driver of Change in the Academy

Law firms, much like law schools, have been slow to embrace formal leadership development training. But that is beginning to change for several reasons. First, law firms are increasingly larger and complex organizations that demand formal leadership and management systems and structures. Second, the kind of informal mentoring that took place in earlier periods has disappeared in many law firms, leaving a void of relationships between more experienced attorneys and young associates that encourage the formation of good habits and ethical practices needed to succeed in law practice and life. Third, legal practices have shifted in ways that require more teamwork and collaboration within firms and across practice groups.

In response to these changes, law firms are establishing leadership programs in collaboration with business schools and consulting firms, and this phenomenon will undoubtedly expand in the next several years. Examples include Reed Smith LLP's partnership with Wharton School of Business to develop leadership curriculum, and DLA Piper's contract with Harvard Business School to teach leadership and management skills to its firm leaders (Rubenstein 2008: xiii). Bar associations also are recognizing this need, and the state bar associations of Wisconsin, Colorado, Oregon, and Alabama now offer leadership education for CLE credit (Rubenstein 2008: xv). In Florida, the Center on Professionalism—jointly created by the Supreme Court and the Florida Bar—is promoting a statewide approach to enlisting the law schools in the state to develop leadership programs as a vehicle for enhancing professionalism. Many other state and local bar associations offer leadership education to affinity groups within the bar, including women lawyers and lawyers of color.

Hildebrandt International, one of the world's largest consulting groups for professional services organizations, hired Dr. Larry Richard (former trial attorney) several years ago to head the firm's Leadership and Organization Development Practice Group. Dr. Richard has worked with hundreds of law firms and corporate law departments to improve human performance, and in recent years, his work has increasingly focused on leadership development. Dr. Richard's expertise includes an understanding of "lawyer personality traits," and the management and leadership challenges and opportunities these traits present in law firm settings.

III. Inquiry and Perspectives on Leadership in the Legal Profession

Recognizing the growing interest in leadership education in the legal academy and broader profession, the Burns Academy undertook a process of inquiry and facilitated a dialogue among leaders in law and leadership studies to explore two central questions:

1. What makes leadership education in law schools necessary at this time?
2. What will make it possible?

In September 2007, Burns Academy Senior Scholar Judy Brown convened a Steering Committee that included representatives of the University of Maryland School of Law, the Center for Law & Renewal and the Burns Academy to design and implement a process of inquiry. The process began with a review of relevant literature. Despite the plethora of literature on leadership studies in other disciplines, the committee found scant literature on leadership in the law, and observed that relatively few law schools have developed leadership curricula or programs for their students.

By contrast, business schools have followed a different pattern of development. A review of *U.S. News and World Report*'s 2007 top ten ranked business schools shows that all offer substantial courses in leadership. Many, such as Harvard Business School, Massachusetts Institute of Technology (MIT)'s Sloan School of Management, and the Tuck School of Business at Dartmouth, are recognized for their historic achievement in leadership education. Other prominent schools are developing innovative and individualized approaches to leadership education. Wharton School of Finance offers leadership development training in the military academy in Quantico, Virginia and partners with the University of Pennsylvania Law School in the America-Mideast Educational and Training Service; the University of California Berkeley's Hass School of Business is partnering with the College of Engineering to launch a program in technology and leadership; Columbia University has designed a New Media Executive Leadership Program in its Journalism School; and Georgetown University's McDonough School of Business offers an Executive Master's in Leadership program. In 2005, the Association of American Medical Colleges sampled Leadership Development programs available to health care professionals. Not surprisingly, the schools taking the initiative in the field were frequently the universities with strong credentials in business leadership education, such as Harvard, Wharton, Duke, Stanford, and Georgetown.

Following the literature review, the Steering Committee proceeded to conduct anonymous written interviews through the "Delphi Process"—named for the Oracle at Delphi who could see into the future. The committee sent a questionnaire to more than 50 students and legal educators, as well as to leadership experts.

Sixty percent responded, and there was general consensus that leadership education is needed for law students.[7]

Key themes that emerged from the survey included:

- Leadership education in the field of law is important because many lawyers end up in public leadership roles for which they have not been prepared.
- Leadership is not only about positional or public authority roles, but also relates to how an individual integrates the different aspects of daily life, manages conflicting demands and recognizes the values underlying choices.
- Leadership principles, consciousness, habits, and skills can be taught.
- Successful leadership curricula and programs must integrate theory and practice.

Leadership development in the law needs to encourage change at three levels: 1) individual, i.e. equipping lawyers to stay connected to their own moral compasses and maintain leadership of their own lives; 2) institutional, i.e. providing skills and tools for lawyers to act as agents of positive change within their organizations; and 3) community, i.e. using legal skills and the law to transform communities and strengthen democracy.

Leadership skills are critical to changing negative trends in the legal profession, including the decline in civility, failure of work-life balance, deterioration of professionalism, and a public service ethic, and steadily declining public trust in the legal system.

The Delphi responses contributed to shaping the agenda and identifying participants for a Roundtable on Law School Leadership Education, hosted by the University of Maryland School of Law on February 19, 2008, in Baltimore. More than fifty leaders attended, including the managing partners and senior partners of prominent law firms, executive directors of nonprofit legal organizations, elected officials, state Supreme Court Justices and other members of the judiciary, law school faculty and deans, law students, and experts from the field of leadership studies.

...

The Roundtable's purpose was to explore the why, what and how of developing leadership programs in law schools. Panels of leaders discussed the current challenges facing the legal profession, including globalization, diversity, profit-driven legal cultures, and a serious erosion of public trust.

...

The Roundtable consisted of five panel discussions with small group break-outs in between. Panel topics included:

---

7   See   http://www.law.umaryland.edu/faculty/conferences/detail.hmtl?conf=63   for Survey: Leaders in Law on Leadership Education.

1. What are lawyers' personal experiences (and observations of others) leading change?
2. What did lawyers learn (or wish they had learned) in law school to prepare them for leadership roles?
3. What do current law students see as present or missing in the leadership dimensions of legal education?
4. What content, skills and experiences should be part of a program on leadership in law school?
5. What can other professional schools suggest about law school leadership programs?

Highlights from the panels included the observations of Frank Burch, managing partner of DLA Piper, the world's largest law firm, who participated on the first panel and noted that many law students enter the profession without the problem-solving and organizational skills needed to work with clients and navigate in large institutions. Martha Bergmark, President of the Mississippi Center for Justice, talked about a "leadership moment" when, as a teenager growing up in Mississippi, she confronted a teacher and engaged in her first act of civil disobedience. John Frisch, Chairman of the Baltimore law firm of Miles & Stockbridge, participated in the second panel and discussed his law firm's recent efforts to transform its institutional culture into one of leadership and professionalism.

During a compelling lunch-time student panel, Andrew Canter, a third year law student at Stanford University School of Law and recent graduate of Harvard University's Kennedy School of Public Policy, called for change in both the measurements and experiences of legal education. This would draw greater leadership talent in prospective students as well as enhanced leadership capabilities upon graduation. He expressed skepticism that law students are likely to become leaders as long as law schools measure success by the incoming LSAT scores and students leave burdened with debt that makes it difficult to consider careers and leadership in other than large, well-paying law firms and corporations. These quantitative and de-personalized forms of measurement spill over into law firm culture, which measures success of lawyers largely by billable hours. In January 2007, Canter co-founded "Building a Better Legal Profession," a national grass roots movement that seeks market-based workplace reforms in large law firms by developing an alternative set of law firm rankings based on pro bono participation, commitment to diversity, and work-life balance.

Michael Kelly, former Dean of the University of Maryland School of Law, who participated on the fourth panel, referenced recent studies of lawyer personalities and contrasted "lawyer traits" with "leader traits." These studies reveal that lawyers tend to be highly competitive, risk-averse, skeptical, and non-collaborative, in contrast to the desired leadership characteristics of team-building, innovation and trust.

...

Dean Donald Polden of Santa Clara University Law School joined Dean Kelly on the panel focused on the content, skills and experiences that should be part of leadership programs in law schools. He described the path of his institution and the four core principles of its approach to leadership development.

...

The last session of the Roundtable featured a presentation by leadership scholars who shared their knowledge and expertise about teaching leadership in other fields, including medicine, business and public policy. These panelists stressed the importance of recognizing leadership studies as an academic discipline with its own body of literature, theory and practice, and one which professional schools are increasingly employing to prepare professionals for their fields.

Burns Academy founder Georgia Sorenson characterized the Roundtable as a pioneering meeting and a memorable launch of a process to shape a broad agenda. She began with a description of leadership studies in ancient Greece, where it was one of four primary fields of inquiry. She then traced the growth of leadership studies in the United States through its emergence at top research universities following the Second World War, and tracked its evolution at top private institutions such as Harvard, Duke, and Princeton. Sorenson noted that most professional schools have now embraced leadership studies, often as a way to bridge the several disciplines that contribute to a field. Law, she recognized, has rarely followed suit, until now.

Burns Academy Director Carol Pearson laid out a process for defining the field-determined core competencies for graduates so as to shape leadership offerings that illuminate and strengthen those competencies. Using the graduate schools of public policy as an example, Pearson traced the work of the federal Office of Personnel Management and The Brookings Institution in identifying "Executive Core Qualifications" which leaders in the government need in order to be successful. Pearson noted that the Burns Academy and the University of Maryland School of Public Policy focus upon shaping leadership education to address those competencies, eighty percent of which specifically bear upon leadership. It is noteworthy that many of the problems identified during the Roundtable have underlying them an implicit sense of the core qualifications that lawyers need as leaders, whether in their firms, with their clients or in the broader society. The Roundtable dialogue also reflected concern that legal education does not currently address those core qualifications. Thus, one path law schools might take is to define the core qualifications for leadership among those trained in the law and design programs to meet those needs.

...

David Mossbarger, Project Director of the Relationship-Centered Care Initiative at the Regenstrief Institute at the Indiana University School of Medicine, outlined the medical school's efforts to address, within the framework of professionalism, many of the elements framed by this inquiry as leadership. At that medical school, in the wake of a curriculum transformation focused on patient-centered care, students began to note that the culture of the institution was inconsistent with the values now promulgated by the curriculum. Those values included compassion, civility and a culture of caring. The transformation at the Indiana University School of Medicine had been one of organizational intervention, in that a change was effected in the teaching and academic culture to comport with the new curriculum. The approach to that change was organic, collaborative and focused on those who wished to participate, and utilized a facilitation approach known as "appreciative inquiry." Mossbarger's remarks signaled a significant issue that this report will return to in a later section: the relationship between professionalism and leadership.

Academy Senior Scholar Judy Brown's role on the final panel was to sketch the work of the MIT Leadership Center as an exemplar among business schools, noting parallels between the challenges that MIT faces, with its high achieving and diverse student body, and those that a law school might experience: a mix of students who have leadership experience as well as those with little interest in the topic. The Sloan Business School at MIT has a half century of history in research on leadership and management, and in 2005, with the launch of the MIT Leadership Center, a new focal point for provision of leadership education at all levels was created. Through the Center, the Sloan School provides all MBA students with a rich leadership program that takes into consideration the wide range of interests and experience levels of participating students. The following dimensions of the MIT Leadership Center seem relevant to address some of the challenges law schools face in developing leadership programs:

- The Center offers a solid intellectual leadership framework developed and tested by the faculty that underlies all of the course offerings. Articulated by Deborah Ancona and other distinguished faculty, the framework emphasizes sense-making, relating, visioning, and inventing, and it provides a coherent point of view about leadership as a way of organizing the wide range of offerings. The framework is detailed in *Leadership in an Age of Uncertainty* (2005) and in "In Praise of the Incomplete Leader" (Ancona et al. 2007).
- All students are required to participate, so the program does not educate only those already attracted to leadership, but ensures that all MIT MBA students graduate with some awareness of the dimensions of leadership skills needed to step into leadership roles.
- Beyond the formal courses required of students, a wide variety of intensive experiences is offered during the "Sloan Innovation Period." These intensives are led by faculty and leaders from the field, and bring additional teaching talent and approaches into the mix.

What the MIT Sloan Business School has in common with law schools is the ability to attract smart, motivated students who display widely divergent interests in and experience of leadership. Given this broad range of leadership aptitude, appetite and experience, the question becomes how to serve all students under a single, powerful conceptual framework of leadership principles. Thereafter, whatever direction a student selects as part of a leadership experience, the framework provides the common and cohesive basis for attitudes, communication and behavior. The MIT Leadership Center is a rich, multifaceted program where students can choose practice activity options, but they end up with a common frame of reference about leadership. From whatever point on the leadership continuum they may have started, they acquire a shared language and framework of leadership.

A current running through the entire Roundtable was the underlying assumption—best articulated by Dean Kurt Schmoke, former Baltimore mayor and current Dean of Howard University School of Law—of a values-based approach to leadership education. The question of "leadership to what end?" is a critical one, said Schmoke, and it must be explicitly declared. Dean Schmoke recounted the story of being challenged by a mentor early in his career to become a modern day biblical Prophet Nehemiah, which requires facing the truth of distress and waste abroad and in the land and gathering people together to rebuild their communities. The normative approach to leadership development once again raises the issue of the relationship between leadership education and professionalism and the ethical formation of the lawyer.

…

Three levels of further inquiry emerged from the Roundtable:

Individual Leadership

There is power in individual reflection upon earlier experiences that have influenced one's sense of leadership. How can we encourage early experience and reflection by our students? What teaching tools and models can be incorporated into curricular and co-curricular activities to facilitate reflection?

Roundtable participants and Delphi survey respondents appreciated the opportunity to reflect on their own leadership stories and to consider the questions of why and how leadership education could be introduced into the legal academy. How can these kinds of individual reflective activities and group dialogues be used to advance the goal of creating more buy-in?

Institutional Leadership within Law Firm Culture

Law firm leaders face significant challenges in work cultures where the predominant individual profile is that of a risk-averse, precedent-oriented, highly skeptical, and marginally social professional. How can leaders in these environments help colleagues see alternative futures? How can law schools prepare students for these kinds of leadership challenges?

Visionary leaders face the challenge of translating their inner passion and deep caring into principles and practices that can be applied in legal institutions filled with strong and diverse personalities. How can law schools develop the capacity to focus on principles before personalities in order to lead change more effectively?

Institutional Leadership within Law School Culture

Success in law school is measured in very limited ways. Are these measurements good predictors of leadership and success in the practice of law? If not, what new measurements should be considered?

Some students come to law school with considerable leadership experience and interest and others do not. How should law schools address this disparity?

Clinical legal education and pro bono work are invaluable in helping students grow comfortable with the wide range of economic and cultural circumstances they are likely to encounter in their clients and communities. How might such experiences be more completely integrated into legal education and linked to leadership programs?

Some lawyers become agents of change. How might leadership education foster that orientation in more of our graduates? What causes that to happen? Early experience? Intention, aptitude, or "hard wiring" from the start? A slower, more coached evolution into a leader? How might the law school experience facilitate this process?

Mentors challenge and support students in their consideration of the applications and uses of legal training. How can law students have more interaction with lawyer-leaders serving in a broad range of professional settings?

IV. Findings

Key findings of the Burns Academy's inquiry, including the research, Roundtable and subsequent reflections, are summarized below:

1. Leadership is a credible field of study, and one in which professional training and education are available at the graduate and professional level in many disciplines, including medicine, business, public policy, and the military.
2. Leadership education is considered to be critically important by many practitioners and public officials who are lawyers. Leadership education and experience as part of legal training would increase the value of those trained in the law, enhancing their effectiveness as leaders in law firms, the judiciary, government, nonprofit organizations, and communities.
3. Law firm demand for lawyers who are effective problem-solvers and navigators of organizational culture has precipitated leadership development programs in an increasing number of large law firms.
4. Leadership can be taught. There are numerous approaches that other professional schools have used successfully. The question becomes how

leadership can best be taught in law schools, or in a specific law school. The case that leadership can be taught in law schools will most successfully be made through law schools' experiences, rather than by argument.

5. Law schools are increasing the variety and dimensions of leadership education offered through new kinds of curriculum in the areas of ethics and professional responsibility, clinics, internships and pro bono opportunities. Few law schools, however, have explicitly integrated these methodologies into a coherent leadership program that includes curricular and co-curricular activity. Here lies a real opportunity for progress.

6. The need to teach leadership skills in law school is more easily accepted by legal educators and practitioners than the need to teach leadership theory. Scholarship in the area of leadership in the law is wide-open territory that presents an exciting new opportunity for legal academics.

7. Much of the pioneering activity in leadership education stems from innovative approaches in "up and coming" law schools. Innovation in the most highly ranked schools tends to lag. This has been the case with many new movements in the law, including alternative dispute resolution, clinics and new approaches to teaching ethics and professional responsibility. Top-tier law schools may have less incentive to innovate. Over time, however, we expect the trend of leadership education in the legal academy to catch on in the most prestigious law schools in the country.

8. Skepticism and a search for precedent are among the characteristics of the trained legal mind that might underlie a search for a template of leadership courses, curricula, or co-curricular experiences. Evidence from leadership programs in other professional schools, however, shows that there is no one right way that fits the unique character and culture of every law school.

9. The leadership approaches most likely to gain traction with students, faculty and administration will have the following qualities:

   • A conceptual and theoretical framework that is authentic for the school, rooted in credible research in the field of leadership studies (and its relationship to the law), that has real intellectual power and coherence.
   • A commitment to identify and develop the existing leadership assets that the law school already possesses: faculty that are interested, alumni that are able to contribute time and money, and administration that will provide a vision and leadership in convening stakeholders to develop "buy in." Other assets including existing theory and practice methodologies, such as clinical programs, externships, and internships that can integrate leadership theory and practice. Assets also include leadership scholars and faculty in nearby professional schools in other disciplines.
   • Support from the local and state bar, alumni, practitioners, and judges.

- An understanding that some faculty and administrators will find leadership education engaging and others will not; a willingness to allow faculty to absorb the intellectual and practical benefits of leadership education at a measured pace and from the experience of the law school as it moves forward.
- The realization that the development of leadership programs may bring about pervasive change in the law school culture over time (creating a culture of leadership throughout the institution).
- A willingness to experiment, run pilot programs, engage in the process of inquiry, seize opportunities, form new partnerships, and evaluate progress and outcomes.

V. Recommendations for Next Steps

Incremental changes in legal education have been under way for several decades. We believe that the release of the Carnegie Report—and the spark it has ignited in the academy and profession—constitutes a tipping point for a much broader and more integrated assessment of the purpose, underlying assumptions and methodologies of legal education. The Carnegie Report has given voice and credibility to the prophecies of a disparate number of individuals and groups that increased in volume and cohesiveness over time. Now, with the imprimatur of the Report, there are formalized processes and opportunities to enter the dialogue at the highest levels of academia and the profession.

Leadership development courses and co-curricular programs provide practical and intellectual tools to facilitate reform of legal education, the practice of law, and legal systems. Our recommended next steps for advancing leadership development in the legal academy include:

1. Enlist the practicing bar in developing leadership programs. Leadership education is an ideal bridge between the academy and the practice. Law schools should reach out to alumni, major donors, law firm leaders, bar leaders, judges, and public officials to seek informed comment on new program and curriculum development. Law school-sponsored leadership forums, such as the Roundtable conducted at the University of Maryland School of Law in February 2008, present excellent opportunities for scholars and practitioners to engage in open dialogue about leadership challenges and opportunities in the profession. Law schools also should engage alumni, major donors, and law firm leaders in fundraising strategies to add faculty and programs in leadership studies. Dedicated funding can provide incentive for faculty and administrators to take risks in developing innovative programs.
2. Engage law students in the design of leadership programs at the outset. That very act will send a clear message—early in their careers—that lawyers are

expected to take on the mantle of leadership. Student participation will add tremendous energy, and it will undoubtedly impact recruiting and help create an institutional reputation for innovation.

3. Establish a process of ongoing legal scholarship that identifies key intellectual paths of inquiry. Areas ripe for scholarly inquiry include the moral dimensions of leadership in the legal profession, "lawyer personality traits" vs. "leader personality traits" and how that disconnect affects client service and organizational management, the impact of women and minority leadership in legal institutions, and how leadership development intersects with the changing roles of lawyers in our society and the global context. Developing an intellectual and scholarly framework will be critical to successfully integrating leadership studies into the legal academy. Law schools on the cutting edge of leadership studies may want to create journals focused on leadership development in the practice and teaching of the law.

4. Make the case for leadership studies and programs as a powerful response to the Carnegie Report. Declare leadership programs as an inherently normative endeavor that can propel movement toward addressing the recommendations of the Report to enhance the moral formation and imagination of the lawyer. Tie leadership development to the teaching of ethics and professional responsibility—while not subsuming one into the other. Teaching in the two fields should be highly complementary—yet distinguished.

5. Early adopters of law school-based leadership studies and programs should network with one another and develop and disseminate best practices. We recommend the convening of conferences about leadership studies in legal education for scholars and practitioners, as well as the publication of articles in legal journals and law reviews. Proponents also should advocate for leadership development in national networks such as the American Bar Association, state bar associations and the American Association of Law Schools. Creating a buzz about law school-based leadership models that catch fire is perhaps the most powerful vehicle for fueling a movement in legal education.

6. Pursue interdisciplinary approaches to teaching and writing in the area of leadership in the law. Proponents should enter the interdisciplinary dialogue by participating in leadership networks, such as the International Leadership Association, to stay current with broader leadership scholarship and practice.[8] This will be particularly useful in developing templates for scholarship, as well as best practices.

---

8   Judy Brown, Bonnie Allen and Angela Oh presented a panel at the International Leadership Association Conference in Los Angeles in 2008 on "Transformational Trends in Law and Justice." Allen also submitted a proposal on "Lawyers as Leaders in Democracy-Building" for the 2009 ILA Conference in Prague.

References

Allen, B., Hager, L. and Myers, R.F. (eds). 2007. *Shifting the Field of Law and Justice*. Kalamazoo, MI: Center for Law and Renewal.

Ancona, D.G. 2005. *Leadership in an Age of Uncertainty*. Massachusetts Institute of Technology Sloan Leadership Center Research Brief. Cambridge, MA [Online]. Available at: http://sloanleadership.mit.edu/pdf/LeadershipinanAgeofUncertainty-researchbrief.pdf [accessed 10 September 2012].

Ancona, D.G., Malone, T.W., Orlikowski, W.J. and Senge, P.M. 2007. In Praise of the Incomplete Leader, *Harvard Business Review*, 85(2): 92–100.

Brown, J. 2007. *A Leader's Guide to Reflective Practice*. Victoria, BC: Trafford Publishing.

Burns, J.M. 1979. *Leadership*. New York: Harper and Row.

Gardner, H. 1983. *Frames of Mind: The Theory of Multiple Intelligences*. New York: Basic Books.

Hall, D. 2005. *The Spiritual Revitalization of the Legal Profession: A Search for Sacred Rivers*. Lewiston, NY: Edwin Mellen Press.

Heifetz, R.A. 1994. *Leadership Without Easy Answers*. Cambridge, MA: Belknap Press of Harvard University Press.

Heineman, B.W. Jr. 2007. Lawyers as Leaders. *Yale Law Journal Pocket Part* [Online], 116: 266–71. Available at: http://yalelawjournal.org/images/pdfs/102.pdf [accessed 10 September 2012].

Kegan, R. 1994. *In Over Our Heads: The Mental Demands of Modern Life*. Cambridge, MA: Harvard University Press.

Kellerman, B. and Rhode, D.L. (eds). 2007. *Women and Leadership: The State of Play and Strategies for Change*. San Francisco: John Wiley & Sons.

King, M.L. 1963. Letter from Birmingham City Jail, *Christian Century*, 80: 767–73.

Kouzes, J.M. and Posner, B.Z. 1997. *The Leadership Challenge*. Hoboken, NJ: Jossey-Bass.

Kouzes, J.M. and Posner, B.Z. 2006. *A Leader's Legacy*. New York: John Wiley & Sons.

May, W.F. 2001. *Beleaguered Rulers: The Public Obligation of the Professional*. Louisville, KY: Westminster John Knox Press.

Pearson, C. 1998. *The Hero Within*. New York: HarperCollins.

Polden, D.J. 2008. Educating Law Students for Leadership Roles and Responsibilities, *University of Toledo Law Review*, 39(2): 353–60.

Rhode, D.L. 2000. *In the Interests of Justice: Reforming the Legal Profession*. New York: Oxford University Press.

Rhode, D.L. (ed.). 2006. *Moral Leadership: The Theory and Practice of Power, Judgment, and Policy*. San Francisco: John Wiley & Sons.

Rubenstein, H. 2008. *Leadership for Lawyers*. 2nd edition. Chicago: ABA Press.

Sells, B. 1996. *The Soul of the Law: Understanding Lawyers and the Law*. Rockport, MA: Element.

Senge, P.M. 1990. *The Fifth Discipline*. New York: Doubleday.

Simon, W.H. 1998. *The Practice of Justice: A Theory of Lawyers' Ethics.* Cambridge, MA: Harvard University Press.

Sorenson, G. and Goethals, G. (eds). 2006. *The Quest for a General Theory of Leadership.* Northampton, MA: Edward Elgar Publishing.

Sorenson, G., Goethals, G. and Burns, J.M. 2004. *Encyclopedia of Leadership.* Thousand Oaks, CA: SAGE.

Sullivan, W., Colby, A., Wegner, J.W., Bond, L. and Shulman, L.S. 2007. *Educating Lawyers: Preparation for the Profession of Law. Carnegie Foundation for the Advancement of Teaching*. Hoboken, NJ: Jossey-Bass.

Index

Page numbers followed by "n" refer to a note at the bottom of the page. Page numbers in **bold** type refer to a figure or table.

AALS Directory of Law Teachers 111
ABA Commission on Women in the
    Profession 254
accountability 82, 217
accountancy 97, 98
accreditation standards 268
active-passivity 28
activism 32, 82, 84, 86
administration 155
advocacy **122**, 125, 169n
    zealous 130, 131, 132, 134
African Americans 240, 242, 245
After the JD – The First 10 Years study
    71, 111
Alabama 270
Alderfer, Clayton P. 103n
Allen, Bonnie 172–3, 174
ambiguity 12, 93, 152
ambition *see* competitiveness
America-Mideast Educational and Training
    Service 271
American Association of Law Schools
    254, 280
American Bar Association 22, 74, 111,
    130, 254, 268, 280
American Civil Rights movement 32, 83
American Lawyer 74
American Railway Union 136
analytical skills 38, 41, 46, 49, **122**,
    145–6, 152, 156, 161, 215
anchoring 142, 151n
Ancona, Deborah 157, 275
anomalies 145
anonymity 181
Antigone (Sophocles) 227, 253, 255

apprenticeships **113**, 114, 115, 117–18,
    169, 191, 210
argument 46, 49, 146, 151, 157
Aristotle 227, 228
Association of American Medical Colleges
    271
asylum 183–4
attitudes 38, 103–4, 106, 110–11, 112, **123**
Attorney Grievance Commission 178
attrition, associate 70n, 72, 73, 74, 76
authority 20n, 43, 81–2, 129, 153–4, 225,
    227, 248
autocrats 20n
automaticity 96, 97
automaticity 96, 97
autonomy 48, 50–51, 84, 156, 157
Avolio, B.J. 204
awareness *see* self-awareness; situation
    awareness
Ayers, William 241

Baltimore 13, 183
Baltimore Freedom Academy 233–9
banking 214n, 218
bar associations 174, 270
    American Bar Association 22, 74, 111,
    130, 254, 268, 280
Barker, Joel 115
Barnett, Martha Walters 254, 258, 259
Bass, Bernard 20, 29, 30, 236n
behavior, organizational 256
behavioral competency 38–9, 93, 103–5,
    107
behavioral event interview (BEI) 36–7, 39
behaviorally anchored rating scales
    (BARS) 38

behavioral theories **26**, 27–8
beliefs 36, 38, 103n, 181, 193
Bergmark, Martha 273
Best Practices for Legal Education, study
    106, 114–15, 169, 170
Bezdek, Barbara 172
bias 142, 143, 152, 153, 154, 160, 242–4
Biden, Vice President 203
Bill and Melinda Gates Foundation 237
Black, Laura 257
Blau, G.M. and Mallery, C. 235n
Blom, Brenda Bratton 174, 207–9
boundaries 176, 189, 190
Boyle, Robin 175
broad partnership business model 61–2
Brown, Judy 271, 275
Brown v. Board of Education 136
"Building a Better Legal Profession"
    (Stanford Law School) 76
Burch, Frank 273
Bureau of Labor Statistics 24
Burke, Edmund 82
Burns, James MacGregor 20, 21, 29–30,
    32, 197, 236n, 265
Burton, Beau 22–3, 31
business development 256, 266
business education 158–9, 214–15,
    216–19
business leaders 155–6
business models 58–65
business partnerships 14
business schools 126, 216, 270, 271,
    275–6

Calabresi, Guido 12
California, University of 76, 117, 271
Caliper Profile 44, 47
Campbell, David 92
Campbell Interest and Skill Survey (CISS)
    107n
Campbell Picture Postcard Deck (CPPD)
    107n
canary in the mineshaft 190
Canter, Andrew 273
Cardin Requirement 174n, 192

career anchors 103
career choice 132, 168–9, 266
career development 57, 59, 61, 62–4, 65,
    87, 173, 187, 207–8, 273
Career Development Office 207
career prospects 114, 243n
caring 247–8, 249, 275
Carle, Susan 180
Carlyle, Thomas 20, 235n
Carnegie Report, *Educating Lawyers:*
    Preparation for the Profession
    of Law 9, 21, 110, 112–17, 167,
    169–70, 191, 266–8, 279, 280
case rounds 178–9
case-based methods 135, 156, 169–70,
    171, 210, 218, 224, 267
casebooks 174n, 182
Center for Courage and Renewal 181
Center for Creative Leadership 94, 105,
    117
Center for Law and Renewal 126, 172,
    173–4, 265, 268n, 271
Center for Public Leadership 254
Center for Women in Law 76
Center for WorkLife Law 76
Center on Professionalism, Florida 270
CEOs 24
chain of command 43
Change = (Dissatisfaction x Model x
    Process) > Resistance 109–10, 114
change, agents of 63, 176, 180, 182, 260,
    269, 272, 277
change, organizational 42, 55–65
change, resistance to 109–10
change, social xxii, 13–14, 32, 84, 85, 86,
    237–8
Change Style Indicator (CSI) 106n
China 13, 19–20n, 25
Chronicle of Higher Education 9, 12
Churchill, Winston 226
cigarette manufacturers 132
Circles of Trust™ model 173, 181
citizenship 82–3, 85, 249
civil courts 266
Civil Justice, Inc. 184

civil rights movement 32, 82, 83, 85
civility 168, 272, 275
    Codes of Civility 176, 178
client relationships
    and law students 179, 257
    and lawyers xxv, 9, 56–9, 62–4, 65,
        71, 150, 153–5, 160–61
    private practice 69, 73–6
clinical education 9, 114, 171n, 206,
        210–11
Clinical Law Program, University of
        Maryland 172n, 174n, 265
Clinton, Hillary 200
clustering 41
cognitive competency 38–9, 46, 52, 92–5,
        103–5, 107, 169, 170n, 191, 204
collaboration 14, 42, 161, 205–6, 209,
        264, 269, 270
collegiality 71, 72, 75, 184, 207
Colorado 270
Columbia University 112, 271
Commission on Billable Hours 74
communication skills 41–2, 64, 65, 111,
        124, 245–7, 256, 264, 265
community, sustainable 14
community involvement 82, 85–6, 173,
        208, 209
    leadership 127, 162, 272
    and personal development 62, 65, 84,
        207–8
    pro bono work 56, 134
    and work-life balance 69, 77
Community Justice Clinic 184, 187, 208
compassion 170, 267, 275
compensation, employee 11, 57, 60–61, 75
    see also salaries
competence 28, 35–53, 92–3, 256, 268
    behavioral competency 38–9, 93,
        103–5, 107
    cognitive competency 38–9, 46, 52,
        92–5, 103–5, 107, 169, 170n, 191,
        204
    emotional competency 38–9, 46, 49,
        51–2
    technical competency 38–9, 92, 93–5,
        98, 105–6, 111, **122**

competency dictionaries 37
competition 11, 29, 57, 70, 71–2, 77, 168
competitiveness 31, **45**, 47
compromise 9, 15, 238
confidence 43, 152, 154, 236, 237–8, 245,
        266
    self-confidence 27, 107, 249
confidentiality 179, 183
conflict resolution 129, 134, 264
conformity 143, 241
Confucius 19, 20
Congress 23, 32, 44, 203
Conley, John and Haskell, Paul 180
conscientiousness 47, 48, 92
consideration 28, 30
consolidation 11, 153
conspiracy, criminal 136
contingency theory 29, **31**, 235n
control, span of 41
cooperation 9, 199
Corey, student 233–5
Corporate Counsel Women of Color 76
Cosby, William 81
costs 70, 71n, 72
counseling 111, 112, **122**, 128, 130
courage 64, 65, **123**, 125, 135–6, 223, 253,
        254
Courage to Lead program 173
Court of Appeals 178
Covey, Stephen 20
Cramton Report 92–3, 110
creativity 63, 65, 97n
    and fee arrangements 57, 60, 69, 75
    and legal training 8, **124**, 125, 209,
        264, 269
    see also thinking
criminal justice 133, 266
criterion-based sampling 35
culture, organizational 39, 136, 152, 265
    law firms 10, 58, 61, 63, 71, 168, 266,
        273, 274–5, 276–7
    law schools 215, 221, 249, 277, 278,
        279
curriculum development 85, 109, 114,
        115–18, 167–93, 197, 213–17,
        219–20, 268–9, 278

Curriden, Mark 24

D'Alamberte, Sandy 91
Darrow, Clarence 84, 136
Dartmouth University 271
Davis, Peter 133–4, 135
Day, D.V. 205
debate 177–8, 186, 187, 197–200, 247
Debs, Eugene 136
debt, student 110, 168, 214n, 215, 266, 273
decision-making 143–4
    ethical 127, 131, 132, 133, 134, 135n, 137
Declaration of Independence 23
delegation **124**
Delphi survey 126–8, 271–2
democracy 175, 187, 266, 272
DeMouy, Maura 257
denial 102
Denver, University of xxivn
Department of Homeland Security (DHS) 183–4
DePree, Max 149
descriptive approach 20–21
desire, objects of 103n
despots 20n
DeStefano, Michele and Bossone, Michael 76
destiny 227–8
detachment 125, 171, 267
determination 27, 146–7, 149, 198, 269
Dewey & LeBoeuf LLP 15n
DiSC Personal Profile System 106n
discipline 145, 178
Disclaimer of Representation 184–5
discrimination 259
distributive justice 134–5
diversified economic business model 60–61
diversity 73–4, 76, 77, 107n, 109, 200, 211, 264
    see also gender issues; racial issues
DLA Piper 126, 257, 270
Drexel University 216n
Duke University 180, 265n, 271, 274
Dworkin, Ronald 21

economic climate 10, 31–2, 44, 55, 57–8, 69, 71, 72
Edwards, Mickey 23
effectiveness 7, 30, 53, 86, 204, 213, 217, 277
efficiency 25, 69, 70n, 199
ego 47, 102, 103n
electoral system 82
Elon University xxivn, 10, 116, 117, 265n, 268
emotional competency 38–9, 46, 49, 51–2
empathy 48, 52, **123**, 125, 129
employees 56, 61–2
    as assets 57, 59
    retention of 69, 71, 73, 74, 75, 77
engineering schools 126
England 81
entrepreneurship 64, 65, 77, 257
equality 30, 131, 133, 239–44, 259
ethics, legal 11–12, 56, 57
    and education 21, 111, 131–6, 167–93, 205, 209–11, 265, 267, 278, 280
        ethical decision-making 127, 131, 132, 133, 134, 135n, 137
ethics, of leadership 7–8, 30, 167–8, 193, 264
Ethics and Professional Responsibility course 171, 268
ethnic issues 71n, 76, 107n, 183–4
evaluation 105, 114, 161, 188–91, 210, 217, 220
examinations 105–6, 112
exception, management by 30
execution skills 218, 219, 220
Executive Core Qualifications 274
experience, lived 9, 15, 108–9, **124**, 217–18
experiences, early life 204
experiencial learning 86, 114, 171, 172–3, 215–16, 218, 230, 249, 267
expertise 41, 71, 75, 93–100, 155, 169, 191, 204, 210
external structure *see* autonomy
externships 59, 86, 118, 215, 216n, 220, 278
extracurricular activities 83, 85–6
extraversion 93

fear 253, 257
feedback 52n, 105, 114, **124**, 157, 210, 234, 247–8
fees 132
   alternative fee arrangement 56–7, 58, 60–61, 64, 72, 73, 74, 75
   billable hours 69, 70, 71n, 74, 77, 132, 168, 266, 273
Fetzer Institute xxiv, 116, 126, 167, 172, 173, 265
Fiedler, Fred 29
FIRO-B (Fundamental Interpersonal Relations Orientation-Behavior) 106n
flexibility 52, 57, 60, 63, 65
Florida 132, 270
Florida Coastal University 117
focus groups 39
followers **26**, 28, 29, 197
Fordham University 267
"Forming the Legal Argument" class 233–5, 247
Fortune 50 companies 24
foundations, charitable 6, 14, 237, 254
framing 149–50, 151–2
Francis King Carey School of Law *see* Maryland, University of
Frank, Jerome 149
fraud detection 97, 98
free agents 72
freedom 22, 30
freedom of the press 81–2
Freud, Sigmund 101
friendships 208, 217, 243
Frisch, John 77, 273
Fuller, Lon 9, 144, 149
"fundamental attribution error" 144

Gandhi, Mahatma 197
Gardner, Howard 170, 267
Gellhorn, Walter 118–19
gender issues 71n, 133, 199–200, 239, 253–60, 270, 280
   diversity 74, 76, 77, 107n, 200, 211
genetics 27, 43, 204
Genovese, Kitty 238
George Washington University 213

Georgetown University xxivn, 117, 267, 271
Gibson, Mel 239
Gilmore, Dorcas R. 207–9
Ginott, H.G. 236–7
Ginsburg, Ruth Bader 259
Gladwell, Malcolm 95, 159n
Globe Project 20
goals 10, 41, 42, 65, 105, **124**, 154, 207, 234, 235
Gohn, Sandy 257
Golden Gate University 117
government leadership 81–7, 129, 155–6
Grant, Ulysses 27
great man theory 27, 235n
Greece, ancient 274
greed 132–3
Groopman, Jerome 143
group understanding 148, 153–4, 156–7, 159, 160–62
group work 216–17, 218, 220, 264
Grutter v. Bollinger 15
Gurnham, David 22

Hall, David 173–4n, 181, 269
Hamilton, Andrew 136
Hamline University 267
Hardaway, Tim 239
Harvard University
   Harvard Business School 126, 217n, 218n, 270, 271
   Harvard Law School 172n, 210, 265n
   Kennedy School of Government 84, 254
Harvey, Michael 19
Hastings College of Law, University of California 76, 117
height 27
Heineman, Ben W. Jr. 19, 21, 268–9
Henry V (Shakespeare) 81, 225–6
Henry VI (Shakespeare) 227
Higginbotham, Leon 83
high school students 233–49
Hildebrandt International 270
Hogan Personality Inventory (HPI) 44–7
Holland & Knight, law firm 200n, 253–4
Hollander, Ed 28

honesty 28, 41, 43, 133, 181
Hornstein, Alan 24
House of Representatives 23, 82
Howrey & Simon 72n, 200n
Hugo, V., *Les Miserables* 84
humanization 236–7

Ibsen, Henrik, *Enemy of the People* 228
identity, personal 237, 238, 239–48, 249
identity, professional 7, 9, 11, 114,
        167–70, 185–8, 191–2, 193, 264
"idiosyncratic credit" 28
imagination 22, 169, 171, 267, 280
Immigration Clinic 183–4
Imus, Don 239
inclusion 15, 106n
independence 51, 157
Indiana University 186–7n, 275
inductive methods 135, 146
influence, idealized 30, 236n
information overload 46
innovation 41, 114, 278
inspiration 28, 41, 42, 198–9, 234
instinct 142, 145, 160, 190–91
Integrated Knowledge, Skills, and Personal
        Attributes Paradigm 116
integrity 27
    personal 41, 65, **123**, 129, 245
    professional 7, 9, 42–3, 125, 132–3,
        153, 168–72, 193
intelligence 27, 93, 223, 224, 238
interests 103–4, 107, 111, 112, **123**, 207–9
international justice 133
International Leadership Association 280
internships 56, 258, 278
interpersonal skills 41–2, 50, 63, 64–5,
        93–5, 98–9, 101, 105–7, 118, **122**
    Hogan Personality Inventory (HPI)
        45, 46
    see also skills, "soft"
interviewing 112, 146, 161
introversion 93, 107n
investment 14, 56–7, 58, 59, 60, 61, 62,
        63, 75
IQ 35

Jackson, Alexina 258n
Jacobi, Maryann 206

James MacGregor Burns Academy of
        Leadership xxiv, 126, 265, 271,
        274
job performance 55
job satisfaction 55, 72–3, 76, 131, 229
Johari Window **100**, 101, **102**
Johnson, Joshua 74
Johnson, Paul 95, 96–8
journal keeping 179–80, 186, 191, 220
judgement 125, 129, 186, 223, 265
judiciary (United States) 23
jurisprudence 21, 161, 240
JustAdvice® service 184
justice 30, 129–37, 170, 186, 237, 266,
        267
Juvenile Law Clinic 233n, 235–9

Kahneman, Daniel 142, 143
Kant, Immanuel 21
Kellerman, Barbara 255
Kelley, Robert 28
Kelly, Michael 11–12, 273
Kennedy, Robert F. 125, 136
Khurana, Rakesh 158
King, Martin Luther, Jr. 226–7
Kirton Adaption-Innovation Inventory
        106n
Klenke, Karin 255
knowledge 92, 96, **123**, 223
Knowledge Paradigm 115, 118
Knowledge Plus Skills Paradigm 115–16,
        118
Kohl, Herbert 245
Kolb, David 108
Kolb Learning Style Indicator (LSI) 107n
Kotter, John 40, 42, 46
Kouzes, James and Posner, Barry 28, 42,
        76, 198n
Kowalski, M. 205
Kronman, Anthony 130, 223

Langdell model 172n
language, use of 237, 246–7
law firms 40–41, 53, 55–61, 69–77, 270,
        276–7
law schools 91–119, 125–37, 160–62,
        167–93, 213–16, 218–21, 267–8,
        277–8

Law Without Walls 76
lawmaking 82, 145, 152, 153, 161
lawyer-leaders 22–4, 156, 200, 203–11,
    223, 265, 266, 272
Leader Motive Profile 31
leadership, collective 32
leadership, definition of 25, 147–8, 155,
    157–8, 213, 255
Leadership, Ethics and Innovation
    workshops 173
leadership, individual 32, 276
Leadership Ethics and Democracy (LEAD)
    initiative xxiv, 6, 7–8, 13–14, 15,
    116, 119, 167–93, 197, 263–80
Leadership Practices Inventory (LPI)
    198–9
Leadership Quarterly 30–31
Leadership Roundtable 117, 127–8,
    272–7, 279
leadership theory 19–32, 91–119, 235n,
    236n, 255
learning approach 45, 46, 49
Learning Retreat Team 217n
learning styles 107, 108, 175
lecturing 185n, 197
legal aid programs 184, 266
legal profession, structure 10–12
Legal Theory and Practice (LTP) course
    174n
Lerman, Lisa 132
Levi, Edward 146
libel 81, 136
Likert-type scales 38
Lingdau 20n
listening skills 10, 15, 50, 65, **124**, 157
literature 223–30
litigation 46, 128, 130, 218
Llewellyn, Karl 9, 97–8
LMX leadership instrument 30
logic 39, 40, 46
Luban, David 168n, 180, 182, 190, 193

McClelland, David 31, 35–7
MacCrate Report 9, 110, 111, 114
Machiavelli, Niccolo 20, 229
Magdalene Sisters, film 241
Maister, David 155
malpractice 184

management skills 111, 112, 155, 159,
    256–7, 264, 265, 273
manipulation 97, 224, 228
Marjorie Cook Foundation 254
Marquette University 267
Marshall, Thurgood 83, 109n
Martyn, S.R. and Fox, L.J. 178
Maryland, University of 216, 223
    Francis King Carey School of Law
        10, 117, 126, 207, 233–49
        Clinical Law Program 172n, 174n,
        265
        Leadership Ethics and Democracy
        (LEAD) initiative xxiv, 6, 7–8,
        13–14, 15, 116, 119, 167–93,
        197, 263–80
    James MacGregor Burns Academy of
        Leadership xxiv, 126, 263, 265,
        271, 274
    Robert H. Smith School of Business
        216
Maryland Code of Civility 178
Maslow, Abraham 103n
Massachusetts Institute of Technology
    (MIT) 271, 275–6
Mathews, Robert E. 21
MBTI (Myers-Briggs Type Indicator)
    107n
Measure for Measure (Shakespeare)
    224–5
media imagery 7
mediation 179, 187
medical schools 126, 214n, 223, 274–5
Medici, Lorenzo 229
mental illness 72–3, 168, 266
mentoring 65, 108n, 136, 206–11, 257,
    277
    in private practice 57, 71, 76, 77, 270
Merrill Lynch 27
Mexico 13
Miami, University of 76
Michigan, University of 27
Miles & Stockbridge P.C. 77
Millemann, Michael 265
Minneapolis University, St Thomas Law
    School xxivn, 116, 265n
minority groups 240, 243n, 246
Minow, Martha 133

misconduct 178
Mississippi 13, 173
Mississippi Center for Justice 127
mobility 70, 71n
Moliterno, James 177
Monopoli, Paula 265
Montgomery, Alabama 32
moral development *see* ethics, legal;
 ethics, of leadership
morale 57–8, 266, 269
Morgan, Charles 74n
Morrison, Toni 241
Mossbarger, David 274–5
motivation 8, 29, 35, 103–4, 269
 inspirational 30, 41, 42
 of students 87, 112, 234, 235, 247
Mudd, Jack 111
Multistate Professional Responsibility
 Examination 176, 177

Namibia 13
National Council of Nonprofits 24n
National Women's Law Center 127, 258
needs 103–4, 106, 112, **123**
negotiation 111, 112, **124**, 129, 146, 149,
 161, 256, 264
networks 65, 174, 217, 243, 257, 258, 280,
 303
New Media Executive Leadership Program
 271
New Orleans 13
New York University 136
Nixon Peabody 126
nonprofit groups 14, 24, 87, 129, 155–6,
 159
normativity 20–21, 27, 276, 280
North Carolina, University of 112n, 180n
Northeastern University 118n, 216n, 267
Northouse, Peter 27, 29
not-learning 245
novices 95–8, 206, 209, 210
Nussbaum, Martha 224

Obama, President 203
objectification 171, 267
observation 95, 108, 220, 273
O'Connor, Sandra Day 109n
Oedipus Tyrannus (Sophocles) 227–8

Ohio State University 27, 116, 117, 265n
online discussion boards 177–8
opportunities, recognizing 63–4, 65
optimism 48, 93, **123**
Oregon 270
"organizational fit" 29
organizations, dynamics of 7, 11–12, 62,
 219
Orwell, George 228–9
outsourcing 58

Palin, Sarah 200
Palmer, Parker 173n, 181
Palmore, Roderick 74
parenting styles 204
partnership 14, 55, 58–9, 61–2, 65
passion 85–6, 87, 200
patience 49, 157
Pearson, Carol 265, 274
Pennsylvania, University of 126, 213, 217,
 217n, 270, 271
people skills 27n, 39
personality measurement tools 44–52
personality traits
 lawyers 10, 43–53, 125, 156–7, 197–8,
  270, 273, 280
 leadership 27, 35, 38, 41, **122**, **123**,
  204, 224–6, 229, 280
 trait theories **26**, 27, 197, 235n
person-job fit 37, **38**, 47
perspective 52, 65
persuasion 1, 8, 146, 151, 255
pessimism 48
philosophy 20, 21, 180–81, 189
Plato 20, 130, 197
Plutarch 228, 229
Polden, Donald 116–17, 269, 274
policy, government 81–7
Pollak, Joanne 258
Posner, Barry 28, 42, 76, 117, 198n
poverty 132, 174n, 184, 240, 242, 243,
 248
practice, professional 181–5
practicum 220, 258–60
predictive methods 35–40
presentations 182–5
presidents of the United States 23, 203
priming 151n

private sector 24, 57, 69–77, 129, 131,
    200, 270
privilege 133, 209, 239, 240–41, 242–4,
    247, 249
pro bono work 56, 59, 134, 217, 254, 277,
    278
    provision 87, 132, 186, 273
    and work-life balance 70n, 76, 77,
        168, 266
problem-solving
    and lawyer-leaders 129, 223, 265
    and lawyers 8–10, 41, 46, 49, 75, 128,
        145–7, 151, 152, 269
    and leadership 41, 151, 152, 204
    and legal education 15, 109n, 111,
        117, **124**, 125, 160–62, 220, 264,
        273
        and mentoring 207, 208–9, 210
        over-emphasis 215, 219
    and relationships 207, 208–9, 210,
        234, 235, 247
procedural justice 134
productivity 57, 58, 72
Professional Conduct, Rules of 130, 167,
    175, 176–8, 188
Professional Responsibility, Rules of 175,
    176, 183, 189–90, 191, 193, 210
Professional Responsibility and Practice:
    The Rules and Reality, lecture
    167–8, 175, 176–85, 188, 191, 193
professionalization process 93n, **122**
profitability 57, 60, 62, 64
Project for Attorney Retention 76
project management 118, 129, 215
Public Interest Mentoring Group 207, 209
public sector 7, 23, 137
public service 82, 83, 84, 87, 209
public-speaking 112, 129

Rabbit-Proof Fence, film 241
racial issues 15, 133, 174n, 255, 270, 280
    and relationships 207–8, 211, 237,
        238, 239–47
ranking 56, 110, 114, 273
rapport 46, 50
reality 149–50
reasoning, abstract 48, 49, 169, 210, 224,
    267

reciprocal justice 134
recruitment 11, 39, 53, 58, 74, 280
Reed Smith 126, 270
reflection 108, 175, 179–80, 181, 189,
    223, 224, 225
    self-reflection 64, 191, 269
Regan, Donald 27
relationships 42, 198–9, 203–11, 233–49,
    265
    and problem-solving 207, 208–9, 210,
        234, 235, 247
    and racial issues 207–8, 211, 237, 238,
        239–47
    and trust 155, 207, 209, 234, 247
relationships, client xxv, 9, 56–9, 62–4,
    65, 71, 150, 153–5, 160–61
    and law students 179, 257
    private practice 69, 73–6
relationships, colleagues/peers **124**, 184,
    207–9, 211, 258, 270
relationships, employees 56, 57, 58, 60–3,
    65
Reno, Janet 254
repression 102
reputation, professional 63, 133, 210, 272
resilience 43, 48, 51–2, 93, 157
Resnik, Judith 254
resources, shared 74–5
respect 199, 209, 217, 247, 249
responsibilitiy 15, 65, 264
    professional 136, 167–93, 268–9, 278,
        280
retention, of employees 58, 59, 60, 61, 69,
    71, 73, 74, 75, 77
reward, contingent 30
rhetoric 226
Rhode, Deborah 24, 117, 132, 168n,
    176–7, 180, 182, 254, 255, 259
Richard, Larry 31, 270
Richard II (Shakespeare) 227
Richards, Michael 239
rights, individual and collective 22
risk aversion 24, 31, 52, 152
risk management 24, 57, 58, 59, 154–5
risk-taking 60, 207, 209, 236
Robert H. Smith School of Business 216
Robinson, Laurie 76
Rogers, Carl 101

Rokeach, Milton 101, 103, 104
Rokeach Values Survey (RVS) 106n
role models 51, 57, 129, 206
Roosevelt, Franklin and Eleanor 30
Rost, Joseph 158
Rotunda, R.D, and Dzienkoowski, J.S. 178
Roundtable on Law School Leadership
    Education 117, 127–8, 272–7, 279
rule-breaking 204
Rutgers University 239

St. Thomas University (Minnesota) xxivn,
    116, 265n
salaries 57, 60, 256, 259n
    see also compensation, employee
Santa Clara University xxivn, 9–10,
    116–17, 265n
Saybolt Bainum, Rebecca 172–3, 174
scale, economies of 58, 60
Schein, Edgar 103
Schmoke, Kurt 276
Schön, Donald 143
self-assessment 105, 106–7
self-awareness 98–107, **122**, **123**, 168–72,
    181, 191, 198–9, 234, 269
self-confidence 27, 107, 249
self-development 41, 42, 110
self-efficacy 93
self-government 82
self-interest 131, 132, 228
self-reflection 64, 191, 269
Seligman, Martin 48
Sells, Benjamin 170, 267
Senate 23, 82
sensitivity **45**, 46, **100**, 101, 107
Shakespeare, William 81, 224–6, 227
Simon, David and Burns, Edward 243,
    244
Simon, William H. 170, 267
simulation 9, 106, 108, 112, 114, 118, 161
situation 27, 29
situation awareness 98–100, 101–3, 108,
    122, 160, 210
situationalism 144, 145, 148
skepticism 31, 46, 48–9, 135, 157, 278
skills, "soft" 56, 57, 64, 127, 128, 217,
    220, 221 *see also* interpersonal
    skills

skills training 9, 10, 110, 116, 216, 255–7
sociability 27, 48, 50, 157
social change xxii, 13–14, 32, 84, 85, 86,
    237–8
social class 174n, 237, 238, 240, 241,
    242–4, 248
socialization 220, 221
Socratic Method 197, 218
Sophocles 227–8, 253, 255
Sorenson, Georgia 117, 265, 274
Southern California, University of 267
Southern Illinois University Leadership
    Symposia 28
Southwestern Law School 187n
speakers, guest 86, 181–2, 183, 186
specialization 77
"spiral of experience" 95n, 106, 108, 118
Spirit of Justice retreats 173
stability 70, 71, 72–3
Standard & Poor's 24
Stanford University 76, 117, 271
stereotyping 142, 145, 148
Stillings, Jenn 257
stimulation, intellectual 30, 236n
Stogdill, Ralph 27
stories 149–50, 160, 180–81, 183–4,
    246–7
strategic planning 129, 160, 161
stress management **124**
Strong Interest Inventory (SII) 107n
Student Affairs offices 268
student loan debt 110, 168, 214n, 215,
    266, 273
students, high school 233–49
subordinates 19, 20n, 29
substance abuse 72–3, 168, 266
substantive law 111–12
success 152–3
supervision 159
Supreme Court 23, 109n
Susskind, Richard 182, 190, 205
sustainability 12, 60, 153

talent 37, 39, 104–5, **123**
task performance 28
Tatum, B.D. 240, 241, 244
Teach For America 242n
team production 213–21

team-based business models 58–9, 64
team-building 8, 65, **124**, 269
teamwork 42, 119, 129, 213, 215, 270
technical competency 38–9, 93–5, 98,
    105–6, 111, **122**
tenacity 93, 223
Texas, University of 76
thinking 28, 141–62
    critical 28, 237, 264
    fast thinking 142, 143–4, 146, 149,
        151, 157, 160
    slow/hard thinking 143, 145, 146, 150,
        151, 154, 157, 160, 161–2
    strategic 118, 151, 210
    see also creativity
"thinking like a lawyer" 8, 97–8, 144–7,
    156, 160, 205, 210, 215, 255
"thinking like a leader" 147–9
Tocqueville, Alexis de 23
"tragedy of the commons" 74–5
training
    in law firms 43, 46, 57, 60, 71, 72, 73,
        75, 77
    skills training 9, 10, 110, 115–16, 210,
        216, 255–7
trait theories *see* personality traits
transactional leadership theory 30, 218
transformational leadership theory 29–30,
    31, 131, 236n
transparency 16n, 114, 134
Travis Simulation 112
trust, in leaders 28, 43, 46, 49, 50, 129,
    131, 149, 272
trust, in relationships 155, 207, 209, 234,
    247
tuition 12–13, 110, 168, 214n, 266, 273
tyrants 20n

understanding 148–9, 153–4, 160
unemployment 168
United States Constitution 23, 81–2
United States Naval Academy 257
universities, role in legal education 12–15,
    83–7

urgency 48, 49–50, 157
U.S. Department of Justice 183
U.S. Information Service (USIS) 35–6
U.S. military 28, 185, 277
U.S. News 110, 114, 271

Valian, Virginia 255
value 63–4, 112, 118, **123**, 269, 276
    and relationships 198–9, 204, 207, 209
    and self-awareness 103–4, 106,
        110–11
value systems 93, 103, 191
"vertical professionalism" 11
video 106, 180
Vroom, V.H. and Jago, A.G. 205

Wal-Mart 73–4
Washington, Isaiah 239
Washington and Lee University 117–18,
    119
Wegner, Judith 112n–13n
West, Robin 224
Wharton School of Business 126, 217n,
    270, 271
White, James Boyd 224
White, James J. 101
Williams, Gregory H. 5n
Wisconsin 270
wisdom 223, 224, 230
women 71n, 74, 76, 199–200, 253–60, 270
Women, Leadership & Equality (WLE)
    Program 254, 258, 265
"Women's Initiative" programs 200
work-life balance 268, 272
    and billable hours 70, 77, 168, 266
    and employee investment 56, 57, 59,
        60, 71, 72, 75, 259–60
Wren, Thomas 25–6

Zaccaro, S.J. 204
zeal 130, 131, 132, 134
Zenger, John Peter 41, 81, 136